Praise for *Complexity Science and World Affairs*

"Complexity can be overwhelming and complexity science can be daunting, and, yet, in Walter Clemens's skilled hands both become accessible, understandable, and useful tools for both scholars and practitioners. Once again, Clemens has shown that sophisticated academic theorizing only benefits from clarity, elegance, and wit. The book is ideal for graduate and undergraduate students as a supplementary text in international relations or comparative politics."

— Alexander Motyl, Rutgers University–Newark

"Clemens offers a fresh, even startling, paradigm and process for analyzing the seemingly unpredictable relations within and among human societies. With impressive clarity he proposes that 'the capacity to cope with complexity' has become a key determinant of success in our intricately interrelated world. Careful study of this capacity in specific contexts can lead to revealing analyses in comparative politics and international relations. A provocative and stimulating treatise!"

— S. Frederick Starr, Johns Hopkins University

"Walt Clemens's provocative new book can be appreciated at several levels: as an analytical framework in international relations—complexity science—that offers a compelling alternative to realism and neoliberalism; as an incisive critique of the 'fitness' of the supposedly most developed societies to deal with our complex world; and as a humanistic value-set that provides better standards for assessing governments than do GDP, trade levels, or military spending. Clemens skillfully integrates theory and practice to explore US 'hyperpower,' the two Koreas, China, and other states from new angles, and with consistent objectivity. IR specialists should find this book exciting, while IR and international studies students will be challenged by the new paradigm it presents."

— Mel Gurtov, Portland State University

"Clemens proposes a powerful new way of looking at international relations and politics, and offers a productive method for assessing the fitness of societies in the early twenty-first century."

— Guntis Šmidchens, University of Washington, Seattle

"You don't have to be a political scientist to wonder why some states succeed and others do not, why some societies flourish while others suffer stagnation and conflict. Employing the relatively new tool of complexity science, Walter Clemens evaluates the 'fitness' of states and societies, i.e. their ability to cope with complex challenges and opportunities. He does so in a way that is erudite—how many studies quote Walt Whitman and Karl Marx in the same chapter?—yet clear and accessible. Clemens challenges both existing political science paradigms and policy perspectives. This is a stimulating, rich volume that can be read and re-read with profit and appreciation for its breadth and depth and most of all for its insistence that we see the world, and the states in it, in all their complexity."

— Ronald H. Linden, University of Pittsburgh

COMPLEXITY SCIENCE
and WORLD AFFAIRS

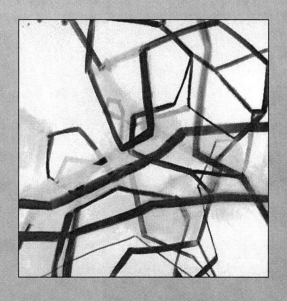

SUNY SERIES, JAMES N. ROSENAU SERIES IN GLOBAL POLITICS

David C. Earnest, editor

COMPLEXITY SCIENCE
and WORLD AFFAIRS

WALTER C. CLEMENS JR.

FOREWORD BY STUART A. KAUFFMAN

SUNY
PRESS

Cover art, *BlueMol 10–13*, by Daniel Kohn.

Cover and interior art by Daniel Kohn is from the series *DataSets*, and is used by permission.

Published by
State University of New York Press, Albany

For information, contact
State University of New York Press, Albany, NY
www.sunypress.edu

Production and book design, Laurie Searl
Marketing, Anne M. Valentine

LIBRARY OF CONGRESS CATALOGING-IN-PUBLICATION DATA

Clemens, Walter C.
Complexity science and world affairs / Walter C. Clemens, Jr.
pages cm
Includes bibliographical references.
ISBN 978-1-4384-4901-2 (hardcover : alk. paper)
1. World politics—21st century. 2. Evaluation—Methodology. 3. Complexity
(Philosophy) I. Title.
D863.C54 2013
909.83'1—dc23

2013002395

10 9 8 7 6 5 4 3 2 1

FOR

Anna, Ali, Lee Lo, Ho Tai,

Lani, Rose, Olivia, Julian, Jeff, Todd, Ben, Julia

Liz and Stu

CONTENTS

List of Figures and Tables   ix

Foreword   xi
Stuart A. Kauffman

To the Reader   xvii

Acknowledgments   xxi

1   Why a Science of Complexity?   1

2   Basic Concepts of Complexity Science   23

3   A Crucial Test Case: Why the Baltic Is Not the Balkans   39

4   Culture and the Capacity to Cope with Complexity   55

5   Complexity Science as a Tool to Understand the New Eurasia   71

6   How Complexity Concepts Explain Past and Present Fitness   107

7   Hyperpower Challenged: Prospects for Americans   121

8   What Future for the American Dream?   147

9   Why Is South Korea Not North Korea?   165

10   Toward a New Paradigm for Global Studies   179

11   Challenges to Complexity Science   201

Afterword: Science and Art in this Book:
Exploring the Genome Together   211
Daniel Kohn

Notes   213

References   227

Index   245

FIGURES *and* TABLES

FIGURES

Figure 1.1   Exploitation, Mutual Gain, and Fitness: Likely Linkages   4

Figure 2.1   Soft and Hard Power Resources: USA, Russia, and China in 2012   32

Figure 2.2   HDI and Honesty Scores for Leading Countries by Cultural and Political Heritage in 2010   37

Figure 5.1   HDI Scores for All Communist and Post-Communist States, 1970-2010   73

Figure 5.2   HDI, BTI, and CPI Scores for Communist and Post-Communist States in 2010   92

Figure 6.1   Bible in the Vernacular vs. HDI, BTI, and CPI Scores for Historically Christian, Post-Communist States   117

Figure 7.1   HDI Trends: Scores for Leading States, 1980-2010   130

Figure 9.1   South Korea compared with North Korea, BTI 2012   167

Figure 9.2   "In the beginning was the Word . . ."—in *Hangŭl*   175

TABLES

Table 2.1   Alternative Scenarios Posited by Complexity Science   34

Table 3.1   Comparative Democracy, Independent Media, and Human Development 2009   43

Table 3.2   Progress in Closing the First 30 Chapters of the *Acquis Communautaire*   45

Table 3.3   Peace and War in Lithuania and Croatia   47

Table 3.4   Economic and Social Development in Estonia
             Compared with Bosnia   48

Table 5.1   Freedom House Democracy Ratings for "Nations in
             Transit" in 2012   84

Table 5.2   Transformation Rankings (BTI) of Communist
             and Post-Communist Countries, 2003-2012,
             by Cultural Heritage   89

Table 5.3   HDI, Transformation, Democracy, Honesty, and
             Economic Freedom, 2011-2012   93

Table 5.4   Purchasing Power Per Inhabitant, Post-Communist
             States Members and Candidate Members of the EU   97

Table 5.5   Suicide Rates per 100,000 Before and After
             Communist Collapse   101

Table 6.1   Percentage of Individuals in Communist or
             Post-Communist Countries Using the Internet in
             2011 (global n = 92)   115

Table 7.1   Parameters of Power, 1776-2000   122

Table 7.2   Parameters of Power, 2008 and 2012   131

Table 10.1   Percentage of Individuals in Islamic Heritage
             Countries Using the Internet in 2011   197

FOREWORD

Walt Clemens is a much admired friend whom I have known since a summer when we both served as counselors in a camp for diabetic children in the Sequoia National Park. I was fifteen, midway through high school, and he twenty-two, a fledgling grad student. Working with these diabetic children planted the seeds for my own future in medical and biological sciences. Before the camp breakfast Walt studied Russian grammar, and later, after these brave kids got their insulin shots, he taught them American Indian lore and dancing. When the camp season ended, Walt and I climbed Mount Whitney and fished in the Klamath River. Years later, he climbed the Matterhorn in the Alps and Mount Pacharmo in Nepal. I wish I had been with him. He tells me that he has studied world affairs because, like mountains, they stand before us—challenging, interesting to explore, sometimes beautiful, potentially useful, and often dangerous. Why grapple with the peaks and valleys of our often messy planet? To understand where humanity has come from and where it can go. To live, prosper, and procreate in realms where, as naturalist John Muir noted, "[w]hen you touch anything, you find it is hitched to everything else in the universe."

The summits of knowledge about human behavior are still distant and enshrouded with mist. The ascent routes are steep and poorly mapped. We would-be climbers and our instruments are clumsy. Our knowledge and tools for learning have improved but remain feeble next to tasks of understanding and perhaps nudging the world to some better place.

Clemens has written an outstanding book—the culmination of a half-century's experience in and analysis of world affairs. Having wrestled with the nostrums of power politics and legal-moralism, he has opted to search for a more comprehensive approach to analyzing world affairs. To this end, he has turned to complexity science in the hope of articulating a new paradigm for the study of comparative government and cross-border relations. Having reached the summit of Mount Whitney and other mountains, he seeks to scale the Everests of global studies with the eyes of a scholar and adventurer utilizing new ideas and tools.

Clemens has performed masterfully in applying the basic concepts of complexity science to confronting and climbing the precarious and often clouded Himalayas of world affairs. But this approach to knowledge still faces severe limits. Complexity science has taken shape for no more than three decades. Still inchoate, it has not yielded any accepted theory. As Clemens writes in his final chapter, complexity science is more like the first efforts at flight by the Wright brothers than by Icarus. The science is primitive but has the potential to become a powerful tool for reaching new heights. Using the existing tools, Clemens provides a strong start. He uses complexity science to generate new insights into the problems and opportunities facing post-communist societies, the much vaunted American dream, and transnational issues ranging from environmental cooperation to metastasizing networks of terror. He has produced a lively book, interesting and deep, bound to interest not only political and other social scientists but all thoughtful persons concerned with understanding and perhaps improving the human condition. He has sketched and outlined a paradigm for social science with fewer limitations than alternative approaches such as structural realism, rational choice, constructivism, or current utopianisms.

Still, complexity science and some forms of social science are constrained by the mechanistic worldview inherited from Sir Isaac Newton and the Enlightenment. In this foreword, I would like to suggest a post-Newtonian and post-Darwinian framework that could enhance the paradigm and insights offered by Clemens. I do so as one not trained in cross-border or comparative politics but as a biologist looking for patterns in all forms of life.

Biology cannot be reduced to chemistry and physics. When students of human relationships seek to mimic physics, they go astray. The realities and potentialities of world affairs cannot be pre-stated. The world is not an optimization or decision problem with a given cost and payoff landscape. Clemens is wise to avoid formal methods not suited to a highly uncertain and variable terrain. International relations refuse to abide within the mooring lines of universal gravitation and integral calculus.

Political life cannot be reduced to the pre-stated payoff matrices of game theory. The values of each actor are hard if not impossible to discern and quantify. Even more important, the adjacent possible space for strategic planning cannot be known or defined in advance. Little or nothing is entailed. Nothing flows ineluctably from anything.

Newton bequeathed to us the view that everything in the universe is entailed by underlying laws of motion and integration. If so, nothing is new or unexpected. There can be no Black Swans. Carrying this view to its logical extreme, Pierre-Simon Laplace in the early nineteenth century imagined a giant computer in the sky. He suggested that if this machine, sometimes called the "Laplacian demon," knew the positions and momenta of all the particles in the universe, it could deduce the entire becoming of the universe. Why? Because everything is entailed. Here began what physics Nobelist Stephen Weinberg called "The Dream of a Final Theory"—a theory so profound it could be written in a compact equation on his T-shirt. Isaac Asimov's *Foundation Trilogy* has Hari Seldon embracing a similar dream for psychosocial history. If this dream corresponded to reality, world affairs could be reduced to a set of decision problems, no more complex than sending a spaceship to Saturn on the basis of Newton's laws.

For better or worse, reality confounds this dream. Many innovations create new adjacent possibles from which can emerge still more possible strategy spaces. A screwdriver, for example, can tighten or release a screw, open a can of paint, wedge open a door, or stab an assailant. It can also spear a fish and so could be rented to fishermen for a share of the catch. It could launch a fish harvesting and sales business. Lacking a screwdriver or other similar, implement, however, a camper might be unable to pry open her last can of tuna.

The number of uses for a screwdriver is not infinite but *indefinite*. More, while the integers are naturally ordered, there is no natural ordering among the uses of a screwdriver. The uses listed here are merely different uses that follow nothing more than a nominal scale. But if the uses of a screwdriver are indefinite in number and un-orderable, we can never be sure that we have listed them all. No effective procedure or algorithm can list all the uses of a screwdriver or—equally important—reveal new uses, as yet unimagined.

The impact of technology on economics and society is equally unforeseeable. No one in the 1930s or 1940s could have envisioned how sophisticated computing machines would shape society. No one foresaw or intended the becoming of the mainframe computer and its evolution into a personal computer used for word processing, file sharing, and accessing the World Wide Web. These unfolding developments generated new sets of adjacent possibles whose impacts have included Google, Facebook, and the Arab Spring. The enabling possibilities that lie ahead outstrip our imagination as well as our knowledge.

Let us shift to life sciences. What if some bacterium takes shape in a new environment? What if some molecular screwdriver finds a use that enhances the fitness of the bacterium? A heritable variation and natural selection may then pull out a new use by selecting at the level of the bacterium. The function of the molecular screwdriver cannot be pre-stated. Once in operation, it changes the very space of possibilities for the future evolution of the biosphere. The new use of the screwdriver, now a reality, creates a new adjacent possible set of opportunities for evolution. This process iterates indefinitely.

If in evolution a niche is thought of as a boundary condition, we cannot pre-state that niche in a noncircular manner. The evolving bacterium, in order to reproduce in its world, achieves a closure in some set of "tasks" or uses of things and processes that pass, in part, through the environment. But there is no noncircular statement of what that task closure is, until selection reveals—*after* the fact—what has worked for the organism in its environment. In short, we cannot pre-state the boundary conditions afforded by the niche.

Because we cannot pre-state the ever-changing phase space of biosphere evolution, we cannot write laws of motion for the evolving biosphere and cannot pre-state the boundary conditions afforded by the "actual" niche, then we have no equations of motion to integrate. Lacking foreknowledge of the boundary conditions, we cannot integrate the laws of motion we do not have.

My conclusion is that the Newtonian paradigm that has reigned for some three hundred and fifty years does not apply to evolution of the biosphere and human relations. No pre-statable laws entail the becoming of the biosphere. Still less do they exist and operate in economic, legal, social, or cultural systems. Enablement—not entailing causal laws—explains the evolution of world affairs.

Social scientists have no reason to suffer physics envy. No one can anticipate the adjacent possibles into which human systems may "become." Moreover, we can form no probability statements on such matters without knowing the sample space. Neither a frequency nor a Baysean sense of probability can apply.

As in biological niches, man-made laws provide enabling constraints that create an adjacent, partially un-pre-statable possible space of actions. If authorities seek to protect the Amazonian forest by conservation laws and satellite monitoring of the canopy, lumber harvesters may get around the law and monitors by cutting trees shorter than the canopy. Man-made rules create an adjacent possible but partially un-pre-statable strategy space of possible actions. Then we cannot know what we enable by our laws, regulations, and policies. Then, what is wise governance? What is wise foreign policy?

Life is a constant becoming of new opportunities—here called *enabling constraint adjacent possibilities*—that enable, but do not cause, innovations in our personal, artistic, scientific, economic, cultural, and political lives. Such typically un-pre-statable innovations, in turn, generate yet new adjacent possible enabling constraint opportunities that people may or may not exploit.

Rational planning has its limits. We must live forward not knowing what will or can happen. The issues that drive world affairs are not pre-statable, optimization problems. We cannot anticipate the novel variables that will become relevant. Clemens agrees with Jean-Paul Sartre on the sources of existential anxiety. Given that we want to live fully, but in a cosmos of unknowns, each must do what he or she regards as meaningful. Beginning in graduate school at Columbia University (interspersed with research at Moscow State University and the Hoover Institution), Clemens chose to study U.S.-Soviet arms control issues in the hope of preserving and then improving the human condition. Later, lecturing under State Department auspices, he was explaining for an audience in Indonesia why only two countries could be regarded as "superpowers." As he rattled off statistics about Soviet and U.S. military and economic power, an earthquake shook the room. Chastened, Walter acknowledged the existence of still greater forces.

Clemens in recent years has looked beyond arms control to search for patterns that govern life in many domains of world affairs. Focusing on issues of societal fitness, he showed in *The Baltic Transformed* (2001) how peoples in Estonia, Latvia, and Lithuania escaped the Scylla of top-down communist rigidity and the Charybdis of anarchy to optimize their political and economic liberation. In the present book he expands his horizon to understand why the Balkans did not follow the Baltic example; why some post-communist societies such as Slovenia and the Czech Republic became more fit in the 1990s and early 2000s while most others stagnated; why the United States dominated the twentieth century but staggered like a blinded giant early in the twenty-first; why South Korea is so unlike the North; and how complexity science illuminates the adjacent possibles generated by technological change in fourteen cases of transnational relations. While eschewing any simple formulas, Clemens combines quantitative measures by the United Nations Human Development Programme, Freedom House, the Bertelsmann Foundation, and Transparency International with his own qualitative research to arrive at balanced evaluations of societal fitness across Eurasia, the United States, and worldwide. Both his quantitative and qualitative assessments point to what Clemens sees as the mother lode of fitness: culture. He notes the interactions between folk mythology and behavior in the Baltic and Balkan lands. For Americans and all peoples, Clemens notes the contributions to "consilience" (E. O. Wilson's term) that radiate from the writings of Herman Melville and Ralph Waldo Emerson.

This book does not offer the last word on complexity science and world affairs. Like the first flights by the Wright brothers, however, Clemens shows brilliantly how theory can illuminate and benefit praxis. His book provides a model—perhaps a paradigm—that researchers in many fields can follow as they depart from simplistic reductionisms, aware and wary of the adjacent possibles that may emerge as humans co-evolve with each other and their ever-changing environment.

STUART A. KAUFFMAN

Stuart A. Kauffman is Professor Emeritus, University of Pennsylvania; Distinguished Visiting Professor, University of Vermont; Affiliate Professor, The Institute for Systems Biology; and former MacArthur Fellow.

TO THE READER

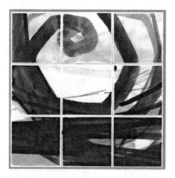

This book is about societal fitness—defined by complexity scientists as the ability to cope with complex challenges. The capacity to cope with complexity, this book argues, hinges heavily on culture—the values and way of life of each society. These values, in turn, arise from the heritage of a broad civilization such as Western Christianity or Islam. To be sure, many other factors shape fitness—including the role of individuals both inside and outside of government. But some cultures give rise to outstanding individuals while others suppress them. Some cultures help people to take advantage of their resources, while others waste and abort them.

Can fitness be measured? The best single measure is probably the United Nations Human Development Index (HDI). The index seeks to evaluate how well each society enhances the range of choice for its members. To do so, it measures health, education, and income in each UN member state.

Since the HDI omits other variables relevant to fitness, this book supplements the UN index by rankings of democratization, honesty, and knowledge-based economics by Freedom House, the Bertelsmann Foundation, Transparency International, and the Harvard-MIT Index of Economic Complexity. All these rankings try to show the absolute and the relative fitness of each actor, for example, changes in life expectancy within each country and how they compare with movements up or down in other states.

A drive to excel—as individuals and as communities—is essential to fitness in the twenty-first century, but so is the ability to create shared values by cooperation. This quality is very different from the brute strength endorsed by

Social Darwinists in the nineteenth century, the rugged individualism favored by Ayn Rand and her disciples, the egotistical "rational choice" expectations of many social scientists, and the "every man for himself" orientation of many politicians.

Two quite different views of reality have guided students of human affairs for millennia. Materialistic realists have assumed that political actors pursue power and wealth; idealists, that humans are—or should be—guided by ideals. Each approach has inspired a *paradigm*—a model of scientific inquiry—that filters and colors our view of human affairs. Materialistic and idealistic paradigms reveal important aspects of reality, but not the "entire elephant." When they miss parts of the whole, narrow-gauge paradigms can blur or even distort our vision. This book searches for a paradigm that moves international and comparative studies beyond traditional versions of realism and idealism-moralism and their "neo" offspring such as structuralism, institutional liberalism, constructivism, and feminism. Complexity science offers a better guide to understanding and changing the world than maxims such as "get rich and grow power" or "pursue your ideals."

Complexity science sees the planet and its inhabitants as interdependent—mutually vulnerable—so closely linked that they can help as well as harm one another. To advance individual and group interests, all parties need to see life not as a zero-sum struggle but as a coordination game aimed at promoting mutual gain.

Relations within and among societies are complex—nonlinear and in many ways unpredictable. Neither realist nor idealist paradigms help scholars to explain the speed, timing, location, and intensity of civil violence, revolutions, and failed democratic transitions. The basic concepts of complexity science outlined below in chapter 2 provide a useful way to analyze and perhaps change the world for the common good. Subsequent chapters apply these concepts to understand the relatively harmonious transformation of the Baltic republics compared with the Balkans; to assess post-communist developments across Eurasia from Albania to Mongolia; to analyze the challenges to America's fitness; and to comprehend the dynamism of South Korea relative to the North. Chapter 10 compares complexity with other paradigms for analyzing fourteen basic problems in world affairs.

The theories and problems discussed here are central to the study of comparative and global politics and, by extension, to social sciences broadly. Historians, psychologists, and philosophers may also find here facts and ideas that confirm, add to, or challenge their existing views.

We shall see that complexity science helps to describe and explain our past and present, but is less useful as a way to prescribe or predict consequences. Still, a better understanding of fitness implies actions that can bolster a society's ability to cope with complexity. While absolute prediction is not feasible, we can say that, all things being equal, if x and y, then z is more likely.

This book suggests that complexity science, despite its limitations, can help explain some of the most vexing questions of political institutionalization, democratization, and development. The concept of fitness, basic to some versions of complexity science, can measure the ability of nations to navigate the complexity and unpredictability of the modern world. At least for now, however, complexity science offers a useful paradigm of world affairs rather than a comprehensive theory. Complexity science can extend the ability of conventional theories of world affairs and increase their power to explain and, to a lesser extent, predict or prescribe.

Some critics ask, "What value does complexity science add to social inquiry?" Many of its basic concepts such as "co-evolution" and "punctuated equilibrium" are adapted from other sciences in the spirit of what E. O. Wilson calls "consilience." Some concepts of complexity science appear to be little more than common sense. Bundle them together and apply them to the peculiarities of human agency and social structures, however, and they provide a valuable way to analyze the fitness landscapes of the twenty-first century. An improved paradigm for the study of world affairs and for social science is surely "value added." Complexity science does not yet soar. Still, its emerging potential is more like the intuitions and know-how of the Wright Brothers than those of Icarus.

Acknowledgments

Deep thanks to Stuart A. Kauffman for his foreword and for his efforts to decode complexity and other fields of knowledge for me over more than half a century. Exploring the ties between art and science, Daniel Kohn provided the book's illustrations. Anshul Jain, Boston University, compressed many numbers to produce the data-rich figures throughout the book. Dino Christenson, also at Boston University, helped me fathom correlations. Neil E. Harrison in Wyoming has encouraged and joined me in proposing complexity as a useful approach to international studies. He edited and contributed to *Complexity in World Politics: Concepts and Methods of a New Paradigm* (SUNY Press, 2006) and organized several panels on this topic at meetings of the International Studies Association. Emilian Kavalski has also been a pioneer in these efforts. He organized a conference at the University of Western Sydney for which I prepared a paper. Daryl Morini in Queensland and Stephen Advocate in New Haven critiqued that essay and several chapters of this book. Ronald H. Linden at the University of Pittsburgh, series editor for my first attempt at applying complexity theory to security and development issues, has also helped me understand Eastern Europe going back to his work-study job in 1968. Alexander J. Motyl at Rutgers University has kept me abreast of developments in Ukraine and has suggested constructive ways to think about agents and structures, contingency and determinism. J. David Singer at Michigan has been a friend for decades and, though not a convert to complexity, has supported my efforts to make studies of Eurasia and the United

States more systematic. Merle Lefkoff and her colleagues in Santa Fe spurred me to think about complexity science and security issues. Yaneer Bar-Yam has broadened my horizons by seminars and international conferences arranged by his New England Complexity Systems Institute. S. Frederick Starr at SAIS has focused on Central Asia and the Caucasus for decades, all the while encouraging me to explore complexity as a way to understand Eurasia. Earlier versions of chapters 3 and 4 were presented at the Conference on Border Changes in Twentieth Century Europe held at Tartu University in February 2005, and the National Meeting of the International Studies Association in Honolulu in March 2005. My thanks to Olaf Mertelsmann and other participants in these meetings for useful suggestions. Adaptations of those papers were later published in *Communist and Post-Communist Studies* and *International Journal of Peace Studies,* whose editors and reviewers made valuable comments. Rein Taagepera in Tartu and Mari-Ann Kelam in Tallinn have supported my studies of the Baltic region for years. Yurim Yi, Ezra Vogel, and Jong-Sung You made useful suggestions for an earlier version of chapter 9 presented at the International Studies Association Annual Meeting held in San Francisco, April 3, 2013. Many chapters benefit from analyses by the United Nations Development Programme, Freedom House, Transparency International, and the Bertelsmann Foundation. My special thanks to Hauke Hartmann at the Bertelsmann Foundation for providing Figure 9.1 comparing South and North Korea.

While I taught at M.I.T. and Boston University starting in the 1960s, my research base all those years has been Harvard University and its Davis Center for Russian and Eurasian Studies, Belfer Center for Science and International Affairs, and Korea Institute. Ideas put forward by Harvard political scientists Joseph S. Nye, Graham Allison, and the late Samuel P. Huntington, not to mention the great "ant man" E. O. Wilson, run through nearly every chapter.

Sharon Donahue, Office Essentials, and Karen Kenney, Organizing Works, provided both moral and technical assistance.

Dr. Michael Rinella at the SUNY Press has been a supportive, patient, and helpful editor. He corralled two reviewers who went over the manuscript with a fine-toothed comb, not once but twice. I am grateful for their judicious, erudite, and constructive suggestions.

Thanks to family—especially Ali and Anna close by, and Lani et al. in California—for indulging my retreats from the world and occasional reentries. Let's hope we all learn how to cope with the challenges of complexity!

chapter one

WHY A SCIENCE OF COMPLEXITY?

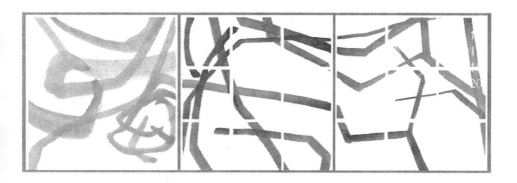

"Quarks are simple but jaguars are complex," explained the Nobel laureate in physics and pioneer in complexity science Murray Gell-Mann (1994). So too, the inner workings of a cell in a worm are more complex than those of the sun. A survey of particle physics research finds that the "universe is a complex and intricate place" (Lincoln 2012).

Humans are even more complex than worms or jaguars—especially in world affairs as individuals and groups of humans deal with one another across borders of culture, language, politics, and geography. As Ralph Waldo Emerson put it 1847, "The last lesson of modern science is that the highest simplicity of structure is produced, not by few elements, but by the highest complexity. Man is the most composite of all creatures"—quite the opposite of the wheel insect, *volvox glob*.

The difference between complexity and complication was made clear in an essay by Daniel Barenboim on Richard Wagner (*New York Review of Books*, June 20, 2013). "Wagner's music is often complex, sometimes simple, but never complicated." Complication implies "the use of unnecessary mechanisms or techniques that could potentially obfuscate the meaning of the music. These are not present in Wagner's work." By contrast, complexity in Wagner's music is represented by multidimensionality—"many layers that may be individually simple but that constitute a complex construction when taken together." When Wagner transforms a theme, he does so by adding dimensions. "The individual transformations are sometimes simple but never primitive. . . ." Wagner's "complexity is always a means and never a goal in itself."

Human society and culture did not just drop from the sky but, like other human activities, arose from beings and processes shaped by millions of years of evolution (Wilson 2012). Humans and the estimated seven million other animals who now roam the planet, from the ocean floor to the highest mountains, evolved from single-celled ancestors who, some eight hundred million years ago, probably resembled today's *Capsapora owczarsaki,* a tentacled, amoeba-like creature barely noticed by scientists until 2002. Animal bodies can total trillions of cells, able to develop into muscles, bones, and hundreds of other kinds of tissues and cell types. From single cells arose a vast kingdom of complexity and diversity (Zimmer 2012).

Humans, however, are not just "wet robots" (Dilbert's term) and social science is not just biology or physics. Still, those who seek to understand political life need an approach to scientific inquiry with strong links to the life and other sciences. They must consider human affairs in the context of other animate and inanimate activities across a shrinking planet.

Scientists from many disciplines now mobilize to study the most complex object in the known universe, the human brain. The brain activity mapping project sponsored by the U.S. government, starting in 2013, and conducted at several universities will study how the brain is wired at all levels—from individual nerve cells to the neuronal superhighways between its various lobes and ganglia. The project will institutionalize the emerging science of connectomics. Brain mapping and the human connectome project should shed light not only on mental processes but also on mental disease, brain injuries, and psychopathologies.

THE COMPLEXITY OF INTERDEPENDENCE

The complexity of global interdependence demands a science of complexity to fathom it. The essence of life is interdependence—every element dependent on every other. Walt Whitman depicted this reality in his *Salut au Monde*:

Such gliding wonders! Such sights and sounds!
Such join'd unended links, each hook'd to the next,
Each answering all, each sharing the earth with all. . . .
I see the shaded part on one side where the sleepers are sleeping,
    and the sunlit part on the other side,
I see the curious rapid change of the light and shade,
I see distant lands, as real and near to the inhabitants of them as
    my land is to me.

A few years before Whitman composed his *Leaves of Grass,* Karl Marx in 1848 described how global economics intensified the planet's "unended links, each hook'd to the next." And long before Thomas L. Friedman (2007) argued that *The World Is Flat,* the *Communist Manifesto* declared: "In place of the old local and national seclusion and self-sufficiency, we have intercourse in every direction, universal interdependence of nations [*eine allseitige Abhängigheit der Nationen voreinander*]. And as in material, so also in intellectual production. The intellectual creations of individual nations become common property. National one-sidedness and narrow-mindedness become more and more impossible, and from the numerous national and local literatures, there arises a world literature."

The *Manifesto* postulated that human history is the story of class struggle rooted in a materialist dialectic. More than two millennia before Marx, Thucydides described a struggle for political hegemony that nearly destroyed the glory that was Greece. The idea that politics is dominated by zero-sum competition was set out again by Machiavelli in Renaissance Florence and by Thomas Hobbes amid England's seventeenth-century civil war. Hobbes postulated a "war of all against all" that can be quelled only by an almighty sovereign who imposes order over anarchy. Twisting Darwin's theory of evolution to rationalize European dominion over Africa and Asia, nineteenth-century Social Darwinists proclaimed that life is a struggle for survival and that might makes right. Jack London in the early twentieth century described life in Alaska as dog-eat-dog. Nazi geopoliticians asserted that East Europeans must give way so the master race could expand.

Contrary to Marx, to Social Darwinists, and to disciples of Ayn Rand, we now see that evolution is complex—shaped by cooperation as well as competition—between and within species (Kropotkin 1904; Minelli and Fusco 2008; Flannery 2011). The red-toothed "survival of the fittest" interpretation of evolution is much too simplistic. Humans, like other living things, often collaborate to increase their survival prospects and other interests. Scientists debate whether cooperative tendencies result from a "selfish gene" or other factors. The Nobel Prize for Economics in 1986 went to James M. Buchanan, who warned that politicians and publics seeking their own self-interest could institutionalize irresponsibility as government outlays exceeded revenue. The Nobel Prize for Economics in 2012 went to an economist and a mathematician, Alvin Roth and Lloyd Shapley, who used cooperative game theory to show how goods could be shared to mutual advantage.[1]

As humans specialized, society became more complex and interdependence mounted. Adam Smith posited an "invisible hand" that served the common good. This was not the whole story, however, for interdependence can cut two ways. The term denotes *mutual vulnerability*—a relationship so close that the parties can help or hurt one another If an actor cannot deflect the changes made by another, it is "vulnerable." If it can thwart the change, it is merely "sensitive" (Keohane and Nye 2011). The policy implication is that the invisible hand may need guidance and even regulation.

A fit society thrives on complexity and its capacity to create values from the challenges and opportunities arising from an ever-changing environment.

Like a coral reef, participants in a fit society exist in a symbiosis that protects and nourishes both individuals and the wider community. Mutual gain and high fitness are the products of self-organization and creative responses to complexity. Diminished fitness, by contrast, is the consequence of a zero-sum, exploitative approach to life—the usual pattern when there is no law or rigid, top-down rule. These concepts are elaborated in later chapters, but the basic argument is summarized in Figure 1.1.

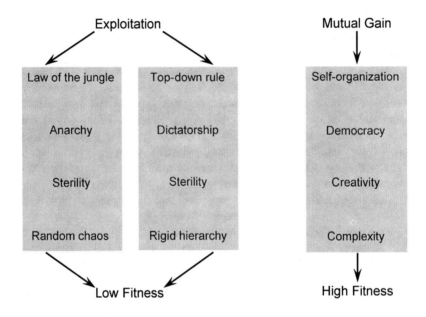

FIGURE 1.1. Exploitation, Mutual Gain, and Fitness: Likely Linkages

CHAOS OR COMPLEXITY?

The deep realities of life are difficult to discern and assess. As John Muir cautioned, "Touch one thing and you find it is linked to everything in the universe." If a butterfly flaps her wings in China, how will this affect the next day's weather in Kansas? As weather develops, it feeds back on itself and influences future weather. The butterfly effect underscores the interconnectedness of all things. Even if we could trace long chains of interaction, however, small errors in initial measurements would multiply and lead to erroneous conclusions. Chaos theorists conclude that the chains of cause and effect in many domains—weather, turbulent rivers, insect populations, stock markets, and others—cannot be accurately predicted. Some chaotic structures may be in principle deterministic, but in practice they are virtually unpredictable (Marshall and Zohar 1997, 81–86; Krasner 1990). A miniscule error in the initial measurement of just one variable will skew the entire calculation.

Complexity science agrees with chaos theory and worldviews such as Buddhism that all things are interdependent. But it avers—or hopes—that common patterns characterize the evolution of all things, and that, with hard work and some luck, we may identify them and begin to fathom their interactions. Thus, complexity scientists have discovered fractal properties within heartbeats as well as in stock market movements and air flow turbulence.[2] They have investigated scalability. It appears that some of the same principles apply to animals of different sizes and species—even to cells. Thus, the metabolic rate is proportional to body mass in everything from a mouse to a goose to an elephant. Organisms reach a certain weight at a certain age. Or look at a forest. At first, it may seem to be a wild thicket, randomly organized, with no structure. But there is structure. A forest has trees of a certain type, size, and age—often spaced at a similar distance from each other, each consuming a similar amount of energy and growing at a similar pace. In bodies, as in entire ecosystems and in sprawling cities, networks provide basic functions that range from blood circulation to irrigation to electric transmission. The pace of life slows as size of organism increases. There are economies of scale. Cities, like organisms, seem to obey power laws of scaling. As cities expand, we see fewer gas stations per capita. With more people, the length of electric lines needed to serve each person decreases. The dynamics of life go beyond mere natural selection (West 2011).

It may appear that complexity can be reduced to regularity and simplicity. Thus, Acemoglu and Robinson (2012) studied many complex and seemingly quite different cases over time and concluded that "nations fail" because their leaders exploit the common good for private gain.[3] Similarly, Emerson (1847) believed that Goethe possessed "a power to unite the detached atoms again by their own law." Goethe contributed a key to many parts of nature through the rare turn for unity and simplicity in his mind.[4]

Following in the footsteps of Goethe and—before him—Leonardo Da Vinci, complexity scientists seek to identify and understand the patterns of behavior common to all forms of life.[5] But many structures—from a beehive to the weather to the human brain—seem to defy any reductive approach. Isaac Newton appeared to have discovered the basic laws underlying the flux of physical motion, but Newtonian physics was later supplemented or supplanted by relativity and quantum mechanics.[6] Reductionism does not work where reality breaks from linear sequencing—with outcomes not proportional to ostensible causes, and where wholes cannot be understood from analyzing their parts (Kauffman 2008).

Classical economics is also reductionist. It assumes that the real value of goods is determined by the price they fetch in the market place. Put into practice, however, this approach is unfair and conduces to huge disparities in income. Theoretically, it is untenable because one cannot know in advance what goods and what supply/demand conditions will exist. Nor, in biology, could we anticipate that from the lungs of lung fish would evolve the swim bladders that assure neutral buoyancy in the water column of certain fish—nor what kinds of creatures would find their niche within those bladders (Kauffman 2008; 2011).

THE EVOLUTION OF SOCIETAL FITNESS

A system of cooperative bands provides the social infrastructure that can nurture creativity. The social institutions and behaviors that differentiate humans from other primates developed in large part because they were enabled by biological and historical accidents. Cooperation is a key behavior that distinguishes humans from other primates. A system of cooperative bands provides the social infrastructure that nurtures human creativity. No individual can construct a rocket ship. To build and fly the International Space Station required the collaboration of thousands of persons, most of whom never met one another, and many of whom came from "tribes" with distinct languages and ways of life.

Social institutions and world affairs, like all evolution, have been decisively impacted by accidents. "Evolution is, fundamentally, a process of cumulative integration: Novel combinations of older material or otherwise ordinary features generate systems of new properties—emergent properties—which in turn promote further evolutionary change" (Chapais 2008, 303). Nothing appears to have been unidirectional or foreordained.

Biology is not physics.[7] Very little in evolution was preset. Little could be prestated or anticipated. Living beings evolve in ways that defy prediction. Each step in evolution is a kind of preadaptation. Each innovation arises from and builds on what precedes it. Each creates an "enablement" or "adjacent possible" from which new adjacent possibles can emerge (Kauffman 2008). Mutant genes gave some individuals traits better adapted to survive and prosper in their environment.

The evolution of society and life itself is impossible to predict because of adjacent possibles. Each new adaptation opens the way to other innovations, as the laptop computer opened the way to iPhones and social networking—all undreamed of by those who, during World War II, sought a mechanical system to break German codes. Who could have predicted Facebook without first anticipating the invention of the Internet and then of miniature computers? We cannot prestate such innovations.

Both serendipity and synergy contribute to unforeseeable outcomes. Still, once a series of enabling conditions has conduced to a new set of conditions, one can look back and say that such-and-such factors seemed to have led to such-and-such effects. In retrospect, it seems clear that growing complexity has bred still more complexity.

Many features that make humans more adaptable than other primates and some human societies more fit than others have resulted from biological and historical accidents. Once humans learned to communicate and plan, some gained fitness by acts of cognition and volition—they made smart (or lucky) choices and tried to execute them. If we go far back in time, however, successful adaptation to a changing environment depended in large part on accident—an opportune conjunctions of self with other.

The distinctive qualities of human behavior derive from many factors. The genomes of humans and chimpanzees are 99 percent the same, but humans learned to cooperate in ways that gave them powers unknown to chimps and any other animals. How did humans—unlike other primates—learn to cooperate? The answer began four to six million years ago when the apelike creatures from which hominoids descended broke off from the ancestral line shared with chimpanzees. Some apelike creatures acquired a more human *form* approximately one hundred thousand years ago, but distinctly human *behavior* did not emerge until about fifty thousand years ago. *Homo sapiens* acquired a more nuanced language about that time and an instinct for reciprocity that governed social relations within the group and trade with outsiders. These people practiced religious rituals and could mobilize for war. The cold and dryness of the great Ice Age had reduced this group to some five thousand individuals, but as the Pleistocene glaciers receded, some recovered and some moved out of Africa. The migrants cohabitated with but eventually displaced two sets of earlier hominids—*homo neanderthalensis* who had emigrated from Africa many thousands of years earlier and settled in the Middle East and Europe, and the *homo erectus* who had found their way to East Asia. These developments have been traced mainly by the studies of the human genome, because written histories of mankind go back only five thousand years and most archeological finds stop fifteen thousand years ago (Wade 2006).

Two foundations of cooperation, fire and weapons, served as adjacent possibles whose consequences could never have been prestated. Having observed how natural phenomena can start fires, early hominids learned to make and sustain fire. As some hominids huddled around a fire, they improved their communications and launched a division of labor. Some continued to hunt and gather but others could plant and harvest. In time, still other enabling conditions permitted some to develop writing, mathematics, and other technologies that permitted even larger and more complex communities (Wilson 2012).

Weapons also generated cooperation. Their advent helps explain why humans—unlike chimpanzees—need not be subject to an alpha male and his allies. When some hominoids became bipedal, they could walk more efficiently than on folded knuckles. Just as important, their hands were liberated to gesture and to manipulate objects—not just digging tools for agriculture but also weapons. Clubs and spears became equalizers. No longer could the physically stronger alphas readily dominate other males and females. When all males were armed, the cost of monopolizing a large number of females became higher.[8] Females became allocated to males more equally. The orgiastic promiscuity of apes gave way to the pair bond between male and female. Each male now had an incentive to guard his mate and his paternity. The deep structure of human society arose from the sequence *male kin group + pair-bonding → exogamy* (Chapais 2008).

Pair bonding opened the way to hominid evolution. Pair bonding transformed a social organization loosely based on kinship into one exhibiting the strong hold of kinship and affinity. Having two parents permitted infants to be dependent for longer periods and, as a result, to enjoy continued brain growth. Bonding also revealed the genealogical structure of the family. Now males could recognize their sisters and daughters in neighboring bands. The presence of female relatives in neighboring bands became a bridge that permitted a new and more complex social structure. Neighboring males could be seen as in-laws rather than as enemies. Bands that exchanged women learned to cooperate. Some formed a group or tribe. Cooperation could become the norm within a tribe, even though one tribe might fight another as relentlessly as chimpanzee bands.

Hominid society entered a runaway, snowballing evolutionary process that conformed to the basic pattern of evolution—integration of old and new material to form emergent properties and new adjacent possibles. The process benefited from many accidental conjunctures: Kinship structures dominated by fathers emerged when fathers could recognize their offspring and by lengthened father-son bonds. Kin-group exogamy and postmarital residence patterns resulted from the merging of pair bonding and kin-group dispersal. Bilateral kinship networks occurred after uterine kin recognition processes combined with consistent paternity recognition and the tribal level of organization (Chapais 2008, 303).

Changes in the environment also pressed hominoids to cooperate. The Ice Age dried up forests, pushing some of our ancestors into the savannah. Those who could walk on two legs could cover larger distances with less energy than those still on four legs. Some learned to cooperate not only to guard against predators but also to hunt and gather food. They became obligate collaborators.

Another accident helped humans to communicate and share their intentions and plans (Tomasello 2009). The whites of human eyes are three times larger than those of any other primate. When a human shifts his or her gaze, others can infer his or her intention. Chimps infer the direction of a gaze by looking at another's head; human infants do so by watching the eyes.

There was no single pressure that made us human, because "human" evolved by a series of accidents. The fact that humans could recognize their patrilineal kind was not selected for. Still, this development permitted movement toward peaceful relations with other groups. *"Effects" had "causes," but the synergistic relationships among coevolving genes, temperaments, and contexts could be perceived only after they took shape.* A multiplicity of factors combined to reduce violence among humans from prehistoric times to the twenty-first century (Pinker 2011). This trend would be invisible to news junkies and could be traced only by historical analysis.

The trends toward less violence and longer life expectancy could be shattered by imaginable events such as nuclear war and pandemics and by unimagined "Black Swans." Would-be forecasters often underestimate the size and frequency of "thick tails"—critical events that occur more frequently than usually believed. People should count on the appearance of more Black Swans, some of them long present but undiscovered, plus others freshly emerged from adjacent possibles. Both thick tails and Black Swans curtail the scope of meaningful prediction (Taleb 2007).

In a world dominated by chaos and uncertainty, some people, systems, and institutions do not succumb but rather manage to benefit from shocks of the new. They resemble the Greek hydra that grew two heads for each one it lost (Taleb 2011; 2012). Antifragility can be seen as a crowning attribute of societal fitness.

Meanwhile, most innovations are Janus-faced. Walking on just two legs freed humanoids to travel far and use their hands, but bipedalism also contributed to back and hip pains. Enablements that permitted each hominoid to wield weapons led to polygyny and later to monogamy, but individuals and groups with the most lethal weapons could still dominate others or die trying. The combination of larger brains and improved weapons produced carnage on scales hitherto unknown. Pair bonding led to cooperation and harmony among ever-larger social entities, but when one large political unit confronted another, whole peoples were decimated, enslaved, or even exterminated. Pair bonding helped defend mothers and infants, prolonging the time when children could develop. But it also fostered jealousy, distrust, and divorce so the point where many people now eschew formal bonding altogether.

Still another paradox remains: Why altruism? If living beings are driven to perpetuate their genes, why do humans as well as ants sometimes sacrifice themselves for others? Humans and certain insects are the only species that form communities that contain multiple generations and where, as part of a division of labor, community members sometimes perform altruistic acts for the benefit of others. Social insects such as bees and ants exhibit the Darwinian paradox of evolved sterility. How could sterility evolve by a process that favors reproduction? For years most scientists answered, "*kin* selection for inclusive fitness." On this view, sterile workers that serve the hive are selected for because they spread their genes through helping their mothers, sisters, and brothers to reproduce. But E. O. Wilson (2012) and some other scientists challenged the consensus with a theory of *group* selection. They attributed "altruism" to a gene-based drive to perpetuate the group. When it is advantageous to cooperate, those genes that promote cooperation will be favored. Competition of one group against others rewards self-sacrificial behaviors by individuals that benefit all group members, even those that are not kin.[9] The gene for high-order sociality is not linked to kinship but to social organization. A gene that guides a human or other animal to help its relatives could spread through the population even if the helping action harmed the animal itself.

But theories derived from insect behavior may not apply to humans. What looks like altruism can arise simply from experience and enlightened self-interest. It is well established that unrelated individuals can benefit from repeated cooperation with one another, so long as there are mechanisms in place to encourage reciprocity and punish betrayal by cheats and freeriders (Bloom 2012).

Altruism can also spring from a sense of human solidarity and empathy—products of nurture as well as nature. Many individuals risk themselves to save absolute strangers and foreigners. Some take risks to assist nonhumans.

Teaching is another form of altruism. Individual teachers and schools donate information to others, including non-kin and even foreigners. According to Tomasello (2009), both teaching and norms of conformity contribute to *cumulative* culture by *conserving* innovations. Like other species, humans learn to exploit to meet their survival needs. But humans seem also born and bred to cooperate. Machiavelli was probably correct when he said that "a prince must learn how not to be good." Babies cooperate as they begin to walk and talk. Their indiscriminate cooperativeness is later mediated by judgments of likely reciprocity and concern for how others will judge them. In time they internalize social norms. Humans imitate to be like others in their group. They develop rules to enforce conformity. These behaviors arise from *gene-culture coevolution* and from processes of cultural niche construction—adaptations to help humans function in any one of the many self-built cultural worlds.

Languages and the cultures that spawn them are also complicated. The world's lingua franca became English in the twentieth century. At some time the balance may shift to Chinese, but—derived from many cultures and emerging sciences—English has acquired a richer vocabulary than any other language. This trove could reduce ambiguity and improve clarity of expression. But to master the meanings of these many words and the irregular grammar that joins them is not easy. The pitfalls were manifest in an announcement posted in a hotel in the former Yugoslavia: "The flattening of underwear with pleasure is the job of the chambermaid. Turn to her straightway." A British motorist in Tokyo might also be taken aback by an instruction to "tootle with vigor" any pedestrian who "obstacles his passage." Even well-versed Americans can confuse meanings. Jimmy Carter said Iran should not "flaunt" the world community when he meant *flout*. George H. W. Bush spoke of the "enormity" of his election in 1988—a term connoting monstrous wickedness (Bryson 1990, 11, 140).

Thus, the history of human culture has been autocatalytic. Jumping ahead to events since the first large human settlements, Jared Diamond (1997) explained how geographical peculiarities such as the existence of cattle and horses in Eurasia bolstered the fitness of Eurasians compared to Americans and other peoples. Cattle and horses proved invaluable both in peace and war. Aztecs and Incas, for example, had nothing comparable. In chapters 3 to 6 below we shall see how, starting six centuries ago, other developments, intangible but not entirely accidental, helped Westerners dominate the world. Mass literacy and free thought took root in Europe and became a force more fundamental than guns, germs, or steel. Literacy and free thought, together with a new respect for individual dignity (of both genders) fed on the synergies of the Renaissance and the Reformation. Martin Luther's demand that all persons read Holy Scripture in their vernacular went against the official language of the established church, incomprehensible to most peoples whose languages had long departed from imperial Latin or Greek. The recently perfected printing press served as an adjacent possible that made mass literacy a feasible ambition. Gold and other riches from the New World funded still other innovations. These riches were a kind of accident, for they might have been acquired earlier by Chinese or Arab sailors had their sponsors possessed the boundless greed and curiosity of Europeans. In the 1830s, Alexis de Tocqueville asserted that two nations were destined to rule the world—one rooted in slavery, the other in freedom. By the 1990s, freedom appeared to have prevailed—thanks in part to geographical factors such as the protection afforded by two oceans.

The future of the twenty-first century will probably be greatly influenced the complex interdependence of China and the United States. Circumstances gave China a huge population of studious and hardworking people but a poor resource base and a diminished moral code. The United States continued to harbor vast hard and soft power assets, albeit vitiated (as we shall see in chapters 7 and 8) by a growing deficit of wisdom and smart power. Depending on many adjacent possibles and their choices, the two countries could build on their complementary needs—or fight. Neither course is predetermined.

Huge mysteries remain: How did some hominids acquire consciousness and, it seems, a conscience? How to explain the "sapiens paradox" that complex civilizations with monuments and astronomy arose in widely separated regions at about the same time? Is increasing complexity tantamount to successful adaptation? Or does growing complexity eventually lead to atrophy and self-destruction? The number of complex entities seems to increase, causing the envelope of complexity to expand, but entropy and other forces may be able to reverse these trends.

IS COMPLEXITY GOOD OR BAD?

Is greater complexity good or bad—in ecosystems and/or in human affairs? Should rule makers try to regulate every contingency or just deal with the basics?

Alan Siegel and Irene Etzkorn (2013) want to conquer "the crisis of complexity." They report that the U.S. tax code tripled in size in the early twenty-first century to nearly four million words. The tax code is not just "complicated" but also complex, as its many elements interact in nonlinear ways. Its complexity generated work for accountants, lawyers, and lobbyists but made it nearly incomprehensible for most taxpayers. The message from Siegel and Etzkorn to governments and other organizations amounted to this: "Strip away the red tape. Be fruitful and simplify."

"Red tape" might be burdensome, but some regulation is necessary. How and where to strike the appropriate balance? The Office of Information and Regulatory Affairs under President Barack Obama backed high efficiency standards for motor vehicles but postponed rules to cut ozone emissions (Sunstein 2013). Did the office regulate too much or too little? Its decisions reflected a complex of interacting economic, environmental, and—in the end—political concerns.

The May-Widmer stability theorem holds that greater complexity in ecosystems, with more species and interactions among them, increases their vulnerability to external shocks. A small perturbation can disrupt a large, complex system. The introduction of an exotic species—a toad, pig, goat, or mongoose—can destabilize an entire ecosystem. Professor May (2012) grants that complex, species-rich ecosystems, such as coral reefs or tropical rain forests, are able to arise and persist in relatively predictable environments, but harsh, unpredictable environments favor simpler life forms. Thus, monocultures of *Spartina alterniflora* flourish in the highly stressed marshlands of New Jersey.

Professor May, a zoologist, suggests that financial systems and products have become too complex and too costly. In finance, as in ecology, complexity adds to system vulnerability. Highly connected structures are best avoided. There is no evidence that big and highly interconnected banks are less liable to failure than small ones. The epidemiology of H.I.V./AIDS shows how "superspreaders" can disseminate infection. "Arguably, the pressures that have driven financial ecosystems to ever-increasing complexity have been more about rent-taking than about optimising the distribution of capital in a free market." The moral—more is less—remains. May recommends smaller agents in simpler systems regulated by simpler and shorter sets of rules.

Some critics contend that the May-Widmer theorem applies only to random systems—not to real-world networks, which have acquired structure.

Indeed, some scientists say that the theorem is wrong, because complex diversity is healthful and increases the overall productivity of ecosystems. Thus, soils with highly complex microbiological communities cycle nutrients more efficiently—as when complex and diverse fungal communities support old growth forests.

Analogous disputes arise in the analysis of international power. Which distribution of power is more conducive to stability and overall fitness—complex multipolarity or simple bipolarity or even simpler unipolarity? A complex multipolar system correlated with the long peace of the nineteenth century. If one power became too strong, others balanced against it. Still, this complex system permitted many small wars and finally erupted in the cataclysm of World War I. A much simpler, bipolar confrontation underlay a cold peace with some small wars from the late 1940s to late 1980s. When the bipolar balance became uncertain in 1962, however, efforts by the weaker side to regain its leverage by deploying missiles to Cuba nearly provoked Armageddon. Some decades later, the collapse of the USSR left just one superpower. Unipolarity promised a new world order but did not prevent Iraq's invasion of Kuwait and subsequent Gulf War. A few years later, jihadists began to terrorize the sole superpower and its allies.

So is complexity a positive or negative force in world politics? A detached observer would probably conclude that there is no simple answer. The unipolar Pax Americana, like the Pax Romana, generated both pluses and minuses both for the imperial power and for others. If China becomes a sort of superpower like the United States, will bipolarity conduce to peace or to conflict? The two countries could focus on their interests in common or on points of discord. Even if the two greatest powers seek peace, however, smaller powers—some with nuclear weapons—could act as spoilers.

Robert Keohane and Joseph Nye (2011) postulated that "complex interdependence" makes war nearly unthinkable. Between the United States and Canada, for example, interactions take place on many levels—governmental, economic, cultural, and social. So many interests fill each country's agenda that no one interest (for example, fishing rights) could be worth fighting for. Thus, complexity fosters peace. This argument is plausible, but Europe's complex interdependence did not prevent war in 1914. And the 2013 travails of "united Europe" point to many downsides of complexity. It was far easier to reach agreements among the six states that formed the European Coal and Steel Community in 1951 than among the twenty-eight EU members in 2013. Greece could more easily be competitive if it controlled its own currency rather than being locked into a common currency.

Bottom line: Complex interdependencies defy simple answers. A progressively fragile and interdependent world means that vulnerable people face an increased risk from shocks and disruptions (Rockefeller Foundation 2012). And yet this world also includes extraordinary growth in human knowledge and technological capacity. There is a race between mushrooming challenges and unprecedented growth in our capabilities. New technologies may bolster or erode psychological, social, and systemic resilience.

In complex systems with elements in dynamic connection, conventional scientific assumptions do not seem to hold. Instead, the behavior of a system "emerges" from the interaction of its elements (Casti 1995; Holland 1998; Levin 1999). Relationships *among* elements rather than the elements themselves become the focus of research. The elements in a complex system adapt in response to the actions of other elements in the system and to their environment—hence the concept "complex adaptive system" or CAS. Each CAS may be embedded in another CAS, as a tree is part of a forest nested in a large ecosystem. Operating through positive feedback loops, small-scale "causes" may be amplified to produce large-scale "effects." Because these interactions are nonlinear, however, study of their components in isolation cannot predict their outcomes (Hendrick 2010, 386).

Goethe's Mephistopheles explained how difficult it is to comprehend complex interdependence. Logicians may posit that life is like a syllogism— "one, two, three." But the fabric of thought (*Gedankenfabrik*) should be like a masterpiece of weaving. One step on the shuttle and a thousand threads arise. Another blow, still more threads emerge and scatter. Would-be philosophers may say things *had* to be thus and thus. But they never learned to weave. Trying to describe a living thing, some analysts begin by driving the spirit from its parts. They may hold all the pieces in one hand. They lack nothing except the essential connections (*Faust* I, 1920–41). Even history is an illusion. Our attempts to capture the spirit of an earlier time become no more than mirrors of our own temperament. As Faust warned a student, the few who see and describe things as they are "have at all times been burned and crucified" (*Faust* I, 570–93). Indeed, said Mephistopheles, "All theory is gray, while life is green like a golden tree" (*Faust* I, 2038–39).[10]

Mephistopheles was on target. "Complect" is to join by weaving. The proto-Indo-European root of complexity is *plek*—a plait, as in duplex or multiplex, and in complex and perplex. John Locke in 1690 noted that complex concepts such as beauty and gratitude are woven from several simple ideas. Thus, our concept of father embodies both guardian and master. Dealing with complexity, both the artist and the scientist weave a unity from many strands and parts. Their skills, said the Unitarian minister James Martineau in 1869, can make complexities vanish.[11]

Is there a "web" across borders? The relationships among some two hundred states and thousands of nonstate actors on the global scene surely produce a complex adaptive system. Global politics and international organization can be and have been studied as systems. Robert Jervis (1997) and other scholars have analyzed "system effects."[12] But explaining cross-border complexity is a complex undertaking. Seeking to cut through the complexity, neorealists apply their version of Occam's Razor: they purport to explain global politics as a set of responses to the hierarchy of power (Waltz 1979; 1986; 2000). Doing so, they ignore other key levels of cross-border relations—from individuals and states to transnational movements and the all-encompassing biosphere. Scientists agree that, if all things are equal, a simpler explanation is preferred to a complex one—but only if the explanation is also *sufficient,* that is, takes account of all the key variables. Since neorealists ignore important explanatory variables, their approach is not sufficient. Their effort at parsimony goes too far.[13] Ironically, Waltz (1959) had earlier demonstrated the importance of analyzing individuals and the state as well as the system.

A generation before Waltz (1979) published the foundational text of neorealism, Morton Kaplan (1957) depicted international relations (IR) as a mechanical system. But his portrait of IR struck many analysts as simplistic and misleading. Standing on the shoulders of Quincy Wright and Raymond Aron, Stanley Hoffmann (1960, 179–84) suggested that scholars instead develop a comparative historical sociology of diplomatic constellations or "fields." Each field needed to be identified by (1) its structure—the major actors, hierarchy of power, and global fault lines; (2) the transnational forces shaping the material and moral context of the field; (3) the internal constitution and culture of each actor as it formulates its foreign policy; and (4) how the actors pursue their goals and how the field accommodates these strivings.

Hoffmann provided a comprehensive check list—but no way to see both the trees and the forest. To compare fields across different eras is possible but difficult. To describe even one diplomatic constellation in Hoffmann's four terms proved a daunting task.[14] And while Hoffmann included two key levels— the state and the global system—he omitted a key variable—the individuals who fillip everything else. Graham Allison's *Essence of Decision* (1971) also focuses on system-level and state-level explanations, mentioning personality factors only in passing. But the Cuban missile crisis would probably have never been initiated without Nikita S. Khrushchev or have been managed without the Kennedy brothers and Robert S. McNamara. Nor would the world scene in the 1930s have been the same without the idiosyncrasies of Hitler, Mussolini, and Stalin.

Given all the "complexities," can complexity science be relevant and useful in international studies? We put off a detailed reply to this question until chapters 10 and 11—after a review of the evidence pro and con. But the reader should be forewarned: some observers believe that "complexity science" is not a science but an illusion. John Horgan (1996) for example, asserts there are no simple, general principles of complexity. While some scholars have found efforts to apply complexity science to world affairs to be stimulating and useful, if only as a heuristic, others have found these efforts turgid and lifeless—evidence that global interactions are even more resistant to deep analysis than many scholars had imagined (Earnest and Rosenau 2006; Rosenau 2003).

Still, leading scientists in many disciplines, including Nobel laureates in physics Murray Gell-Mann and in economics Kenneth J. Arrow and Thomas C. Schelling contributed for years to complexity science, believing it to have great promise.

Aware of the difficulties, analysts of world affairs should at least consider whether complexity science (or *sciences,* since there is more than one branch) could offer them a useful tool kit—perhaps even a basic approach to studying the turbulence and nonlinearity, the cascades, and macro-micro linkages of world affairs (trenchantly described by Rosenau 1990; 2003).

THE NEED FOR A SOUND PARADIGM

Scholars of comparative politics, international relations (IR), and other social sciences could benefit from the late Saul Bellow's message to his students: "We are here, in this fallen state, riven by contradictions, given to understand some things but never others, faltering in our wills, flawed in our abilities, uncertain in our actions. But that is where we must begin and there is no excuse for not taking the task seriously" (Rothstein 2005). People expect from the social sciences the knowledge to understand their lives and control their futures. They want to know what will happen if society and its leaders opt for one course of action over another. Even with recent advances, can any social science contribute to that kind of knowledge?

Despite the dangers of reductionism, scholars (as well as political leaders) often succumb to hubris. Hoping that they have discovered the essence of things, students of politics, as in other domains, may proclaim, "I have found it!" Often, however, they have identified only the tail or an ear of the elephant—one facet of a much larger and more complicated whole (Hawkings 2002, 148). In politics, as in physics, it is difficult to reconcile theories with underlying uncertainties. In both disciplines the apparent realities are often contradictory. For example, Newton's theory of gravity does not mesh with Einstein's on relativity and neither seems to harmonize with quantum mechanics.

Scientists need a dependable paradigm (Kuhn 1970). Ideally, a paradigm should help scholars to organize their findings and guide their research. It should reflect the present state of knowledge; conduce to testable, falsifiable propositions; function with parsimony—require relatively few variables to explain outcomes; and connect with other branches of science (Singer 1970; Vasquez 1997). These criteria present high standards for students of human behavior. Some analysts doubt that essential human behaviors can be quantified or predicted. Good social science, they say, need not—probably cannot—match the precision of natural science.

Even economists, apparently the most rigorous social scientists, disagree on the most basic questions, for example, whether it is more useful to study macro trends or individual and group psychology. Confronted with recessions, economists debate whether governments should "prime the pump" or cut spending. Joseph Schumpeter, a rival of John Maynard Keynes, argued that Keynes's *General Theory of Employment, Interest and Money* (1936) offered not a general theory but a treatise concerning the special case of a decaying civilization.[15]

Based on the ancient Greek word for "pattern," the word *paradigm* implies a standard way to do science in a particular field of knowledge such as physics or astronomy. This standard (or "normal") form of science starts with a consensus on the puzzles to be solved, the methods for solving them, and the standards by which to measure scientific success. For Kuhn, the word paradigm also implies a universally recognized scientific achievement embodying the standard approach. For a time it provides model problems and solutions to a community of practitioners. That achievement may be expressed in a theory believed to express the relationships between the objects studied.

A *paradigm shift* occurs when the standard approach is challenged, modified, or even supplanted by another. Thus, Ptolemy's earth-centered view of astronomy was replaced by the heliocentric view of Galileo, Copernicus, and Kepler. If their heliocentric view were correct, the earth-centered view had to be wrong. All efforts to study the stars and planets will be confounded by a false paradigm. By the same token, if human motives and activities deviate sharply from an existing social science paradigm, research based on that approach will be off base.

Some paradigms seem not to be commensurate. They may even appear to contradict one another. Still, incommensurate paradigms help to highlight black holes in our knowledge or suggest unexpected linkages. Theories of gravity, relativity, and quantum mechanics appear to be incommensurate but each nonetheless captures major aspects of reality. Meanwhile, some scientists look for a theory that will unify all of physics.

Kuhn (1970, viii) noticed that psychologists and social scientists disagree about the nature of legitimate scientific problems and methods with far greater intensity than do astronomers, physicists, chemists, and biologists. In effect, social scientists recognize no standard, normal way to do science in their domains. Perhaps, Kuhn speculated, their subject matter is too complex and value-laden to generate consensus about scientific achievements or methods. Still, political and other social sciences can probably benefit from explicit description and analysis of their existing or proposed paradigms.

The present book expects a theory to be more precise than a science. Ideally, a theory should be testable and capable of prediction. Science, by contrast, is a branch or body of knowledge about facts and principles gathered by observation and experimentation. Complexity science is itself emerging and probably too young and diffuse to claim the existence of any agreed theory.[16] The situation resembles cosmology and physics where "one could never hope to construct a complete unified theory of everything all at one go."

Instead, researchers progress by "partial theories that describe a limited range of happenings and neglect other effects, or approximate them with certain numbers" (Hawkings 2002, 147). "The theory of evolution by cumulative natural selection is the only theory we know of that is in principle capable of explaining the existence of organized complexity" (Dawkins 1986).

Complexity science, as developed by Stuart Kauffman (1993; 1995; 2000) and others associated with the Santa Fe Institute, seeks to update, qualify, and enhance Darwinism by refining the concept of fitness and showing more clearly how it can be attained. If IR scholars gained nourishment from complexity science, this nexus would also tie their discipline more closely to the most significant and most widely accepted (by scholars) scientific discovery of recent centuries—evolution.[17]

While George Modelski (1996) and some other IR scholars have written on evolutionary paradigms in the social sciences, few IR specialists have pursued this path. The failure to link IR and comparative politics more closely with evolution is ironic given that many students of world affairs focus on the struggle for power. Many study human behavior without paying much attention to how other species or early humans have evolved and behaved.[18] To be sure, IR scholars rightly distanced themselves from "Social Darwinists" of the late nineteenth century. Given the advances in all the life sciences in recent decades, however, it is surely time for IR scholars to step up their efforts to learn from Darwin and neo-Darwinians (Wilson 1975, 1998; Somit and Peterson 1992, 2008). Social scientists should not ignore the capacity of biology and related scientists to understand and better the human condition (Hatemi and McDermott 2011; West 2011). At the same time, however, they must avoid any simplistic extrapolation from the behavioral patterns of other species to homo sapiens—equipped both with consciousness and some elements of free will.

The founding father of neorealism in IR called his seminal book *A Theory of International Politics* (Waltz 1979). But it is premature to suggest that any approach to the study of world affairs amounts to a scientific *theory*.[19] While neorealism and other purported "theories" do meet a basic definition as a "set of statements or principles devised to explain a group of facts or phenomena," none has been universally accepted. None has been subjected to rigorous testing over times with many variables. Most have been falsified—given the lie—by experience, not just once but often. Meanwhile, IR specialists disagree even on which are the basic actors, which of their interactions are relevant, and what methods to pursue in studying them.

Still, most IR scholars do pursue identifiable orientations that resemble paradigms. This book urges that interdependence and complexity be treated as valid paradigms—no less useful and perhaps more so than the various schools of realism, idealism, constructivism, and Marxism.

This book expresses aspiration rather than any claim for achievement. Complexity science underscores that purported explanations of world affairs are often too simple: many ignore the spatial organization of actors, temporal effects, and other features known to shape international behavior. An explanation should be as simple as possible *but no simpler*.

Neither complexity science nor its possible applications in IR can overcome what Karl Popper called the problem of *practical falsifiability*. Thus, scientists might aver that that the Earth will suffer a new Ice Age in forty million years. In theory, this prediction can be confirmed or falsified by experience. In practice, we can do neither for eons. Complexity science helps us to identify conditions under which practical falsifiability is impossible. It predicts the unpredictability of world affairs due to chaotic dynamics, feedback mechanisms, and the power of small events. Unlike chaos theory, however, complexity scientists believe—or hope—that significant patterns can be identified in the swirl of inanimate and living things.

EITHER/OR PARADIGMS IN INTERNATIONAL STUDIES

For millennia, many philosophers and analysts of world affairs have been trapped in a false choice between materialist and idealist paradigms.[20] They have asked: Are humans evil or good? And which is most basic—matter or form? Rooted in a materialist philosophy, realists explain all politics as a quest for power and wealth. Idealists, however, turn this picture upside down. Followers of Plato and Hegel portray human history as the reflection of ideas or a contest between opposed ideologies. Liberal idealists say that IR is—or should be—a pursuit of universal values, while other idealists campaign for the hegemony of one religion, civilization, nation, race, or class. Talking past one another, most realists focus on "what is," while most idealists emphasize "what should be" (Carr 1940).

Discontented with his ivory tower pursuits, Goethe's Faust doubted that "in the beginning was the Word." Instead of "Word," Faust wondered, should the all-creating source be rendered as "Mind [*Sinn*]"? No, he went on, everything starts with "Force [*Macht*]." But that concept also seemed too narrow. Mindful that a spiritual power helped him to write, Faust concluded, "In the beginning was the Deed [*Tat*]" (*Faust* I, 1224–37).

High above quotidian events, political philosophers debate the relevance of epistemology to world affairs. Can our knowledge come close to approximating reality, or can we do little more than test hypotheses about objects we cannot really observe (Jackson 2011)?

Since life consists of both material and spiritual elements, neither materialism nor idealism can capture reality in all its complexity.[21] World affairs are shaped by many forces—some material and deterministic, while others are intangible—ideational, moral, sentimental, spiritual. Karl Marx and Hegel latched onto quite different parts of the elephant; so did Machiavelli and Kant; Bismarck and Woodrow Wilson; Henry Kissinger and Jimmy Carter;

Niall Ferguson and Francis Fukuyama. While the various realisms and idealisms may describe aspects of IR, they usually fail to provide a comprehensive picture. To see the entire "elephant" becomes more difficult due to the rise of nonstate actors, the "flatness" of a world in which technology transfer becomes easier, and other features of globalization (Bennendijk and Kugler 2006). To understand not just the entire elephant but also the ways it may twist and turn is probably beyond scientific reach in the foreseeable future. Still, complexity science provides a framework for understanding how whole systems come to exceed their parts—and how these parts interact with each other. The basic concepts of complexity science, summarized below, provide a far more nuanced approach to understanding IR than the realist maxims of Hans J. Morgenthau (1978) or the idealist postulates of Johan Galtung (1996) and Richard A. Falk (2008).[22] Liberal institutionalism includes elements of realism and idealism. It helps explain movement in some domains, such as environmental protection regimes, but is too narrow to comprehend other dimensions of IR (Keohane 1989).

The realist and idealist paradigms widely used in political analysis appear to be not only incommensurate but contradictory. Still, major failings in the study and practice of IR have resulted from seeing, thinking, and acting as if world affairs were one-dimensional—either one thing or another. And while most global relationships are interdependent and variable-sum, actors have often seen them as zero-sum and acted accordingly—often to their disadvantage. Two analysts at the U.S. National Defense University have attempted to show the relevance of both Kantian idealism and neo-Hobbesian realism to U.S. security policy. Their book, appropriately, is entitled *Seeing the Elephant* (Binnendijk and Kugler 2006).

Complexity science accepts that power politics and various idealisms have played key roles in shaping world affairs and will continue to do so. Some realisms and idealisms help to describe IR at certain times and places, but—rooted in either matter or form, and in a Manichean choice between evil and good, they tend to be too reductionist. A monocausal paradigm limits any theory's potential for general explanation, projection of alternative futures, or sound policy advice. The more advanced a species in the chain of evolution, the greater the chance that a variety of factors shape its behavior.[23]

Despite the advent of various "neo" realisms and idealisms, most IR theorizing continues to present such dichotomies. To be sure, many new approaches to IR have evolved in recent decades—from the roles of gender and social constructs to polyheuristic analysis of decision making.[24] But none offers a basic paradigm like those articulated by classic writers such as Thucydides. Some can be construed as applications of realism or idealism. Some articulate a grand theory akin to a philosophy of history; others present a micro- or intermediate-range theory. Few show much recognition of advances in the life sciences, anthropology, or other disciplines likely to illuminate the interactions of humans across borders.[25]

One of the either/or questions for IR is the relative weight of hard and soft power. Realists say that material power, especially when wielded by states, is king. Idealists trust intangibles—the soft power of ideas, argument, and example (though neo-Kantian Woodrow Wilson also called for a war to end war). Many idealists disdain states and expect broader, transnational forms of unity to prevail. Complexity science accepts that IR, like all of life, contains both tangible and intangible elements that condition one another. Pursuit of power without vision is fatuous. But so is the quest for ideals without regard for material capacity. A League of Nations without effective power could not stop aggression. Goals must be adjusted to means and means to goals (Carr 1940). Neither hard nor soft power will be useful unless mobilized. Fitness requires *smart* power—the capacity to convert hard and soft assets into influence and wise policy (Nye 1990; 2004; 2011).

A related controversy is that between the proponents of determinism and voluntarism. Marxists assume that production forces and production relations are decisive and determine the superstructure of politics and culture. Similarly, neorealists contend that the structure of material power among states is the key force in IR. Inspired by Thomas Hobbes, neorealists contend that anarchy prevails except where power has imposed order on a state of nature in which life is nasty, brutish, and short.[26] By contrast, voluntarist historians stress the weight of ideas and free will. They argue that great men are decisive in human affairs.

Some historians also allow important roles for a few women such as Catherine the Great and Margaret Thatcher. The empire-expanding tsarina and Great Britain's "iron lady" prime minister remind us how difficult it is to stereotype what is "feminine" in IR. The same difficulty is illustrated by Israel's "iron lady," Golda Meir, also called the "grandmother of the Jewish people"; Madeleine Albright, regarded as more "hawkish" than most males in Bill Clinton's administration; and by the three women who urged President Barack Obama to intervene in Libya in 2011—Hillary Clinton, Susan Rice, and Obama's "humanitarian hawk," Samantha Power.

Complexity science challenges every "either/or" worldview—indeed, any monocausal model of individual or group behavior. To understand human societies and their interactions we must examine the complex interactions of actors on many *levels*—individuals, clans, regions, classes, societies, governments, states, civilizations, the international system of states, international organizations, and transnational organizations and movements (from IBM and Greenpeace to al-Qaeda). Beyond these levels on which humans strut and fret, the entire biosphere is another crucial level that shapes and is shaped by politics (Clemens 2004). Most realisms and idealisms go off track by failing to take account of one or more of the many levels of actions that shape world affairs (Singer 1970). Also, given the "extraordinary complexity" that characterizes today's world, analysts "must treat feedback loops as no less central . . . than linear sequences" (Rosenau 2005).

Alert to the interactions among all levels of action, complexity science looks beyond every form of dichotomous thinking. Complexity challenges several favorite theories of political scientists. It questions the "rational choice" theory that political decisions represent calculations designed to maximize private or group utility.[27] It also rejects the near fatalism of structural realism, which, asserting the primacy of material power, allows little room for individual agency or soft variable such as culture. Instead, complexity weighs the interactions of both material and intangible forces. It analyzes the broad context in which decisions take place as well as the idiosyncrasies of human choice. It studies patterns and trends but also "chance" events and rare but transforming "Black Swans" such as "fifty-year floods" (recognizing that the old "fifty" may be the new "five" or "ten"). It grants that world affairs are often shaped by exceptions to accustomed patterns—not by the mean or steady drip, but by unprecedented catastrophes such as the scope and destruction of World War I (Taleb 2011).

Complexity science readily accepts the importance of values, beliefs, and perceptions in social action and policymaking, emphasized by constructivist theory. But complexity resists any suggestion that actors and forces in IR are not real. Constructivist theorists also refuse to accept realism or idealism/liberalism as a guiding paradigm in international studies. Constructivists hold that beliefs and perceptions are key, because "reality" is what we make of it (Wendt 1999). Hamlet anticipated constructivist theory as he welcomed two visitors and asked what brought them to Denmark:

> HAMLET: What have you, my good friends, deserv'd at the hands of Fortune, that she sends you to prison hither?
>
> GUILDENSTERN: Prison, my lord?
>
> HAMLET: Denmark's a prison.
>
> ROSENCRANTZ: Then is the world one.
>
> HAMLET: A goodly one, in which there are many confines, wards, and dungeons, Denmark being one o' th' worst.
>
> ROSENCRANTZ: We think not so, my lord.
>
> HAMLET: Why then 'tis none to you; for *there is nothing either good or bad, but thinking makes it so.* To me it is a prison.[28]

No radical subjectivism can serve as a basic paradigm in social science. On the other hand, the emphasis of some constructivists on the interaction between actors and structures is essential to grasping the complexity of world affairs.

Before comparing the various approaches to international studies in case studies, let us try to summarize some key concepts of complexity science that can and should be incorporated into a paradigm for analysis of world affairs.

chapter two

BASIC CONCEPTS OF COMPLEXITY SCIENCE

Fitness is the capacity to cope with complex challenges and opportunities to enhance one's own survival and other interests. The fitness of every organism, including whole societies and the international system, is found somewhere on the spectrum between rigid order and chaos (in politics, anarchy)—but usually closer to the edge of chaos.[1] The Greeks said that Alexander went as far as Chaos. According to Emerson (1847), however, Goethe—one of the most creative spirits ever—went that far and then hazarded one step farther, but brought himself safely back.

This view of fitness is close to what Folke et al. (2002) call "resilience"—the capacity to buffer change, learn, and develop. But "resilience" connotes a defensive stance, while "fitness" suggests an ability not only to withstand pressure but also a capacity to create values and alter the environment. In short, the concept of fitness offers a framework for understanding how to sustain and enhance adaptive capacity in a complex world of rapid transformations.[2]

How to achieve fitness? There are at least three answers (Mitchell 2009):

Natural selection. Small-scale, genetic mutations and recombinations help some individuals and, in time, larger groupings to adapt, survive, and multiply in their ever changing environment. Mutations occur at random and are not biased toward improvement or degradation. An apparently fit species (such as dinosaurs) may disappear if it cannot adapt. Humans have proved adaptable and resilient. Apart from formal organizations and signed documents, states and nonstate actors often coalesce for shared purposes, for example, the tendency of states worried about the rise of China to gravitate toward Washington.

Historical contingency. History usually moves more like a ponderous freighter than a nimble kayak. Profound turning points in human affairs are rare. They usually emerge as a consequence of many factors accumulating and multiplying over time. Whereas natural selection operates slowly and gradually, the life cycle of systems is often characterized by punctuated equilibrium—a pattern of rapid growth, followed by a long plateau, terminated by an often rapid decline or upsurge—sometimes brought about by critical threshold effects (Gould 1989, 2002; Somit and Peterson 1992). Biology remains constant but prospers or wanes in a changed environment. Change may come suddenly like a thief in the night. More grains of sand can make entire systems lurch in a nonlinear fashion into a new phase space.

This concept may help explain the rise and fall of states, and empires as well as movements and fashions. The historian Niall Ferguson (2011, 257–59; 2012) argues that the greatness that was Rome collapsed suddenly. The USSR disappeared not with a bang but a whimper. As we shall see in chapter 7, the United States shifted in just a few years from being an awesome but widely respected hyperpower to one widely despised and sometimes ignored. Both the USSR and U.S.A. suffered from many small and large burdens including the consequences of military and political overreach.

Structures. The key to fitness is self-organization—a capacity by members of a group to cooperate for shared goals without top-down commands. Self-organization can take place without natural selection or historical catastrophes or boons. Scientists find abundant instances in nature of "order for free"—as when corals, polyps, fishes, mollusks, worms, crustaceans, sponges, and other life forms cohabitate in positive symbiosis. The coral reef is a complex adaptive system that provides mutual gain for its inhabitants. Even closer integration is practiced by ants and termites as they build their nests, feed, and procreate. Humans can think and plan what kind of order to pursue, but often they too move in similar directions or even coordinate their actions with no discussion or commands from above.

Self-organization often gives rise to power laws in social systems, because of "preferential attachment"—the principle that in a network, a node with more connections is likely to attract more connections in future. This explains the rich-get-richer effect. Studying the evolution of the most common English words and phrases over five centuries, Perc (2012) found that power laws were at play Along with the steady growth of the English lexicon, his study confirmed that writing, although undoubtedly an expression of art and skill, is not immune to the same influences of self-organization that are known to regulate processes as diverse as the making of new friends and World Wide Web growth.

Self-organization can occur within and among groups—inside and across state borders. Members of a community can self-organize to clean up a riverbank and clean up fallen trees. They can initiate a petition to remove a governor and back a candidate to replace him or her. The thirteen units under the Articles of Confederation approved a constitution bringing them into a federal union. Much later, states on each side of the Atlantic self-organized to form an alliance, NATO, whose most powerful member could lead but not dictate—unlike the Warsaw Pact in which the USSR exercised strong top-down control. Europeans formed and gradually expanded the European Union, an entity with considerable flexibility but limited capacity to take decisions binding on all members. Members of the United Nations have generated a host of international agencies. An even larger multitude of nonstate actors has formed networks of transnational agencies and movements, from Greenpeace to al-Qaeda.

Each of these processes—natural selection, historical events, and self-organization—has shaped the fitness of human and other societies over time. But does change always point to something better? Mutations and historic events often appear like accidents on the path of evolution. Still, humans seem to have outstripped the mold from which they emerged. As Ralph Waldo Emerson noted in 1847, man's self-registration in the historical record is more than the print of the seal. "It is a new and finer form of the original. The record is alive, as that which it recorded is alive. . . . The man [presumably both genders] cooperates. He loves to communicate; and that which is for him to say lies as a load on his heart until it is delivered. But, besides the universal joy of conversation, some men are born with exalted powers for this second creation." Some men, Emerson wrote (with Goethe in mind) "are born to write."

HOW TO MEASURE FITNESS?

For some life forms, survival and procreation provide indicators. For humans, fitness requirements are far more nuanced. The size and growth of gross domestic product "does not add up" to indicate societal well-being—even when converted into real purchasing power per capita (Stiglitz, Sen, Fitousi 2010). The best single indicator of fitness is probably the Human Development Index (HDI) constructed by the United Nations Development Programme (1990-). It seeks to measure the conditions that enhance the realm of choice for individuals within each society. To do this the index aggregates information on per capita income (parity purchasing power in dollars), education (mean and expected years of schooling), and health (life expectancy at birth).[3] Here too, GDP is not decisive. Wealthy countries such as Singapore and Saudi Arabia rank lower on the HDI than their income rank because of weaknesses in education or health. Thanks to its strengths in education and health, low-income Cuba ranks higher on the HDI than Saudi Arabia in 2011. (For the most recent HDI statistics, see http://hdr.undp.org/en/reports/).

Since income, education, and health are often distributed unevenly, the UNDP adds indexes adjusted for gender and gender empowerment. In 2010 it introduced another auxiliary tool—the Inequality-adjusted HDI or IHDI. The highest-ranked country on the HDI in 2011 was Norway. Its IHDI showed only a 5.6 percent loss The IHDIs of the United States and Russian Federation experienced losses of 15.3 percent and 11.3 percent. The lowest-ranked country on the HDI, Democratic Republic of Congo, suffered a 39.9 percent loss on the IHDI. The income disparities in these four countries were manifest also in their Geni coefficients: Norway, 25.8; the United States, 40.8; Russia, 42.3; and DRC, 44.4. In the top thirty countries on the HDI, only Hong Kong (ranked thirteenth overall) came close to the U.S. level of inequality with its Geni coefficient of 43.4.

Another indicator of fitness is the Index of Economic Complexity (IEC) (Haussman and Hidalgo 2011), based on the variety and uniqueness in the products produced and exported by a country. Each product surveyed by the IEC depends on knowledge as well as material assets The IEC rankings are similar but not identical to those of the HDI. Each index takes into account intangible as well as tangible factors.

A broad view of fitness should also incorporate concepts of political rights, civil liberties, transparency, and subjective well-being.[4] Confirming the importance of self-organization, the fittest countries in the world—the top-ranked twenty on the Human Development Index—all get perfect scores on the Freedom House Index of Political and Civil Liberties (2010). Confirming the importance of trust in overall development, the top ten countries on the HDI are also ranked among the most honest (least corrupt) by Transparency International (2009). For some 128 "developing and transitional" countries the Bertelsmann Foundation has generated a Transformation Index (BTI) that provides a mean score for both democracy and free market economics. This index also tries to measure how things are ("status") and how they can develop ("management"). Most of the BTI rankings correlate strongly with the HDI and Freedom House rankings. Thus, the Czech Republic and Slovenia vied for top place on the Bertelsmann index, while North Korea and Somalia brought up the rear (http://www.bti-project.org/index/).

It is more difficult to measure competitiveness, education, creativity, sustainability, and—not least—happiness. Analysts struggle to find objective measures, as in the following examples:

- Competitiveness, which may be indicated by how "wired" a society has become; the number of patents its people file; the extent to which the economic system is free and open; and the sophistication of the products produced and traded;

- Education, by test scores and rankings of schools and universities;

- Creativity, by Nobel and other prizes for science and the arts;

- Sustainability, by estimates of resources consumed or enhanced;

- Transparency, by surveys of how business people perceive corruption;

- Happiness, by survey questions and by statistics on crime and suicide.

All these indicators hint at fitness, but all are subject to debate and often contradict one another.[5] Surveys of happiness may be skewed by local culture or politics;[6] indexes of perceived corruption, by subjective experiences and limited sampling.

"Fitness" is a relative concept. The Human Development Index permits comparison of a country's performance from year to year *and* in relation to other countries. It shows their rank (a relational measure) based on their absolute scores. Thus, the U.S. human development score improved steadily from 1980 to 2011 (from 0.837 to 0.910) but rose less than the average for other advanced industrial (OECD) countries (which increased from 0.749 to 0.873 in those years).

The difficulties in measuring fitness increase manyfold when we assess not only a country's performance but also its record in relation to other actors on the world scene and to their shared environment. Because Norway scored high on life expectancy and other factors, it ranked number one on the HDI in certain years. These scores permit the HDI to compare small Norway with the much larger United States, at least on some dimensions. Most of the political and other rankings of fitness cited in this book are also based on absolute scores.

Besides indicators of fitness at home, however, a comprehensive view must include *external* fitness—the country's ability to protect its people and territory, exert influence beyond state borders, and take advantage of opportunities on the world scene. Domestic fitness is probably a precondition for long-term fitness in the international arena. But domestic fitness does not guarantee that an actor can or will cope effectively with internal violence or external threats to its security—from forces of nature (climate change, tornadoes, drought), nonstate terrorism, or coercive moves by other states.

To assess external fitness is difficult. Elements of hard, soft, and smart power must be considered—each in relation to the global environment. What works for one country may not be appropriate for another. The demands of military security can differ from economic. The United States in 2012 spent many times more than China on "defense" but owed China more than $1.5 trillion—making debtor and creditor vulnerable to each other. Looking at these two countries alone and in relation to each other, the quality of education and political cohesion also shaped their fitness—at home and across borders. But even the largest and weightiest actors can usually shape the global landscape only at the margins. The external fitness of most countries depends heavily on their domestic fitness—including their ability to adapt to what is out there. Most actors can aspire only to resilience—not to be a game changer.

Norway's HDI scores do not show the country's ability to cope with external threats without assistance from the United States and other NATO members. Most OECD countries spend a smaller portion of their GDP on defense than the United States. The U.S.A. pays disproportionately for the security of itself and its partners—reducing resources that could otherwise be used to improve human development at home.

The fitness of Norway and most countries reflects their ability to develop and advance their interests within the global system as they find it. But the highest-ranked country on the HDI was unable in June 2011 to prevent a terrorist from detonating a bomb in front of the prime minister's office and, less than two hours later, shooting many children at camp on an island. Without a helicopter or boat available, police took more than an hour to arrive at the scene, where they arrested not only the shooter but, by an egregious error, an innocent teenager who had seen killings in his native Chechnya and did not become hysterical like most other campers.

A not so obvious measure of external fitness is the compatibility between a country's modus operandi and international institutions. The United States, for example, has done much to shape the structure and policies of the International Monetary Fund and World Bank (each headquartered in Washington), while Russia and China have not. Even so, many Americans fear that UN "blue helmets" are ready to suppress U.S. sovereignty.

No simple number such as defense outlays or battle deaths can suffice to measure external fitness. Do high defense outlays signify high fitness or the opposite? Answers must consider the entire context—political, economic, military, environmental. Evaluations of fitness should also weigh a country's ability to meet challenges and opportunities in the near, intermediate, and long term.[7]

Nor can fitness be gauged by public opinion, and expert polls on any actor's popularity or influence are also unreliable. Most of the world thought the USSR ahead militarily and scientifically in the late 1950s. Many experts and publics judged Japan an economic dynamo just before it entered a long period of stagnation. Many people admired the United States under Bill Clinton and reversed their opinion in the George W. Bush era, and shifted again when Barack Obama became president. The Nobel committee awarded Obama its peace prize for his encouragement of negotiation—just before he became another war president.

Even in retrospect it is difficult to assess the wisdom of policies intended to buttress fitness. Long after the fact, we may decide that London and Paris were wrong to "sleep" while Hitler menaced, but is it so clear that the United

States needed to ally with Stalin to defeat the Axis? Did Ronald Reagan's defense buildup help destroy an evil empire or put off the day when both nuclear superpowers could cooperate for mutual gain? The George W. Bush and Barack Obama administrations invested heavily to shape events in Afghanistan and Iraq and to prevent more deaths caused by foreign terrorists within the United States. Long after September 11, 2001, however, partisans and critics could debate whether the war against terrorism bolstered or weakened U.S. fitness at home and abroad. The interactions between U.S. domestic strength and its position in world affairs are discussed by Brzezinski (2012) and Kagan (2012) and in chapters 7 and 8 below.

Coevolution

Actors coevolve with one another and with their environment. Coevolution can imply a positive symbiosis for mutual gain. But coevolution is also illustrated by the Lotka-Voltera equation relating to predators and their prey. Let us assume that a population of foxes depends on a supply of rabbits for sustenance. In the model system, the predators thrive when prey are plentiful. However, if foxes eat too many rabbits, or if other factors reduce the supply of rabbits, the prey population shrinks. If the prey collapse in numbers, so do the predators. In the Lotka-Voltera model, the prey recover first. The predators recover only when the prey regenerate. These dynamics may continue in a cycle of growth and decline. Population equilibrium occurs in the model when neither of the population levels is changing, that is, when both of the derivatives are equal to zero.

The equations drawn from the animal world may be relevant to relationships within and between human societies. John Whiteman (2012) argued that "too much government policy is focused on imposing austerity on a population already at risk, rather than on helping their recovery." Such policy amounted to culling an already depleting population." An investor, Whiteman suggested, would "go long on rabbits and short on foxes."

If a society's richest elements exploit the middle and lower classes, the rich may in time weaken or destroy the sources of their own wealth. If a few metropoles at the core of an imperial system exploit poorer and weaker societies on the periphery, the rich may impoverish not only their subjects but also themselves. Before the poor die out, however, they are likely to rebel and change the system. This kind of challenge and response, predicted by Karl Marx in the nineteenth century, also concerns social scientists studying inequality in the twenty-first century.

Emergence

Coevolution shapes and generates emergent properties—structures and systems whose totality cannot be predicted from summing their constituent parts. Human emotions and ideas may be seen as emergent properties—not predictable from genes or neural connections (Marshall and Zohar 1997, 299–301). Emergent structures can enhance individual and group capabilities, but may also threaten the well-being of others. Networks of believers, for better or worse, can subvert existing orders. "Group-think" can limit creative problem solving but the collective intelligence of any group—whether in a boardroom, a diplomatic forum, or a social network—can sometimes produce constructive solutions to complex problems (Klein 2011; Keller 2011; Holman 2011).

AGENT-BASED SYSTEMS

Agents exist in and depend on systems, but systems are built and changed by agents. Independent agents often practice self-organization—a major contributor to system fitness, as in a coral reef. Top-down organization is usually less fit than self-organized cooperation.

Earnest and Rosenau (2006) complain that agent-based modeling omits the role of political authority—operating as though all actors were equal. But this deficit is not inherent or necessary. To be sure, not all agents have the same clout. Also, their relative weight can change. But complexity science is well suited to capture these nuances. Most realist and idealist models of politics miss the dynamism and flux of real life interactions captured in agent-based studies. If complexity fails to pay due deference to the state, most realisms go overboard in the other direction.

SELF-ORGANIZED CRITICALITY

Balanced between order and chaos, a fit organism—even an entire society or social system—may resemble a sand pile with a fragile equilibrium. As more sand is slowly added to the top of the pile, it spontaneously evolves into a conical shape. If more weight or stress is added, a critical threshold may be passed, leading to system collapse. Again, structure interacts both with actor choice and with chance. Operating through loops of positive feedback, small causes can produce large, system-wide effects.

The concept of self-organized criticality illuminates the problems facing a country (such as Ireland in the early twenty-first century) that takes on great debt or an empire (such as the Soviet or the American) that reaches beyond its means. The concept sheds light on how much stress any system can endure before breaking—from a fish stock or a wheat field to a multinational alliance to the mind of a decision maker bombarded with often conflicting bits. Ironically, fitness may thrive at the edge of chaos, but disappear over the cliff if a few more grains of sand break its equilibrium.

FITNESS LANDSCAPES

The *relative* fitness of diverse actors can be mapped as a rugged landscape of peaks and valleys. Human migrations and explorations have caused many if not most polities to be linked along several dimensions.[8] A fitness landscape for two or more actors can depict their relationship to each other, to their physical environment, and to exogenous forces that become relevant. For a population of fruit flies and their predators, fitness could be measured by plotting their coevolving reproductive capacities over time. But even this graph could mislead, because an exploding population of either species could wipe out its food supply and trigger its decline and possible extinction. Among human communities, a fitness peak would need to reflect the many qualities that condition both domestic and external fitness. To graph the relative size of the actors' populations, their GDP, and their armed forces would not suffice. To capture the essence of global affairs, the landscape would have to show multiple peaks that reflect soft and smart power as well as material assets.

Fitness can be assessed both at the actor level and the system level among actors. The fitness of post-communist Russia declined on each level. The country's life expectancy as well as its GDP declined sharply in the 1990s. This happened at the same time that the assets of China and the United States were rising. Russia's fitness shriveled both in absolute and in relative terms, that is, in relation to its public health and economic strength in earlier decades, *and* relative to other great powers.

No country's "peak" is carved in granite. It may be more appropriate to imagine the peak as the top an iceberg that can melt or grow. If an actor gains or loses fitness in relationship to other actors, its peak can be said to rise or fall. If a country's relative fitness declines, its people and leaders may wander as in a valley, looking for ways to rebuild their ability to cope with complex challenges. Alternating between top-down order and centrifugal disorder, many Russians in the early twenty-first century hoped that the iron fist of Vladimir Putin would restore the relative fitness that went missing in the chaotic 1990s under Boris Yeltsin. But Putin's Kremlin did little to rebuild the country's fitness. Higher prices for oil exports brought in more cash but did little to boost overall fitness. Russia placed only sixty-sixth on the HDI in 2011. Tsarist Russia in the early twentieth century was more dynamic than Putin's early in the twenty-first.

How to regain lost fitness? This topic is addressed in later chapters, but the task can be Sisyphean. Focused on reducing government debt, the U.S. Congress allowed federal spending for job retraining in 2012 to decrease by 18 percent below 2006 levels, even though there were six million persons seeking retraining in 2012. The National Skills Coalition argued that the government should be spending significantly more to retrain dislocated workers. Even if spending increased, it would hard to catch up with demand.

When many aspects of fitness must be considered, a one-dimensional landscape cannot show a complex picture of rise and decline. However, a radar graph, with many axes running from the center to the periphery, can portray diverse aspects of fitness (Maruca 2000, 24). Figure 2.1 summarizes the assets of the United States, the Russian Federation, and the People's Republic of China in 2013. Scaled from zero to 100, the graph shows great strengths for each country.[9] Failed or failing states such as Somalia would rank low on most measures. North Korea would rank medium or medium-high on military assets but very low on economic power and compatibility with international institutions. Just a few nuclear weapons could provide Pyongyang a minimum deterrent, but a credible delivery system must also be part of the package.

SELF-ORGANIZED FITNESS VERSUS DESPOTISM AND ANARCHY

Complexity science contends that top-down rule is inimical to human development and that self-organization is the key to societal fitness. High levels of fitness and human development are most likely to be found in communities

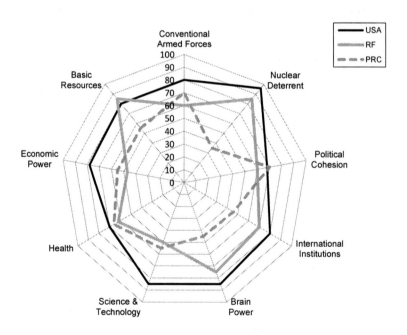

FIGURE 2.1. Soft and Hard Power Resources: USA, Russia, and China in 2013.

Sources: Author's estimates based on data published by International Institute for Strategic Studies, World Economic Forum, World Bank, The Economist, and other periodicals.

that practice self-organization while avoiding the polar opposites of anarchy and despotism. As outlined in Table 2.1, this diagnosis describes and explains the main obstacles to development and to world peace. It also generates a foundation for assessing alternative futures and policy recommendations.

While self-organization implies some form of democracy, it does not signify egalitarian leveling. A healthy society will provide incentives and rewards to innovators and leaders, but extreme inequalities are not compatible with self-organization. If rich minorities can buy ads that sway election results, this vitiates the principle of broad participation. If privileged elites exploit their positions to extract value for themselves, overall fitness will suffer (Acemoglu and Robinson 2012).

Long before the advent of anything called complexity science, both Plato and Aristotle warned about the dangers of power concentrated in a small elite and, at the other extreme, the diffusion of power through a crowd. Both Plato (*The Statesman*) and Aristotle (*Politics*) favored a mixed polity that represents the rich and the poor or, better still, a moderately wealthy middle class. A system based on despotism or rule by the poor masses could not endure for long, according to Aristotle.

As conditions in the 1960s spawned rebellions across the planet, Samuel P. Huntington cautioned that political stability in a modern state requires institutional complexity and flexibility—the multiplication and differentiation of subunits in the polity. How could Japan in the late nineteenth century survive the overthrow of the shogunate that had ruled for many centuries? The country's modernizing samurai could proclaim the "restoration" of the emperor who had reigned while the shogun ("great general") ruled. "The greater the number and variety of subunits, the greater the ability of the organization to secure and maintain the loyalty of its members." An organization with many purposes will be more capable of adjusting itself to the loss of any one purpose than an entity with just one purpose. Thus, having achieved its goal of independence for India in 1947, the Congress Party reoriented its mission to governing (Huntington 1968, 17–19).

A self-organized society is pluralistic. Its members have a say in politics and a meaningful opportunity to choose what they do in economic and cultural life. There is strong synergy between economic and political institutions. Extractive political institutions concentrate power in the hands of a narrow elite. If political power is wielded by a narrow elite, as in North Korea, broad participation in public life will be limited. Absolutist regimes tend to extract value mainly for the privileged few. Value-claiming in this vein could persist for long times in previous eras, but tends to backfire in an era of global interdependence and rapid information transfer (Acemoglu and Robinson 2012).

Somalia is at the opposite pole from North Korea. Power is not concentrated at the center but is distributed among several rival absolutists. This is not quite anarchy, because the power of one clan is constrained by the guns

TABLE 2.1. Alternative Scenarios Posited by Complexity Science

Political Condition	Anarchy	Top-Down Rule	Self-Organized Polity
Stability/instability	Unstable chaos	Rigid but fragile stability	Dynamic equilibrium near the edge of chaos
Outlook	Zero-sum	Zero-sum	Variable-sum but seek mutual gain
Value orientation	Self-help value-claiming	Self-help value-claiming	Create values to expand the pie
Legal climate	Law of the jungle	Diktat	Impartial justice
Social consequences	War of all vs. all fostering demands for top-down rule	Repression with risk of insurgency	Consensual democracy
Creativity	No art, technology, or science	Limited art, technology, and science	Innovation in art, technology, and science
Wealth and incomes	General poverty with a few pockets of wealth	Some wealth but with great inequality	High incomes with relative equality
Human development index	Very low rank (e.g., Somalia)	Low to medium rank (e.g., Russia)	High rank (e.g., Norway)
Fitness	Unfit: no collective capacity to cope with challenges and opportunities	Unfit: little capacity to cope with challenges and opportunities	Fit: strong capacity to cope with challenges and opportunities
Role in world affairs	Negative and destabilizing	An obstacle to development and danger to peace	Positive

of another. This distribution of power leads not to inclusive institutions but to virtual chaos—making it difficult to conduct a normal business, trade, or maintain basic security. Failed states such as Somalia are exceptions in world affairs. The gradual emergence of global governance by states and nonstate actors in recent centuries belies the assumption that, lacking a supranational authority, IR is anarchy.

Today's realists and neorealists agree with Hobbes that IR resembles a state of nature where the key actors—states—vie for power either alone or with allies. Each actor tries to prevent any shift in the balance of power—relative as well as absolute—to its disadvantage. Struggling for marginal gains here and now, states give less attention to remote dangers. Some neorealists expect the global system to self-regulate. The gradual emergence of global governance by states and nonstate actors in recent centuries belies the assumption that, lacking a supranational authority, IR is anarchy.

Complexity science agrees with Hobbes about the perils of chaos but not with his proposed remedy of absolute top-down rule. Rather, complexity concurs with liberal peace theory: republics rarely if ever fight one another and suffer less internal violence than authoritarian regimes. The originator of liberal peace theory, Immanuel Kant, counted on a system of self-organization similar to that practiced for centuries by the Hanseatic city-states.[10] Republics fought back when attacked in the twentieth century and won most of the century's major hot wars and the long cold war—in part because they were more fit than their adversaries.

THE MATRIX: CULTURE

Far more than other species or life forms, humans use their intellectual and creative powers to alter their capacity to cope with challenges and opportunities. Unlike the denizens of a coral reef, humans can contemplate alternative futures and plan coping strategies and tactics. How effectively they use these powers depends heavily on the culture—the society's values and way of life.[11] Some cultures have proved far more fit than others.

A culture that endorses and rewards cooperation and mutual trust is likely to be more fit than one that spawns narrow self-seeking and diffidence. As Huntington noted, "The public interest of a complex society is a complex matter." Communal well-being requires that most individuals bridle their private impulses for the sake of general political objectives. "Morality requires trust; trust involves predictability and predictability requires regularized and institutionalized patterns of behavior." To confine morality to relations within one's own family, clan, or class will impede not only communal unity but also development (Huntington 1968, 24–25).

Figure 2.2 correlates cultural heritage with HDI and Transparency International's Corruption Perception Index (CPI) rankings as of 2010.[12] It shows the highest-placed country on the HDI from each major civilization and how it correlates with rankings, high or low, on the CPI. Most Western Christian countries ranked high on both the HDI and CPI. Norway ranked first on the HDI and tenth in honesty (opposite of corruption). The United States, not at the top but included here to give comparative perspective, placed fourth on the HDI but much lower on honesty—twenty-second. The highest ranked non–Western Christian country was Japan, with Shinto-Buddhist traditions. It placed eleventh on the HDI in 2010 and seventeenth on the CPI—higher than the United States.[13] Israel, with Jewish and heavy Western influences, ranked fifteenth on the HDI and thirtieth on the CPI. The highest-placed Orthodox Christian country was Greece—twenty-second on the HDI but seventy-eighth on the CPI. The Czech Republic ranked twenty-eighth on the HDI—highest for Western Christian/post-communist countries, but fifty-third on the CPI. The highest placed Islamic heritage country on the HDI was the United Arab Emirates—thirty-second on the HDI and twenty-eighth on the CPI. Of Western Christian countries in Latin America, Chile ranked highest on the HDI—forty-fifth, but with an excellent honesty ranking—twenty-first in the world. Of Orthodox Christian/post-communist countries, Montenegro scored highest on the HDI—forty-ninth. Like other post-communist countries, it ranked very low on honesty. China, with its unique Confucian/Buddhist/Taoist/Communist heritage, placed eighty-ninth on the HDI and seventy-eighth on the CPI. Gabon was the highest ranked Western Christian/African country—ninety-third on the HDI. Hindu majority/Islamic minority India ranked 121st on the HDI. Nigeria—Islamic, Western Christian, and African—placed 142nd on the HDI. Ethiopia—Islamic, Orthodox Christian, and African—ranked 157th. Of course, geography and other factors condition HDI and honesty rankings, but *we must ask why most countries with an Orthodox Christian, Muslim, or other heritage ranked far behind those with Western Christian or East Asian traditions.* To respond fully to this question properly would require another book (or more), but subsequent chapters 3 to 6 suggest parts of the answer.

Each culture embodies both structure and choice in ways that affect its capacity to cope with change. Sociobiology explains that each culture is shaped by the genes of the individuals who have survived and have, over generations, shaped its epigenetic rules (Lumsden and Wilson 1981; Durham 1991). Memetics suggests parallels between culture and the evolution of species (Gabora 1997). Here is open terrain where social and complexity sciences can and should work synergistically with biology and sociobiology (Axelrod 1997b).

Culture is the matrix of fitness. Certain kinds of culture seem necessary though not sufficient for high levels of human development and political freedom. The logic can be captured in one line:

Culture → high HDI and freedom → fitness, the ability to cope with complexity

This linkage, if valid, presents major policy implications for all societies—those that now rank high on the HDI as well as for those that would climb

37

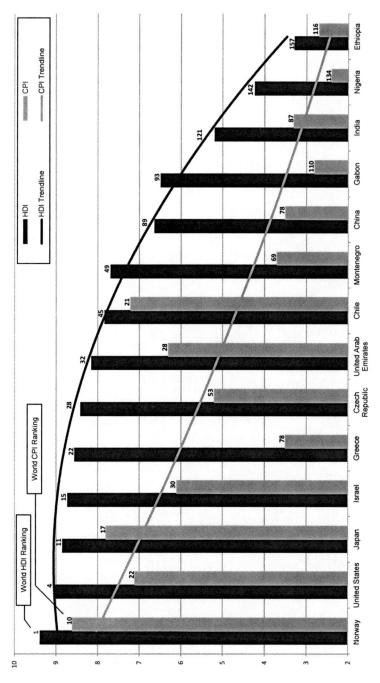

FIGURE 2.2. HDI and Honesty Scores for Leading Countries by Cultural and Political Heritage in 2010.

higher. To support this view, we begin with a detailed juxtaposition of happenings in the Baltic and the Balkans since 1991; move on to a broader survey of patterns across Eurasia since the collapse of communist rule; analyze the challenges to U.S. fitness in the twenty-first century; compare fitness levels in South and North Korea; and conclude with a still broader tour of global issues as seen by other schools of thought and by students of complexity.

chapter three

A CRUCIAL TEST CASE:
WHY THE BALTIC IS NOT THE BALKANS

I want to say something . . . for the NEWS! I recently saw on TV. . . . Did you know, wretched girl, that the Serbs are the oldest nation? While the Kraut and English and American, six hundred years ago were eating pork with their fucking hands, we had this, and we'd gallantly . . . pick! At the Serbian court we ate with a fork and the Kraut with his damn fingers. Serbs . . . the oldest nation!

[New speaker]

It's this fork that drove us in here, into a cave.

—From the Serbian film *Pretty Village, Pretty Flame*
[*Lepa sela lepo gore*] (1996)[1]

Here is a test for complexity science. Can it explain why, as communist rule collapsed in Eastern Europe, human development advanced relatively steadily in the Baltic region—but languished in most of the Balkans? Both regions had been repressed by alien despots for centuries; both were inhabited by combustible mixes of ethnic and religious groupings. Why then the near absence of ethnic violence in Estonia, Latvia, and Lithuania while most of the former Yugoslavia roiled in civil and cross-border war? Why the rapid consolidation of democracy and market economics in the Baltic countries compared to halting movements toward political and economic freedom—not only in Yugoslavia but in most Balkan polities? This chapter examines several potential explanations including those from complexity science. It concludes that divergent profiles in societal fitness go far toward explaining divergent patterns of development in the Baltic and Balkan regions. Contrasts between political leaders in the two regions were also critical, but they served as immediate causes that reflected long-term, underlying differences in political cultures and societal fitness.

A glance at other post-communist regimes helps to put the Baltic and Balkan cases in perspective. As detailed in chapter 5 below, transitions in the Czech Republic, Hungary, Poland, and Slovakia went relatively smoothly. For Russia and most other former Soviet republics, many aspects of post-communism were difficult and remained so in the twenty-first century. So this chapter focuses on two sets of *outliers*—the Baltic republics and the states that emerged from Yugoslavia, with some references to other Balkan states—Albania, Romania, and Bulgaria. Two other Balkan states, Greece and Turkey, with no heritage of communist rule, are mentioned only in passing.

Why study these contrasts? Is this a meaningful case or just a straw man? In 1988–1991 it was not clear that the Baltic peoples—Estonians, Latvians, Lithuanians—could or would reemerge, without war, as modern nations. Their successes may suggest lessons for others—in the Balkans and elsewhere—struggling to restrain ethnic conflict and develop in freedom.

HOW TO MEASURE TRANSITIONS IN THE BALTIC AND THE BALKANS

CASUALTIES FROM ETHNIC AND POLITICAL CONFLICT

The three Baltic republics regained independence from Moscow with little violence and soon flourished in conditions of political and economic freedom. Many Balkan communities, by contrast, suffered years of civil and cross-border violence. The most telling comparison between the two regions is the number of persons killed in ethnic or political fighting during the transition from communist rule. None died in Estonia and fewer than forty altogether in the other two Baltic republics—all killed by Soviet troops. In the former Yugoslavia, by contrast, more than one hundred thousand civilians and soldiers died fighting in 1991–95. The conflict forced nearly 2.2 million people to flee their homes, moving mostly to regions within the country controlled by their own ethnic group, but with many moving abroad (Judah 2000, 101, 133–34, 361; Tanner 1997, 278).

Besides physical suffering, there was also great psychological trauma. (Flögel and Lauc n.d.) Considerable ethnic cleansing and rape took place. Long after the 1995 Dayton Peace Accords, many thousands of persons remained uprooted in the Balkans—Europe's largest refugee population since the 1940s.

Ethnic minorities in Slovenia constituted only 13 percent of the population, but they too faced severe challenges in the early twenty-first century (Lük et al. 2000; Klemenčič and Žagar 2004).[2]

Hundreds died as communist regimes were overthrown in the 1990s and replaced in Albania and Romania, but that violence had little *ethnic* content compared to what happened in the former Yugoslavia.[3] A notable exception was the conflict that took place over three days in several places in Transylvania in March 1990. In the county seat of Targu Mures, for example, some five thousand Hungarian ethnics faced off against some two thousand Romanian ethnics. At least six people were killed and hundreds injured. The repercussions of these clashes were remembered for years afterward.(Kostecki 2002).

The lack of political violence in the Baltic was the more remarkable because ethnic differences there were sharp and could have exploded, as they did in much of the Balkans. The 1989 Soviet census showed that barely half of Latvia's population was "Latvian," while just over three-fifths of Estonia's residents were "Estonian." By contrast, the census reported that four-fifths of Lithuania's population was "Lithuanian." Rates of intermarriage between different nationalities were low in all Baltic republics. (*Naselenie SSSR 1988* [1989], 276, 286, 318).

Having regained their independence in 1991, the three Baltic republics accommodated and gradually integrated Slavic speakers with very little overt physical violence. Balts commemorated Soviet-era deportations and took some measures to ostracize if not punish former KGB agents accused of serious human rights. Lithuania enacted lustration laws in the 1990s, but they were directed mainly at Lithuanians. However, when Estonia in 2007 moved a Red Army memorial from the center of Tallinn to the outskirts, this action triggered demonstrations by Russian speakers in Estonia, in which one person died, and by *Nashi* youth in Moscow. It also led to days of cyberwar attacks that nearly paralyzed Estonia's computer networks.

Unlike patterns in Central Asia, relatively few Russian speakers moved away from the Baltic republics after the collapse of Soviet rule. To be sure, speakers of Slavic languages were slow to apply and qualify for citizenship in Estonia or Latvia.[4] By 2005, however, naturalized Estonians outnumbered noncitizens. (Freedom House 2006, 243). By 2008, native Russian speakers made up 30 percent of the population (down from circa 40 percent in 1991). Disputes over citizenship, language rights, and minority education continued to flare. Following ethnic disturbances in 2007, the Estonian government intensified its efforts to integrate minorities and cultivate proactive programs to reduce tensions.

Latvia had a larger percentage of noncitizens than Estonia. In 2005 some 42 percent of Slavic speakers living in Latvia were noncitizens (down from nearly 50 percent in the last years of communist rule. This group—nearly half the population—lacked the right to vote even in municipal elections.[5]

Emigration plus slight changes in birth rates raised the percentage of native Latvian speakers from 52 percent in 1989 to 58.5 percent in 2004 (Freedom House 2004, 334). In 1995–2005, however, the proportion of noncitizens decreased from 29 to 19 percent (Freedom House 2006, 354–55). Each year more residents of Latvia became citizens. By 2008 some 82 percent of the population (1,857,508) were citizens, ethnic Latvians or naturalized. About 2 percent held foreign citizenship, and 372,421, or 16.4 percent, were "noncitizens." People of Latvian ethnic origin formed roughly 60 percent of the population in 2008. As native Russian speakers and other non-Latvians obtained obtain the right to vote, their potential political weight increased. Their influence was bolstered by the Russophone focus of a single party, the Harmony Center, which led all other parties in the polls. Leaders of the First Party-Latvian Way and the People's Party expressed their willingness to cooperate with the Harmony Center. (Freedom House 2009, 313).

The pattern was different in Lithuania where, facing comparatively small and diverse communities of Polish and Russian speakers, the post-Soviet regime granted citizenship automatically to most residents in the early 1990s. In 2008 lawmakers amended the Law on Citizenship to extend the right of dual citizenship to children of Lithuanian nationals born abroad, but nationalist resentments and ethnic intolerance grew stronger. The Migration Department reported that some 1,500 citizens were stripped of their Lithuanian passports. Also in 2008, the replacement of Polish and Russian street names with Lithuanian ones by the Vilnius region administration sparked disputes over the rights of ethnic minorities. Disregarding possible obligations in human rights treaties, the Constitutional Court ruled that the official state language had to be used in public to ensure smooth governance. The Parliament, however, did not specify the circumstances for use of ethnic minority languages, though ethnic minorities, mainly Poles, constituted more than 50 percent of the Vilnius region population. Many Lithuanians displayed their dislike of minority ethnicities and cultures, especially Roma, Jews, and immigrants. There were more reports of hate speech against minorities, some of which was attributed to new forms of electronic communication (Freedom House 2009, 347).

POLITICAL, ECONOMIC, AND HUMAN DEVELOPMENT

Nearly two decades after the implosion of communist regimes in Europe, most Balkan states except Slovenia registered low scores for democracy, media freedom, and human development. These outcomes are tracked in Table 3.1.

Independence regained, the Baltic republics and Slovenia quickly became what Freedom House termed "consolidated democracies." Their political rights and civil liberties were comparable to those in the Czech Republic, Hungary, Poland, and Slovakia. Early in the twenty-first century most former Yugoslav republics remained at best "semi-consolidated democracies" (Croatia, Macedonia, Montenegro, Serbia) or "transitional-hybrid" (Bosnia) or "semi-consolidated

TABLE 3.1. Comparative Democracy, Independent Media, and Human Development 2009

Country	Democracy Scores (1 = highest, 7 = lowest)	Independent Media Scores (1 = freest, 7 = least free)	Human Development Index Ranks (n = 182)
Baltic Region			
Estonia	1.9 consolidated democracy	1.5	40th (0.883)
Latvia	2.9 consolidated democracy	1.8	48th (0.866) + 2 places since 2006
Lithuania	2.3 consolidated democracy	1.8	46th (0.870)
Balkan Region			
Albania	3.8 semi-consolidated democracy	3.8	70th (0.818)
Bosnia	4.2 hybrid, transitional regime	4.5	76th (0.812)
Bulgaria	3.0 semi-consolidated democracy	3.8	61st (0.840) −2
Croatia	3.7 semi-consolidated democracy	4.0	45th (0.871)
Kosovo	5.1 semi-consolidated authoritarian regime	5.5	Not a UN member
Macedonia	3.9 semi-consolidated democracy	4.3	72th (0.817)
Montenegro	5.8 semi-consolidated authoritarian regime	3.8	65th (0.0834)
Romania	3.4 semi-consolidated democracy	3.8	63rd (0.837) + 1
Serbia	3.8 semi-consolidated democracy	3.8	67th (0.826)
Slovenia	2.5 consolidated democracy	2.3	29th (0.929)
Neighbors			
Belarus	6.6 consolidated authoritarian regime	6.7	68th (0.826) +1
Russia	6.1 consolidated authoritarian regime	6.3	71st (0.817) +2
Ukraine	4.4 hybrid, transitional	3.5	85th (0.796) −1

Sources: Democracy and Independent Media Scores from Freedom House, *Nations in Transit 2009* at http://www.freedomhouse.org/uploads/nit/2009/Tables-WEB.pdf, accessed April 19, 2010. Human Development Index from United Nations Development Programme, *Human Development Report 2009* (New York: Palgrave, 2009), Tables G and H. The number in parenthesis = aggregate score for life expectancy, years of education, and GDP per capita, where 10 is highest possible. Plus sign = number of places improved 2006 to 2007; minus sign = number of places declined; blank = no change. Norway placed first on the index (0.97) and Niger last, 182nd (0.340).

authoritarian" regimes (Kosovo). Bulgaria, however, joined the "consolidated democracies," while Albania and Romania ranked among "semi-consolidated democracies."

Reporting on the years 2008 to 2012, Freedom House registered improved democracy scores for Croatia and Serbia. Despite public aspirations for joining the European Union, most reforms stagnated in the Balkans, with multiple declines in Albania, Bosnia and Herzegovina, Kosovo, and Macedonia.[6] Albania received a downward trend arrow due to the killing of opposition protesters in January 2011, the politicization of electoral mechanisms surrounding municipal balloting in May, and the failure of the courts to impartially adjudicate a corruption case against a senior government politician.

Of the former Soviet republics, the three Baltic states enjoyed the highest rankings on the UN Human Development Index (HDI). Of formerly communist states, Slovenia achieved the highest HDI ranking.[7] The other former Yugoslav republics ranked quite low—as did Balkan neighbors Albania, Bulgaria, and Romania. Russia and all the other traditionally Orthodox Christian units of the former USSR ranked much lower. The former Soviet republics with an Islamic heritage ranked lower still. Another Balkan nation, Greece, Orthodox Christian and never burdened with communist institutions, ranked among the top twenty-five on the HDI, while adjacent Turkey—Muslim and never communist—placed seventy-ninth (United Nations Development Programme 2009).

Freedom House surveys of the press found that by 2005 the media in all consolidated democracies such as the Baltic republics and Slovenia were "free." The media in Ukraine and Georgia were "partly free," while the media in Russia and all nine other ex-Soviet republics were "not free." Slovenia aside, the media in all other ex-Yugoslav republics were "partly free"—as also in Bulgaria and Romania. In 2006–08, however, Freedom House found that fifteen of the formerly communist countries slipped backward, due to politicization of public broadcasting. Media independence declined not only in Bulgaria, Romania, Serbia, and Montenegro (not to mention Russia), but also in Slovakia and even Slovenia. Only one country in the region experienced some improvement in the mid-2010s—Ukraine.

PARTICIPATION IN WESTERN INSTITUTIONS

Another indicator of political and economic development was the admission of transitional states into NATO and the European Union. Following the path taken by former Soviet satellites Poland, Hungary, and the Czech Republic in 1999, the three Baltic republics plus Slovenia, Slovakia, Bulgaria, and Romania joined NATO in 2002–04. By contrast, NATO judged it necessary to attack Serbia in 1999—the only military action ever waged under NATO command until its Libya campaign in 2011. Of course, strategic calculations as well as estimates about political development colored NATO thinking. Regardless the low democracy scores of Ukraine and Georgia, NATO pledged on April

3, 2008, to admit them some day (Bucharest Summit Declaration 2008)—a promise that inflamed Russian sensitivities.

The prospect of membership in the EU acted as both carrot and stick—pushing aspiring states to reform and to satisfy the requirements of thirty-one chapters in the EU *acqis communautaire*. Ten countries joined the EU in 2004—including the Czech Republic, Estonia, Hungary, Latvia, Lithuania, Poland, Slovakia, and Slovenia (Mrak et al. 2004), They were followed by Bulgaria and Romania in 2007. Table 3.2 shows their progress in closing the first thirty of thirty-one chapters. As we see, the frontrunners were the Czech Republic, Estonia, Hungary, Slovenia, and Poland. Next came Latvia, Lithuania, and Slovakia—followed by the late movers Bulgaria and Romania. The first group needed five years to clear these hurdles; the second group, three years; the third set—Bulgaria and Romania—started later but also needed five years.

Persistent problems in Bulgaria and Romania led some observers to ask if they had not been admitted too early to the European Union—a symptom perhaps of Western expansionitis. When they joined the EU on January 1, 2007, Brussels opined that both countries still needed to make progress in judicial reform and in fighting corruption and organized crime. Accordingly, the EU established a special "cooperation and verification mechanism" to help Sofia and Bucharest address these issues. Indeed, the EU Commission threatened sanctions if they failed to do so. Some progress took place, but in 2011 the EU Commission voted to continue its assessment of each country's administrative and judicial systems. The Commission said that "progress on judicial reform, corruption and organized crime will allow Bulgarians and Romanians to enjoy their full rights as EU citizens." (EU Commission 2011) These persistent problems cast doubt on the high rankings given by Freedom House to Bulgaria and Romania.

TABLE 3.2. Progress in Closing the First 30 Chapters of the *Acquis Communautaire*

	1998	1999	2000	2001	2002	2003	2004
Czech R	3	10	13	24	30		
Slovenia	3	9	14	26	30		
Poland	3	9	13	20	30		
Estonia	3	8	16	20	30		
Hungary	3	8	14	24	30		
Slovakia			10	22	30		
Latvia			9	23	30		
Lithuania			8	23	30		
Bulgaria			8	15	22	25	30
Romania			6	9	15	21	30

Source: Appatova 2008.

Croatia joined the European Union in July 2013. Negotiations for accession were underway with Macedonia, Iceland, Montenegro, Serbia, and Turkey. Negotiations could begin with Albania, Bosnia, and Kosovo when they are ready. But there were no guarantees: Turkey became a candidate member in the mid-1980s but remained in limbo thanks to issues with Cyprus, human rights, and Turkey's non-Western culture.

More than a decade after most fighting stopped, the political entities created by the 1995 Dayton Accords and subsequent NATO support for an independent Kosovo left the region a powder keg brimming with elemental nationalisms. In 2012–13, however, the European Union mediated talks between Serbia and Kosovo on outlines for a modus vivendi. The EU also pressed Sarajevo to hold a census in Bosnia and Herzegovina in 2013, its first since 1991. Muslims feared that their numbers had declined relative to Serbs and Croats, but detailed population data was required to receive EU funding for candidate members. Montenegro in 2012 held elections to firm up the government, and expected to conduct membership negotiations with the EU in 2013.

In the years after communist rule collapsed, all the nations between the Baltic and the Black Sea experienced contractions as well as expansions of good governance. The frailties of human nature did not disappear. Czechs and Slovaks continued to antagonize each other so much that the two peoples split and formed separate countries. Polish leaders sometimes overplayed their hand in EU affairs. Hungarian leaders admitted lying to their public and to the EU about the country's financial situation. Voters in the Baltic lands sometimes rejected liberation politicians and voted again for those who promised bread over freedom. Russian mafias penetrated Latvia and Lithuania, leading, inter alia, to the impeachment of one Lithuanian president. Estonians irritated Moscow unnecessarily when they moved a Red Army war memorial. Neither the Balts nor their neighbors in Eastern and Western Europe were doing much to forge a united strategy to cope with energy shortages exacerbated by Moscow's manipulation of its oil and gas levers. Of course human foibles appeared worldwide—including the United States. Balts were not alone in falling short on political vision.

POTENTIAL EXPLANATIONS

Many schools of thought seek to explain ethnic violence and other issues in post-communist transitions. Realists and neorealists focus on tangibles such as the structure of military and economic power. Some claim that the behavior of various actors should be viewed as a rational choice aimed at maximizing its gains and minimizing its losses. Constructivists, however, argue that subjective factors are decisive. They examine the ways that various actors—elites and publics, majorities and minorities, haves and have-nots—perceive and discourse about each other (Kolsto 2002).

Many psychologists and historians stress the role of free will—the impacts of individuals who work for social peace as well as entrepreneurs of ethnic discord. Some individuals and parties strive to create values for all while others claim them for a particular group.

This study acknowledges the role of all these factors—their weight differing across time and place. It suggests, however, that the overall fitness of each society was crucial in blocking or allowing destructive forces to prevail and permitting constructive individuals, policies, and forces to prevail. Every society has its apostles of hate but not every public embraces and follows them. How these many factors came together to shape the prospects for nonviolent separation and subsequent political-economic development in two sets of contrasting cases are outlined in Tables 3.3.

The same congeries of theories can be applied to explain divergences in economic and social development—as in Table 3.4.

TABLE 3.3. Peace and War in Lithuania and Croatia

Potential Explanations	Nonviolent Independence in Lithuania, 1988–1991	War and Chaos in Croatia in 1990s
Imperial center	Strong but divided Kremlin	Resolute Belgrade
The West	Moral support and nonrecognition of Soviet annexation	Moral support and prompt diplomatic recognition of Croatia
Military strength	Puny	Moderate
Economic strength	Fair with hope of improvement	Fair with hope of improvement
Ethnic diversity	20% non-titular	12% Serb and 4% other non-titular
Clash of civilizations	Yes. Western Christianity vs. Orthodox	Yes. Western Christianity vs. Orthodox
Historical grievances	Yes. Past and present.	Yes. Past and present.
Ethnic (vs. civic) nationalism	Yes	Yes
Militant ideology	No	Yes
Commitment to ethnic harmony	Some	Little
Societal security dilemma	Moderate	Strong
Leadership	Moderate, farsighted	Chauvinist, myopic
Societal fitness	Fair to moderate	Poor to fair

Source: Author's estimates.

TABLE 3.4. Economic and Social Development in Estonia Compared with Bosnia

Potential Explanations	Rapid Development in Estonia after 1991	Slow Development in Bosnia after 1995
Former imperial hegemon	Weakened Russia	Resolute Serbia
Military strength	Puny	Moderate
Economic strength	B– with hope of improvement	C– with hope of improvement
Ethnic diversity	Over one-third non-titular	Over half non-titular
Clash of civilizations	Latent Western-Orthodox	Latent three-way
Ethnic (vs civic) nationalism	Yes, among titulars and many Slavs	Moderate/strong
Militant ideology	No	Chastened
Commitment to ethnic harmony	Moderate	Weak/moderate
Societal security dilemma	Moderate	Strong
Leadership	Free enterprise and smart	Uncertain and divided
Societal fitness	B–/B	C–/C

Source: Author's estimates.

Each table represents a highly simplified rendering of a nuanced reality. Let us now examine each potential explanation in more detail.

THE STRUCTURES OF POWER

Neorealists argue that, absent supranational government, the hierarchy of power determines how nations behave (Waltz 1979). Neorealism treats individual and societal variables as irrelevant to world politics. Could the theory be adapted to explain what happened in the Baltic region and the Balkans in the 1990s?

The imperial hegemon ruling the Baltic republics was a military superpower whose troops had repressed nationalists in Kazakhstan in 1986 and in Georgia in 1989. Balts realized they had no chance to prevail in war against Soviet power. Even the largest and least Russified Baltic state, Lithuania, had no possibility of prevailing against the Soviet juggernaut. Instead, Balts looked for nonviolent solutions. They took advantage of the Gorbachev regime's interest in glasnost and perestroika to build a base for secession. Even after Soviet troops killed fourteen civilians, the parliament in Vilnius on February 2, 1991, called on Lithuanians to use their sole "effective and undefeatable weapon, expressive of Baltic and Christian culture—that of nonviolent protest, of people's self-control and calm endurance."

Seeing the so-called superpower in retreat, long-repressed peoples did not compromise. Balts spurned Gorbachev's 1991 proposal for a confederation. When the USSR dissolved, Balts also spurned its weak replacement, the Commonwealth of Independent States. Granted that Soviet hard power was ebbing, the neorealist thesis does not does not explain why the USSR, still a military Goliath, failed to use decisive force to crush moves by the Baltic Davids to regain independence. It does not explain why—before and after 1991—Moscow did not do more to help Russian "compatriots" in the Baltic. Moscow maintained large numbers of troops (formerly Soviet, now Russian) in the Baltic republics for three to four years after they regained independence. Alternatively, if we view Russian power as a feeble ghost of the erstwhile superpower, why did Estonians and Latvians not exploit Russian weakness after the withdrawal of Russian troops to cleanse their lands of Russian speakers?

In retrospect, we may say that Mikhail Gorbachev and later Boris Yeltsin lacked the will to keep the empire together by force.[8] But Balts could not know whether they would or would not be crushed by the large alien army based on their soil until the mid-1990s. The West offered only moral support to the Baltic republics as they struggled to regain independence. The George H. W. Bush administration warned the Gorbachev regime not to use force against Balts, but did little to roll back the Soviet empire.

While Yeltsin's Russia wished to dissolve the USSR, Serbia wanted to keep its realm intact. But if Croatia or Bosnia insisted on splitting, Belgrade demanded that they surrender Serb-populated lands to Serbia. Unlike the divided leadership in Moscow, most leaders in Belgrade backed Slobodan Milošević in his determination to fight for a greater Serbia. The Croats, Bosniaks, Kosovars, and others who defied Serbia also defied hard power. Serbs constituted only a plurality of the Yugoslav population but Serbs led the "Yugoslav" army, which provided extensive support to the Bosnian Serbs. Unlike Moscow under Gorbachev, the Belgrade government led by Milošević did not lose its imperial will. Belgrade too ignored the logic of hard power when, in 1998–99, it refused NATO's demands to give way on Kosovo.

Structures of hard power influenced but did not control the thoughts and actions of actors in the Baltic and the Balkans. Intangibles—courage, perceptions, emotions, cultures—overrode the threat and even the use of brute force. If raw power always prevailed, the weak would never revolt or, if they did, the strong would always win.

SECURITY DILEMMAS AND COMMITMENT

A "societal security dilemma" may develop when one ethnic group feels its identity threatened by another and then takes countermeasures that provoke a tough response. Whether the societal security dilemma fans violence or not depends on many factors—one of them the perceived commitment of each group to respect the other's political, economic, and cultural interests (Posen 1993; Johnson 2008). Where there is a history of abuse by either side, avowed commitments to peaceful coexistence may be doubted.

In Transylvania the security dilemma was underscored by a 1990 law that permitted Hungarian-language schools and required local Romanian speakers to study Hungarian. Some Romanians perceived these changes as precursors to secession. Their hostile responses drove some Hungarian speakers to demand not just cultural autonomy but independence (Roe 2002).

Similarly, violence in Croatia's Krajina ("border") region in August 1990 derived mainly from a struggle by Serbs to maintain their identity within a republic they saw as being increasingly "Croatized" (Roe 2002, 65). A tipping point was reached when Serbs felt they were losing their ability to control education in their region. Only then did secession become an explicit goal for Croatia's Serbs. At the same time, actions by Serbian leaders gave non-Serbs reasons to fear Belgrade. Education and ideology in Serbia became increasingly chauvinist if not xenophobic—illustrated by some examples given below.

While some security dilemmas are fanned by misperception, some fears of an impending confrontation are well founded. Such troubled relationships need not become zero-sum conflicts, but if the dominant power is intransigent, the weaker may need to struggle—even fight—to protect its interests. Kosovars were correct to fear that Belgrade under Milošević meant to repress them. Belgrade was right to think that Kosovars wanted to secede. Self-righteous to the hilt, each side took deliberately hostile moves against the other until an outside power—NATO—intervened.

The societal security dilemma was much less acute in the Baltic. To be sure, Soviet leaders in Moscow and the large Slavic-speaking populations of the Baltic countries correctly perceived in the late 1980s that "popular fronts" in Estonia, Latvia, and Lithuania were setting the stage for secession. If this happened, the privileges enjoyed by Slavic speakers could suffer. Worried Slavs took countermeasures. Many—encouraged by Moscow and local organizers—backed an "Interfront" to counter the popular fronts.[9] While Estonians, Latvians, and Lithuanians clearly meant to recreate ethnic states and cultures, their words and actions did not provoke violence. Slavs perceived that they would not automatically become citizens of the new states but neither would they be persecuted. No tipping point occurred.

ECONOMIC DETERMINISM

A neo-Marxist might note that the most affluent republics of the former USSR and Yugoslav Federation led the breakup of each empire. Estonians, Latvians, Lithuanians, Slovenes, and Croats were the richest nations in their multinational states. They believed they could become still more prosperous if free to go their own ways. Balts used Gorbachev's perestroika to break out in new directions, but still felt hamstrung by Moscow's centralized controls. Meanwhile, Yugoslavia was the only major country in Eastern Europe to experience a net decline in GDP per capita in the 1980s. Slovenes inferred that the ruling elite in Belgrade would never take more than trivial moves toward a market economy. Thus, economic downturns helped stoke political crisis in Yugoslav as well as the Soviet realm.[10]

But economic determinism fails on many counts. It does not explain why Balts *risked* their relative affluence by defying Soviet power and by cutting economic links with the USSR. Balts were quite aware that the other Soviet republics provided nearly the only markets for their products. Equally important, Moscow controlled the oil spigots on which Latvia and Lithuania depended.[11] Balts hoped to do better economically if they broke from Moscow's grip, but they also knew that the costs of freedom would be severe—perhaps unsupportable.

Similarly, Slovenes and Croats jeopardized their relative prosperity by challenging the local hegemon and by daring to compete in world markets. Still ruled from Belgrade in the 1990s, much poorer Kosovars also ignored economic logic by cultivating their own networks of schools and social services, not paid for by Serbian authorities.

When cross-border war and ethnic cleansing began in the Balkans, thoughts about material gain and loss usually played a very subordinate role. Deeper emotions were at work. Independence movements in the Baltic and the Balkans differed from civil wars in Africa and Asia, where many insurgencies were driven by poverty, unequal distribution of wealth, rough terrain, and large populations as well as by political instability (Fearon and Laitin 2003).[12]

Having avoided major ethnic and major cross-border violence, Balts could concentrate on development. Many people in the Balkans, however, had to cope with the consequences of civil war.[13] These included heavy economic and social costs, mutual distrust and fear, bad governance, disease, and disrupted education. Leftover munitions and landmines left enduring hazards. Memories of violence made it harder for people to live peacefully with one another, build civil society, and develop economically. Civil war is development in reverse. It represents both a failure *of* development and a deep problem *for* development. Its ripple effects trouble not only the peoples directly involved but also the region where they live and sometimes the entire world. (Collier 2003). Once civil war has begun, it often continues—if not overtly, then in its long-term consequences.

CLASHES OF CIVILIZATIONS

In much of the former Soviet Union and Yugoslavia, the fight against the imperial hegemon correlated with religious differences. This correspondence led

Huntington (1996) and other observers to exaggerate the weight of cultural differences. Clashes across the erstwhile Communist realm arose primarily from political and economic disagreements—*reinforced* by religion and other cultural differences. The clash of civilizations argument, like neorealism and neo-Marxism, oversimplified. It elevated one factor and asserted its decisive impact. In reality, conflicts between and among individuals, clans, nationalisms, financial and trading interests loomed as large or larger than any clash of civilizations.[14]

The ethnic conflict in Transylvania pitted Hungarian ethnics with a Roman Catholic tradition against Romanians with an Orthodox heritage. The case was significant because it provided an iconic interethnic dispute in Eastern Europe. An Orthodox priest was seen egging on Romanian demonstrators as they clashed with Hungarians in March 1990. His rallying call, however, was not that the other side consisted of heretics but that the "Hungarians" sought to take away Transylvania. The catalysts for the conflict were language and politics—not religion (Roe 2002, 58, 73).

To be sure, rival faiths have fueled nationalist fires. Before, during, and since the years of communist rule, Orthodox Russia has often supported Orthodox Serbia and Armenia. But many people in Orthodox Belarus, Ukraine, Moldova, Romania, Georgia, and even in Armenia have at times opposed Russia—not for its religious heritage but for more tangible reasons. Similarly, in the Balkans, it was not only Catholic and Muslim societies that resisted Orthodox Serbia. So did Orthodox Montenegrins, Macedonians, and Bulgarians.

So long as the central government did not discriminate against any constituent group in Yugoslavia, no clash of civilizations surfaced. An uneasy social peace prevailed in Yugoslavia from 1945 until 1980. Intermarriage across cultures was common. But when Slobodan Milošević began playing the nationalist card in 1989, he alienated non-Serbs and provoked them to split from Serbia—not just Catholics and Muslims but also Orthodox Christians in Montenegro and Macedonia. For them, local rights trumped cultural solidarity. Slovenes and Croats were consciously Western in their orientations, but their major complaints against Serbia were political.[15]

The 1990s did not witness any upsurge in religious fervor among the warring nations of the former Yugoslavia (Perica 2002). But in 1993 the Ministry of Education began to foster the "Serbian" language over Serbo-Croat. School textbooks suggested that relationships between different social groups are, as a rule, conflictual. Textbooks suggested that cooperation with other groups can be no more than short-term alliances against a shared foe. A kind of literary ethnic cleansing of non-Serbian writers eliminated most of their contributions. For reasons of ideological cleansing, many essays on Tito were also excluded (Rosandić 2000, 18–19).

Regardless of ethnic and other differences, however, the granddaughter of Yugoslavia's late president found in 1990s plenty of "good people in times of evil." There were countless "Schindlers"—Croats, Serbs, Bosniaks, Jews, and others who risked their own lives to help designated enemies (Broz 2001, 46–78).

On the other hand, many clashes over religion took place *within* some Orthodox countries. The tight links between church and state—especially since the collapse of communist rule—led to discrimination against other faiths. Romania, for example, recognized eighteen denominations, but only the Orthodox church—treated as the national church by the constitution—could receive state support. Similarly, Bulgaria treated Orthodoxy as the county's traditional faith and enacted a law allowing only denominations registered at the local and national level to perform public activities outside their places of worship. Path dependency played a role: Christian churches in most Balkan countries had struggled to survive under Ottoman rule, whereas Christianity (at first Catholic, then Protestant) was imposed and then fostered by the Germans and Swedes who ruled what later became Estonia and Latvia.

Resistance in the three Baltic republics to Russian domination corresponded with the cleavage between Western and Orthodox Christianity. But religion seldom aggravated Baltic-Russian relations unless tied to political maneuvers.[16] Differences between Western and Eastern Christians did not provoke communal strife *within* the Baltic republics.[17]

Politics—not faith—shaped Baltic attitudes toward other independence movements. Thus, Balts supported self-determination in Muslim as well as Orthodox regions of the former USSR, including Kazakhstan, Chechnya, Ukraine, and Georgia.[18] Lithuania and Latvia, along with Ukraine, extended diplomatic recognition to Slovenia and Croatia in 1991 even before Germany and Iceland. Estonia followed suit two weeks later. While traditional religion enjoyed a revival in Russia and some other parts of the former USSR, it lost its drive for most Balts. As in much of Europe, hope for salvation in a future life gave way to hope for a "normal" life without interference by a tyrannical government (Ferguson 2003).

The United States also drove a nail into the coffin of the clash of civilizations thesis. The "Anglo-Saxon Protestant" superpower intervened to defend the human rights of Muslims in Bosnia, Kosovo, and Macedonia even though these lands—unlike Azerbaijan. Kazakhstan, and Kuwait—lacked any material resources coveted by Americans. Washington in 2011 joined Paris and London in actions meant to help Libyan rebels. The trigger was fear of massacres by the Gaddafi regime, though concerns about Libya's oil wealth were not distant. The West welcomed democratic upsurges in Tunisia and Egypt but did little to help dissidents in Syria or Bahrain. Whether the West intervened or held back, religious identity played a minor role. As new governments replaced autocracies in Arab countries and as rebel forces grew stronger in Syria, Washington worried that Islamic militants would prevail over moderates.

chapter four

CULTURE AND THE CAPACITY TO COPE WITH COMPLEXITY

Greater societal fitness would make it easier to moderate ethnic conflicts and to advance human development. How to move in this direction? Culture matters. As Daniel P. Moynihan noted, conservatives believe that culture determines the success of a society, but liberals know (or hope) that politics can change a culture and save it from itself (L Harrison 2006; L. Harrison and Huntington 2000). In most societies both culture and politics needed enlightened change.

MYTHS AND MYTHMAKING

Myths make nations and nations make myths. Within each culture, behavior is shaped by beliefs nurtured by myths. Orthodox Christianity combined with political mythology to shape Balkan identities through the sacralization of politics, a process rooted in the Byzantine concept of *symphonia* between Orthodox religion and the state (Leustean 2008). In the erstwhile Yugoslavia, mythology served not to unite but to divide three religious communities, for each had its own myth of national origin (Perica 2002, 5). For centuries, Serbs have been raised to believe that they are a "heavenly people" led by saints but oppressed by infidel Turks, harassed by heretical Catholics, and often betrayed by perfidious Russians. Like some Shiite Muslims, many Serbs have acted as though, suffering from a persecution complex, they wanted pity and expected to be martyred. Their "Kosovo Pole" and related myths bespeak "a land of ceaseless resentment inhabited by eternal losers" (Perica

2002, 229). Serbs have been taught to fight and kill for their just cause even when the odds are stacked against them. Believing they have been wronged, but confident that God is with them, they expect sooner or later to regain Serbia's former glory. Obsessed by such myths, many intellectuals such as the writer Dobrica Ćosić (first president of rump Yugoslavia, 1992–93) abetted atrocities against other ethnic groups (Zimmerman 1999, 93–94, 201). The 1996 Serbian film *Pretty Village, Pretty Flame*[1] depicts a Bosnian Serb soldier, his unit facing extermination by Muslim fighters, proclaiming, for all to hear, that Serbia is the "oldest nation."

Undaunted by time or circumstances, a Serbian choir entertained the United Nations General Assembly in January 2013 and ended with the song *March on the Drina*. First written to honor Serbian soldiers killed in World War I, the march became a kind of unofficial anthem among Serbian forces that carried out massacres of Muslims at Srebrenica and other sites in 1995. Not understanding the words or the background, UN Secretary General Ban Ki-moon and other UN officials gave the choir a standing ovation. The General Assembly president at the time, Vuk Jeremić, a former Serbian foreign minister (with a Harvard Kennedy School of Government degree, Master in Public Administration in International Development) stated "We are very proud of it [the song] and wanted to share it with the world" with a message of "reconciliation [sic]" (*New York Times,* January 18, 2013).

The upshot was that Serbs and some others in the Balkans have hoped for glory and valued honor far more than Balts. Like Iranians, many Serbs have expected to die fighting as martyrs for a just if losing cause. Of course Serbs are not alone in such feelings. Some nationalists in Croatia, Poland, Slovakia, Ukraine, and elsewhere have also indulged in self-pity—portraying their own nation as the ultimate victim. Some Polish historians described their Poland as the "Christ of nations"—victimized by its neighbors. Many Romanians, like Serbs, spoke about their nation's destiny to save Christian civilization from Ottoman invasions and their differences with Russia. After all the established certainties have been shattered, nationalism has offered a soothing balm for a disaffected community (Tismaneanu 1998, 84–85). Far from the Balkans, some U.S. patriots take comfort in putative American values and virtues. For Romanians, Transylvania occupied a role in historical mythology similar to that of Kosovo for Serbs. Transylvania was said to have been the cradle of the Romanian nation, where indigenous Dacians mingled with Romans many centuries before the arrival of Hungarian speakers. In point of fact, however, this "cradle" was ruled from Budapest for long periods of time, giving rise to irredentist sentiments on both sides of the Romanian-Hungarian border.[2]

In the post-communist politics of the 1990s, weak civic traditions in the Balkans provided a precarious basis for tolerance of alterity, acceptance of ethnic diversity, and commitment to full equality under the law. Many intellectuals in the Balkans labored to cover up the shameful pages of national history and to fabricate new messianic, self-indulging fantasies (Tismaneanu 1998, 82).

The situation was different in the northern parts of the communist realm, where dissidents established freedom as the basic value of post-1989 politics. Unlike the Balkans, few mainstream intellectuals in Central Europe and the Baltic region pandered to the populist Right. Instead, most saw that the main conflict of the twentieth century was between collectivism, whether communist or fascist, and liberal individualism. Their commitment to nonviolence was expressed in peaceful metaphors coupled with an underdog ethos that empathized with more than it demonized its opponents. Their nonviolent rhetoric appeared in the retellings of stories about three national heroes: *The Son of Kalev* (*Kalevipoeg,* first published serially in 1857–1861) in Estonia, *The Bearslayer* (*Lāčplēsis,* 1888) in Latvia, and King Mindaugas in Lithuania. The retellings minimized violence in the central allegory of Baltic nationhood. Yes, all three heroes were warriors when they emerged as national symbols in the nineteenth century. Through a series of adaptations, however, they lost their militant characteristics. Enemies too, lost their demonic qualities and became easier to forgive. Female characters gained in importance as they steered the hero from violence (Šmidchens 2007, 485).

Many Estonians, Latvians, and Lithuanians also saw their nations as victims, but few focused on past misfortunes or glories. Monuments such as Latvia's Occupation Museum sought to ensure that past horrors were not forgotten. Medieval guild houses and churches were restored or rebuilt nearly from scratch. Independence regained, however, most Balts looked to the future—one in which their national values could thrive in a supranational context along with those of other European nations. Lithuania had a privately owned park containing communist-era statues, but it did not signify nostalgia for communism. It probably signified forgetfulness more than remembrance.

For Estonians and Latvians, the second millennium yielded few national heroes or claims to martial glory. They had no epic to unite them until the second half of the nineteenth century. Even so, Estonia's *The Son of Kalev* turned out to be an awkward giant who managed to cut off his own legs with his own sword. Crippled, he stands guard at the Gates of Hell. Latvia's *Bearslayer* fights the Black Knight but both fell beneath the waves of the Daugava where they continue their struggle. Both the Estonian and the Latvian epics promised a form of national redemption *some day,* but each cultivated patience more than militancy. Neither suggested that Estonians or Latvians are God's Chosen People. Neither fostered a superiority or a persecution complex. Neither extolled violence against neighbors. Unlike the *Marseillaise* or *Star Spangled Banner,* Estonia's national anthem and national hymns had no martial themes.

Like Serbs, Lithuanians could recall their medieval glory. But they did not dwell on any event such as Kosovo Pole which, for Serbs, evoked suspicions of treason from within as well as hatred toward an external foe. Lithuanians, after all, surrendered their primacy voluntarily in an alliance with Poland, an arrangement that worked fairly well for several centuries before it collapsed in the late eighteenth century. The erstwhile commonwealth with Poland left some Lithuanians with dreams of a renewed confederation with neighbors—not with hope for renewed empire.

Lithuanians had no epic comparable to *The Son of Kalev* or *The Bearslayer*. But in 1898 a play about King Mindaugas, written by a Polish romantic in 1823, was translated into Lithuanian. The 1823 play presented this medieval character as a brave but savage ruler. His character changed as Lithuanian authors recast the king to fit the *Zeitgeist*. In the 1930s Mindaugas was an autocrat who used force to accomplish his goals, though he failed due to his weakness for women. A more humane autocrat appears in a 1968 retelling. Inspired by his wife, this Mindaugas performs his first act of nonviolent heroism: mercy. A monument to the king unveiled in 2003 shows him seated, holding an orb and scepter—unlike earlier depictions with a sword (Šmidchens 2007, 503–504).

Lithuanian popular culture for centuries has been expressed in roadside shrines to Christ. The shrines, like the Estonian and Latvian epics, exude patience under duress. They were sometimes torn down by tsarist Russian and Soviet officials, but were often rebuilt (Richardson 2003). Lithuanians trusted that God was on their side but felt no call to violent action.

The epic heroes of the Amber Coast stood for redemption but not for revenge or militant expansion. Serbs, by contrast, were taught that they are God's chosen people—wronged and entitled to settle old scores and regain lost lands. There is no analogue in the Baltic traditions—not even in Lithuania, once part of Europe's largest and most powerful state. Yes, the country and its people have been abused, but the culture gives no impetus to regain a lost imperial glory.

In short, mythology helped sustain destructive behavior in the Balkans but not in the Baltic. The narratives summarized here were part of a national civilizing process that culminated in the late-1980s Singing Revolution. The Baltic heroes offered a new litmus test for the sustained future of nonviolence (Šmidchens 2007 and 2013; Clemens 2009).

INDIVIDUAL LEADERS

Individuals can lead the way to peace or war. They can inflame hostility or reconcile differences.

Ethnic conflict can be triggered from within by elite- or mass-level factors, or from without by bad neighbors and bad neighborhoods (Brown 2001, 14–15). All these factors contributed to ethnic conflict among the South Slavs and Albanian-speaking communities of the Balkans. Inflammatory words and deeds by elites, however, were crucial. Absent these sparks, the Balkan peoples would probably have been spared the costs of war.

"Yugoslavia was destroyed from the top down." Its "death and the violence that followed resulted from the conscious actions of nationalist leaders who coopted, intimidated, circumvented, or eliminated all opposition to their demagogic designs." This was the conclusion of Warren Zimmerman, the U.S. ambassador to Belgrade from 1989 to 1992, who saw it all happen (Zimmerman 1999, vii).

The South Serbs had long lived under power-hungry despots. The fathers, sons, and brothers at the helm of Serbia's medieval kingdom (founded 1159, withered after 1389) often killed one another and then claimed sainthood. After most of the region fell to Ottoman Turks in the fifteenth and sixteenth centuries, Serbs and some other Balkan peoples were dominated for centuries by far-off sultans and their local pashas. As Ottoman control weakened in the nineteenth century, the rival Karadjordjević and Obrenović dynasties in Serbia took turns murdering each other and confronting Turks. Following World War I, the Kingdom of Serbs, Croats, and Slovenes ("Yugoslavia" after 1929) endured another set of royal authoritarians until 1939, though one was assassinated in 1934.

Each of the rival Yugoslav resistance movements during World War II was dominated by a strong personality—the Partisans by Josip Broz Tito and the Chetniks by Dragoljub-Draža Mihailović. Tito's Partisans prevailed and hunted down the remaining Chetniks and executed their leader Mihailović. In Croatia, meanwhile, Ante Pavlović, the same man who commissioned the Yugoslav king's assassination in 1934, returned from Italian exile and became the Croatian *Poglavnik* [*Führer*]. His Ustaša movement served as Hitler's puppet regime until May 1945.

Individuals can also be important for what they do *not* do. The leading churchman of Croatia during World War II and for decades thereafter, Alojzije Stepinac, privately condemned Ustaša brutality and managed to save some Jews and other minorities from Croatian Fascists.[3] While Stepinac did little in public to restrain the Ustaša, in 1946 he led other bishops in condemning communist atheism.[4] These facts were recalled by protestors against beatification of Stepinac by the anticommunist Pope John Paul II (Perica 2002, 229–30).

Marshal Tito (part Croat, part Slovene), having become president, held Yugoslavia together from 1945 until his death in 1980. He succeeded by dint of his own personality and adroit management of ethnic issues and foreign policy. But when Milovan Đjilas in 1957 accused Tito of breeding a new privileged class, Tito locked up his longtime comrade twice—for a total of nine years. Tito used the slogan "Brotherhood and Unity," reinforced by a heavy police apparatus, to crush the old nationalisms. But this approach probably helped germinate their reemergence after his departure. More glasnost some years earlier might have released mounting tensions before they exploded.

Tito's passing left a vacuum that other power-hungry individuals sought to fill. Many of them exploited long-repressed ethnic grievances, both real and imagined. Their ranks included Milošević, Radovan Karadzić, and Ratko

Mladić. Milošević paid lip service to Yugoslav unity, but he spun plans for a Serb-dominated dictatorship—the very actions that soon destroyed the federation. As in Saddam Hussein's Iraq, the families and associates of Serbia's top leader became richer thanks to sanctions. Allied with gangsters such as "Arkan" and Aleksandar Knežević, and with the banker Dafina Milanović, they cornered the black market in cigarettes, liquor, and other valuable goods. Even after Milošević was ousted, gangland and political murders continued in Belgrade.

Croatia in the 1990s had its own despot, President Franjo Tuđman, who, reviving Ustaša symbols, exploited local nationalist cards, much like Milošević. Tuđman's declaration of Croatian independence—issued with no promise to protect the country's 12 percent Serbian population—gave Milošević a pretext to attack Croatia. Tuđman, in turn, responded to irredentist pressures in Herzegovinan towns such as Ljubuški, Široki Brijeg, and Mostar for Serbia to annex Croatian-inhabited areas there, thereby extending and prolonging the wars of all against all.

Both Milošević and Tuđman embraced and employed communist techniques of control—mass parties, control of the media, and centralized economic power. Both communists and Balkan nationalists asserted that the individual counts for nothing compared to the collective. Balkan nationalism rejected communist internationalism and cloaked itself in the local religion and values—stamped, however, with the habits and assumptions of Leninism. It demonized dissidents, minorities, and any groups associated with pro-Western pluralism. It resurrected pre-communist collectivist traditions and hailed post-communist leaders as saviors from traitors within and implacable foes without (Zimmerman 1992, 252). Ex-communists exerted significant influence over mostly communist parties. Tuđman's Croatian Democratic Union (HDZ) used war to impose a semiauthoritarian system that weakened the electoral prospects of its main rival, the Social Democratic Party in the 1990s. After Tuđman died in 1999, the SDP-led coalition won the 2000 elections, enabling a deeper democratization in Croatia that helped the country meet EU requirements. Thus, Croatia broke with path-dependency (Pickering and Baskin 2008).

Bosnia also had its charismatic president, Alija Izetbegović. Like Tuđman, Izetbegović had served time in prison for nationalist tendencies. Though accused of espousing Islamist fundamentalism, in the 1990s Izetbegović championed democratic pluralism.

Slovenia benefited from the presidency of Milan Kučan, a former communist elected on a pro-Yugoslav platform in 1990, who despised Milošević, and that of Janez Stanovnik, "a wise and compassionate man," married to a Serb, who believed that the South Slavs needed to learn to live together, and from Prime Minister Janez Drnovšek, who labored in 1992 to save the country from violence (Zimmerman 1999, 112–13; also Tismaneanu 1998).

Zimmerman found heroes among Yugoslav's leaders, such as former prime minister Ante Marković, a Croatian businessman who sought in 1989–1991 to launch the most liberal economic reforms in Eastern Europe. Zimmerman respected the erstwhile Yugoslav foreign minister Budimir Lončar, who resigned when Milošević ordered his ministry to spread nationalist Serbian propaganda abroad. Zimmerman found most Yugoslavs to be decent people "without a trace of the hostility on which nationalism feeds." Many capitulated to the passions whipped up by engineers of violence, but many resisted the incessant racist propaganda spewing from their television sets.

Was Yugoslavia's breakup inevitable? No, but for some Yugoslavs—especially those living in mixed neighborhoods, ethnic hatreds and cultural clashes were simply repressed by Tito's strong hand. When Tito died, the resulting power vacuum permitted aspiring leaders to stoke the fires of animosity.

Conversely, the relative ethnic calm of Romania after 1989 illustrated the positive role that individuals can play. Romania's first leader after Nicolae Ceaușescu, Ion Iliescu, moved in the opposite direction from Milošević. As president, Iliescu attempted to reduce if not eliminate ethnic tensions. To be sure, his language-law reforms in 1990 had the opposite effect, because Romanian ethnics feared a cascade leading to the secession of Transylvania.[5] On balance, however, Iliescu helped to subdue ethnic tensions. He was also the first Romanian head of state to participate in the Jewish community's annual commemoration of the Holocaust. In 1996, he signed a friendship treaty with Yugoslavia, paid an official visit to Moldova, and signed a treaty with Hungary designed to end historic conflicts and boost each country's chances of joining NATO and the EU.[6] Despite this treaty, however, a majority of Romanians continued to believe that Hungary wanted to regain control of Transylvania. Some 43 percent of Romanians in Transylvania surveyed in 2001 thought that relations with the Hungarian minority were "cooperative," but only 22 percent thought interethnic relations had improved since 1989 (Kostecki 2002, 41–42).

Balts were not angels, but the Amber Coast had not seen such brutal contenders for power as those in the Balkans for five hundred years—not since fights to the death within Lithuania's Jagiello dynasty. Authoritarian leaders did emerge in each Baltic republic between the two world wars—championed in some cases by sycophantic journalists and academics. But their goals and methods were mild compared to the personality cults and bloody tactics used for centuries in what became Yugoslavia.

In post-Tito Yugoslavia the top leaders had professions—banking, history, even psychiatry—but each came at politics with the zero-sum mentality nurtured by their rise within the *kto kovo* (who will do in whom) culture of the Communist Party.

Some Baltic politicians such as Arnold Rüütel and Algirdas Brazauskas had been Communist leaders, but those in the vanguard of Baltic independence movements had never joined the Party and made their careers without Communist patronage. They included music professor Vytautas Landsbergis, filmmaker Lennart Meri, historians Mart Laar and Tunne Kelam. Social scientist

Rein Taagepera, folklorist, Vaira Vīķe-Freiberga, environmental manager Valdas Adamkus, and other émigrés returned from abroad—not primarily for personal gain but to help rebuild their homelands. To be sure, some businessmen such as Andris Šķēle in Latvia became rich in the 1990s and then entered politics. Some Baltic politicians took bribes; some aligned with local and Russian mafias; but none abetted bloodletting to get rich—as happened among the South Slavs.[7] No major leader in the Baltic hitched his or her fortune to calls for action against ethnic aliens. Some even joined with Russian-speaking politicians (already citizens by virtue of long residence in the Baltic) to promote "Unity" parties devoted to enhancing the rights of Russian-speaking residents.

No Baltic leader aspired to dictatorship in the wake of Soviet rule. Of course each rising figure had an ego to polish, but most sought first and foremost to serve their fellow citizens There were no power-hungry megalomaniacs like Milošević. The Lithuanian leader Vytautas Landsbergis had a fiery tongue but an impish face—a deeply cultured person who had learned from the nonviolent tactics of Solidarność.[8] Nor did Balts yearn for a strong hand. Indeed, every few years after 1991 Balts often seemed ready to "throw the bums out"—Landsbergis included, and bring in a different set of personalities and promises.

THE CAPACITY TO COPE WITH COMPLEXITY

Many factors help explain differences between the Baltic and Balkan regions, but the fundamental difference has been their relative fitness—each society's capacity to cope with complex challenges, process information, and create and utilize opportunities at home and abroad. A fit society is more able to cope with ethnic and other differences and to prosper in a market economy. This kind of fitness, according to complexity science, requires self-organization—not just in politics but in all dimensions of life—economic, social, and cultural. This capacity cannot be realized in conditions of anarchy or rigid order—the poles of political life, as in Russia. It is more likely to bubble close to the edge of apparent chaos, as in the United States.

Unfit societies experience a vicious circle of poverty and perceived discrimination that provokes scapegoating and ethnic violence. A fit society, by contrast, cultivates a virtuous circle: social peace → political and economic advance → deeper harmony. Such a progression requires a way of life that generates values for all stakeholders.

A fit society will help talented leaders emerge while limiting the options for destructive individuals. Energetic individuals can undermine or enhance societal fitness. But they will not come to the fore in a static society. That the traditionally white Anglo-Saxon, male-dominated United States could consider Catholics, Jews, blacks, and women for high positions showed that the country was becoming not only more tolerant but also more fit. Increasingly it could draw on the talents and energies of persons long denied access to influential positions—nonwhites and "the weaker sex." That Estonians would accept a young historian such as Mart Laar as prime minister and let him push the country rapidly into a free market democracy bore witness to the openness and creativity of a long repressed but potentially fit society. A fit society will eschew Pied Pipers of negativity such as Milošević and Tuđman and listen instead to leaders such as Meri and Landsbergis, whose policies aimed at mutual gain.

Cultural and ethnic diversity can boost or undermine fitness. For Canada and the United States, diversity generated a mosaic of mutual enrichment. For the USSR, diversity strongly correlated with inequality. Most Balkan nations did little to foster a multicultural mosaic. A fit society can minimize the security dilemmas and commitment problems that disrupt unfit societies.

Self-organization implies some form of democracy. But democracy can have negative as well as positive outcomes. As liberal peace theory suggests, democracies are more likely to resolve their domestic disputes without violence and to avoid war when interacting with other democracies. On the other hand, societies making the transit to democracy (or from democracy to authoritarianism) are likely to be unstable and prone to violence (J. Snyder 2000; Mansfield and Snyder 2005). Democracy can foster compromise among diverse groups but it can also spawn a dictatorship of the majority—often sharpening security dilemmas at home and across borders. When a democracy is both proud and powerful, it may seek to impose its will on others (S. Harris 2011).

SELF-ORGANIZED FITNESS IN THE BALTIC REPUBLICS

Self-organization had a long running start in the Czech lands, Poland, Hungary, the Baltic countries, and Slovenia relative to the lands to the south and east, most of which adhered to Orthodox or Muslim traditions. Self-organized fitness depended on high levels of literacy, devotion to free thought, and respect for individual dignity.

Alien rule left a more positive legacy in the Baltic than in the Balkans. The Hanseatic city-states along the Baltic coast offered models of self-organized fitness (Clemens 2001, 21–38; Cederman 1997). They were exemplars of the republican, commercial, and cosmopolitan qualities that Immanuel Kant later prescribed for "eternal peace" (Kant 1983, 107–43). The German-speaking Hansas in city-states such as Reval, Dorpat, and Riga gave little scope to the *Undeutsche*. Nonetheless, indigenous Estonians and Latvians came in time to build on the legal order and other institutions pioneered by Hansas.

Respect for the local language was manifested in the late thirteenth and fourteenth centuries as local authorities required sermons to be preached in Estonian and Latvian. Catechisms in the local tongue were published in the

1530s. Jesuits in the 1580s, followed later by Swedes, founded colleges in Tartu. When Swedish rule supplanted Hanseatic in the seventeenth century, German elites still dominated the region, but Protestant Sweden promoted education in its Baltic provinces. Balts got the Bible in their own languages less than two centuries after Martin Luther—Latvians in 1685, southern Estonians in 1686, and Lithuanians in 1701.[9] Sweden surrendered its Baltic provinces and parts of Finland to Russia in 1721, but Swedish administration had given Finns and Balts a head start in literacy over other subjects of the Russian tsar.

Self-organization among Balts gradually increased in the nineteenth century. Russia ended serfdom in what became Estonia and Latvia in 1816–19—long before its demise elsewhere in the empire (1861). Free Estonians and Latvians traveled by rail to meet their kinsmen. Awareness of a shared heritage grew in the second half of the century as choirs from diverse parishes took part in song competitions across Russian-ruled Estonia and Latvia[10] This process deepened awareness of national solidarity for generations to come—in times of tsarist occupation, interwar independence, under Nazi occupation, and during a half-century of Soviet rule. In the late 1980s and early 1990s this process culminated in a Singing Revolution for independence.

Self-organization took a different shape in Lithuania. Unlike Estonia and Latvia, Lithuania enjoyed several centuries of great power status—first as a Grand Duchy and then as partner in the Polish-Lithuanian Commonwealth. This empire reached from the Baltic to the Black Sea, but embodied high levels of religious-linguistic tolerance and considerable self-organization. Three Christian faiths—Catholic, Uniate, and Orthodox—flourished. Both Latin and Chancery Slavic served as official languages. Nobles from Lithuania as well as Poland had a powerful voice in state affairs.

The Reformation also shaped Lithuanian culture. Several Protestant sects were active in Lithuania and made many converts, especially among the nobility. To counter these influences, Jesuits founded a college in Vil'no in 1579 that was revived in the early nineteenth century by a friend of Tsar Alexander I. Vil'no University then became the largest in the Russian empire, even though instruction (in Polish) served to codify the legacy of the recently defunct Polish-Lithuanian Commonwealth. One Vil'no graduate, the poet Adam Mickiewicz, kept alive the spirit of tolerance and unity across cultural and linguistic divides.

The movement toward literacy was so strong that by the late nineteenth century most Estonians and Latvians, of both genders, could read—a much larger percentage than in Russia proper.[11] By then each people also had its epic, *The Son of Kalev* and *The Bearslayer,* to buttress perceptions of a shared destiny. Progress toward universal literacy advanced more slowly in Lithuania, in part because St. Petersburg tried for decades to substitute the Cyrillic alphabet for Roman.

Self-organized fitness helped give rise to a professionalized middle class in Baltic cities with expectations that life should be governed by law and by merit—not by authoritarian whims and personal patronage. This transition got underway in the Baltic region in the latter decades of the nineteenth century and underlay the basis for independent statehood in 1920.

When the Russian, Austrian, and German empires perished in World War I, Józef Piłsudski and other leaders strove once more for a federation uniting Poles, Lithuanians, and Belarusians (T. Snyder 2003, 26–27). Failure to federate, however, set the stage for stubborn and sometimes violent responses. Foreigners had exploited the Baltic peoples for centuries, but as World War I ended, Estonians, Latvians, and Lithuanians looked forward more than backward. They fought local Germans and Soviet Russians who sought to regain or gain hegemony in Baltic lands. When those battles ended in 1920, their heritage of empire left Balts with little hate but much hope.

Like most of Europe, the Baltic republics experienced authoritarian and often myopic governance in the 1930s. They failed to coordinate their assets— internally, regionally, internationally—to resist takeovers by Stalin, by Hitler, and again by Stalin. Following a half-century of Soviet occupation, however, all three Baltic republics broke from the USSR by developing Popular Fronts that fused the energies of noncommunists and national communists (Clemens 1991; Lieven 1993). The fronts became major expressions of a civil society long repressed by communist rule. Complexity science would see them as "emergent structures"—the outcomes of a self-organizing process that became larger than the sum of its parts. The wide-scale, participatory nature of the Baltic independence movements provided a healthy basis for the civil and political freedoms achieved in the years after 1991.

If cooperation is common, its beneficiaries may take it for granted, not recognizing its importance.[12] The Baltic republics experienced much cooperation—with each other as well as internally—in the runup to independence regained, but very little before or after that time. Among the South Slavs, it was precisely the failure to cooperate among themselves that repeatedly set the stage for war.[13] The one South Slav nation spared great violence in the 1990s was Slovenia—referred to in one book title as a "Land of Cooperators" (Čujeŝ 1985). Helping to undergird this outlook, Slovene folk tales (Kavčič 1969) are notable for their "Horatio Alger"–type messages—how hard work and virtue conduce to middle-class prosperity and respectability.

Top-Down Rule in the Balkans

Communists tried to extirpate free thought and expression in the Baltic and other lands shaped by the Reformation and Counter-Reformation, but could not overcome a heritage stretching back nearly five hundred years. Communism fostered mass literacy in the Balkans and across the Soviet empire, but without freedom of thought or much respect for individual human dignity. Not only were Serbian children taught to expect conflict with other social groups, but they were also taught—at least through the 1990s—to obey authority and not think for themselves. Pupils were socialized to accept conformity as a virtue and to follow directives unquestionably (Rosandić 2000, 16).

History and culture left the Balkan peoples with a much weaker basis for self-organization than in the Baltic. Most Balkan states arose from the ruins of multinational empires. Most have held irredentist claims against neighbors because some portion of their population was incorporated into another state (Larrabee 1977, 1–2). Ottoman rule was more oppressive in Serbian lands than in other Turkish provinces. It was much tougher than what Baltic peoples endured under various foreign rulers or what Slovenes and Croats experienced under Habsburg domination. Ottoman rule subjected the Serbian church (proud of its autocephalous status) to control by unpopular Greek Phanariots. Serbian ways interacting with Ottoman administration left a legacy of hate.

The Ottoman millet system permitted non-Muslims to practice their faith and use their language so long as they paid their taxes (often double those imposed on Muslims). But the system also bolstered ethnocentrism throughout the Ottoman Empire. Like the Soviet and Yugoslav federalist approach to ethnicity, the millet deepened each community's sense of identity, setting the stage for struggles such as those between Serbia and Bulgaria over Macedonia.

Ottoman rule hindered modernization and helped to keep Balkan peoples undeveloped economically and poorly educated. After 1815, the Obrenović dynasty imported educated Serbs from Austrian lands to staff government bureaucracies and schools. Though they contended for supremacy, each rival dynasty in Serbia sought a patriarchic alliance between the central state and the peasantry. In power, each dynasty used the growing grid of public schools to inculcate the claim that only a strong unified state could project the Serbian nation from foreign domination. Serbia's rulers used nationalism to buttress central authority over local elites and justify taxes to support the government, and its military programs (J. Snyder 2003, 172–73).

In Bosnia-Herzegovina both Muslim and Serb elites also practiced top-down politics from the early nineteenth century into the 1980s, setting the stage for communal distrust and conflict in the 1990s (Burg and Shoup 1999). As Belgrade's central control weakened and republics such as Croatia became bolder, "Yugoslav" fitness declined. Any semblance of Rousseau's ideal "general will" disappeared as each actor sought to maximize its particular interest.

Reformation influences favoring self-organization rather than top-down rule were felt most strongly in Slovenia, less so in Croatia, and still less in Serbia. Protestant forces in Austria shaped Slovenia for fifty years in the sixteenth century (Berčič 1968). The New Testament was published in Slovene in 1557 and in Croatian in 1562. The entire Bible was published in Slovene in 1584 but not until 1831 in Croatian. Between 1580 and 1700, spurred by the Counter-Reformation, three Catholic secondary schools were established in Slovenia and seven in Croatia. The Croatian Diet in 1606–08 denied toleration to Protestants and in 1627 an imperial edict from Vienna banned

Protestantism throughout the Hapsburg realm. Later, Empress Maria Theresa promoted schooling in these regions, albeit in German.

Much later than in the Baltic and Hapsburg lands, the groundwork for higher and for mass education developed in nineteenth-century Serbia. Early in the century, Serbia's first institution of higher learning was established in Belgrade. By 1813 there were forty schools attended by 1,500 pupils in Serbia. The first printing press opened in 1831; the first bookshop in 1837 (Judah 2000, 55). The New Testament was published in Serbian in 1824 (abroad) and the entire Bible in 1868.[14] The last Turkish soldiers departed in 1867, but Serbia won international recognition only in 1878.

Cultural foundations known as *maticas* were established in Balkan lands to promote the publication and distribution of books and related cultural activities in the vernacular. For Bulgarians, one was established in 1847; for Slovenes, in 1852; for Romanians, in 1861; for Croats, in 1868. An academy of sciences was founded in Belgrade in 1864 and in Zagreb four years later. A university was established in Zagreb in 1874 and in Belgrade in 1905. A secondary school *lycée* for Muslims was founded in Bosnia in 1864. From 1607 to the nineteenth century, a dozen such schools were established for Croats. Starting with a school dating from 1728, Serbs had seven *lycées* by the late nineteenth century (Magocsi 2002, 54–56, 100–103).

Many Slovenes and Croats—even Josip Broz—fought with in the Austro-Hungarian Army in World War I. When the war ended, however, Slovenes and Croats sought self-determination. In 1920 they settled for junior roles in a Serbian-led "Kingdom of Serbs, Croats, and Slovenes."

Peoples without strong self-organization are vulnerable to manipulation by strong leaders, such as those who led the struggles for Serbian independence in the nineteenth century and ruled the South Slavs after 1918. But non-Serbs chaffed at centralized control and the kingdom splintered. Starting in 1945, however, Tito's strong hand kept Yugoslavia together for thirty-five years. His regime was probably the least tyrannical in the communist world, but depended on an individual feared and respected if not loved. After Tito's passing, the federation of South Slavs again fell apart.[15]

In the Balkans some potentially positive processes became negative. Whereas literacy fostered liberation in northern Europe, Balkan leaders used it to bolster authoritarian rule. State control of the media in Serbia and Croatia permitted political authorities to whip up nationalist fervor against minorities and neighbors. Struggling against these trends, students from the University of Belgrade organized in 1998 what became a powerful tool in national and even international affairs. The group, known as *Otpor!* [Resistance!] took shape to oppose repressive university and media laws introduced by the Milošević regime. During the presidential campaign of September 2000, *Otpor!* mobilized a broad-based resistance to Milošević using slogans such as *Gotov je* ["He is Finished"]. It challenged falsified election results and helped Vojislav Koštunica to replace Milošević as president. Some *Otpor!* tactics were inspired by Serbian translations of Gene Sharp's writings on nonviolent action, but *Otpor!* also received funding from U.S. National Endowment for Democracy and other U.S. agencies (Arrow 2011). Some *Otpor!* leaders exploited their prominence to enter politics, business, or diplomacy. But some organized a Center for Nonviolent Resistance that supported groups around the world in learning *Otpor!* methods. These included Georgian *Kmara* ["Enough"], a driving force in the 2003 Rose Revolution that removed Eduard Shevardnadze from power; Ukraine's *Pora* ["It's time"], which powered the 2004 Orange Revolution; and Kyrgyzstan's *KelKel,* which helped to oust President Askar Akayev in 2005. The center's efforts in Russia, Venezuela, and Belarus were less successful, but *Otpor!* tactics and advice guided some Egyptians struggling to oust President Hosni Mubarak in 2011.

HUMAN CAPITAL

The key to moving beyond Malthusian stagnation is human capital (Galor 2011). Slovenia in the 1980s ranked higher than other Yugoslav republics on most economic and social measures. In 1986, per capita income in Slovenia averaged one-third higher than in Vojvodina or Croatia, twice that of Serbia, and three times that of Bosnia or Macedonia, and seven times higher than in Kosovo. Slovenia had five times as many telephones per capita as Kosovo. While Slovenia had twelve stillborn babies per one thousand inhabitants; Serbia had twenty-two and Kosovo fifty-one.

These differences could be predicted by literacy levels in each republic. Less than 1 percent of Slovenia's population over age ten was illiterate in 1981. Kosovo had the highest percentage of illiterates—17.6 percent, followed by Bosnia, 14.5 percent; Serbia, 11.1 percent; Macedonia, 10.9 percent; Montenegro, 9.4 percent. Two republics once governed from Budapest came next. Vojvodina (5.8) and Croatia (5.6) had only half the illiteracy rate of Serbia, but neither came close to the near universal literacy of Slovenia—the only ex-Yugoslav republic to have directly experienced the Reformation.

Relatively high incomes in Slovenia developed in tandem with a more liberal political culture oriented to Western rather than to Balkan norms. The material conditions for Slovene youth were much better in the 1980s than for other Yugoslav youth, but the Slovenes were far more critical of their own status and their society as a whole. Thus, they pushed for democratic change, preferring nonviolent methods. At the other extreme, Kosovar youth, the poorest and most repressed, opted for violent rebellion.

Elsewhere in the Orthodox realm, as we shall see in the next chapter, Russia's failure to cast off top-down government reduced its ability to harness the country's human and material resources, and obstructed its acceptance as a legitimate member in the community of nations (Neumann 2008). While authoritarian rule undermined societal fitness in Russia and Belarus, oscillation between authoritarianism and anarchy weakened Ukraine.

ALTERNATIVE FUTURES

Along with devotion to one's one local community and religion, varieties of nationalism and internationalism have alternated in the region between the Baltic Sea and the Balkans for many centuries.[16] Nationalisms in the three Baltic republics in the late twentieth and early twenty-first centuries were closer to traditional patriotism than to the aggressive ethnic nationalism experienced in most of the former Yugoslavia. Devotion to one's own culture and land can, but need not, imply a claim to superiority or disdain for other cultures and lands. Patriotic nationalism can coexist with a cosmopolitan humanism. Such a worldview helped the uniting of Europe after World War II. It also permeated the consciousness of most Balts in the late twentieth and early twenty-first centuries.

The three Baltic peoples managed to extract positive strains from their historic inheritance so as to live in peace and benefit from political and economic freedom. Slovenes did much the same. Many Croats and Serbs moved in this direction in the early twenty-first century, but many leaders and publics in Balkan countries remained mired in history. Many still acted as though their peoples and cultures were superior to their neighbors'. Efforts to promote peace education in Serbia in the late 1990s received some marginal support from the Serbian Ministry of Education but made little progress. Teachers were limited by a traditional, aggressive, argumentative understanding of conflict and the use of withdrawal as reserve mechanism. The social reality of the school system reflected that of the larger society. Pupils absorbed a threatening, impoverished, and highly simplified picture of the world. They acquired belligerent, war-induced values about civilization and humanity from the media and much adult communication (Rosandić 2000, 9).

A Bulgarian film, *Whose Song Is This?*, documented how the same melody but with different words was regarded as "theirs" by Turks, Albanians, Greeks, Bulgarians, Serbs, Macedonians, and Bosnians. Each claimed the song was part of their tradition and if used by others it was "stolen" and "unworthy." None of the interlocutors perceived that the song could be regarded as a shared heritage (Rosandić 2000, 15).

Despite the heavy toll of communal violence, many people in the Balkans were not ready for peaceful coexistence. Even after a more democratic regime was elected in October 2000, many Serbs refused to acknowledge any responsibility for atrocities such as Srebrenica (Dimitrijevic 2008). Large numbers of displaced persons feared to go home. Elections in Bosnia, Kosovo, and Macedonia showed that many voters preferred their own kind. Many Serbs in Kosovo were afraid or unwilling to send their children to schools with Albanian-speaking majorities.

To save themselves, the Balkan peoples (like all others) needed to reject leaders who seek popularity by exploiting ethnic grievances. Aspiring peacemakers—the EU, United States, and others—needed to isolate and constrain fomenters of ethnic violence. Conflict prevention requires reining in domestic elites who spark internal conflicts to advance their personal agendas. Reformers need to neuter the ethnic scapegoating, hate mongering, and propagandizing that often precede violence (Brown 2001, 24). But it will never be easy to know when, how, or where to intervene. American efforts at nation-building in Iraq and Afghanistan did not encourage confidence in such ventures.

chapter five

COMPLEXITY SCIENCE AS A
TOOL TO UNDERSTAND THE NEW EURASIA

Why did the Soviet empire and Yugoslavia collapse? What forces within and without shaped these momentous events? And what happened afterward? Which peoples became more free? More prosperous? Better able to fulfill their ambitions and potential? Which achieved higher levels of human development and individual dignity—and which did not? Our focus is on the USSR and its successor states, all members of the former Warsaw Pact, Yugoslavia and its successor states, Albania, and Mongolia. To gain perspective, we include data and analysis of other former and present communist countries—Cambodia, China, Cuba, Laos, North Korea, and Vietnam. Reviewing these many cases, we see a pattern: societal fitness—the ability to cope with complex challenges and opportunities—seemed to align with culture. Societies with a heritage of Western Christianity proved far better able to engage complexity than those with an Orthodox Christian, Muslim, or other tradition. Starting in the fifteenth and sixteenth centuries, peoples in East Central Europe were energized by revolutionary demands for mass literacy, free thought, and respect for individual human dignity. Their past became both present and future.

Following the collapse of communist regimes across Eurasia in 1989–1991, some successor states avoided or minimized ethnic conflict while others suffered ethnic fighting at home or across borders. Still others managed to prevent or repress both internal and external conflict. Two leading authorities argue that democratization is the key variable that accounts for these divergent outcomes (Snyder 2000; Mansfield and Snyder 2005). The present book, however, argues that achievements and difficulties on the path from communist rule to a new way of life are more fully explained by each society's relative fitness. A fit society can deal constructively with ethnic as well as with other political, economic, and cultural problems. If a society fails on any of these fronts, internal grievances are likely to become more acute and may even explode in violence. When this happens, the society's ability to cope with many other problems also declines. Thus, societal fitness is both cause and effect of overall development. The key to fitness, according to complexity science, is self-organization. This quality, in turn, depends heavily upon culture. Cultures long devoted to universal literacy, independent thinking, and individual dignity have a far greater capacity for self-organization than those that resisted free thought and human rights.

TRENDS IN HUMAN DEVELOPMENT: VARIATIONS THAT NEED EXPLANATION

The huge area to which we shall try to apply insights from complexity science extends from Albania to Vietnam. To identify trends across Eurasia, we begin by tracing the rise and fall of each country's score on the UN Human Development Index (HDI). Later we will follow the patterns in each country's political and economic evolution. To set the stage, Figure 5.1 shows changes in HDI scores for all these countries at five junctures: 1970—the onset of Brezhnev-era stagnation in the Soviet empire; 1990—as communist systems in Europe collapsed; 1995—the economic nadir for most Soviet and Yugoslav states; 2000—when many began to recover or even move ahead; and 2010—when some prospered and others backpedaled. China, of course, was on a different trajectory. Mao Zedong in 1970 still presided over a chaotic Cultural Revolution. By 1990 Deng Xiaoping had unleashed the slogan "glorious to be rich." By 2010 the resultant system of Leninist capitalism helped China become the world's second-largest economy. Vietnam, though hostile to China, also embraced Leninist capitalism.

Each of the states that took shape in Eurasia in the 1990s and early twentieth century had its own unique qualities, assets, and problems. Still, we can identify six groups of countries distinguished by the way they dealt with ethnic issues and development in the first decades after the collapse of communist rule. Several zones were dominated by countries with the same cultural heritage—buttressing this book's contention that cultural patterns go far toward shaping societal fitness.

ZONE A: PEACE, PROGRESS, AND DEMOCRACY

Zone A consisted of societies and states that, in the 1990s and early twenty-first century, experienced almost no ethnic violence and made strong progress

73

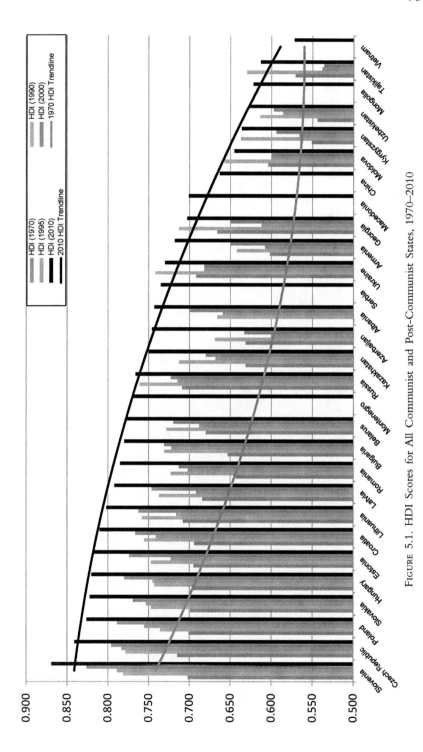

FIGURE 5.1. HDI Scores for All Communist and Post-Communist States, 1970–2010

toward democratic institutions and economic development through market economics. Listed by their Human Development Index rank in 2011, these countries were Slovenia (21), Czech Republic (27), Estonia (34), Slovakia (35), Hungary (38), Poland (39), Lithuania (40), and Latvia (43). Each was a "consolidated democracy," according to Freedom House (Table 5.1). Each had a Western Christian heritage, Catholic or Protestant. Each placed no lower than the mid-40s on the Human Development Index (Table 5.2). As we see in Table 5.3, most zone A countries also placed relatively high on the Bertelsmann Index of Political and Economic Transformation, the Heritage Foundation Index of Economic Freedom; and the honesty/corruption ratings of Transparency International.[1] They also placed relatively high on the UN Gender-related Development Index (GDI), not shown on the table.

Slovenia was the only successor state from the former Yugoslavia to be found in zone A. Its HDI score in 2011 was the highest of any formerly communist society. Slovenia joined the EU in 2004 and the euro zone in 2007. But the euro brought easy credit and fueled a construction bubble that inevitably burst. Slovenia in 2011–12 faced one of the worst recessions of the seventeen nations using the euro currency. It risked becoming the first former socialist state in the Eurozone to need a bailout. Slovenia's economy shrank by more than 8 percent in the years 2009–2012, resulting in a sharp drop in exports and living standards and a surge in unemployment, which reached 12 percent in 2012. The government imposed harsh austerity measures—spending cuts and tax hikes—which protestors claimed targeted the poor and spared the rich. Slovenia's voters in 2011 and 2012 shifted their allegiances between center-left and center-right parties claiming to have the right stuff to fix the economy. The poster child for progressive development was faltering. A professor of physics in Maribor commented (e-mail, December 14, 2012): "Slovenia is now going through a difficult time. The prevailing public opinion here is, and I would agree, that there is simply nobody competent enough around to run the country (or those that are competent are simply not willing or unable to step up). When I do watch the news and listen to their debates, I can't get rid of the feeling that I am listening to a bunch of poorly educated self-centered wannabes, and with that opinion I am definitively not alone."

From erstwhile Soviet allies in Eastern Europe, zone A included the Czech Republic, Slovakia, Poland, and Hungary. The fitness landscape appeared to be path-dependent. Each country in zone A had ranked higher than other communist countries even under communist rule. The Czech Republic's HDI score ranked highest in the region in 1970 but Slovenia took the lead in 1995. In 2011 the Czech Republic ranked 27th in the world. Hungary and Poland followed similar HDI trajectories from 1970 to 2010. By 2011 Hungary placed 38th in the world; Poland, 39th.

Of former Soviet Union Republics, only Estonia, Latvia, and Lithuania were in zone A. Even under Soviet rule, the three Baltic countries made a great ascent from 1970 to 1990. Their HDI scores fell sharply in the early 1990s but resumed their upward climb from 1995 to 2011. Estonia's global HDI ranking rose from 38th in 2009 to 34th in 2010 and 2011. Lithuania placed higher than its two Baltic neighbors in 1970 but advanced more slowly after 1991. In 2009 and 2010 Lithuania's global rank was 44th but climbed to 40th in 2011—three places higher than Latvia.

ZONE B: FLAWED FREEDOM

The four countries in zone B approached those in zone A in terms of democracy, but they lagged in most other respects. Romania (HDI 50), Bulgaria (55), Albania (70), and Mongolia (110) were semi-consolidated or hybrid democracies but each suffered extensive corruption. None endured large-scale ethnic violence, as in the former Yugoslavia. Except for Mongolia, however, each experienced ethnic or other civil violence in the 1990s or early twenty-first century—violence far more serious than anything that happened in zone A countries.

Romania and Bulgaria, each with Orthodox Christian traditions, were admitted to NATO in 2004 and with some misgivings in Brussels, both joined the European Union in 2007. A former fireman, judo coach, and bodyguard, Boyko Borisov served as Bulgaria's prime minister, 2009–2013, but was accused of illicit activities not only before but also throughout the time he headed the government and attacked some of the country's "godfathers." Albania in 2009 became (after Turkey) the second country with a Muslim majority to join NATO, but EU members did not think either country ready to join their union.

There were few conflicts between Albania's Muslim majority and its Orthodox and Catholic minorities. But in January 2011 the Republican Guard fired on a crowd of opposition protesters, killing four people and wounding dozens others. Local administrative elections in May 2011 saw many violent incidents. One judge was assassinated in 2011. Fifteen other judges received official protection. The judiciary was under constant pressure to favor the ruling party. In 2013 the president would be elected for the first time by parliament through a simple majority vote. Time would tell whether the process would become more open.

Separated from Europe by Russia, Mongolia (Buddhist) could not be considered for membership in any Western organization. For many decades a Soviet dependency, Mongolia's HDI in 1990 was lower than that of any Soviet republic and declined still more in the following decade. In the early 2000s Mongolia's HDI increased but its global rank then fell from 100th in 2010 to 110th in 2011. Life expectancy was fairly high; education middling; but income low—despite some earnings from gold and mineral exports. In November 2012, a Chinese power company in Inner Mongolia agreed, after prolonged haggling over terms, to supply electricity to the Oyu Tolgoi copper-gold mine, source of one-third of Mongolia's GDP.[2] Mongolia experienced no direct clashes with China despite some irredentist and expansionist pressures on each side.

Mongolia had a weak infrastructure but few ethnic problems. Some 90 percent of the population was Mongolian; 4 percent Kazakh; 2 percent Russian; 2 percent Chinese; 2 percent other. Its Buddhist traditions remained so strong in the twenty-first century that one in three young men wanted to become monks. Corruption, however, became more pervasive in the first and second decade of the twenty-first century.

ZONE C: TURMOIL AND SLOW DEVELOPMENT

Zone C was a shatterbelt of ethnic conflict and material regress. Ranked by their HDI placement in 2011, these countries included Croatia (46), Montenegro (54), Serbia (55), Bosnia and Herzegovina (74), Macedonia (78), Georgia (75), Armenia (86), and Moldova (111). Croatia had a strong Catholic heritage while the other six countries were traditionally Orthodox. All became embroiled in severe ethnic fighting in the 1990s and its bitter consequences in the early twenty-first century. Georgia fought with Russia in 2008. The four Balkan countries stopped fighting in the late 1990s, but relations between Serbia and its two neighbors, Croatia and Kosovo, became more tense in 2012. As of 2013 Armenia continued to clash with Azerbaijan as did Moldova with the breakaway Transnistrian region.[3] Some countries in this zone were traditionally Orthodox; others, Muslim; one was Catholic.

Each of these societies showed a very low capacity for coping with ethnic differences or with the problems of establishing a viable economy and a stable democracy. In each case, as Mansfield and Snyder argued in 2005, partial democratization probably aggravated ethnic tensions. Some leaders tried to rally support by invoking external threats and resorting to belligerent, nationalist rhetoric. In Armenia, for example, populist pressures made it harder for leaders to negotiate any kind of compromise with Azerbaijan over Nagorno-Karabakh. Popular sentiments in Georgia, Abkhazia, and South Ossetia obstructed any accommodation of their differences. This discord set the stage for a brief war between Georgia and Russia in 2008 that resulted in de facto autonomy for Abkhazia and South Ossetia under Russian protection.

By 2000, these countries had achieved only middling rankings on the HDI. Most lost ground on the HDI from 2010 to 2011 In that one year Montenegro dropped from 48th to 54th, Bosnia from 68th to 74th, Georgia, from 74th to 75th, Macedonia from 71st to 78th, Armenia, from 76th to 86th, Moldova, from 101 to 111; Croatia, however, jumped from 51st to 46th in just one year—just a few places below Latvia, while Serbia advanced from 60th to 59th. A referendum in 2012 cleared the way for Croatia to become the twenty-eighth member of the EU in 2013.

Armenia in 1970 had the lowest HDI score (0.602) of any Christian-heritage republic of the former USSR. It suffered a big decline in the early 1990s, in part due to hostilities with Azerbaijan, but rose substantially in the late 1990s. Armenia placed 74th in the world in 2009 and 76th in 2010 but fell to 86th in 2011. Georgia in 1970 (0.666) scored much higher than Armenia; but declined drastically in the 1990s; and then rose only to 0.703 by 2009, compared to 0.718 for Armenia. Georgia ranked 78th in 2009 and 75th in 2011.[4]

Moldova in 1970 scored far below its neighbor and cultural cousin Romania. By 2011 its score of 0.649 was the lowest of any Christian heritage country in Europe and placed just ahead of Uzbekistan (0.641). Moldova's world ranking on the HDI was 111 in 2011. Moldova showed the least economic advance of any European successor states from the former Soviet Union. Twenty years after the Soviet breakup, Moldova had the lowest GDP per capita in Europe—just over $2,000. An official estimate showed that one-fourth of the population was working abroad—often illegally. More than 78 percent of the population was Moldovan/Romanian. Nearly 16 percent were Slavs—some 8 percent Ukrainians, 6 percent Russians, and 2 percent Bulgarians. Another 4.5 percent was Gagauz—Turkic Christians. Nearly the entire population had roots in Orthodox Christianity, but some Orthodox believers bowed to church authorities in Moscow; others, to Bucharest.

Despite substantial ethnic and cultural homogeneity, Moldova was paralyzed by the determination of some speakers of Russian and Ukrainian to establish an autonomous Transnistrian Republic. More than two years of intermittent fighting began in November 1990 between Moldovan troops and the Transnistrian Republic Guard plus Cossack units, supplied and backed by locally based Russian Federation and Ukrainian forces. An uneasy ceasefire in July 1992 halted the fighting, but—as of 2013—mediation efforts by the Organization for Economic and Security Cooperation in Europe and by the Russian Federation achieved few positive results. Meanwhile, Abkhazia and South Ossetia, having declared their independence from Georgia, recognized the "Pridnestrovian Moldavian Republic" (PMR) as an independent state and established diplomatic relations in return for PRM recognition of them via the Community for Democracy and Rights of Nations (known also as Commonwealth of Unrecognized States), founded in Nagorno-Karabakh in 2001.

Kosovo might logically have belonged to this grouping. It was backed by the West but kept in limbo by Moscow. Unable to become a UN member-state, Kosovo had no HDI rank. Political and other problems in Kosovo, Bosnia-Herzegovina, and Macedonia curtailed both democracy and human development.[5] In the early twenty-first century, however, there were signs that Croatia (Catholic) along with Albania (mostly Muslim), Bulgaria, Romania, Montenegro, and perhaps even Serbia (all of them Orthodox) might edge into another zone. By 2010 and again in 2011–12 Freedom House ranked each of these countries "free," despite a host of shortfalls in political liberties and civil rights.

Serbia made important strides toward democracy and peace with its neighbors in 2011 but Belgrade in 2012 still had unresolved tensions with Kosovars and the Hungarian speakers (14% of the population in Vojvodina). Relations between Serbia and Croatia cooled in 2012 when Tomislav Nikolić, a former extreme nationalist, became president of Serbia and Ivica Dačić, the former spokesman of Slobodan Milosević, the wartime of leader of Serbia, became prime minister. In the 1990s Nikolić was a member of the extreme nationalist Serbian Radical Party, which aimed to create a Greater Serbia in Bosnia and Croatia. In May 2012 he told a German newspaper that Croats should not return to live in Vukovar, the town in Croatia that Serbian and Yugoslav army artillery had reduced to rubble in 1991, because it was a Serbian town.

In November 2012 Serbs again felt unfairly treated when the United Nations Yugoslav war crimes tribunal acquitted two Croatian generals of war crimes against Serbs. Ante Gotovina and Mladen Markač had been convicted in 2011 but their successful appeal meant that *no* Croats were convicted by the UN tribunal of any crimes against Serbs in Croatia during the war years. The tribunal found no "joint criminal enterprise" designed to drive out some two hundred thousand Serbs from the Krajina region in 1995. The court ignored that when the Croatian army retook most of the territory in the Krajina region in 1995 almost all the inhabitants fled, or were ethnically cleansed, few to return. Serb president Nikolic Nikolić complained that Croatians were celebrating not just the acquittal but also what they called the liberation of Krajina. Now, Nikolić complained, Croatian president Ivo Josipović, wanted to talk again—as the leader of a people not convicted of anything, with the president of a people convicted of war crimes. Josipović, replied that he could not believe that such statements "were being made 'by a politician at the head of a country which wishes to be European," adding that such statements did "not contribute to good relations and reconciliation." Croatia would "not succumb to such hysteria."

Rubbing more salt into Serbian wounds, the war crimes tribunal in November 2012 acquitted Ramush Haradinaj, a former Kosovo prime minister, for the second time, of murdering and torturing Serbs, Albanians, and others in 1998. The verdict was issued in the UN court's first-ever retrial, which was ordered after appeals judges overturned the 2008 acquittals of Haradinaj because of alleged intimidation of prosecution witnesses.

Croatia was on track to join the EU in 2013, while Serbia remained on the waiting list. Croatian leaders said they would not use their position inside the EU to impede the EU accession of any of its neighbors as Slovenia had done for Croatia. Money still talked. In November 2012 both the Serbian and Croatian ambassadors to London attended an event to mark a €307m

($399m) financing package to Atlantic Grupa, a Croatian company, by the European Bank for Reconstruction and Development. Atlantic Grupa was heavily invested in Serbia, and the rest of the former Yugoslavia and aimed to expand significantly in Russia and the CIS countries.

The passage of time and prospect of money also opened new avenues between Serbia and Kosovo. Personal chemistry also helped. In December 2012, Ivica Dačić, Serbia's prime minister, dined with Hashim Thaçi, prime minister of Kosovo, and Catherine Ashton, the EU foreign policy chief. in Brussels. Each man had been reviled as a gangster by the other side but now their personalities clicked. Dačić, said he was "ready and prepared for a permanent and final solution" between Kosovo and Serbia. "It needs to be just, to respect the legitimate interests of Serbs and Albanians. We need to reach a solution acceptable to both sides." Both Belgrade and Pristina wanted closer ties with the EU and sought EU funding for reconciling their differences. Top Serbian and Kosovar leaders reached a modus vivendi in 2013 that helped their EU prospects. But their accord lacked popular support and Belgrade still did not recognize Kosovo as an independent state.

ZONE D: STATISM AND STAGNATION

Zone D was a set of seven former Soviet republics virtually frozen in time— with little ethnic conflict but also little economic advance. Each was strongly authoritarian. These seven states (with their HDI scores in 2011) were Belarus (65), Kazakhstan (68), Azerbaijan (76), Turkmenistan (108), Uzbekistan (115), Kyrgyzstan (126), and Tajikistan (127). Moscow's former client state, Cuba (51), was also statist and stagnant. Most of these states were poor except where oil and gas earnings and foreign investment enriched elite coffers. All these states were traditionally Muslim except for historically Orthodox Belarus and traditionally Catholic Cuba.

Freedom House ranked Belarus as Not Free—more authoritarian even than Russia. Other indices showed Belarus with less economic freedom than Russia and higher levels of corruption. In some respects, however, Belarus was more egalitarian than Russia. The gap between the UNDP's Inequality-adjusted HDI and basic HDI was less in Belarus than in Russia. Belarus in 1970 (0.680) scored lower on the HDI than Ukraine (0.692) and just slightly below Latvia (0.684). Belarus and Ukraine were nearly tied in 1995 but then Belarus moved ahead while Ukraine stagnated. By 2000 Belarus scored 0.720; Ukraine 0.682. By 2010, Belarus advanced to 0.777 while Ukraine moved to 0.730. Belarus placed 54th in the world in 2009, but fell to 61st in 2010 and 65th in 2011. Ukraine placed 70th in 2009 but 76th in 2011.

In most zone D countries erstwhile communist leaders became dictators claiming to be both nationalist and democratic. Worried about internal challenges to stability, they repressed Islamic fundamentalists and gave some support to compliant Islamic leaders obedient to the state. In the 1990s Tajikistan experienced much fighting between political rivals, but ethnic differences were not at issue. Kyrgystan had a free press for a time, but this ingredient of a true democracy disappeared in the mid-1990s. Tensions over land and housing led to violent clashes in 2005 and again in 2010 between Kyrgyz (nearly 70% of the population) and Uzbeks (15%) concentrated in the fertile Ferghana Valley. Hundreds died in each encounter.

Nearly all countries in zone D suffered human development losses from 2010 to 2011. The HDI rank of oil-rich Azerbaijan declined from 67th to 76th and Kazakhstan from 66th to 68th—two places behind Russia. Tajikistan declined bv thirteen places and Kyrgyzstan (site of a hopeful "Tulip Revolution" in 2005) by fifteen. Kyrgyzstan and Tajikistan placed lower on the HDI in 2011 than any other former Soviet republics.

Moscow's former client state Cuba also belonged to the zone of stagnation. Cuba's political life was "not free" and data on the economy were sketchy. But Cuba's systems of health care and education helped it move from 53rd on the HDI in 2010 to 51st in 2011.

ZONE E: BETWEEN AN IRON FIST AND ANARCHY

Zone E was a hybrid where two major countries—the Russian Federation (HDI rank 66 in 2011) and Ukraine (76)—shared some but not all characteristics of states in other zones. Both had an Orthodox Christian heritage, though other faiths also existed, as in predominantly Muslim Tatarstan and in Greek Catholic western Ukraine.[6] By the early twenty-first century neither Russia nor Ukraine had achieved a real democracy or a strong market economy. Neither Russia nor Ukraine nor the other Eastern Slav nation, Belarus, came close to fulfilling its economic or human potential. A complexity scholar might observe that while Belarus continued to endure a harsh variant of top-down rule, both Russia and Ukraine suffered from alternating bouts of near anarchy and rigid authoritarianism.

Having experienced a chaotic semblance of democracy in the 1990s, Russia moved toward dictatorship under Vladimir Putin (President, then Prime Minister, then President again), while Ukraine oscillated between dictatorship, a short-lived Orange Revolution, and more authoritarian rule. But neither Russia nor Ukraine suffered from large-scale ethnic violence, with one major exception—Russia's wars against Chechnya (1994–96 and again 1999–). Chechnya became less fevered in the early twenty-first century, but embers burned and occasionally flared in nearby North Caucasus communities. In June 2011, Muslim religious leaders from each republic in the North Caucasus gathered in Dagestan to concert their efforts against extremism. They chose not to invite representatives of Salafi communities, however, because they were unwilling to condemn terrorism. In the weeks before the conference, several

Dagestani officials were assassinated and more than a dozen Federal Security Service officers killed fighting militants. As noted earlier, Russia also fought a short war against Georgia in 2008.

Nationalisms in the Russian Federation were both civic and ethnic in nature. Nationalism in the RF was "civic" in so far as citizenship did not depend on ethnicity. The word *Russian* within the Russian Federation was rendered as *Rossiskaia*—not as *Russkaia*. The term *Rossiskaia* was the more inclusive—as "British" includes not only English but also Scottish, Irish, Welsh, and was even applied to the erstwhile British Empire. In the 1990s any reference to "nationality" (such as Tatar or Jewish), a hangover from Soviet times, was dropped from RF passports. The Boris Yeltsin presidency recognized Tatarstan's "sovereignty," though Putin later placed the Tatar Republic within a Volga Federal District headed by a Kremlin appointee. On the other hand, chauvinist appeals to Russian glory multiplied in the Putin era and the Duma debated whether to require that any would-be Russian citizen be fluent in Russian.

In 1970, the Russian Federation (RF) at 0.709 ranked second in the region on the HDI—just below the Czech Republic (being subsidized by Moscow after Soviet tanks crushed "socialism with a human face" in 1968).[7] Twenty years later, as the Soviet empire imploded, the RF (then the RSFSR) placed third on the HDI in the region, behind the Czech Republic and Slovenia. Russia's absolute score on the HDI then fell sharply in the 1990s. One key indicator was life expectancy for Russian men—down by five years during the 1990s. By 2000 the RF score was eclipsed by ten other countries in the region. Its global rank fell from 54th in 2010 to 66th in 2011—its HDI score in 2011 (0.755) lower than in 1990 (0.761). Meanwhile, the HDI score of the other superpower, the United States, rose from 0.790 in 1970 to 0.910 in 2011.

The "commodity curse" helped undermine democracy in Russia and Eurasia's other major exporters of oil and gas—Kazakhstan, Azerbaijan, and Turkmenistan. When oil prices began to rise in 2002–03, democracy shriveled. Transparency and accountability were already weak, but floods of petrodollars allowed dominant elites to tighten their grip on individuals and institutions.

The HDI scores of Russia and other oil exporting countries were skewed upward by the fact that the HDI gave equal weight to its three components—income, education, and life expectancy. Since more than half of Russia's export earnings derived from oil and gas, high prices for these commodities boosted the country's HDI ratings, helping to make up for its deficits in education and life expectancy. On the other hand, if oil prices fell or production declined, the country's HDI score would decrease. Many Russians became multimillionaires in the 1990s and early 2000s thanks to their access to oil and other mineral wealth. Still, Russia's HDI adjusted for inequality showed a loss of only 11.3 percent in 2011—less than the United States (15.3%) but greater than Slovenia (5.3%), Estonia (7.9%), Lithuania

(9.8%), or Latvia (10.9%), none of them endowed with oil or other valuable commodities. Russia's Geni coefficient (42.3), however, showed slightly more income inequality than the United States (40.8).

In 1970 Ukraine (at 0.692) ranked on the HDI about the same as Croatia (0.694). Like Croatia, Ukraine's score improved greatly by 1990. But by 1995 Ukraine's score collapsed to 0.682 and did not rise in the late 1990s. Ukraine's score of 0.682 in 2000 was lower than thirty years before—1970 (0.692). Ukraine's HDI rank fell from 69th in 2010 to 76th in 2011. (For comparison, the rank of Belarus declined from 61st in 2010 to 65th. The Inequality-adjusted HDI in the Ukraine in 2010 was only 9.1 percent lower than its basic HDI score. Gender inequality in Ukraine was not much greater than in Russia and less than in Romania.

Kyiv's leaders sought a kind of civic nationalism incorporating native Russian and Ukrainian speakers, but for a time denied voting rights to Tatars returned to Crimea from exile in Central Asia. Ukraine's political alignments and voting patterns strongly reflected differences between liberal and Russophobic elements in western Ukraine and the more statist and Russophile regions in the east. Ukraine's most intense nationalist and ethnic conflicts took place in Crimea—officially transferred by Soviet leader N. S. Khrushchev from Russia to Ukraine in the 1950s, but where Russian speakers outnumbered Ukrainians. Many of these Russians wanted Crimea to rejoin Russia while many Tatars, some 12 percent of the Crimean population, demanded some form of self-determination. Complicating these complications still further, both Kyiv and Moscow contested the Black Sea naval base at Sevastopol. Kyiv managed to mollify Ukraine's Russian irredentists and to negotiate an arrangement to share facilities with Russia at Sevastopol. Like Russia, however, Ukraine failed to utilize effectively its vast natural resources and highly educated workforce. While Russia's HDI rank fell only one place from 2010 to 2011, Ukraine's fell by seven ranks—to ten places below Russia's.

ZONE F: ECONOMIC ADVANCE WITHOUT POLITICAL FREEDOM

Last but not least was an East Asian zone F dominated by China. No formerly communist country in this region was free except for Mongolia.[8] Some countries were dynamic but others moribund. All shared a Buddhist and/or a Confucian heritage coupled with strong local traditions. In many of these countries communist education and materialistic-hedonistic values had undermined traditional beliefs and morals. Still, the past shaped both present and future.

Starting in the late 1970s and continuing for more than three decades, China consistently achieved the world's highest rates of economic growth— averaging close to 10 percent a year. China used its growing wealth far more efficiently than oil-rich Azerbaijan or Kazakhstan. China's HDI score rose from 0.404 in 1980 to 0.687 in 2011—placing it at 101st in the world, but down by twenty-six places from 2010.

Starting a few years after China's opening to markets, Vietnam's economy also expanded at a fast clip. Vietnam's HDI and that of Laos, each still ruled by communists, nearly doubled between 1970 and 2011. Vietnam's rank rose to 128th and Laos to 138th while Cambodia, no longer ruled by communists, placed 139th. The Democratic People's Republic of Korea, now on a short leash from China, managed to develop an incipient nuclear missile force, but struggled to feed its own people. Indeed, more than one million North Koreans starved to death in the mid-1990s and many were again eating grass and roots in 2011. Few reliable statistics were available on the DPRK, but surely its HDI rank was "low." Freedom House ranked all these Asian regimes as "not free," with North Korea at the bottom.

DEMOCRACY RATINGS BY FREEDOM HOUSE

The Human Development Index aims to measure conditions that expand human choice, but it does not directly address political and other institutions that shape human choice. For countries in zone A, the pattern was a virtuous circle: HDI scores tended to parallel ratings in political and economic development. In other zones, correlations were more jagged. Table 5.1 shows how Freedom House rated "democracy" in Eurasia's "nations in transition."

ZONE A

The eight consolidated democracies scored high on political rights and civil liberties. Still, politicians and publics remained subject to all the human frailties and uncertainties. Thus, starting in 1990–91, voters in Lithuania could not decide if they wanted to be ruled by free market conservatives who opposed the former imperial power or by welfare-minded leftists who tilted toward Moscow. Paradoxes were abundant. The ostensibly conservative President Rolandas Paksas was impeached in 2004 for violating the constitution by granting citizenship to a Russian businessman. Dr. Algirdas Butkevikius, a leader of nonviolent resistance to Soviet rule and a former defense minister, was jailed for allegedly fraudulent dealings in arms purchases. Released on parole in 2000, he later became leader of the Social Democrats and a leading candidate for prime minister in 2012. He wanted his party to rule in a coalition with the Labor Party but its Russian-born leader had fled to Russia to escape criminal proceedings against him. The Order and Justice Party headed by Paksas, who never quit politics even as he continued to fly the world as a stunt pilot, could also partner with the Social Democrats and Butkevikius.

84

TABLE 5.1. Freedom House Democracy Ratings for "Nations in Transit" in 2012 (from highest 1 to lowest 7)

Consolidated Democracies (1.00–2.99)	
Slovenia	1.89
Estonia	1.93
Latvia	2.11
Poland	2.14
Czech Republic	2.18
Lithuania	2.29
Slovakia	2.50
Hungary	2.86
Semi-Consolidated Democracies (3.00–3.99)	
Bulgaria	3.14
Romania	3.43
Croatia	3.61
Serbia	3.64
Montenegro	3.82
Macedonia	3.89
Transitional Governments or Hybrid Regimes (4.00–4.99)	
Albania	4.14
Bosnia and Herzegovina	4.36
Ukraine	4.82
Georgia	4.82
Moldova	4.89
Semi-Consolidated Authoritarian Regimes (5.00–5.99)	
Kosovo	5.18
Armenia	5.39
Consolidated Authoritarian Regimes (6.00–7.00)	
Kyrgyzstan	6.00
Russian Federation	6.18
Tajikistan	6.18
Kazakhstan	6.54
Azerbaijan	6.57
Belarus	6.68
Turkmenistan	6.93
Uzbekistan	6.93

CODE: The ratings are based on a scale of 1 to 7, with 1 representing the highest level of democratic progress and 7 the lowest.

Source: Freedom House, *Nations in Transit 2012* at http://www.freedomhouse.org/report/nations-transit/nations-transit-2012 (accessed 10/22/2012).

Butkevikius became Lithuania's prime minister in December 2012. Because of his criminal activities, Lithuania's legislature and top courts had banned Paksas from taking part in political life, but the European Court of Human Rights ruled in 2011 that this punishment was disproportionate and thus violated the European Convention on Human Rights. A country led by unblemished patriots such as Vytautas Landsbergis and Valdas Adamkus in the 1990s now chose convicted criminals as its leaders. Some of the other contenders also had very shady records. In 2011 one-fifth of the assets of Lithuania's third-largest bank disappeared. Lithuania was ranked forty-eighth out of 176 countries surveyed in Transparency International's 2012 Corruption Perceptions Index.

Freedom House credited Slovakia for amending its press act in 2011 so as to protect the media from political influence and intimidation and for improving the judicial independence. Among most of the newer EU members, however, Freedom House said that Hungary led a decline in democratic practices.[9] Hungary's parliament, on March 11, 2013, defied international pressure and passed constitutional amendments that could undermine democratic checks and balances, deepening the rift with the country's European partners and further worrying investors concerned by the recent appointment of György Matolcsy, known for an unorthodox "postmodernist policy," to head Hungary's central bank.

The quality of self-government in the region declined due to a combination of poorly rooted democratic traditions, resilient networks of corruption, low levels of public trust, and shaky economic conditions. Democratic institutions, especially judicial independence, were jeopardized across Eurasia. In 2011 a total of eight countries—Albania, Azerbaijan, Belarus, Bulgaria, Hungary, Kazakhstan, Russia, and Ukraine—regressed on judicial independence. At the end of this chapter we consider another paradox: Traditionally Catholic Lithuania placed just behind Belarus as the *world* leader in suicide, with Russia and many but not all other post-communist countries not far behind.

ZONE B

Using its scale of 1 to 7 (best to worst), Freedom House in 2012 gave Romania a democracy score of 3.43 but a rating of 4 for corruption and for independent media. Tensions between Romanians and ethnic Hungarians did not erupt again after 1989–1990, but distrust and resentments persisted. The major internal cleavage in 2010–12 arose from the economic crises confronting all of Europe. Romania's center-right ruling coalition imposed an austerity package aimed at restoring fiscal balance. These measures achieved some success but were implemented with minimal public consultation. The opposition seized the opportunity presented by the unpopular fiscal restraints and demanded the resignation of the government and the president. Civil society and the media suffered from the withdrawal of foreign financial support.

Bulgaria's electoral process got high marks from Freedom House in 2012 but its overall democracy score was 3.14, while independent media and corruption ranked close to 4. Since 1989 Bulgaria had consolidated its system of democratic governance with a stable parliament, sound government structures, an active civil society, and a free media. Power changed hands peacefully, allowing more than a decade of stable, full-term governments. In 2011, however, a series of small bombings targeted opposition-oriented media and political parties. Also, the killing of an ethnic Bulgarian youth in September triggered a series of street protests against local organized crime and the Roma minority. EU authorities believed that corruption in Bulgaria and Romania got worse in 2011–12.

The year 2012 marked one hundred years of independence since the establishment of the modern state of Albania. One of the poorest countries in Europe, Albania placed 70th on the HDI in 2011. In 2011, Freedom House lowered Albania's electoral process rating from 4.00 to 4.25 but still classified Albania as "free," albeit with a "transitional" form of governance. Albania joined NATO in 2009 but failed to properly address the twelve key priorities identified by the European Commission to begin EU accession talks. As a consequence, the country's bid for official EU candidacy was rejected for the second time in October 2011.

Freedom House rated Mongolia "free" but Transparency International lowered its honesty rating from 116th in 2010 to 120th in 2011.

Zone C

Freedom House in 2012 classified four of the protagonists in the Yugoslav wars of the 1990s—Croatia, Serbia, Montenegro, and Moldova—as "semi-consolidated democracies." Two of the societies still mired in conflict got very low marks for democracy: Armenia and Kosovo were labeled "semi-consolidated authoritarian regimes." Three countries—Bosnia, Georgia, and Moldova—were called "transitional or hybrid regimes." In October 2012 Georgia experienced its first peaceful transfer of power by election in modern history. How the new government, headed by a little-known billionaire, would perform was unknown. Voting patterns in Bosnia and Herzegovina, however, showed each ethnic group voting for its own.

Zone D

Freedom House in 2012 judged Belarus and all five Central Asian states "Not Free." In all these countries dictators suppressed ethnic or other challenges to their rule. Still, Belarus placed 65th on the HDI in 2011—ahead of Russia at 66th. At times, President Aleksandr Lukashenko tried to russify Belarus and negotiate its union with the Russian Federation. On some occasions, however, Lukashenko bridled at Moscow's demands that Belarus pay more for oil and gas. His opponents sought to establish and maintain a clear Belarusian identity and/or to practice self-rule, but Lukashenko held on with an iron fist. For its part, the near-dictatorship in Moscow lost patience at times with the even tougher dictatorship in Minsk. The relationship resembled that between Beijing and Pyongyang. Neither Big Brother liked its semi-client, but neither knew how to change things for the better.

Freedom House reported a downward trend in Azerbaijan because authorities launched attacks on civil society. These included the unlawful detention and imprisonment of political activists, opposition embers, local and international journalists; restrictions and violent dispersals of public protests; and unlawful evictions of citizens from their homes. Kazakhstan also received a downward trend arrow due to new legislation restricting public expression of religious belief and the right to form religious organizations.

ZONE E

In the 1990s Freedom House ranked Russia as "partly free." With Putin at the helm, Russia was judged to be "not free"—grade 6 on political rights and 5 on civil liberties. Despite charges of unfair and even rigged elections, Freedom House judged Ukraine to be "partly free" in 2010.

In 2004 Ukraine experienced a democratic upsurge called the "Orange Revolution." The next decade, however, witnessed a return to the admixtures of authoritarianism and chaos that prevailed in the 1990s—both poles of societal malaise. By 2012, Freedom House rankings for democracy in Ukraine approached their pre-2004 levels. Freedom House downgraded Ukraine in all dimensions of democracy except "civil society" and "local democratic governance." Authorities in Kyiv sought to crush the opposition by politicizing the courts, cracking down on the media, locking up former prime minister (in 2005 and 2007) Yulia Tymoshenko in 2011, and using force against demonstrations. Meanwhile, the Index of Economic Freedom rated Ukraine 163 places from the top.

ZONE F

Freedom House found that China, Vietnam, Laos, Cambodia, and North Korea were "not free." North Korea was rated worst of the lot—grade 7 on political rights and 7 on civil liberties. As China prepared in late 2012 for the sixteenth party congress and decennial turnover at the helm, repression intensified. Taxi drivers were told not to take pigeons aboard lest they be used to disseminate antiregime propaganda. Ping pong balls were also suspect. China's neighbor Mongolia, as we have seen, was ranked free. Distant Cuba, statist and stagnant, was also labeled "not free."

POLITICAL AND ECONOMIC TRANSFORMATIONS

While Freedom House focused on political rights and civil liberties, the Bertelsmann Foundation's Transformation Index (BTI) sought to measure movement toward political democracy under the rule of law *and* toward a market economy flanked by sociopolitical safeguards. While the UNDP and Freedom House developed global indexes, the BTI analyzed "developing and transition countries." The BTI sought to foster what complexity science would see as "fitness." The project aimed to help improve political management processes and optimize outside support by identifying and facilitating the transfer of best practices among a broad spectrum of countries in transition. Much broader than the laissez-faire orientation of the Heritage Foundation Index of Economic Freedom, the BTI assumed that development entails not only economic growth but also overcoming poverty while extending freedoms of action and choice to the largest possible share of the population. It further assumed that a responsible market economy implies not only free markets and property rights but also principles of social justice, equal opportunities, and sustainability. The BTI posited that democracy and a market economy are interdependent and mutually reinforcing. Only a democracy based on the rule of law can ensure the equal playing field for all citizens that is essential to sustained development. Only a market economy with sociopolitical safeguards can provide all citizens with opportunities to realize their potential in the open market place of goods and ideas that is essential to a prosperous democracy. The BTI manifesto thus laid out a teleology to which most European Social Democrats and many Christian conservatives would subscribe.

The Bertelsmann Transformation Index averaged political and economic transformation scores.[10] Of 128 countries on the BTI in 2010–12, the Czech Republic ranked highest, but most of countries surveyed had never been communist. Thus, the top twenty countries in 2012 included Taiwan, Uruguay, Chile, Costa Rica, South Korea, Mauritius, Brazil, Botswana, and Turkey. Given the handicaps imposed by decades of communist rule, it was a major achievement for countries such as the Czech Republic and Estonia to rank at or near the top of the BTI.

The BTI gave each of 128 countries a score and divided them into five categories. There were "highly advanced" countries such as the Czech Republic; second, "advanced" such as Hungary and Macedonia; third, those that had made "limited" progress, such as Serbia; fourth, those that made "very limited" progress such as Russia and China; and fifth, those "failed or blocked" such as Belarus, Cuba, Uzbekistan, and North Korea.[11] Rather than using these classifications, Table 5.2 organizes communist and former communist states by their scores and by cultural heritage.

The Bertelsmann Index took into account a wider number and range of criteria than the HDI or Freedom House Index. With regard to former

TABLE 5.2. Transformation Rankings (BTI) of Communist and Post-Communist Countries, 2003–2012, by Cultural Heritage

Cultural Heritage	2012 n = 128	2010 n = 128	2008 n = 125	2006 n = 119	2003 n = 116
WESTERN CHRISTIAN					
Czech Republic	1	1	1	3	2
Slovenia	3	2	2	1	2
Estonia	5	4	3	2	6
Poland	6	10	11	9	7
Lithuania	7	7	6	7	2
Slovakia	8	6	7	6	2
Hungary	12	8	5	5	1
Latvia	13	13	13	14	12
Croatia	15	15	14	11	15
Cuba	106	107	95	96	91
ORTHODOX CHRISTIAN HERITAGE	2012	2010	2008	2006	2003
Bulgaria	14	14	15	15	18
Romania	16	16	17	19	21
Serbia	21	24	31	33	29
Macedonia	25	21	22	29	34
Montenegro	27	25	30	n.a.	n.a.
Moldova	43	61	60	75	79
Ukraine	55	37	35	32	34
Georgia	58	52	38	61	79
Russian Federation	60	65	59	43	41
Armenia	66	62	41	44	46
Belarus	101	96	89	83	85

continued on next page

TABLE 5.2. (*Continued*)

Cultural Heritage	2012 n = 128	2010 n = 128	2008 n = 125	2006 n = 119	2003 n = 116
MUSLIM HERITAGE	2012	2010	2008	2006	2003
Albania	31	30	33	n.a.	n.a.
Bosnia Herzegovina	39	39	40	33	29
Kosovo	41	38	n.a.	n.a.	n.a.
Kyrgyzstan	76	83	63	73	69
Kazakhstan	79	76	68	66	61
Azerbaijan	85	86	87	82	72
Turkmenistan	116	115	115	109	96
Tajikistan	117	118	106	102	100
Uzbekistan	123	120	111	103	93
BUDDHIST OR CONFUCIAN HERITAGE	2012	2010	2008	2006	2003
Mongolia	51	46	44	43	29
China	84	88	85	85	77
Vietnam	86	91	92	n.a.	n.a.
Cambodia	105	100	88	87	74
Laos	112	114	112	106	111
North Korea	125	126	122	116	100

http://www.bti-project.de/index/status-index/(accessed 10/24/2012) and current communist states, however, the results dovetailed. They supported the identification of certain states with certain cultures into five zones. Thus, the Czech Republic and other countries with a Western Christian heritage ranked at or near the top. Bulgaria and Romania placed 14th and 16th but other Orthodox countries placed much lower. Despite their enormous human and material assets, Russia and Ukraine moved backward from 2003 to 2012. Albania placed 31st and Bosnia 39th but other Muslim heritage countries stagnated or lost ground from 2003 to 2012. All Asian countries including Mongolia regressed. Cuba (with its Western Christian heritage) ranked 51st on the HDI but placed only 106th on the BTI. Good medical services did not fill the voids in political and economic freedom.

Table 5.2 permits us to track which communist and ex-communist countries made progress in democratization and which lost ground from 2003 to 2012.

Little moved (no more than two places): Czech Republic, Slovenia, Estonia, Poland, Latvia, Croatia, Albania, and Laos

Upward trajectory: Bulgaria, Romania, Macedonia, Serbia, Montenegro, Georgia, Moldova, Vietnam

Downward trajectory: Slovakia, Lithuania, Hungary, Cuba, Ukraine, Armenia, Russia, Belarus, Bosnia, Kazakhstan, Kyrgyzstan, Azerbaijan, Turkmenistan, Tajikistan, Uzbekistan, Mongolia, China, Cambodia, and North Korea.

TRANSPARENCY

Honesty in business and politics tends to correlate with high human development and democracy.

Thus, Norway, Iceland, Sweden, and Denmark dominated not only the top ranks of the HDI and Gender-related HDI but also the honesty rankings compiled by Transparency International—the converse of its Corruption Perceptions Index. Testimony to the endemic corruption of Communist systems, decades after the collapse of the USSR and Yugoslavia, every post-communist and communist society registered a worse score on the Corruption Perceptions Index (CPI) in 2010 than they did on the HDI or BTI. The trend lines are shown in Figure 5.2.[12]

Table 5.3 shows the same indicators as they evolved in 2011–12. It adds a fifth indicator, Economic Freedom, as calculated by the Heritage Foundation.

Even the Czech Republic and Slovakia, world leaders in democratic transformation, experienced high levels of corruption. Pervasive corruption kept Bulgaria, Romania, Albania, and Mongolia in zone B. Corruption remained deeply entrenched in all sectors of life in these countries, negatively affecting economic and political development as well as the consolidation of democratic

92

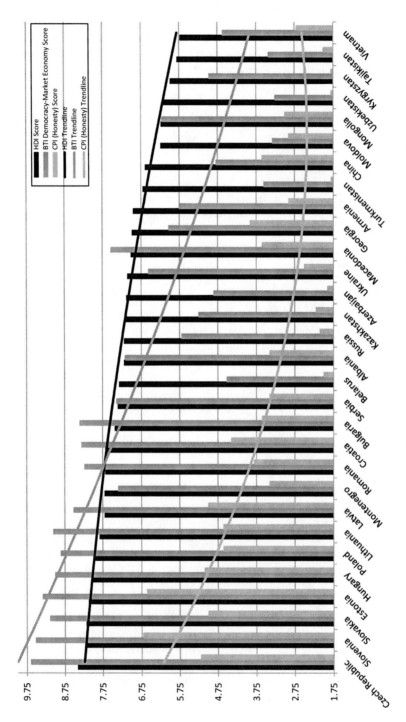

FIGURE 5.2. HDI, BTI, and CPI Scores for Communist and Post-Communist States in 2010

TABLE 5.3. HDI, Transformation, Democracy, Honesty, and Economic Freedom, 2011–12

	HDI Rank n = 187 2011	Transformation Rank n = 29 2012	Democracy n = 182 2012	Honesty n = 179 2011	Economic Freedom 2012
WESTERN CHRISTIAN HERITAGE					
Highest	Norway (1)	n.a.	Free	New Zealand (1)	Australia (3)
For comparison, USA	4	n.a.	Free	24	10
Slovenia	21	3	1	35	69
Czech Republic	27	1	5	57	30
Estonia	34	5	2	29	16
Slovakia	35	8	7	66	51
Hungary	38	12	8	54	49
Poland	39	6	4	41	64
Lithuania	40	7	6	50	23
Latvia	43	13	3	61	56
Croatia	46	15	11	66	83
Cuba	51	106	Not Free	61	177
ORTHODOX CHRISTIAN HERITAGE					
Highest:	Greece (29)	n.a.	n.a.	Cyprus (30)	Cyprus (20)
Romania	50	16	10	75	62
Montenegro	54	27	13	66	72
Bulgaria	55	14	9	86	61
Serbia	59	21	12	86	98
Belarus	65	101	27	143	153

TABLE 5.3. *(Continued)*

	HDI Rank n = 187 2011	Transformation Rank n = 29 2012	Democracy n = 182 2012	Honesty n = 179 2011	Economic Freedom 2012
ORTHODOX CHRISTIAN HERITAGE					
Russian Federation	66	60	23	143	144
Georgia	75	58	18	64	34
Ukraine	76	55	17	152	163
Macedonia	78	25	14	69	43
Armenia	86	66	21	129	39
Moldova	111	43	19	112	124
MUSLIM HERITAGE					
Highest:	UAR (30)	n.a.	UAR (Not Free)	Qatar (22)	Bahrain (12)
Kazakhstan	68	79	25	120	65
Albania	70	31	15	95	57
Bosnia Herzegovina	74	39	16	91	104
Azerbaijan	76	85	26	143	91
Turkmenistan	102	116	29	177	168
Uzbekistan	115	123	28	177	164
Kyrgyzstan	126	76	22	164	88
Tajikistan	127	117	24	152	129
Kosovo	n.a.	41	20	112	n.a.

BUDDHIST OR CONFUCIAN HERITAGE

Highest:	Hong Kong (13) S. Korea (15)	n.a.	n.a.	Singapore (5)	Hong Kong (1) S. Korea (31)
China	101	84	Not Free	75	138
Mongolia	110	51	Free	120	81
Vietnam	128	86	Not Free	112	136
Laos	138	112	Not Free	154	150
Cambodia	139	105	Not Free	164	102
North Korea	n.a.	125	Not Free	182	179

Sources: (all accessed 10/24/2012): HDI: http://hdr.undp.org/en/reports/global/hdr2011/download/; Transformation: http://www.bti-project.de/index/status-index/; Democracy: http://www.freedomhouse.org/article/freedom-house-releases-nations-transit-2012; Honesty: http://cpi.transparency.org/cpi2011/results/; Economic Freedom: http://www.heritage.org/index/.

institutions. Thus, Albania was the hub of the global trade in human trafficking but prosecutors were reluctant to bring charges against police abuse or corruption. High-level corruption remained largely untouched. In 2011 there was growing political interference in institutions, legal immunity for a wide range of officials, a lack of transparency in accessing information. Freedom House rated Albania's corruption at 5.00 and Transparency International in 2011 rated Albania 95th ninety-fifth in honesty.

In 2011 the Russian Federation placed 66th on the HDI and on the BTI, but 143rd in honesty. Ukraine placed 76th on the HDI but 152nd on the CPI. The largest losses in honesty in 2010–11 took place in Belarus, down from 127th to 143rd, while its HDI rank fell from 61st to 65th. Azerbaijan ranked 91st on the HDI but 143rd on the CPI. The disconnect was less severe in China, which placed 101st on the HDI and 84th on the BTI and 75th on the CPI. By contrast, Hong Kong, with residual elements of British law and values, ranked as relatively clean on the CPI—18th. Only two post-communist countries broke with this pattern. Estonia paced 29th on the CPI—far ahead of its HDI rank of 34th, while Georgia placed 64th on the CPI and 75th on the HDI.[13]

Kazakhstan's honesty placement fell from 105 to 120 in 2010–11. Cuba and China, by contrast, climbed a few places on the Corruption Perceptions Index moving from 69 to 61 and 78 to 75, while the United States fell from 22 to 24—far below that of most Western democracies.

INCOMES

Behind the other ups and downs of societal fitness loomed the issue of material wealth and how it was distributed. Most EU member states, like most other countries, suffered large declines in their GDP in 2009–2010. For post-communist members or candidate members of the EU, the pattern of growth and decline is shown in Table 5.4, which shows purchasing power per inhabitant. Expressed in purchasing power, the numbers for poorer countries look higher than if rendered in official currency exchange rates. These numbers, however, are averages and do not show how GDP was shared.

Estonia and Latvia, the table makes clear, suffered large economic losses in 2009–2010. Economist Paul Krugman (2012) blamed the declines in both countries on government-sponsored austerity programs. But affluent Norway, without much austerity, experienced even larger declines in its GDP in 2009–2010 than either Estonia or Latvia. In 2011 inhabitants of Slovenia, the Czech Republic, Slovakia, Hungary, Poland, and Lithuania regained purchasing power equal to or higher than in the pre-crisis year 2008.[14] In late 2012, however, most of the world's economies including the vaunted German powerhouse began to contract once more.[15] If Germany sneezed, its smaller neighbors could get the flu.

TABLE 5.4. Purchasing Power per Inhabitant, Post-Communist States, Members and Candidate Members of the EU (in thousands of 2012 Euros)

	2002	2004	2008	2009	2010	2011	HDR Rank 2011
WESTERN CHRISTIAN HERITAGE							
For comparison, Norway	31,7	35,8	48,0	41,2	44,2	47,5	1
For comparison, USA	31,6	34,0	36,7	34,3	36,0	37,1	4
Slovenia	11,1	12,3	18,1	17,0	17,9	18,4	21
Czech Republic	15,0	16,9	20,2	19,4	19,6	20,2	27
Estonia	10,2	12,4	17,2	14,8	15,7	16,8	34
Slovakia	11,1	12,3	18,1	17,0	17,9	18,4	35
Hungary	12,5	13,6	16,0	15,2	15,7	16,4	38
Poland	9,9	11,0	14,1	14,3	15,3	n.a.	39
Lithuania	9,1	11,0	15,4	12,8	14,1	16,6	40
Latvia	8,3	9,9	14,1	12,0	12,6	14,8	43
Croatia	10,7	12,2	15,8	14,6	14,5	15,5	46
ORTHODOX CHRISTIAN HERITAGE							
Highest: Cyprus	18,0	19,7	24,9	23,2	23,6	23,6	29
For comparison, Greece	18,5	20,3	23,1	22,1	22,4	20,1	31
Romania	6,0	7,4	11,7	11,0	11,4	n.a.	50
Bulgaria	6,5	7,5	10,9	10,3	10,7	n.a.	55
Macedonia	5,2	5,9	8,4	8,5	8,9	n.a.	78

Source: http://epp.eurostat.ec.europa.eu/tgm/ (accessed 10/24/2012)

Statistics could mislead by ignoring the larger context. Thus, Latvia seemed to recover economic vitality in 2012, but lowered rates of unemployment resulted in part from emigration westward. Even after declines from very high rates, unemployment in 2012 among workers remaining in Latvia was about 20 percent. Even as Greece and other countries considered ditching the euro in 2012–13, some small countries wanted their prosperity linked to the common currency. Estonia benefited from joining the Eurozone in 2010 and Latvia opted in 2013 to do the same. Latvia made austerity pay. The government laid off one-third of its civil servants, slashed wages for the rest, and sharply reduced support for hospitals. But the cuts eased fears that Latvia would go bankrupt and helped the government and firms to obtain the loans they needed to stay afloat. Lower wages made exports more competitive and helped companies to rehire workers in 2012–13.

FITNESS CHALLENGED: EACH UNHAPPY IN ITS WAY

What do all the indicators mean for human happiness? Tolstoy began *Anna Karenina* with the claim: "Happy families are all alike, while every unhappy family is unhappy in its own way [*po-svoemu*]." Does his principle apply also to countries? The first half of the *Karenina* axiom does not fit. Nations (with much variation among their members) may be cheerful and contented due to many diverse factors—child upbringing, cultural values, worldview, lifestyle, climate, wealth, pride, or sense of well-being. But global statistics on suicide bear out the second part of Tolstoy's aphorism. Most of the leading counties by suicides per capita in the early twenty-first century were quite different from one another.[16]

More than one-half of the top thirty-two leaders in suicide shared a communist heritage. But they had inherited many different cultural traditions and were experiencing quite different patterns of transition. The world champions included Catholic heritage Lithuania, Hungary, Slovenia, and Croatia plus Lutheran majority Estonia and Latvia (each in zone A or moving that way); Orthodox Belarus, Russia and Ukraine, and Serbia (zones D, E, and C).; Muslim majority Kazakhstan (zone D). Rankings shifted throughout the two thousands, but the world leader in 2011 was Belarus (with 36.9 suicides per 100,000 population), followed by Lithuania (31.9 per 100,000), next by Russia (31.7), and then by Kazakhstan (28 suicides per 100,000). Apart from Kazakhstan, 4th or 5th in the world,[17] and Muslim plurality Bosnia (36th), no other Muslim heritage country placed above 50th (Kyrgyzstan). Hungary, the world leader in earlier decades, placed sixth in 2011 (La Vecchia et al. 1994). The noncommunist leaders in suicide also derived from a variety of cultures—from Lutheran Finland in the north to Buddhist/Hindu Sri Lanka in the south (numbers two and three after Hungary before 1989 (according to La Vecchia). Two countries still ruled by communists also ranked high— China (shaped by Confucian, Buddhist, and animist traditions) ranked 26th while Cuba (Catholic) ranked 32nd, well above its long-time antagonist, the United States (42nd).

The World Health Organization noted that suicide rates rose by 60 percent worldwide from the mid-twentieth century and were spiking for teenagers in the early twenty-first. They were responsible for about 2 percent of the global burden of disease. Rates were shaped by a complex of psychological, social, biological, cultural, and environmental factors.[18] Despair is more extensive than shown by successful suicides, because most attempts (at least nineteen of twenty) fail.[19]

As we shall see, many suicides were by persons aged seventy-five and older, but teenage suicides were rising worldwide and in post-communist countries. In the mid-2000s nine of the top twenty countries in teenage suicides (age fifteen to nineteen) were post-communist.[20] In 2011 the world leaders were

Kazakhstan, Belarus, and Russia—each with rates three times above the world average.[21] The problems ran deep. The head of a counseling center in Moscow, Kiril Khlomov, observed: "When a person commits suicide he forgets about his own life, and his goal is to punish other people. . . . It's very specific for teenagers, this feeling of almightiness and infinity" (Kates 2012).

Responding to a spate of teenage suicides, Russian president Dmitri A. Medvedev in April 2012 urged news media not to make too much of the deaths, for fear of attracting more imitators. The attitudes of teenage suicides in postconmunist milieux surely differed from those of the young Lev Tolstoy in the 1840s. Yes, his expectations of universal harmony and virtue were shattered when his family moved from their country estate to Moscow in his late teens, but he continued striving to better himself and the world. Still, recalling his anger toward girls who, he thought mocked him, and a teacher who, he thought, had no goal except to punish him, Lev Tolstoy noted that persons aged twelve to fourteen often consider committing violent acts—partly out of curiosity, partly from a felt need to act, and without any thought about past or future (Tolstoy 1852, 160).

SPAWNING CONDITIONS

The huge variety of cultures and circumstances shaping the leaders in suicide confirms the axiom: each unhappy in its own way. How explain that the free and prosperous nations in Zone A experienced high rates of suicide? Progress and pain can coexist. Leaders in societal fitness such as Finland and Japan (each at the top in life expectancy) were also leaders in self-destruction. Affluence is no barrier to despair. South Korea, Belgium, Switzerland, and France also ranked among the top twenty countries for suicide. (Sweden, once a world leader, dropped to 30th.)

In many cases, the malaise was rooted in money—too little or too much of it. Too little for those with no jobs or low wages, particularly if they saw others advancing in wealth or prestige. However, the world's poorest countries did not record high suicide rates Mortality statistics were probably incomplete or misleading, but traditions may have made suicide unthinkable. Also, lifespans did not extend so long that older people opted to end it all.

Affluent as well as generally poor countries may experience suicide because of gaps between haves and have-nots. On the other hand, inequality expanded in the United States for decades but the country had much lower suicide rates than most of Europe, East Asia, and even Cuba. Many Americans resented inequality but some (a diminishing percentage) continued to hope that they would one day "make it."

Too much money—"affluenza"—can challenge the nouveaux riches. The sudden wealth syndrome may provoke agonizing questions: With whom can I now associate? What should I do with my new opportunities? Some newly rich may ask, "Is this all there is?" Some seek refuge in the bottle, in cocaine, or in other gods that fail.

Is geography the culprit? Do high rates of suicide occur due to nonpolitical factors such the weather? People in northern climes such as Finland and Russia often complain about gray skies and long winter nights, but these issues are absent for other leaders in suicide—Sri Lanka, Guyana, Uruguay, Hong Kong, Surinam, New Zealand, or Cuba. These small countries, however, were literally outliers on a globe where high suicide rates were concentrated in Eurasia. Why were the peoples of Eurasia, more than half of them in countries once ruled by communists, more inclined toward suicide than those in Africa, the Americas, the Middle East, and (apart from Sri Lanka) the Indian subcontinent?

Heedless of incomes and geography, many people consider suicide in response to illness, depression and other mental health issues—often made more painful by lack of support from friends, family, or medical and counseling facilities. Some individuals ask, like Hamlet, why continue to suffer the slings and arrows of outrageous fortune? Why not put an end to heartache, and the thousand natural shocks that flesh is heir to. Why

> bear the whips and scorns of time,
> Th' oppressor's wrong, the proud man's contumely
> The pangs of despised love, the law's delay,
> The insolence of office, and the spurns
> That patient merit of th' unworthy takes.
> When he himself might his quietus make. . . .

Such questions arise in every society regardless of politics. Still, given that seventeen of the top thirty-two countries that lead in suicide had been ruled by communists, it is fair to ask: Did the legacy of communist rule contribute to the high suicide rates? Or was it the *end* of communist rule and the challenges inherent in transition to a new way of life that led some people to end it all? The complex factors shaping suicide defy any simple explanation. While we cannot identify a single factor sufficient and necessary to account for suicide rates, it is clear that communist and post-communist systems incubate a disproportionate share of the world's suicides. High suicide rates in these countries implied that, even in zone A countries such as Lithuania and Hungary, aspects of societal fitness were lacking.

Most of the post-communist leaders had high rates of suicide even before the demise of communism—at least twice the world average of sixteen per one hundred thousand. In most cases the rates increased in the early 1990s but declined in the late 1990s and the early 2000s. For some countries—the top four in Table 5.5—the levels reached in the late 2000s were higher than in the late 1980s; for others, including noncommunist Finland and the United States, included here for comparative purposes, the later rates were lower.

TABLE 5.5. Suicide Rates per 100,000 Before and After Communist Collapse

Country	1990	2008/2009
Lithuania	26.1	34.1
Russian Federation	26.5	30.1
Belarus	20.4	28.4
Kazakhstan	19.1	25.6
Latvia	26.0	22.9
Slovenia	27.7	21.9
Estonia	27.1	18.1
China	14.5	13.9
Cuba	21.3 (1992 data)	12.3
Finland	*30.3*	*19.3*
USA	*12.4*	*11.0 (2005 data)*

Source: World Health Organization, 2012, Country Reports, at http://www.who.int/mental_health/prevention/suicide/country_reports/en/(accessed 11/14/2012)

For most people living under communist rule, life was tough, but there were also consolations. Most people in the former Soviet empire realized that they were poor and had little freedom relative to Western democracies.[22] Food and housing were usually mediocre but sufficient. Health care and education were "free" albeit with pressure to bribe for good treatment. Some survivors recalled, "We pretended to work and they pretended to pay us." Despite a somewhat drab and monotonic existence on the outside, many disgruntled people found release and deep pleasure in small, close-knit groups of friends with whom one could drink and talk (though not too loudly, lest neighbors hear). The end of communist rule in 1989–1991 opened new opportunities to travel, speak openly, and create new sources of income. But it also meant an end to job security and a need to pay more for everything—from food and transport to health care and schools. People with skills and energy (or useful political connections) could climb while those without such assets felt they were landing on the scrap heap of history. Pensions were low and few older people had the money and know-how to exploit the newer technologies. Even middle-aged people were often left without means when state-owned enterprises shut down and startups wanted younger skill sets. Fifty-year-olds living on the streets of Riga told me in 1999 how some of their friends suffered frostbite or froze to death in winter.

If both God and hope were dead, why live? Communists waged a long struggle against traditional values, religion, and—indeed—any philosophy except "*diamat*"—atheistic dialectical materialism. Decades of communist rule left most people with little faith in or dedication to the collective. Instead, they developed a sense of *sauve qui peut*—every man and woman for themselves. Neither honesty nor hard work was rewarded. Economic and social advance often depended on what Russians called *blat*—connections and bribes. In persons for whom nihilism had replaced any positive worldview, there might seem no reason to continue the struggle.

Some dissidents wanted to change the systems that crushed human rights and individual creativity but their struggles achieved very little for decades. Like Sisyphus, they continued to push against the weight of totalitarian oppression. Still, a few prevailed over the *ancien régime*—Vaclav Havel, Vytautas Landsbergis, Lech Walesa. Some escaped, such as Eduard Kuznetsov and Chen Guangcheng. Some did not win much in their life times but, like Andrei D. Sakharov, left a strong imprint. Few if any dissidents under Soviet rule committed suicide, but many Tibetans burned themselves to raise awareness of Chinese oppression.[23]

LEADING CASES

Lithuania

To deepen our understanding of the cases summarized in Table 5.5, let us add some detail. We begin with Lithuania, a country whose Catholic traditions strongly opposed suicide but yet became a world leader in self-destruction. Suicide rates fell from 33.6 per one hundred thousand in 1981 to 26.1 in 1990 as Lithuania pulled away from the USSR, only to rocket to 45.6 in 1995. The rate then declined till it reached 34.1 in 2009—with male deaths exceeding female by six to one. The highest rates were among men and women aged forty-five to fifty-four. Many men in the countryside had access not only to alcohol but to weapons. Suicides among young people aged fifteen to twenty-four were among the highest in the world, accounting for about one-tenth of the Lithuanian total.

The Russian Federation

Trends in the core of a former superpower were nearly identical to those in Lithuania. The suicide rate in 1980 was 34.6. It steadily declined to 26.5 in 1990. It then jumped to 41.5 in 1995 and slowly lowered to 30.1 in 2006—somewhat beneath the 1980 rate. Men and women aged forty-five to fifty-four and those over seventy-five had the highest rates. The younger group aged fifteen to twenty-four was responsible for one-seventh of total suicides—a larger share than in Lithuania. Rates in the Far East were higher than average among indigenous peoples and also among Russians. As in Lithuania, the highest rates were for men and women aged forty-five to fifty-four and for those over seventy-five.

Belarus

No country suffered greater devastation in World War II—heart of what historian Timothy Snyder (2010) called the "bloodlands." The trajectories in Belarus resembled those of Lithuania and Russia except that the peak years came later—plateauing from 2000 to 2003 at about 35 per hundred thousand. The rate declined to 27.4 in 2007 and then rose to 28.4 in 2009—much higher than in 1981. The implication: life had become more burdensome for many people. Female rates were higher than in Lithuania or Russia—ranging from one-fourth to one-third of the total. Rates for men were highest in the age group thirty-five to forty-four—slightly higher than for those seventy-five and more.

Kazakhstan

The largest and most ethnically diverse country in Central Asia experienced less of a decline in suicides in the 1980s than did Lithuania, Russia, or Belarus. The rate was 22.5 in 1981 and reached 19.1 in 1990. It then rose steadily to 29.9 in 2000 and slowly declined to 25.6 in 2008—somewhat higher than it had been in 1981 before the petrodollars started to roll in. As in Russia, the highest rates were among men twenty-five to thirty-four. For men fifty-five and older, however, suicide rates were lower. Even after age seventy-five, Kazakh men killed themselves less frequently than in the other cases reviewed here except for Estonia, Cuba, and the United States. The suicide rate for men over seventy-five was twice as high in China as in Kazakhstan (70.7 versus 33.5). For Kazakh women, however, the rate doubled from 8.3 to 16.8 after age seventy-five. Considering all age groups, female suicides accounted for not quite one-fifth of all suicides in Kazakhstan, while young suicides (age fifteen to twenty-four) accounted for nearly over one-fourth of the total in 2008.

Latvia and Estonia

Latvia's rate declined from 32.6 in 1980 to 26.0 in 1990. It then rose in the early 1990s to 40.7 in 1995 but then moved steady downward to 22.9 in 2009. Estonia's rate declined from 36.7 in 1981 to 22.3 in 1985. As talk of perestroika and independence gained steam, Estonia's suicide rate went up to 27.1 in 1990. Estonia differed from Latvia and the other cases studied here in that its rate rose in the five years *before* independence. Was it that Estonia's Slavic speakers (two-fifths of the population) were becoming disoriented? Perhaps, but suicide rates in Latvia *declined* during this period (the Gorbachev era), even though half Latvia's population spoke Slavic tongues. As elsewhere, Estonia's rates increased sharply after 1990. They peaked at 40.1 in 1995 and then fell in three stages to 18.1 in 2009.

Slovenia

Still part of Yugoslavia, Slovenia experienced a steady decline in suicides from 32.8 in 1985 to 27.7 in 1990, just before independence. Unlike the former Soviet republics, there was no upsurge in suicides after the end of communist rule. Rates rose to 29.7 in 2000 and then slid to 21.9 in 2009. Starting at age forty-five, however, rates for men and women steadily increased and then rose dramatically for those over seventy-five—some 78.2/100,000 for men and 20.6 for women. By 2009 females accounted for nearly one-third of the total, while youth (aged fifteen to twenty-four) provided less than one-twentieth of the total.

China

The suicide rate "in selected rural and urban areas" gradually declined from 17.6 in 1987 to 13.9 in 1999—a victory, it would seem, for Deng Xiaoping's economic liberalization. Women, however, accounted for *half* of all suicides—without parallel in any other country. Indeed, women aged fifteen to thirty-four accounted for more suicides than any cohort, male or female, in China. The WHO data stop with 1999 but there is no reason to expect that pressures on women diminished after that date. Some Chinese were becoming prosperous (e.g., families of "princelings") but most—in urban ghettos as well as in the countryside—were poor. Chinese sociologists estimated that some five hundred riots, collective protests, and strikes were occurring every day in 2012—up nearly fourfold from a decade earlier—often coordinated by cell phones (Pei 2012). Still lacking much "voice," many educated and well-to-do Chinese resorted to "exit." Ever greater numbers studied or moved to the United States and other Western countries in 2011–12. Chinese was joining Russian and Spanish among the languages that cohabitated on the sandy shores of Walden Pond.

Cuba

Using data that go back nearly to Castro's victory in 1959, we find that suicide rates rose from 10.2 in 1963 (just after the missile crisis) to 17.2 in 1975 and peaked at 21.3 in 1992 (just after Soviet subsidies stopped). Starting about 1995, rates gradually decreased and leveled off at 12.3 in 2008, with women making up one-fifth of the total. Regardless of the reported consolations of family ties, when Cuban men passed age seventy-five, their rates jumped from 36.4 to 82.8. The group aged fifteen to twenty-four made up less than one-twentieth of the total in 2008.

Finland

A country noted for its high life expectancy and superb education system, Finland suffered the highest suicide rate of any country without a communist heritage. Its suicide rate was high in 1950—15.5—and gradually rose to 24.6 in 1985. As in Lithuania, the rate shot up in the late 1980s and peaked at 30.3 in 1990s. It gradually declined to 18.9 in 2005 but then rose to 19.3 in 2009. Rates were highest for men aged forty-five to fifty-four. Rates did not rise appreciably for men over seventy-five and decreased for women. Young people aged fifteen to twenty-four accounted for just over one-tenth the total in 2009.

United States

U.S. rates rose from 7.6 in 1950 (as the Korean War began) to 10.2 in 1955 (the Eisenhower years) and peaked in 1975 (as the Vietnam War ended) at 12.7. Rates declined to 11.8 in 1980 but rose to 12.4 in 1990. They declined to 11.9 in 1995; fell to 10.4 in 2000; rose to 11.0 in 2005. Women accounted for one-fifth of suicides in 2005 and young people aged fifteen to twenty-four for one-eighth of the total. Males aged forty-five to fifty-four and above seventy-five were at greatest risk.[24] But U.S. rates for men over seventy-five were 37.8—not half those in the communist paradises of China and Cuba. U.S. rates rose again in tandem with unemployment in President Obama's first term. In the United States, as in some other countries, a 1 percent uptick in joblessness correlated with a 1 percent rise in suicides.

Suicide rates in the United States remained low compared to many other countries, but the statistics showed a 28 percent rise in suicide rates for Americans aged thirty-five to sixty-four between 1999 and 2010, led by deaths of white men in their fifties. The numbers prompted concern that a generation of baby boomers who had faced years of economic worry and easy access to prescription painkillers might be particularly vulnerable to self-inflicted harm. In 2010, more Americans killed themselves (38,364) (often using guns) than died in motor vehicle crashes (33,687). Though still a magnet for immigrants, as we shall see in chapters 7 and 8, the American dream was under siege.

PARADOXES PREVAIL

No problem illustrates the fragility and complexity of societal fitness better than the non-patterns of suicide. Unable to provide any all-encompassing answers or remedies, this chapter ends by noting the many paradoxes: A happy and generally affluent society can have high rates of suicide. People in Utah and Hawaii are among the most contented in the United States, but these states are also leaders in suicide; New Yorkers, facing many stresses, have among the lowest rates. Finland and Japan lead the world in life expectancy, but are also leaders in suicide. Norway and Sweden rank high on the HDI but also experience high suicide rates. Some of the most successful post-communist societies on the Transformation Index are also leaders in self-destruction—Lithuania,

Slovenia, Estonia, and Latvia. The highest-ranked Central Asian country by GDP, Kazakhstan, is the only one with a high suicide rate. Belarusians tell pollsters they are content, despite or due to political dictatorship, but they are also world leaders in self-destruction.

Former Soviet republics or client states were leaders not only in suicide but also in alcohol consumption. The World Health Organization reported in 2013 that Moldovans, the poorest ex-Soviets, were the most bibulous people in the world—consuming 18.2 liters of alcohol per capita each year--nearly three times the global average of 6.1 liters. Adding to paradox, however, the second ranked ex-Communist country on the HDI, the Czech Republic, placed second in the world in alcohol consumption with some 16.4 liters per capita. Did drinking matter? In Russia and some of its former client states one in five male deaths was associated with drink. Moldovans' habits were especially lethal, because 10 liters of annual intake was home-brew. Such "unrecorded" liquor accounted for nearly one-third of global alcohol consumption and 2.5 million premature deaths per year--more than AIDS or TB. Australians and South Koreans also consumed a great deal of alcohol, but little was home-brewed, and they had good medical facilities to cope with some of the consequences. Americans and Japanese consumed a little more than the world average; citizens of most Islamic countries and Israel, far less.

chapter six

HOW COMPLEXITY CONCEPTS
EXPLAIN PAST AND PRESENT FITNESS

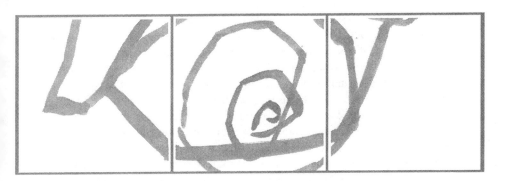

Basic concepts of complexity science offer a powerful way to explain the movement toward or away from understanding and coping with ethnic and other problems in emerging countries. These concepts do not contradict explanations rooted in democratization but enrich them and offer linkages to other fields of knowledge. They start with a wider lens than democratization but include it. The concept of societal fitness, a major concern of complexity science, *subsumes* political, economic, and cultural strengths. The precise weight of each strength in shaping societal fitness becomes an important but secondary question.

THE DANGERS OF TRANSITION

The diverse experiences of states in zones A, B, C, D, E, and F raise questions about the key postulate of liberal peace theory: that established democracies seldom if ever make war on one another (Doyle 1997; Elman 1997; Brown 1996). Is the theory not falsified by the intermittent fighting between Armenia and Azerbaijan, each of which—independent since 1991—has claimed to be democratic? Or by the fighting between Georgia, on the one hand, and Abkhazia, South Ossetia, and Russia on the other? And what about the occasional stresses bordering on a new cold war between Russia and the United States with its allies?

Seeking to show the limits of liberal peace theory, Jack Snyder (2000) explained the presence or absence of ethnic peace by treating democratization as the key independent variable. Thus, he attributed the absence of ethnic violence in Estonia since 1991 to successful democratization. Ethnic calm in Uzbekistan, on the other hand, resulted from an efficient dictatorship. Between these extremes was the persistent ethnic strife pitting Armenians against Azeris and Georgians against their neighbors. Snyder traced these ethnic conflicts, as well as the wars between Russia and Chechnya, to partial but unsuccessful democratizations.

To explain the successes and failures of democratization Jack Snyder considered many economic and cultural as well as political variables. For example, he weighed the impact of early versus middle or late economic development. The violent ways of Serbian nationalists, he argued (Snyder 2000, 207), reflected their society's early but partial democratization—manipulated by rival dynasties while fighting the Ottomans and later by President Tito. Snyder's broad treatment helps us to grasp the context but it leaves the reader unsure which factor, if any, determines whether there is ethnic calm or conflict.

Taking partial democratization as a source of nationalist violence is the more complicated because, Snyder conceded, it can cut in opposite directions. President Boris Yeltsin sent Russian troops into Chechnya in 1994 hoping to rebuild his popularity by appealing to nationalist sentiment. Instead, partially democratized Russians objected to this campaign and pressed the Kremlin to end it. "Thus, Russia's fragile democratic institutions could be mobilized in crisis against imperial excesses, but they were less effective in scrutinizing nationalist mythmaking on a day-to-day basis" (Snyder 2000, 236–37).

Snyder's leitmotif of democratization—whether successful, partial, or nonexistent—serves as a heuristic organizing principle for assessing a wide range of past and present cases of political and economic development. But this approach embodies a tautology: "Successful democracy equals ethnic peace." We can know that democracy has taken root because there is no ethnic conflict; where ethnic strife appears, democracy is shallow. The independent variable becomes the same as the dependent.

Contrary to Snyder and Mansfield (2005), the harmony and vibrancy of countries in Eurasia's zone A appear to confirm liberal peace theory. Consolidated democracies do not fight one another and tend to rely on established methods of conflict resolution to deal with internal disputes. Societies in zone A achieved high levels of fitness on many fronts after the demise of the Soviet empire and Yugoslavia. Success in one domain helped them cope with problems in others. Ethnic peace made it easier to raise living standards, consolidate democracy, and nourish creativity. Economic advances in Estonia, for example, make it easier for Tallinn to provide welfare benefits for Russian speakers residing in Estonia but who were not citizens. On the other hand, countries in zones B, C, D, and E displayed low levels of overall fitness even though many possessed material assets lacking in zone A. Thus, Azerbaijan, Kazakhstan, and Russia had energy resources far superior to those in any zone A lands. Parts of Ukraine and Russia had far better soil for farming than most countries in zone A. China, dominant in zone E, generated and managed great wealth but its leaders feared freedom and tried—even in the age of the Internet, to limit and control information flows.

Because they were more homogeneous, most countries in zones C, D, and E faced less severe ethnic challenges than in many zone A or B countries. Relative to Latvia and Estonia, ethnic minorities were very small in Belarus, Moldova, the South Caucasus, and in most of Central Asia except for Kazakhstan. About four-fifths of the *Rossiskaia Federatsiia* population was Russian (*russkii*) but most other groups spoke fluent Russian. A million or so Chechens occupied only a dot on the Federation's huge periphery. Still, the governments in zones C, D, and E as well as in B experienced great difficulty in accommodating ethnic minorities. In Kyrgyzstan, for example, more than 350 people died in ethnic fighting between Kyrgyz and Uzbeks in Osh and two other southern cities in 2010, where each group made up about half the local population and had coexisted in relative harmony for generations (McGlinchey 2011). By contrast, Estonia and Latvia in the 1990s faced anxious and somewhat restive minorities of Slavic speakers that made up more than one-third of the resident population. Estonia and Latvia instituted a naturalization process that required and assisted aspiring citizens to pass residency, language, and civic tests. Estonia even permitted noncitizens to vote in local elections. The city councils in Riga as well as Tallinn were sometimes dominated by coalitions of old leftists and "unity" parties devoted to the interests of Russian speakers.

China's population was more than 90 percent Han, but Beijing needed all the levers of modern totalitarianism to control the subject peoples of Tibet, Xinjiang, and Inner Mongolia. In China's rural areas and even in cities, kidnapping and buying and selling children for adoption did not diminish in the twenty-first century. Female infanticide, sex-selective abortions, and the abandonment and neglect of baby girls also persisted. Chinese security forces reportedly committed arbitrary or unlawful killings.

Militant Islam combined with other grievances to trigger violence from western China to the eastern United States, where, in 2013, two ethnic Chechens set off bombs at the Boston Marathon.

COMPLEXITY PERSPECTIVES

SELF-ORGANIZATION

Self-organization takes in more than democratic politics. It entails also a market economy and a system that, from the bottom up, produces innovation and ways to meet needs and exploit opportunities. The centralized regimes in zones B, C, D, and E attempted to direct economic and cultural life as well as politics from the top down. As in Soviet times, they squeezed out newspapers and news media that contradicted the official line. After Vladimir Putin succeeded Boris Yelstin as RF President (and appointing a lapdog successor), Russia became essentially a one-party (or one-faction) state—nearly another oriental despotism. Privatization in Russia and most other countries in zones B, C, D, and E permitted privileged insiders to seize and exploit public resources at low cost.

COEVOLUTION

Coevolution explains several features of post-Soviet Eurasia. Most countries close to Western Europe coevolved with the West more quickly and thoroughly than those more distant. They shared the economic crises as well as the prosperity of the West. Belarus abuts Poland and Lithuania, but the Minsk government's orientation toward Moscow served to minimize productive exchanges between Belarus and the wider world. Western-style institutions of higher learning were taking root in parts of Central Asia, but most of the region's people and institutions were isolated from the West and engaged with China only in very narrow realms. Kazakhstan "coevolves" with foreign oil drillers—Chinese as well as Western, but this is a very limited facet of coevolution.

EMERGENCE

Nowhere in the formerly communist lands did there emerge strong patterns of cooperation. Nowhere did the whole amount to more than its parts. Instead, the guideline seemed to be "every state for itself"—indeed, "every national and subnational group for itself." Even in zone A, each state focused on joining Western Europe and NATO—not on cooperating for shared ends with its immediate neighbors.

Failure to cooperate curtailed fitness within and across state borders in Eurasia. The Kremlin-backed Commonwealth of Independent States produced many accords registered on paper but not in practice. Rivalries in the Trans-Caucasus persisted even though both Georgia and Armenia needed the energy that Azerbaijan could provide. For its part, Azerbaijan could find suitors for its products elsewhere, but it needed peace with its neighbors to secure its pipelines. Conflicts between Georgia and Russia also hurt both sides—especially Georgia. Despite much palaver, Central Asian states did little to stop the shrinkage of the Aral Sea, an environmental disaster affecting the whole region. However, the Shanghai Cooperation Organization (China, Russia, Kazakhstan, Kyrgyzstan, Tajikistan, Uzbekistan) helped Beijing and Moscow to constrain Western influences in Central Asia.

Whatever the shortfalls of the European Union, the EU was a triumph of rationality and cooperation for mutual gain compared to the beggar-thy-neighbor behaviors of ex-communist societies. Indeed, it was EU and NATO demands for settled borders and ethnic peace that persuaded Hungary and Romania to patch over their differences and convinced Estonia and Latvia to renounce some border regions seized by Moscow in the 1940s.

AGENT-BASED SYSTEMS

Individuals and institutions in zone A were agents within larger, agent-based systems, over which there was no dictator—not even the United States or Germany. "Europe" had no supranational, unitary, or federal government. Still, its overlapping institutions and authorities provided a flexible but relatively stable framework in which individuals, corporations, and governmental bodies could initiate and conduct their affairs. The effect was not quite "order for free," which complexity scientists see in ecosystems such as coral reefs. Nor did it assure the positive gains for all that Adam Smith expected if agents were allowed to do what they do best—as if guided by an "invisible hand." Compared with the disasters resulting from economic anarchy between the world wars, however, the agent-based, agent-bound system to which zone A actors belonged functioned quite well.

Economic crises, however, put great strain on governments, intergovernmental institutions, and nongovernmental actors. Problems that could be finessed in times of prosperity can drive political and economic systems nearly to a breaking point when times become tough. Arrangements to promote economic coordination in Europe faltered without comparable political unification. Debtor nations such as Greece needed aid that economic colossus Germany was reluctant to offer except on tough conditions.

The IMF and European Central Bank (ECB) could be seen as "agents" able to influence if not dictate actions by other actors. Belonging to such institutions generated potential benefits but also limitations and risks. Thus, when the Eurozone debt crisis rippled into Eastern Europe, Hungary in 2006 felt obliged to borrow up to five billion euros from the ECB to avoid the fate then befalling Iceland. Hungary suffered not because its banks invested in bad mortgages, but because credit markets dried up, depriving it of the ability to service debts denominated in currencies other than the Hungarian forint. The ECB's loan gave Hungary the means to meet its obligations directly even though harder currencies were flowing *out*. To obtain the loan, however, the Hungarian central bank had to deposit collateral, denominated in euros, with the ECB. As in Greece and other parts of southern Europe, Hungary's problems did not go away. The IMF was reluctant to back up Hungary's currency unless Budapest adopted strict austerity measures. In 2011 the ECB threatened to sue the Hungarian government because its actions threatened the independence of the Hungarian central bank. These pressures grew at the same time that Freedom House noted a sharp decline in democratic practices in Hungary. In July 2011 both the Hungarian forint and Polish zloty fell to record lows against the Swiss franc, with Romania's currency potentially the next domino. In late 2011 Hungarian authorities hoped for a new form of "insurance" loan from the IMF. In 2012, however, negotiations between the IMF and Hungary broke down, each side accusing the other of bad faith.

Even as Greece and other countries considered ditching the euro, some countries wanted their prosperity linked to the common currency. Estonia benefited from joining the Eurozone in 2010–11. Leaders in Latvia, Poland, and Lithuania wanted to follow suit, though many of their citizens harbored deep doubts. Provided that the Eurozone survived, it might expand. By 2013 it was nearly "too big to fail."

SELF-ORGANIZED CRITICALITY

Complexity science warns that societies may be less fit than they appear. Fitness depends on the harmony of many factors. Just as an extra grain of sand may cause a sand pile to collapse, a new or heavier burden can weaken an apparently fit society. How would Lithuania have responded if its Ingalina nuclear power plant, the only one in the Baltic region and the source for 70 percent of Lithuania's energy supply, suffered a meltdown and spread poison to the air and soil? Some Lithuanian engineers argued that an accident was unlikely, but the EU demanded that Lithuania close the plant (similar to that at Chernobyl) as a condition for Lithuania's joining the EU. Lithuania dutifully closed the plant in two stages, 2004 and 2009, with some of the costs subsidized by the EU. Vilnius, in turn, complained that nuclear plants planned in nearby Belarus and in Kaliningrad, RF, did not meet international safety standards.

Even as Japan in 2011 wrestled with its Fukushima disaster, Lithuanian authorities asked General Electric and Hitachi to build a new nuclear power plant at Visaginas (near Ingalina). Construction could begin in 2015 but the plant would not produce energy until 2021. The project was backed by Estonia and Latvia and by a consortium headed by the Rothschild investment bank. Some energy would go to Sweden and Finland as well as Estonia and Latvia, helping Nordic as well as Baltic countries to rely less on Russian energy. Many economic, financial, and environmental institutions in Lithuania and the EU had to approve the project. Energy from the new reactor would flow over the European Network of Transmission System Operations. But the Visaginas reactor also required approval from the Lithuanian public, more than 60 percent of whom voted against the project in an October 2012 referendum. Some counted on electricity that began to flow from the Lietuvos Energia AB cycle gas turbine that same October.

Meanwhile, Lithuania and its neighbors became more dependent on Russia for energy. What if Moscow again turned off the spigots as it did several times since 1991? One could not be sure what grain of sand might start an avalanche. The Eurozone itself was in danger.

PUNCTUATED EQUILIBRIUM

The concept of punctuated equilibrium warns us not to expect steady progress. Following a prolonged plateau, fitness can improve or fall quickly. The unification of Europe after 1945 looked like a gradual process, but it took place with many big jumps and some steps backward. Meaningful social change often requires a long period of preparation. New generations must be trained in new ways. Long plateaus without improvement may drive some people to take drastic steps to effect change. Regress is also possible. How long would persons uprooted from the former Yugoslavia or those who fled to Baku from Nagorno-Karabakh have to wait to return home?

FITNESS LANDSCAPES

Like the foxes and rabbits mentioned in chapter 2, the relative fitness of a fruit fly and a frog population may be portrayed as "peaks" that rise and fall with coevolution. Can we graph changing patterns of fitness among the societies of post-Soviet Eurasia? This would not be a simple task, if only because fitness among humans is multidimensional. The HDI provides a solid starting point to measure public health, education, and material living standards. But this is not the whole picture, which should also include measures of political, environmental, and emotional well-being. The Economic Complexity Index (discussed in chapter 2) generated rankings similar to those of the HDI, but with some major exceptions. Belarus looks retrograde on the HDI but strong on the ECI.

If we focus on ethnic problems, we need measures not only of ethnic harmony but also of its opposites—injury, dislocations, and deaths caused by ethnic unrest. Low fitness in this domain probably correlates with low HDI scores, lack of political and civil liberties, low technological achievement, and abundant corruption. Though it is difficult to show all these variables in a single peak, a cobweb graphic can illustrate such complexities, as suggested in chapter 2.

The most basic element of fitness—security from internal and external threats—remains nearly impossible to quantify. Norway, highest ranked on the HDI but 33rd on the ECI. Norwegians needed sixty-one minutes to stop a shooting rampage on an island near Oslo in July 2011. The police lacked a working helicopter and had to bail out a leaking boat to reach the island. The police assumed they needed a squad to subdue a lone killer. Having failed to prevent the Marathon bombings in 2013, Americans mobilized a small army to find and subdue the two bombers.

PREDICTING ETHNIC VIOLENCE AND PRESCRIBING REMEDIES

Complexity science provides useful concepts for analyzing ethnic issues and other ingredients of societal fitness. But it offers only general principles for anticipating future outcomes or prescribing constructive policies. In this regard, however, it does no worse than most competing theories—few of which provide useful handles for predicting or shaping the future (Singer 1999). Indeed, if complexity is correct about the role of self-organization in cultivating societal fitness, Social Darwinists and ultra-realists are wrong: Success in politics does not derive from raw power plus cunning. "Bowling alone" or "singing alone" can be a sign of declining fitness (Putnam 1993; 2000).

A fundamental insight of complexity science is that fitness is likely to be found neither in rigid hierarchy nor in anarchy but close to the edge of chaos. This insight helps explain why Central Asia is frozen in time, why the Caucasus explodes, and why Russia resorts to an iron fist to overcome chaos. This insight has clear policy implications: The leaders and publics of societies seeking high levels of human development should eschew the extremes of dictatorship and anarchy. They should reduce, not add to, social and economic inequalities. To generate a healthy and innovative community, they must cultivate self-organization—not a system steered and manipulated from on high, geared to extracting value for power holders. When Western policymakers and investors look at new countries such as Kazakhstan and Azerbaijan, they should not assume that authoritarian regimes can maintain order forever. Their apparent equilibrium could be punctuated in short order. It is shortsighted to try and prop up local dynasties in the hope of securing privileged access to oil and gas. Outsiders cannot compel internal reforms but should do what they can to nudge these societies toward wider participation by all stakeholders. Countries such as Azerbaijan suffer not only from top-down control but from a rent-seeking mentality by those who covet the nation's wealth. Cultural values and public attitudes as well as formal structures will determine whether Azerbaijan and Kazakhstan use their petrodollars to create values for the entire community and promote creative life (as in Norway) or succumb to the "curse of oil."

In the twenty-first century self-organization and human development require connection to the world. As we see in Table 6.1, the communist and ex-communist states with high Internet usage were also the most free and ranked among the highest on the HDI. Thus, nearly three out of four Slovenes used the Internet in 2011, while their country ranked 21st in the world in human development. One in two Russians used the Internet while their country ranked 66th on the HDI. At the other extreme, one in three Vietnamese used the Internet while their country placed 128th on the HDI. Of course, Internet usage was not the only variable. Slovenia had enjoyed more than sixty years of relative peace while Vietnam was still recovering from many decades of war.

TABLE 6.1. Percentage of Individuals in Communist or Post-Communist Countries Using the Internet in 2011 (global n = 92)

Internet Usage Rank	Country	Percentage	HDI Rank
1 (highest)	Iceland	95.0	14
23 (for comparison)	United States	77.9	4
26	Estonia	76.5	34
28	Slovakia	74.4	35
30	Czech Republic	73.0	27
31	Slovenia	72.0	21
33	Latvia	71.7	43
34	Croatia	70.7	46
40	Lithuania	65.1	40
42	Poland	64.9	39
44	Bosnia	60.0	74
45	Hungary	59.0	38
58	Bulgaria	51.0	55
59	Azerbaijan	50.0	76
61	Russia	49.0	66
62	Albania	49.0	70
65	Kazakhstan	45.0	68
67	Romania	44.0	50
71	Serbia	42.2	59
77	Montenegro	40.0	54
78	Belarus	39.6	65
80	China	38.3	101
81	Moldova	38.0	111
82	Georgia	36.6	75
87	Vietnam	35.1	128
92 (for comparison)	Guyana	32.0	117

Source: http://www.broadbandcommission.org/Documents/bb-annualreport2012.pdf (accessed 10/30/2012)

Complexity science buttresses the conviction of many political scientists that institutions of civil society are needed to help buffer the ravages of free markets and curb the excesses of willful governments. The stronger and more diverse the independent agents shaping the formerly communist societies, the healthier and fitter they will be. Constructive policies will cultivate creative individuals, businesses, and NGOs that enhance public goods and are not dominated by government. These independent agents face a difficult struggle against the moral legacies of communism—corruption, group-think, and a welfare mentality that discourages grassroots initiatives.

Even if the goal of self-organization seems clear, questions arise about the road to this goal. What if democracy kills democracy—as happened in interwar Germany? Is self-organization desirable if the majority votes against the minority, as happened in Sri Lanka and as Serbs feared would happen in a democratic Bosnia? And what if the majority brings in a government that imposes the laws and mores of one religion, as in parts of the Islamic world?

HOW TO ACQUIRE AND NURTURE FITNESS

Culture matters (Grondona 1996; Jacquin-Berdal, Oros, Verweij 1998; Harrison and Huntington 2000). All the societies in zone A were shaped by three revolutions that began more than five hundred years ago: demands for universal literacy, freedom of thought and expression, and respect for the dignity of every individual, female as well as male, regardless of his or her ethnicity or religion. The societies in zones B, C, and D did not start to drive for universal literacy until the late nineteenth or twentieth century. Many regimes in these zones still discourage or try to prevent open debate on policy and other important issues. Most show scant respect for individual dignity.

Following the leads of John Wycliffe, Jan Hus, Martin Luther, and other reformers, each society in zone A acquired its sacred religious texts in the vernacular between the fifteenth and seventeenth centuries. For the first time in history, some princes and religious leaders also urged individuals—female as well as male—to read and interpret sacred texts on their own. After the Peasants' Revolt in 1524–25, however, Luther feared that he was provoking chaos. He then wrote his *Short Catechism* instructing people what to believe. But Luther could not stop the transformation he had unleashed. The synergies of literacy and individualist thinking were empowered by the printing press, the Renaissance, the discovery of New Worlds, and growing refinement of scientific methods. Catholic France and Italy had Bibles in the vernacular even before Luther's challenge to Rome. In the seventeenth century Sweden's monarchy and state church wanted their subjects—even servant girls—to read and discuss the Bible. Bibles in the vernacular also helped cultivate a sense of national identity (Hastings 1997; Lepore 2002). Emerging across many centuries, these developments helped to liberate and energize the communities who now live in zone A.

Certainly, many factors shape human development, but Figure 6.1. shows a strong correlation between early publication of the Bible in the vernacular and high ratings for human development, political-economic transformation, and honesty. Where Orthodox Christianity prevailed, Bibles in the vernacular were not widely published until the late nineteenth or twentieth century. The sole exception was Romania, which published both the New and Old Testaments in the seventeenth century. Wide-scale literacy came to the Orthodox countries much later than in Protestant and Catholic countries or in Jewish communities.

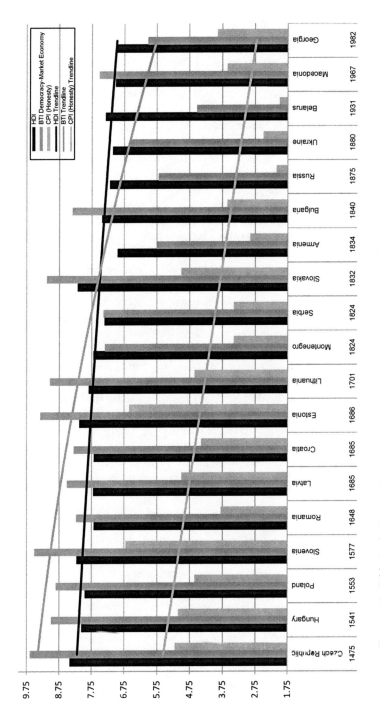

FIGURE 6.1. Bible in the Vernacular vs. HDI, BTI, and CPI Scores for Historically Christian, Post-Communist States

By the 1950s communism brought near universal literacy to the USSR and Eastern Europe. But communist regimes and schools discouraged free thinking. Centralized controls channeled thought and discouraged debate. Even when communist regimes sought to foster technological innovation, this proved difficult, because of state secrecy and communications networks that ran vertically but not horizontally.

Despite the reactionary impact of Russian Orthodoxy and its contribution to Russian imperialism, President Vladimir Putin in 2012 praised Russia's "unique civilization" and sought to employ this rubric to dilute other cultures and languages within the Russian Federation, where 19 percent of the people said they were not Russian (Clover 2012).

What about sacred texts and literacy in non-Christian countries? Unlike the Christian Bible, the language in which the Qu'ran was first written is regarded by Muslims as the only truly accurate way to express God's word and will. Islamic societies did not encourage literacy or individual interpretation of sacred texts. For Arabs as well as non-Arabs, memorization and recitation of the Qu'ran have been far more important than discussion. Few Bosnians, Azeris, or Central Asians have been able to read classical Arabic. Until recent times translations of the Qu'ran into Persian, Turkish, and Chinese were largely in the form of paraphrase and commentary (Swartz 2002)—not the entire text. The classical Arabic of the Qu'ran is difficult to understand for most Arabs living more than a millennium after it was written. The spurs to literacy in Islamic countries in the twentieth and twenty-first centuries arose mainly from secular imperatives—not from a drive to read and interpret God's word for oneself.

THE UPSHOT

In the early twenty-first century most governments in zones B, C, D, and E still did not encourage free thought and debate. Failing to do so, they lacked an essential for societal fitness. Comparatively unfit, they would continue to lag freer societies in many ways. In the language of complexity science, they would wander in valleys, searching in vain for ways to push their peak(s) upward. Bereft of self-organized economies and governments, they would continue to encounter great difficulty dealing with complex issues such as ethnic differences. Even those that were democratic in form were authoritarian in substance—inclined to repress dissent rather than create solutions for mutual gain.

At the onset of the twenty-first century most Russians still hoped that a vigorous leader, Vladimir Putin, like a legendary *vozhd,* would unite and mobilize the people for a better life. A few years earlier, Georgians had entertained similar hopes when Eduard Shevardnadze returned from Moscow to Tbilisi, promising to end a reign of chaos. After a few years, however, they ousted him in favor of a U.S.-trained lawyer, Mikheil Saakashvili, who proved equally despotic and corrupt. In Georgia, as elsewhere, reliance on top-down leadership did not end turmoil. Rather, it added to the already heavy burdens of corruption at the center.

Georgia in 2012 became a poster for the dangers of dictatorship and chaos. Revelations of the Saakashvili regime's brutality and abuse of the courts over the past nine years fanned protests that led to his party's defeat in parliamentary elections. For the first time in Georgian history, power passed peacefully from one party to another by means of an election. However, the new prime minister, Bidzina Ivanishvili, a little known billionaire with close business ties to Moscow, proceeded to prosecute what he regarded as the criminal actions of Saakashvili's associates. Meanwhile, the Georgian constitution provided that Saakashvili remain president until October 2013. Western officials warned Ivanishvili that his zealous attacks on political rivals could obstruct Georgia's bid to join NATO. Observers in Tbilisi explained that demands for revenge against Saakashvili were widespread and often justified. Politics in Georgia, some said, had long been a winner-take-all contest. Meanwhile, many of Saakashvili's associates wondered if they might be summoned the next morning by the new state prosecutor.

America's post–September 11, 2001, war on terrorism raised hopes among some Russians, Georgians, Uzbeks, Kyrgyz, and other denizens of the former Soviet Union. Washington needed allies and bases close to Taliban strongholds in Afghanistan. Perhaps America's strategic requirements would generate more foreign assistance for some former Soviet republics. But outside aid can be counterproductive—the nemesis of self-reliance. Greater dependency on the United States could harm self-organized fitness. Lacking internal strength, each people's capacity to cope with ethnic diversity could well decline—especially if exploited by political entrepreneurs hoping to gain power and wealth from others' differences.

By 2013, the big picture was that many individuals and some societies in post-Soviet Eurasia were benefiting from the opportunities and challenges of new freedoms acquired since 1989–1991. However most residents and most countries in the former Soviet empire continued to live under dictatorships that smothered their minds, bodies, and spirits.

While U.S. security officials benefited from consultation with Russia regarding the two Boston Marathon bombers, many observers warned Washington not to become too close. The United States, they said, should not emulate Putin's brutal ways of dealing with terrorists in the North Caucasus and elsewhere. Gideon Rachman (*Financial Times*, July 17, 2013) advised the West instead to "confront Putin's lawless Russia."

Analysis of trends across Eurasia suggests that the tools of complexity science can enhance our ability to describe and explain the past and present. However this approach has much less utility for projecting alternative futures or prescribing policy. Still, the basic concepts of complexity science can enlarge our vision and complement other approaches to social science. The next chapter develops this argument with respect to a large democracy that opposed and helped to weaken communist networks.

chapter seven

HYPERPOWER CHALLENGED: PROSPECTS FOR AMERICANS

The twentieth century, as Henry Luce predicted, proved to be an American century. The United States amassed and deployed its power to coerce and to persuade in ways that permitted the country to play decisive roles in war and peace. More important, Americans and their leaders—in culture and business as well as in government—set standards by which all nations and their actions would be judged. In the early twenty-first century, however, America's power and influence declined sharply. "Is America over?" asked the journal *Foreign Affairs* (November-December 2011). Some economists lamented what they called a "lost decade." Thomas L. Friedman and Michael Mandelbaum (2011) pondered "How America Fell Behind in the World It Invented" and offered suggestions on "How We Can Come Back." Other analysts such as Carla Norrlof (2010), however, argued America's continuing "global advantage." A reporter for the *Financial Times* opined that the American dream was unraveling and that it was time for Americans to "start thinking" (Luce 2012a; 2012b).

Could complexity science shed light on these issues? If complexity science could not foretell the future, might it help to understand the past and present? Could it suggest roads to greater fitness?

UNDERSTANDING THE PAST

The nearly steady growth of American assets from the colonies' Declaration of Independence to the country's status as the world's sole superpower is summarized in Table 7.1. By 1962 U.S. strength ranked high in nearly all

TABLE 7.1. Parameters of Power, 1776–2000 (H = high; M = medium; L = low strength)

	Actor	Basic Resources	Economic Power	Political Cohesion	Military Power	Brain Power	International Institutions	Fitness at Home	External Fitness
1776	USA	H	L	M	L	H	L	M	L
	Russia	H	L	L	M	L	M	L	M
USA	Prussia	M	L	M	M	M	M	M	M
Declaration of	Britain	M	H	M	H	H	H	M	H
Independence	Japan	L	L	M	L	L	L	L	L
	China	M	L	L	L	L	L	L	L
	Ottoman Empire	H	M	L	M	L	M	L	L
1914	USA	H	H	M	L	H	M	M	M
	Russia	H	M	L	M	M	M	L	M
Eve of	Germany	M	H	H	H	H	M	H	H
World War I	Britain	M	H	M	H	H	H	M	H
	Japan	L	M	H	M	M	L	M	M
	China	M	L	L	L	L	L	L	L
	Ottoman Empire	M	L	L	M	L	M	L	L
1939	USA	H	M	M	M	H	M	M	M
	USSR	H	M	L	M	H	M	L	M
Eve of	Germany	M	H	H	H	H	M	H	H
World War II	Britain	M	M	M	M	M	H	M	M
	Japan	M	M	H	M	H	L	M	M
	China	M	L	L	L	M	L	L	L

1962								
USA	H	H	H	H	H	H	H	H
USSR	H	M	M	M	H	M	M	H
European Community	M	M	M	M	M	M	M	M
Japan	L	M	L	M	H	L	M	L
China	M	L	M	M	M	L	L	L
Cuban Crisis; Great Leap Forward in China. Sino–Soviet Rift								
1976								
USA	H	H	H	H	H	M	M	H
USSR	H	M	M	M	H	M	M	H
European Community	M	H	M	M	M	H	H	M
Japan	L	M	H	H	L	M	M	L
China	M	L	M	M	M	L	L	L
After the Vietnam War								
1990								
USA	H	M	H	H	H	M	M	H
USSR	H	L	L	L	H	L	L	M
European Community	H	H	H	H	M	M	M	M
Japan	L	M	M	M	L	H	H	M
China	M	M	M	M	L	L	L	M
After the Afghan War								
2000								
USA	H	M	H	H	H	M	M	H
Russia	H	L	L	L	H	L	L	M
European Union	M	M	M	M	M	H	H	M
Japan	L	H	H	H	M	M	H	M
China	M	M	M	M	M	L	L	M
After the Gulf War, the dissolution of the USSR, and the wars in former Yugoslavia								

Sources: Estimates drawn from historical surveys such as Kennedy 1987; from annual reports such as International Institute for Strategic Studies, *The Military Balance*; *The Statesman's Year-book*; and the World Bank, *World Development Report*; and from periodicals such as *The Economist*.

domains. Soon, however, during and after the Indochina War, two dimensions of power declined—political cohesion and internal fitness. In the last four decades of the twentieth century, Europe and Japan, followed by China, became stronger. Russia's assets, except for basic resources, went into a tailspin—even before the Soviet collapse. As of 2000 the potential assets of Brazil and India were vast but not yet realized.

The six types of assets listed in Table 7.1 contributed both to America's ability to coerce (hard power) and to inspire and persuade (soft power). Though U.S. brain power remained high at all levels for most of the twentieth century, this asset did not guarantee that U.S. leaders and the American public would possess *smart* power and use it to employ hard and soft assets to enhance their basic objectives.[1] Indeed, the United States entered and remained in its Indochina quagmire thanks in part to some of the "best and brightest" advisers the White House could muster. On the other hand, the gut instincts of presidents Gerald Ford and Ronald Reagan, neither a renowned intellectual, proved well founded in many cases. Whatever their strong and weak points, America's leaders and public managed for most of the century to convert their assets into high levels of fitness both at home and abroad. "So long as humans strive," the Lord reminded Mephistopheles, "they will make mistakes."[2]

BALANCE SHEET ON THE TWENTIETH CENTURY

The century saw Americans raise their living standards, reduce income gaps, expand education at all levels, reduce infant mortality, and extend lifespans. Like the peoples of most industrialized countries, Americans suffered greatly during the Great Depression, but they voted for a dynamic leader willing to risk bold remedies to alleviate economic and social malaise. The New Deal saved America's free market economy even as it established significant social safeguards. Americans emerged stronger from World War II and its aftermath. Their responses to these challenges both tapped and strengthened the deepest potentials of U.S. economic and brain power. The United States accounted for one-fourth to one-fifth of world GDP in the decades before 1941. By 1946 the share rose to one-half. As the world recovered from World War II, the U.S. share declined again to one-fourth or one-fifth—even though the U.S. population only amounted to one-twentieth of global. For most of the century the United States had the world's best educated work force as well as multiple centers of scientific excellence. Americans, native or naturalized, won the lion's share of Nobel prizes. Policy innovations such as the G.I. Bill, the Fulbright and other exchange programs, and, later, the Peace Corps, infused America's higher education with a wide range of experiences and insights.

The European Recovery Program was the outstanding achievement of U.S. foreign policy in the twentieth century—probably ever. It was a model of open diplomacy and mutual planning, pooling of resources, and mutual gain. It cost between 2 and 3 percent of American GDP for three years, but quickly paid for itself as Europeans bought goods and services from America and formed a strong anti-Soviet alliance with the United States. Containing the USSR without war was another major achievement, though purchased at the cost of a growing military-industrial complex and several trips to the brink of nuclear Armageddon. The Kennedy team managed the 1962 Cuban crisis skillfully, having helped to provoke it by committing to one thousand Minuteman missiles and by showing weakness when JFK met Khrushchev in 1961.

Of course, power does not guarantee wisdom. The greatest failure of U.S. foreign policy in the twentieth century took place in the aftermath of the Cuban crisis—a decade of futile and destructive fighting in Indochina.[3] A related failure was the long delay in coming to terms with communist rule in China. These and the many boomerangs that followed interventions in Iran, Guatemala, Cuba, and elsewhere derived from a blind hostility to revolution. Somehow Americans ignored their own struggles for national liberation and sought, often using dirty tricks, to hold back history (Clemens 2000).

Other shortfalls: Americans did little to protect the environment. They continued their madcap uses/abuses of energy in ways that fueled global warming and made the United States increasingly dependent on foreign oil. Despite early signs of Islamic jihad against the West, the United States continued to coddle the Arab sheikdoms and Israel. Despite mounting signs of American interests and vulnerabilities worldwide, neither the U.S. government nor America's educational systems did much to encourage mastery of Chinese, Japanese, Arabic, Farsi, and other important languages or the cultures they represented. The demise of the USSR also triggered a decline in study of Russian.

THE AMERICAN CENTURY IN THE LIGHT OF COMPLEXITY SCIENCE

SELF-ORGANIZED FITNESS

The key insight of complexity science is that the fitness of social and political bodies, like that of other organisms, depends on their ability to cope with complex challenges in an ever-changing environment. Optimal fitness cannot be found in a rigid order or its opposite—anarchy. Fitness is most likely to be found near the edge of chaos, where conditions of freedom and an environment welcoming to learning and creativity permit individuals and groups to defend and maintain their security but also to cultivate and make the most of opportunities at home and abroad. To be sure, Americans were sometimes straitjacketed by religious and political dogmatisms, and sometimes stepped close to anarchy. But much of their success in times past derived from a capacity to draw on their material bounty and huge cultural diversity to innovate and create close to the edge—but not over the edge—of nearly boundless freedoms.

Tied to the theory of evolution, complexity science posits that fitness requires not just brute strength but also a capacity to cooperate for shared objectives. The key to fitness, according to complexity science, is self-organization. Buttressed by a pioneer spirit, Americans long believed in self-help and often practiced self-organization—a tendency noted by Alexis de Tocqueville in the 1830s. Farmers organized coops. Workers joined trade unions. Volunteers initiated and sustained all kinds of self-help organizations. At the turn of the nineteenth century the "gentle anarchist" prince Petr Kropotkin saw the Harvard Coop as a model of mutual aid.

Cooperation and self-organization require trust—confidence that neighbors and fellow citizens will do their share and not free ride on others' sacrifices. American history is dotted with many cases of rugged individualism, criminality, and exploitation of the many by the few. Still, Americans tended to trust and cooperate with each other more than in other industrialized societies. Automaker Henry Ford believed workers should be paid so they could buy the products they produced. Both political parties fashioned a shared responses to the challenges posed by post–World War II reconstruction and Soviet expansionism. After the war, the Truman administration persuaded the French to trust the Germans and the Belgians and Dutch to trust the French—essential fundamentals for Europe's peace and prosperity. Establishing its own bilateral alliances with Tokyo and Seoul, Washington also managed to foster some cooperation between the former occupying power and its long-time colony.

INTERDEPENDENCE

Americans' fitness benefited from a wide recognition of their interdependence with one another, with nature, and with other societies and ways of life. One of their greatest poets, Walt Whitman, and one of their greatest philosophers, Henry David Thoreau, along with one of their greatest novelists, Herman Melville, recognized that each of us is part of nature and all humanity. Naturalist John Muir and President Theodore Roosevelt implemented this insight, memorialized by photographer Ansel Adams. Roosevelt and most subsequent presidents promoted international law and organization—the League to Enforce the Peace, the League of Nations, and the United Nations. Eleanor Roosevelt, wife of Franklin D., contributed mightily to UN covenants on human rights. Four U.S. presidents and one former vice president won the Nobel Peace Prize. Political realists such as Henry Kissinger saw that tightening the web of interdependence could reduce the danger of war and bring the USSR and China into the community of nations.

COEVOLUTION

Most U.S. presidents have known that their society does not just evolve. It *coevolves* with other societies and with the global environment. Some U.S. politicians preferred to go it alone, but most saw that global problems could not be adequately met by any one nation, no matter how powerful, but required cooperation with others—even with adversaries. The United States became a leader not just in forging alliances to contain aggression but in networks to preserve species and conserve the environment.

EMERGENCE

The United States, like most societies, is far more than the sum of its parts. Despite lapses of "Know-Nothing" intolerance, the United States enjoyed success in tapping the synergy of its component cultures. It did so despite the narrow provincialism of its first European colonists and a long history of aggressive behavior by whites toward Native Americans, African slaves, imported workers from Asia, and immigrants from southern and eastern Europe and from south of the border. Despite this history and its painful memories, many if not most nonwhites came to share in the American dream. They joined and enriched the cultural, economic, and political life of their adopted country. Many also served patriotically and effectively in war. The contrast with other multicultural societies underscores these realities. The USSR and, on a smaller scale, Yugoslavia, also could draw on the strengths of many peoples and cultures, but did not. Held together by strong fists, the USSR and Yugoslavia eventually collapsed.

AGENT-BASED SYSTEMS

Americans have usually rejected any idea that they could be saved by a great man on horseback or by the nature of their system. They have seen that fitness requires gifted and energetic leaders to help society utilize and improve its political and economic structures. Political rivalries have been intense since the times of Jefferson and Adams, but were usually kept in check so that elected leaders could nudge the system to foster the common good.

SELF-ORGANIZED CRITICALITY

Americans have seldom dwelled on limits. They pushed bison and other life forms to the brink of extinction or beyond. They used water and other resources as though the wells could never run dry. This was a dark side to the optimism that spurred material progress. Americans' behavior sometimes ushered in a real or figurative "dust bowl," but the land was so abundant that they often managed to move on and develop some other plot or resource. Some listened to Rachel Carson's admonition in 1962 that chemicals were producing an ever more silent spring. Some harkened to the MIT/Club of Rome warning in the 1970s that there are finite "limits to growth." Most Americans, however, ignored such cautions or trusted that technology will remedy any shortfall. The twenty-first century promised to test whether there are limits to what humans may do to their environment and survive.

FITNESS LANDSCAPES

Except for the Depression years, Americans for most of the twentieth century were confident about their place in the world. They assumed an expanding "pie" in the United States and usually paid little attention to their standing relative to other countries. The Soviet *Sputnik* launching in 1957 gave them a sharp wakeup call. They labored to upgrade America's education system. Soon, the Kennedy administration aimed at—and reached—the moon. Americans often focused on GDP and other dimensions of material power while taking for granted their intangible assets. By the 1990s Americans were pleased to be the only superpower. Some assumed that history had "ended."

CULTURE

The American way of life and deepest values were crucial to meeting the demands of a complex world. Nothing was perfect. The strengths and weaknesses of America's political culture as described by de Tocqueville in the 1830s were still at work in most of the twentieth century. Each U.S. president embodied a strain of American culture. One of the most effective presidents represented the everyday values of middle America—Dwight D. Eisenhower. He lacked the flair and zeal of an Ivy League Woodrow Wilson, FDR, or JFK. Ike lacked the religiosity of Jimmy Carter and ideological intensity of Ronald Reagan. Eisenhower indulged the Dulles brothers and failed to condemn McCarthyism, but he helped normalize relations with Moscow; tried to curtail expansion of America's military-industrial complex; and catalyzed construction of the interstate highway system. In the Eisenhower years corporate executives earned no more than forty times the income of their lowest paid workers—a time when Republicans and Democrats often gravitated toward compromise for the common good (Packer 2011).

PUNCTUATED EQUILIBRIUM

Confident of their manifest destiny, Americans expected a steady expansion of their wealth, realm, and influence. They trusted in God but also labored to keep their powder dry. They denied or rationalized away any signs of failure.

Never expecting a slowdown in their own expansion, they were shocked when Europe, Japan, and China, wasted by war and myopic policies, recovered and began to rival the United States in some realms. Americans were not primed for the possibility that their long hegemony could evaporate. The "unipolar moment," some commentators warned, might not endure.

THE EARLY TWENTY-FIRST CENTURY

The United States in the early twenty-first century was still "number one" in many respects, but it also manifested significant declines relative to some other countries. The U.S.A. in 2010 ranked fourth on the HDI but its rate of advance had slowed since 1980.[4] Figure 7.1 contrasts China's rapid ascent from a lower base and the slowing advance of the United States on the HDI. It records Russia's descent in the 1990s and weak recovery.

The Brookings Institution "How Are We Doing?" surveys found mounting concerns about the U.S. economy, fears about America's place in the world, flagging confidence in Congress and in President Obama.[5] Negative attitudes were reflected also in "Occupy Wall Street" demonstrations that flared and persisted in many U.S. cities in late 2011. When we compare U.S. assets in 2000 next to those a decade or so later, as in Tables 7.1 and 7.2, we see declines from high to medium strength in America's economic power, political cohesion, brain power, and congruity with international institutions. These losses both reflected and led to reduced U.S. fitness at home and abroad. The first eight years of decline took place on the watch of George W. Bush, but weaknesses persisted in Barack Obama's first term. Defenders of Obama said that the Bush legacy could not be readily undone, while critics blamed Obama and his policies.[6]

BASIC RESOURCES

In the early twenty-first century America's strengths in basic resources remained at a high level, though topsoil was being depleted and clean water sources endangered. New ways were found to extract natural gas and oil, though at great risk to environmental well-being. More reliance on fossil fuels could reduce attention to conservation and to alternative energy sources. Air and water quality improved in some ways even as many Republican politicians tried to weaken safeguards. The twenty-first century would test whether there are real limits to what humans can do to their environment and maintain or improve their lifestyles. Some analysts (e.g., McKibben 2010; Wilson 1993) worried that Americans were leading the world to a tipping point collapse. Concentrations of carbon dioxide in the atmosphere, a primary "greenhouse gas," reached a daily average of four hundred parts per million in 2013—the highest level in at least eight hundred thousand years.

130

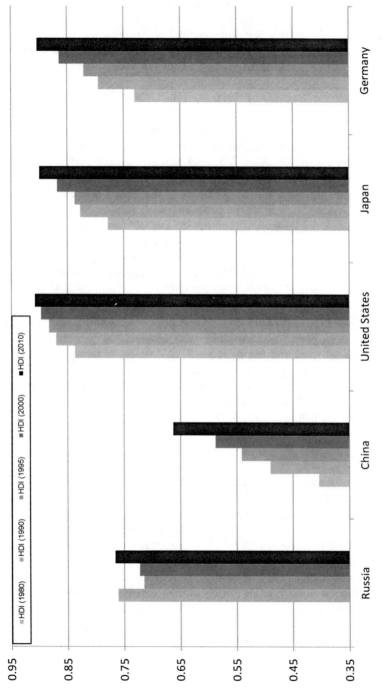

FIGURE 7.1. HDI Trends: Scores for Leading States, 1980–2010

TABLE 7.2. Parameters of Power, 2008 and 2012 (H = high; M = medium; L = low strength)

Actor	Basic Resources	Economic Power	Political Cohesion	Military Power	Brain Power	International Institutions	Fitness at Home	External Fitness
2008								
USA	H	M	M	H	M	M	M	M
Russia	H	M	M	M	M	L	M	M
EU	M	H	M	M	H	H	M	M
Japan	L	M	M	M	M	L	M	M
China	M	M	M	M	M	L	L	M
India	L	M	L	L	L	L	L	L
Brazil	H	M	M	L	L	L	L	L
2012								
USA	H	M	L	M	M	M	M	M
EU	M	M	M	M	M	H	M	M
Japan	L	M	M	M	M	L	L	L
China	M	M	M	M	M	L	L	M
India	L	M	L	L	L	L	L	L
Brazil	H	M	M	L	L	L	L	L

2008 — Bush war on terror; US and global financial crisis; Rise of the BRICs

2012 — War and peace under Obama; Economic stagnation in US, EU, and Japan; Rapid growth in China and India; "Arab Spring"

Sources: Same as previous table plus World Economic Forum 2011 and 2012 and other materials cited in the rest of this chapter.

ECONOMIC POWER AND WELL-BEING

The United States continued to produce the world's largest GDP. But money proved no cure-all. The United States spent far more for security, for health, and for education than most other societies, but did not gain proportional results. Thus, the average Cuban lived longer than his or her U.S. counterpart. Smarter uses of U.S. assets would have garnered better results—and greater fitness.

Tax cuts and elective wars eliminated the budget surpluses achieved in the late 1990s. Indeed, America's relative economic power shriveled as budget and trade deficits widened; as income gaps between the very rich and everyone else became chasms; and as unemployment rose toward 10 percent of those filing. Gross government debt in Greece, Italy, and Ireland exceeded that in the United States in 2010, but U.S. debt as a share of GDP was higher than in the Euro zone—93 percent compared to 85 percent. The U.S. budget deficit in 2011 was 9.1 percent—nearly that of Greece (–10%) and more than double the EU average (–4.2%).[7] Chinese and other foreigners were still buying U.S. Treasury bills but grew increasingly frustrated as dollars lost value. America's greatest potential adversary was also its major creditor.

In 2011, the U.S. current-account deficit was $470 billion or 3.3 percent of GDP. This imbalance was low next to Greece (–8.2%) and Turkey (–9.7%). Meanwhile, however, many other countries ran large current-account surpluses relative to GDP—China (4%), Germany (5.1%), Netherlands (7.4%), Venezuela (8%), Switzerland (12.1%), Malaysia (12.3%), Norway (12.8%), Singapore (15.5%), and Saudi Arabia (24.9%). Switzerland and Singapore achieved large surpluses even without oil exports that benefited Saudi Arabia and Norway. Manufacturing productivity increased about 5 percent per year in the United States from 2008 to 2010, but jumped some 15 percent in Taiwan and Japan.[8]

Another way to look at "who owes whom what" is to consider the foreign debt relative to each citizen. For Americans in 2011, this was just over 35,000 euros; for Greeks, 38,000; for Germans, 50,600; for the French, 66,500. Japanese had by far the largest government debt relative to GDP of any developed economy, but foreign debt amounted to only 16,000 euros per capita.[9]

Though the American economy staggered, the country's richest became much richer. From 1979 to 2007, real (inflation-adjusted) average household income, measured after government transfers and federal taxes, grew by 62 percent. Across nearly three decades, the share of income going to higher-income households rose, while the share going to lower-income households fell. Most income growth went to the top 1 percent of the population. The top fifth of the population saw a ten percentage point increase in their share of after-tax income. All other groups saw their shares decline by 2 to 3 percentage points.

Here is the breakdown. Income grew by:

- 275 percent for the top 1 percent of households,
- 65 percent for the next 19 percent,
- Just under 40 percent for the next 60 percent, and
- 18 percent for the bottom 20 percent.

These trends sharpened as the George W. Bush administration introduced tax changes that favored the wealthy. Between 2005 and 2007, the after-tax income received by the 20 percent of the population with the highest incomes exceeded the after-tax income of the remaining 80 percent. By 2011, the upper 1 percent of Americans were now taking in nearly one-quarter of the nation's income every year. In terms of wealth rather than income, the top 1 percent controlled 40 percent. Twenty-five years ago, the corresponding figures were 12 percent and 33 percent.[10] The combined assets of the owners of Walmart equaled those of America's bottom 150 million people—roughly half the population—for whom they provided cheap goods and low-paying jobs with few fringe benefits (Luce 2012a).

"Of the 1%, by the 1%, for the 1%"—this is how Nobel laureate Joseph E. Stiglitz summed up America's political economy (2012). He warned that growing inequality is the flip side of something else: shrinking opportunity. Whenever we diminish equality of opportunity, it means that we are not using some of our most valuable assets—our people—in the most productive way possible. Many of the same distortions that lead to inequality—such as those associated with monopoly power and preferential tax treatment for special interests—undermine the efficiency of the economy. Many politicians ignored the need for collective action—government investment in infrastructure, education, and technology. They focused on helping a minority to extract value from the labors of the many. Inequality challenges basic morality and helps a money-driven political system to grant excessive power to the most affluent. Those with power use it to insulate themselves from competitive forces by winning favorable tax treatment, government-protected market share, and other forms of rent seeking. The result was a new plutocracy basking in private jets and other perks that exceeded those of the Gilded Age (Freedman 2012). Stiglitz, Krugman, and other liberal economists reinforced the warning of Acemoglu and Robinson (2012) that nations fall because their rulers focus on extraction of wealth for their private gain. Stepan and Linz (2011) showed that, among industrialized democracies, the United States led in many dimensions of inequality.

Stiglitz showed that the federal government manipulated both laws and regulations to benefit the top 1 percent. It lowered tax rates on capital gains, giving the wealthiest Americans close to a free ride. It loaned money to financial institutions at close to zero percent interest and provided bailouts on favorable terms if they failed. The Supreme Court in 2010 enshrined the right of corporations to buy government, by removing limitations on campaign spending.[11] Under the aegis of the Supreme Court, special interest spending spun out of control. Republicans in many states passed voting registration rules to keep poor people away from the polls. The personal and the political evolved in perfect alignment. Most of Congress and top economic officials were members of the top 1 percent when they arrived in Washington; they were kept in office by money from the top 1 percent; and knew how to serve the top 1 percent so they would be rewarded by the top 1 percent when they left office.

Ideology also played a role, as predicted by Karl Marx. Many political and economic figures in the top 1 percent were devoted to rugged individualism, minimal regulations, and small government—provided their special interests were helped or not harmed. They ignored or sought to minimize the "Hamiltonian" vision of what government could do for society—a vision carried forward by Abraham Lincoln during the Civil War, both Teddy and Franklin D. Roosevelt, and by all of F.D.R.'s successors until the great dismantling launched by Jimmy Carter and Ronald Reagan. The Hamiltonian vision lay behind many achievements from the Erie Canal to the Internet, invented at the Pentagon (Lind 2012). Worried about deficits and inflations, many wealthy Americans and their representatives called for cuts in taxes and welfare; others (backed by liberal economists) wanted higher taxes on the most affluent, more government services, and more economic stimulus. The great divergence between America's top 1 percent and the 99 percent below had many sources (Nash 2012). Increased productivity due to automation meant higher profits for some and prolonged unemployment for others. Legally mandated minimum wages did not keep pace with inflation. Trade unions atrophied even as immigration laws permitted an influx of unskilled labor and many firms outsourced to countries with low wages. Imported products at big box stores permitted savings for U.S. consumers but cost U.S. jobs. All these trends were amplified as U.S. educational standards lagged rival systems abroad.

POLITICAL COHESION AND JUSTICE

Of all the costs imposed on American society by the top 1 percent, Stiglitz cautioned in 2011, one of the greatest was growing alienation—"the erosion of our sense of identity, in which fair play, equality of opportunity, and a sense of community are so important. America has long prided itself on being a fair society, where everyone has an equal chance of getting ahead."

Political cohesion began to fall apart during and after the Vietnam War. After the Gerald Ford interregnum, U.S. voters flip-flopped between a liberal Jimmy Carter and conservatives Ronald Reagan and George H. W. Bush. Bipartisan cooperation in the U.S Congress came to a dead end after liberal centrist Bill Clinton defeated the elder Bush in 1992. When Republicans regained control of the House in 1994 and installed Newt Gingrich as Speaker of the House in 1995, he immediately abolished the Democratic Study Group, long trusted by Republicans as well as Democrats for its analysis of proposed legislation. Gingrich halted the previous practice of providing several alternative bills and instead presented one rather partisan bill that members could either approve or reject. Confrontations between Gingrich and President Clinton over budget appropriations led to brief government shutdowns in 1995 and 1996. The take-it-or-leave-it approach continued when Democrats retook the House in 2006 (Cooper 2011; Nocera 2011).

Political tensions deepened in 2000 when Democrats concluded that that Al Gore—not George W. Bush—won the 2000 election, only to be outmaneuvered by Florida Republicans who, Democrats complained, rigged the ballot process, followed by a five to four intervention by a politicized U.S. Supreme Court. Installed in the White House, Bush championed policies that deepened political divisions (Clemens 2004b). The next presidential election (2008) was also disputed—this time because Republican authorities in the crucial state of Ohio kept many blue collar workers and blacks from voting.

Gone were the days when liberal Republicans and conservative Democrats nudged the two parties together. The prospect of legislation achieved by rational discussion to enhance the public good appeared very dim. Use of the filibuster to block legislation in the Senate rose to 70 percent of proposed bills in 2008 from just 8 percent in the 1960s (Luce 2012a). Two long-time observers of Washington concluded in 2012 that "it's even worse than it looks." By Obama's first term the Republican Party had become an insurgent outlier—"ideologically extreme; contemptuous of the inherited social and economic policy regime; scornful of compromise; unpersuaded by conventional understanding of facts, evidence and science; and dismissive of the legitimacy of its political opposition, all but declaring war on the government." In these conditions it became "extremely difficult to enact policies responsive o the country's most pressing challenges" (Mann and Ornstein 2012).

Asymmetrical polarization took shape as swords were drawn for the 2012 elections. Many Republican politicians seemed to place a greater value on defeating Obama than on fostering national fitness. Their August 2011 conditions for raising the debt ceiling led—for the first time—to a downgrading of the country's credit rating. Lowering the U.S rating to one notch below AAA, the rating agency Standard & Poors explained that "political brinkmanship" in the debate over the debt had made the U.S. government's ability to manage its finances "less stable, less effective and less predictable." The AA credit rating was lower than that of Canada and other U.S. partners.

Defying the Keynesian logic of most leading economists, Republicans rejected programs to stimulate the economy and preferred budget cuts even though reductions in government spending would cost jobs and economic growth. Many Republicans in 2011 and 2012 attacked government guarantees of health care for the elderly and the poor; sought to abolish or neuter the Department of Education, Environmental Protection Agency, and Federal Reserve; tried to deregulate the financial industry as well as the environment. Many but not all Republican leaders also strove to maintain discrimination against gays and lesbians in the military; deport immigrants; cut unemployment and insurance and nutrition programs; in effect raise taxes on the poor and lower them on the rich. Lacking a system of compulsory voting, as in New Zealand, U.S. politicians ran hard on hot-button issues calculated to fire up the base and get them to vote (Friedman 2012).

Congress shortchanged the future. It added to the defense budget while cutting domestic non-defense discretionary spending, which accounted for only 12 percent of the pie. It continued obligations from the past such as Social Security while reducing outlays for R&D, infrastructure, and education. (A large part of funding for higher education went to for-profit institutions despite their generally below-par education and a high dropout rate.) Private funding for the future also fell short: annual fundraising in Silicon Valley was running at less than 15 percent of the 2000 level just before the dotcom bubble burst (Luce 2012a). Meanwhile, many town planners invested in casinos and sports stadiums as ways to provide bread and circuses. They ignored the reality that casinos create few jobs, most of which are low paid, and drain the economy. Tax receipts are minimal next to the costs of coping with negative social effects. Casinos on Indian lands only add to the pressures eroding Native American cultures. Newt Gingrich, however, gladly accepted millions from a casino billionaire who bankrolled his campaign to be Republican presidential candidate in 2012. Another would-be candidate was himself a casino mogul—Donald Trump.

As Karl Marx expected, America's system of justice as well as economics seemed to favor entrenched elites. For America's Founding Fathers, law was to be the great equalizer in American life—guarantor of a common set of rules for all. But the principle of equality before the law was degraded when, in the aftermath of Watergate, President Gerald Ford pardoned President Richard Nixon in 1974. A few years later, Congress ignored President Ronald Reagan's involvement in the Iran-Contra affair. This pattern continued when—three decades later, President Obama shielded Bush-era officials from prosecution for torture and other alleged crimes.[12] No banking executives went to jail for misrepresenting their derivative offerings and mortgage loans. A two-tiered system of justice emerged to make the country's political and financial class virtually immune from prosecution—licensed to act without restraint, while the politically powerless were imprisoned with greater ease and in greater numbers than in any other country in the world. Not only the courts but also both political parties and the media abetted a process that produced torture, war crimes, domestic spying, and financial fraud (Greenwald 2011).

A sense of injustice led many Americans to fill the streets in Autumn 2011 in demonstrations against Wall Street and the dominant political-economic system. The "Occupy Wall Street" movement could be seen as a desperate search for self-organization. People from many walks of life, age groups, and social classes coalesced to protest a political-economic system that profited its elites but left most citizens without voice and many without jobs. Their demands for "justice," however, focused on a core challenge to American fitness—the undue influence of corporations (Bar-Yam 2011). True, the demonstrators put forward no agenda of practical steps to change the system. Still, the singer Makana managed to tell President Obama and other Asian Pacific leaders in November 2011 that "the time has come for us to voice our rage. . . . We'll occupy . . . until you do the bidding of the many, not the few."[13]

While many Americans continued to think of themselves as "my brother's keeper," many relished the prospect of vanquishing their neighbors. How else explain the popularity of *The Hunger Games*? (first in a trilogy of books by Suzanne Collins launched by Scholastic [*sic*] Press in 2008 and the title of a number one box office hit film in 2012). In this dystopian tale, far more sadistic than *1984* or *Brave New World*, two dozen young people fight each other on reality TV until one survives and wins food for the oppressed and hungry people of her district.[14] Many critics praised the writing as fast-paced and engrossing, but *New Yorker* critic David Denby (2012) compared the spectacle with television's myriad "Survivor" shows and sado-Trumpian elimination contests. By early 2012 the trilogy had sold 24 million copies in the United States (including seven purchased for the Harvard University libraries) and had been translated into many foreign languages—another example of U.S. influence, for better or worse, on the world.

Perhaps the popularity of the *Hunger Games* expressed the pressures of high school bullying and cliques, but it could also be a metaphor for cutthroat capitalism—or for politics in the United States. The same syndrome was strong in sports. Some colleges masked damage to their football players from concussions. Some baseball stars and cycling champions were defrocked for doping. When seven-time winner of the Tour de France Lance Armstrong was barred for life from any official role in any Olympic sport in August 2012, Travis Tygart, head of the United States Anti-Doping Agency, called it a "yet another heartbreaking example of how the win-at-all-costs culture, if left unchecked, will overtake fair, safe and honest competition."

Adding still another input to the declinist analysis, Charles Murray (2012) claimed that America was falling apart because the white working class has become alienated from "the founding virtues" of civic life. "Our nation is coming apart at the seams," Murray warned, "not ethnic seams, but the seams of class." The upper class, he said, no longer demanded that everyone apply themselves to study and work as they do. Liberal elites, while themselves living lives of probity, refused to proselytize for bourgeois virtues (study, work, save, invest) to which they subscribe, thus leaving their less discerning fellow-citizens to flounder in the antibourgeois legacy of the countercultural 1960s. Many observers questioned Murray's diagnosis but shared his judgment that American society was fragmenting along many lines.

MILITARY MIGHT

The United States still stood as a military Goliath in the early twenty-first century, but its assets were stretched very thin. America faced not one but many Davids—some equipped only with suicidal fanaticism and improvised explosives, but others reaching for mass destruction weapons.

Federal budget deficits notwithstanding, America's defense spending under presidents George W. Bush and Obama equaled military outlays by all other countries combined. Prolonged wars in Iraq and Afghanistan depleted the Pentagon's human and material reserves. Instead of raising taxes to fund these wars, the Bush team lowered taxes—giving a double whammy to the federal deficit. The Bush team also shortchanged returning veterans and failed to deal adequately with their post-traumatic stress. Challenged on many fronts, the Pentagon shifted U.S. troops from South Korea to the Middle East even though North Korea continued to act like a rogue regime acquiring nuclear weapons. The long-term costs of the Iraq and Afghanistan campaigns could easily reach three to four trillion dollars (Stiglitz and Bilmes 2008).

The Bush administration also spent heavily to fight terrorism. It funded a huge Department of Homeland Security destined to occupy more office space than the Pentagon. The president and Congress established a new Director of National Intelligence supposed to coordinate the work and findings of more than a dozen intelligence agencies. Goaded to share information, the various agencies began to talk more to one another but coordination remained weak. Reconnaissance satellites and wiretaps multiplied but smart power in Washington remained in short supply.

The costs of defense amounted to far more than the 3 or 4 percent of GDP officially acknowledged. If outlays for intelligence, homeland security, nuclear weapons research, and space warfare were included, "defense" spending amounted to more than 6 percent of GDP. Including interest payments on debts accumulated on arms buildups since the Reagan era, the total exceeded 7 percent. Despite promises to cut defense spending, the Obama administration funded nuclear submarines and long-range bombers ill-suited to the post–cold war era and likely to provoke Chinese countermeasures.

BRAIN POWER

Of all the factors weakening U.S. fitness, none was greater than the mismatch between young people's skills and the abilities required by a twenty-first century economy (Goldin and Katz 2008; also Noah 2012). Measures of U.S.

brain power were contradictory. Americans continued to win the lion's share of Nobel prizes. High tech companies in Seattle, Silicon Valley, Boston, and North Carolina led the world in innovation. But one erstwhile incubator of innovation and Nobel laureates, the Bell Labs, lost its drive and sponsor when its mother ship, AT&T, lost its monopolistic position in the Reagan years. From the 1920s to the 1980s, Bell Labs had been arguably the most innovative scientific organization in the world. Steven Chu, named Secretary of the Department of Energy in 2008, won a Nobel Prize for his work at Bell Labs in the early 1980s. In its heyday the Bell Labs developed not only incremental laboratories but breakthroughs in basic science and technology (Gertner 2012).

Scientists around the country were attempting to do basic research on fundamental problems. Some were well financed, such as those studying genomics at the Broad Institute associated with M.I.T. and Harvard University. But federal funding and popular support on the scale given to the Apollo Program were missing. "Will America kill the curiosity that landed the rover on Mars?" asked Nobel laureate Ahmed Zewail (2012), worried that U.S. leadership in science was threatened by decreased funding and mounting bureaucracy. He found that curiosity-driven research was no longer looked upon favorably. Research proposals had to address "broad relevance to society" and provide "transformative solutions" even before research could begin. Universities had to raise funds just to keep operating. Professors had to spend more time writing grant requests, reducing the time available for creative thinking. Many were involved in commercial enterprises. Gone was the broad-based, curiosity-driven structure of Bell Labs. Most industrial labs focused research on market-ready products.

The Federal Budget provided few resources to protect fresh water or desalinate ocean water, even though—in Winter 2012—more than 60 percent of the United States suffered drought conditions and more than a billion people worldwide lacked clean drinking water. Did more oil mean less clean water? Washington did little to regulate hydraulic fracturing ("fracking") despite its heavy use of fresh water and threat to drinking supplies. Republicans wanted to pipe Canadian carbons through Nebraska regardless of its impact on the water table.

"Why We Can't Solve Big Problems," by Jason Pontin, was the lead essay in a special issue of *MIT Technology Review* (November–December 2012) devoted to Big Problems and Big Solutions. Pontin wrote that Silicon Valley may have been the planet's lead incubator of new technology in recent decades, but it had not addressed, much less solved, the world's most pressing problems. As Peter Thiel, a co-founder of PayPal, put it, "We wanted flying cars—instead we got 140 characters." The Internet is a net plus," he conceded, "but not a big one."

Pontin complained that "Silicon Valley's explanation of *why* there are no disruptive innovations is parochial and reductive: The markets—in particular, the incentives that venture capital provides entrepreneurs—are to blame." Venture capitalists in recent years have supported marginal rather than fundamental improvements in how the world works. They lost the nerve as well as the broad ambitions that drove Bill Gates and Steve Jobs in earlier decades.

Pontin continued: "These things are complex and . . . there is no one simple explanation." The issues extend far beyond Silicon Valley. First, sometimes we choose not to solve difficult technological problems. We could travel to Mars if we wished but choose to do other things. Second, our politicians often fail the demands of the age. Public investment for energy research and development fell from 10 percent in 1979 of total R&D spending to just 2 percent in 2012 (about $5 billion). Third, some problems turn out to be more political than technological. Famines often result from distribution problems—not from a shortage of food. Finally, scientists and engineers sometimes fail because they do not properly understand the problem. Cancer, for example, turns out to be a foe far more hydra-headed than imagined when President Richard Nixon proclaimed a war on cancer in 1971.

Other contributors to the debate said that political leaders no longer inspired publics and scientists to do big things such as go to the moon. Mitt Romney got big guffaws from the Republican National Convention in 2012 when he said Barack Obama wanted to turn back the seas—this at a time when the convention itself was nearly washed out! Some comments on Pontin's essay complained that he omitted the role of many plutocrats who care nothing for the public good.

The percentage of Americans graduating from college diminished relative to China and some other countries. Fewer Americans took up science in graduate school. Many believed that science was "hard" and that rewards were much greater in other fields. Slashed budgets for the National Science Foundation, NASA, and the National Institutes of Health implied less priority for science (Borrell 2011). U.S. graduate faculties in science would wither without foreign students, many of whom later returned home, where opportunities and needs appeared greater and where authorities welcomed them instead of harassing them about work permits. Yes, their home countries had paid for their early years of education, but U.S. taxpayers had subsidized their advanced studies.

Most Americans enjoyed the material benefits of technological innovation, but many disdained scientific expertise. Nearly half the U.S. Congress and much of the public claimed not to accept the (just another) "theory" of evolution.[15] To be sure, former vice president Al Gore shared the Nobel Peace Prize 2007 with the Intergovernmental Panel on Climate Change (IPCC), "for their efforts to build up and disseminate greater knowledge about man-made climate change, and to lay the foundations for the measures that are needed to counteract such change." Obama's Secretary of Energy, Stephen Chu, shared the Nobel Prize for Physics in 1997. But Chu's calls for alternative energies ran up against Stone Age lawmakers who denied the existence of man-made climate change and resisted measures to curtail global warming.[16]

While Google and Apple generated new apps that mesmerized millions, most pupils in U.S. elementary and high schools performed poorly relative to those in Singapore and other industrialized countries. The George W. Bush "No Child Left Behind" and Barack Obama "Race to the Top" programs tried to raise standards but may well have done more harm than good, because they placed excessive emphasis on testing and, in any event, never received the funding on which they had been predicated.

Howard Gardner (2011) urged Americans to reframe their thinking about truth, beauty, and goodness. This was surely a worthy goal, but what about the here and now? According to Richard Pérez-Peña (2012), the Josephson Institute of Ethics found that about three-fifths of high school students admitted to having cheated in the previous year, while four-fifths said their own ethics were above average. Large-scale cheating occurred—sometimes by teachers and principals as well as by pupils—all the way from elementary schools to Stuyvesant High School in Manhattan to the Air Force Academy and Harvard. Gardner said that over the twenty years he has studied professional and academic integrity, "the ethical muscles have atrophied," in part because of a culture that exalts success, however it is attained. He believed that students at elite colleges reasoned, "Our colleagues are cutting corners, we'll be damned if we'll lose out to them, and some day, when we've made it, we'll be role models. But until then, give us a pass."

Other studies found that American students needed a stronger capacity for self-regulation. They needed noncognitive traits such as resilience, integrity, resourcefulness, persistence, professionalism, and ambition. Programs such as "OneGoal" in Chicago demonstrated that developing these traits could help students in school and in life (Tough 2012). Still other studies found a steady rise in diagnoses of Attention Deficit Hyperactivity Disorder and in the use of drugs to help students concentrate, whether or not they suffered from ADHD.

Like other forms of wealth, education was uneven. Rich suburbs enjoyed better schools than inner cities. Some regions were stronger than others. Nationwide, the average rate of adults with college degrees was 27 percent, but the rate was less than 20 percent in three states and more than 35 percent in five others and the District of Columbia.[17] Texans, gagging in smog and forest fire smoke, three times elected a climate change skeptic, James "Rick" Perry, to be their governor, abetting his efforts to torpedo the Departments of Education and Commerce and—when he could remember his third target (in the debates among Republican candidates for the 2012 presidential election)—the Environmental Protection Agency.

Of course all learning is shaped by forces outside the classroom—by family, neighborhood, the media, the Zeitgeist. As unemployment approached 10 percent in the late Bush and Obama years, many of these influences became more negative. The foundations of learning trembled under the weight of mounting poverty, worsening health, deeper financial worries; rising domestic conflict, and more homes with just one parent or with both parents working.

There were few "tiger moms." Each day American adults on average spent 2.7 hours watching television and socialized for about forty-five minutes. Time spent reading for personal interest and playing games or using a computer for leisure varied greatly by age. Individuals aged seventy-five and over averaged 1.1 hours of reading per weekend day and eighteen minutes playing games or using a computer for leisure. Conversely, individuals ages fifteen to nineteen read for an average of six minutes per weekend day while spending 1.1 hours playing games or using a computer for leisure.

PUBLIC SAFETY

Deep social malaise was manifest also in America's incarceration rates—highest in the world. Fully one-fourth of the world's documented prison population was in the United States. In 2009 more than 7.2 million people were on probation, in jail or prison, or on parole—one in every thirty-two adults. The total number of adults under correctional supervision increased from just over one million in 1980 to over four million in 2009.[18] One in nine black men between ages twenty and thirty-four was behind bars—often on drug-related charges.[19] The United States incarcerated more of its youth than any other country—nearly one hundred thousand juveniles in the early twenty-first century.

Not only was incarceration costly (some 7 percent of state outlays in 2008), but it also deprived society of whatever goods and services those imprisoned could have produced. The money used to imprison someone for year could have paid their tuition, room, and board in most colleges. In California, the cost of incarcerating one person approached $50,000 a year—in Louisiana, $14,000. A higher than average rate of incarceration, as in Kentucky, did nothing to lower recidivism.[20] Some reformers suggested diverting nonviolent offenders away from prison, but many Americans favored punishment over rehabilitation—as did the owners of privatized prisons.

Worried about crime, many Americans kept their own weapons. Many demanded and in all states enjoyed the right to carry concealed weapons in public places, including college classrooms. Of course, hunters, collectors, and sportspeople had their own reasons to keep weapons, but most gun owners trusted that having their own firearms enhanced their security. Gun sales spiked after each shooting incident.

Americans possess more guns per capita than people in any other country—eighty-nine guns for every one hundred Americans in the early 2000s. (Next came Yemen, Switzerland, Finland, and Serbia—each with about fifty guns per one hundred citizens.) Guns kill more than thirty thousand Americans each year—nearly as many as the number who perish in auto accidents and a much higher percentage than in other industrialized countries. More gun deaths occurred by suicide than homicide.[21] More U.S. soldiers died by suicide, usually by guns, than in battle. As suicide rates mounted in the U.S. armed forces, military authorities wanted to monitor personnel who kept a weapon at home and who showed signs of stress.

State-by-state analysis by the Centers for Disease Control and Prevention showed that that the more guns, the more gun deaths. Both Alaska and the District of Columbia suffered some 20 gun deaths per 100,000 population—twice the U.S. national average of 10.3. Some 61 percent of Alaska's residents owned their own weapons and had the third highest gun death rate—17.62 per 100,000. Alabama placed second in gun ownership—57 percent. Its gun death rate was just under Alaska's—17.55. Lousiana placed third in gun ownership, but topped all states in gun deaths—19.87 per 100,000. Mississippi ranked third in gun ownership and second in gun deaths. Nevada, Wyoming, and Montana ranked just under the champions in gun ownership and gun deaths. Western states also led the nation in suicide.

Looking at the other end of the spectrum, the states with the lowest gun death rates also had some of the lowest rates of gun ownership. Hawaii had the very lowest rate of gun ownership, 9.7 percent and the lowest gun death rate—2.82 per 100,000. Massachusetts was second from the bottom in gun ownership—12.8 percent—and had the third lowest gun death rate—3.83 per 100,000. Rhode Island's rate of gun ownership was 13.3 percent. It registered the second lowest gun death rate—3.51. Connecticut, site of a school massacre in 2012, had a 16.2 percent rate of gun ownership and 4.27 gun deaths per 100,000. Despite their reputations for harboring organized crime, New Jersey and New York had about 5 gun deaths per 100,000 residents. Only 11 percent of New Jersey residents had guns, while 18.1 percent of New Yorkers did so (many of them upstate, where hunting was popular).

Between the extremes of Louisiana and Massachusetts came Colorado, site of two large-scale shootings in recent years. It had 11.6 gun deaths per 100,000 residents—just above the nation's overall rate of 10.19 for gun deaths. But Colorado placed just thirty-sixth in the nation in gun ownership—34.5 percent of residents are armed.

A strong exception to this pattern emerged in the nation's capital. Gun ownership in the District of Columbia was low—about 4 or 5 per 100,000 residents—much lower even than in Hawaii or Massachusetts. Despite a low rate of gun ownership, the nation's capital has been called "murder capital" of the United States. The murder rate rose to 80 per 100,000 residents in 1991 but then declined to about 20 in 2006–08. The key factor was probably the rise and fall of a crack cocaine epidemic.

A Gallup survey released in October 2011 found that 47 percent of American adults reported that they had a gun in their home or elsewhere on their property. This was up from 41 percent in 2010 and the highest rate recorded since 1993, when 54 percent reported owning guns. Another Gallup study found that support for stricter gun controls declined from 60 percent of Americans in 1959 to just 26 percent in 2011. Outright opposition to gun controls grew from 36 percent in 1959 to 73 percent in 2011. Since the mid-1990s more than one-half of Americans have declared their opposition to any law banning the manufacture, sale, or possession of semiautomatic rifles.

In 1991 some 68 percent of Americans favored stricter gun laws and 43 percent favored a ban on handguns. Those percentages fell to 43 percent and 26 percent in 2011. Support for stricter gun controls is strongest in the East, among women, and among Democrats. But Democrats as well as Republicans in Congress tend to follow the recommendations of National Rifle Association lobbyists. President Barack Obama in his first term toed the NRA line.

Did weapons make Americans any safer? The state-by-state comparison of guns and gun violence gave a clear answer, "No." As Mephistopheles informed the Lord, "Humans call it 'reason,' but use it only to be more brutish than any beast."

> Er nennt's Vernunft uns braucht's allein
> Nur um tierischer als jedes Tier zu sein. (Faust, ll. 285–286)

CONGRUITY WITH INTERNATIONAL INSTITUTIONS

America's ties with and shared vulnerability with the rest of the planet continued to deepen in the early twenty-first century. Instead of working to create mutual gain with other actors, however, the George W. Bush administration preferred to go it alone. A major disconnect developed between U.S. policies and international institutions—most of which had been sponsored by the United States. The words and deeds of the Bush administration destroyed the sympathy for America expressed around the globe after the 9/11/2011 attacks. The Bush entourage disdained not only the United Nations and international law but also the NATO alliance. The Bush administration "un-signed" the U.S. commitment to the International Criminal Court. It scorned the Kyoto Protocol. The president probably violated the U.S. Constitution by abrogating the anti-ballistic missile treaty without consulting Congress. When America went to war, it did so alone or with a "coalition of the willing"—heedless the views of "old Europe." To justify the Iraq invasion the White House had Secretary of State Colin Powell perjure himself at the United Nations, as if neither he nor anyone else in high places had read the National Intelligence Estimate of October 2002.[22]

Hopeful Europeans awarded Obama the Nobel Peace Prize in 2009 for encouraging negotiated solutions to the world's problems, but few positive results ensued. Israel's relations with its neighbors got worse. Iran and North Korea continued their nuclear programs. The United States gradually withdrew most of its fighters from Iraq and "surged" U.S. forces in Afghanistan, but much killing continued in each country. Pakistan remained a danger to itself and the world. American Special Forces killed Osama bin Laden and other terrorist leaders but al-Qaeda and the Taliban remained virulent. The Obama administration resolved to pull most U.S. troops from Afghanistan in 2014 but—especially as "green-on-blue" killings increased, many observers called for the earliest possible withdrawal.

THE SCORECARD

America's economic stagnation persisted in Obama's first term despite several stimulus packages that liberals lamented were too small and conservatives complained were the wrong medicine entirely. Whiffing blood on the horizon and hoping to retake the White House, Republicans labored to block any program that might help Obama win reelection—never mind the cost to the economy and body politic or America's standing in the world. Despite these blocking efforts and richly endowed "SuperPacs" working against him, Obama was reelected in November 2012. Both parties then pledged to cooperate to rebuild the U.S. economy, but leaders on both sides of the aisle continued to look for ways to eviscerate their opponents. Traditional morality and the security of classified information also became issues in late 2012 as scandals brought down the country's most renowned general, David Petraeus, not long after he became director of the CIA. On the other hand, voters in South Carolina forgave their ex-governor who had turned "hiking the Appalachian Trail" into a euphemism for infidelity. Regardless of his divorce, disgrace, and censure, Mark Sanford readily defeated his Democratic challenger in a special election for a seat in the U.S. House of Representatives in 2013. Sanford explained, "I am an imperfect man saved by God's grace." Petraeus, for his part, agreed in 2013 to share his knowledge of the world as a visiting professor at the City University of New York. Despite his pact with the spirit of negation, Faust too was forgiven.

chapter eight

WHAT FUTURE FOR THE AMERICAN DREAM?

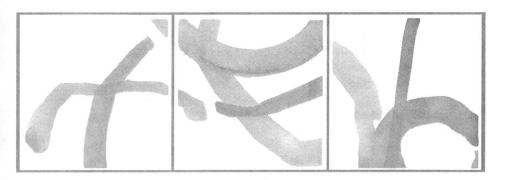

The American dream proved elusive. Asked to join in a discussion of why the United States is the greatest country, the news anchor on Aaron Sorkin's HBO television drama *The Newsroom,* shocked his audience on the show's season premiere in 2012, After attempting a few jokes, he declared: "There's absolutely no evidence to support the statement that we're the greatest country in the world. We're seventh in literacy, twenty-seventh in math, twenty-second in science, forty-ninth in life expectancy, one hundred seventy-eighth in infant mortality, third in median household income, number four in labor force, and number four in exports. We lead the world in only three categories: number of incarcerated citizens per capita, number of adults who believe angels are real, and defense spending, where we spend more than the next twenty-six countries combined."

The National Research Council reported in 2013 that, on average, Americans die sooner and experience higher rates of disease and injury than people in sixteen other high-income countries This health disadvantage existed at all ages and affected even those with health insurance, college educations, higher incomes, and relatively healthy behaviors. Car accidents, gun violence, and drug overdoses cut short the lives of many Americans before age fifty. But disease also took a heavy toll. Americans had among the highest rates of heart disease, lung cancer, diabetes, and sexually transmitted diseases. These trends started in the late twentieth century but grew stronger in the twenty-first. Many factors contributed to this situation. The United States had the highest level of poverty in the countries surveyed. Public policy left the U.S. health care system fragmented with many people uninsured. A "don't tread on me" culture was manifest not only in wide opposition to mandatory health insurance but also in resistance to laws requiring motorists to wear seat belts and motorcyclists helmets (*U.S. health in international perspective 2013*).

Americans spend far more than on education and health than citizens of most high-income countries but learn less and lead shorter lives. Though many Americans are proud of their democracy, they participate less and enjoy fewer real electoral choices than people in other industrialized democracies (Friedman 2012).

The World Economic Forum (2012) also took a dim view of America's trajectory. In 2008 the forum ranked the United States as Number One in "global competitiveness." But the former hyperpower declined along many dimensions. By 2012 the country's competitiveness ranking slipped to 7th—behind Switzerland, Singapore, Finland, Sweden, the Netherlands, and Germany, but ahead of the United Kingdom, Hong Kong, and Japan. It placed 140th out of 144 countries on its government deficit as a percentage of GDP—down from 97th just four years earlier. "Public trust in politicians" fell from 41st to 54th. The ranking on government wastefulness fell from 67th to 76th. On freedom from government regulation, the U.S. economy fell from 50th to 76th. The sole superpower began to look like a banana republic: favoritism in decisions by government officials, 59th; public trust in politics, 54th; bribery, 42nd; diversion of public funds, 34th. The country placed second in the percentage of its population in tertiary education, but only 47th in secondary and 58th in elementary education. The quality of U.S. elementary education ranked 38th, with math and science education ranked at 47th. U.S. citizens ranked 24th on Internet access.

The U.S. business community was critical toward public and private institutions. Despite its fondness for legal remedies, the United States ranked 29th in protection of intellectual property. But macroeconomic stability remained the country's greatest area weakness—111th, down from 90th in 2011. The national savings rate was 114th in the world. The bottom line: the U.S. credit rating slipped to 11th in the world.

Given its many problems, how could the United States rank even seventh in global competitiveness? The World Economic Forum pointed to the sheer size of the U.S. domestic and foreign markets—largest in the world. The United States also ranked first in available airplane seats. It suffered the least business costs due to malaria. Labor market efficiency was another plus (much greater freedom to lay off workers than in Europe). The United States was no longer the undisputed leader in innovation, but continued to benefit from good cooperation between universities and business in research and development.

Why this precipitous decline? Many factors played a role. The German news weekly *Der Spiegel* (November 5, 2012) pointed to a key element:

"The hatred of big government has reached a level in the United States that threatens the country's very existence. Americans everywhere may vow allegiance to the nation and its proud Stars and Stripes, but when it comes time to pay the bills and distribute costs, and when solidarity is needed, all sense of community evaporates." Any semblance of the "general will," Rousseau might say, was subverted by pursuit of personal gain and the narrow agendas of many advocacy groups.

Could these trends be reversed? What perspectives could complexity science offer?

PUNCTUATED EQUILIBRIUM

Evolution can be seen as a gradual, incremental process or as a set of sudden changes followed and preceded by long periods of equilibrium. Could it be that human history is not cyclical and slow-moving but rather, as Ferguson put it in 2010, "arrhythmic"—capable of accelerating like a sports car or stalling? Could America's collapse, like that of the USSR, arrive suddenly—like a thief in the night?

The notion of abrupt change contradicts the widely shared image of gradual change brought on by the relentless wearing away of the wheels on which societies move. But some portents in the early twenty-first century suggested that U.S. fitness was in a downward spiral The federal balance sheet shifted in just a few years from surplus to a huge and expanding deficit. Unemployment, hovering around 4 or 5 percent for decades, suddenly jumped to 9 or 10 percent (though declining in 2012 to just below 8%). More and more Americans were living in poverty—part of an expanding malaise—and angry about it.

The United States appeared to be very fit in 2000 but quickly came to resemble a sand pile with a fragile equilibrium. A heavy dose of hubris-fed arrogance by the George W. Bush administration after 2001 threatened to collapse the sand pile—in ways reminiscent of the Athens described by Thucydides and, in 2010, by Ferguson. The Obama White House rode in on the "audacity of hope" but barely kept the economy from collapsing as Republicans killed most proposals to fire up the economy.

A complex adaptive system is at risk when its components lose faith in its viability. The hopes inspired by Obama in 2008 morphed into fears, anxiety, and anger. The American public as well as investors in China and Japan began to wonder if the United States would rebound or stumble downward. Historians knew that prolonged war, economic stagnation, and hedonism had pushed other empires over the brink.

Wise Cassandras disagreed about the prospects of growth. Martin S. Feldstein (2010) predicted an annual GDP growth rate of 2.6 percent in the new century's second decade based on expansion of the labor force, the growth of capital stock, and the increase of multifactor productivity. But Robert Gordon (2012) aligned with the sudden decline camp and, in effect, supported the punctuated equilibrium model. Gordon argued that earthshaking innovations had ceased and that economic expansion was inexorably slowing in the United States. Given that Europe and North America had experienced virtually no economic growth in the centuries before 1750, "the rapid progress made over the past 250 years could well turn out to be a unique episode in human history."

Gordon analyzed the impact of three industrial revolutions. Starting in England, the first Industrial Revolution (circa 1750–1830) saw steam engines and railroads generate increases in productivity and improved living standards. The second (1870–1900) saw the introduction of electricity, internal combustion engines, running water, indoor toilets, communications, entertainment, chemicals, and petroleum. This second revolution, led by the United States, triggered eighty years of rapid productivity growth between 1890 and 1972. Once its spin-off inventions—airplanes, air conditioning, interstate highways—ran their course, however, U.S. productivity growth during the years 1972–1996 was much slower than before. The increase in U.S. life expectancy in the first half of the twentieth century was three times as fast as in the last half. The third Industrial Revolution (1960 to the early twenty-first century) was based on computers, the Web, and mobile phones. It created only a short-lived growth revival between 1996 and 2004. Many of its spin-off inventions could happen only once—urbanization, transportation speed, the freedom of females from the drudgery of carrying tons of water per year, and the role of central heating and air conditioning in achieving a year-round constant temperature.

Even if innovation were to continue into the future at the rate of the two decades before 2007, Gordon believed that the United States faced six "headwinds" likely to reduce long-term growth to much less than the 1.9 percent annual rate experienced between 1860 and 2007. The headwinds included less population growth, a leveling off of education, greater inequality, global competition, energy shortfalls and costs, and the overhang of consumer and government debt. Elites might still prosper, but growth in consumption per capita for the bottom 99 percent of Americans could fall below 0.5 percent per year for many decades.

Why the slowdown? Growth is powered by the discovery and subsequent exploitation of specific technologies and—above all—by "general purpose technologies" that transform life in ways both deep and broad. The IT revolution centered on communication and entertainment devices—useful and pleasant but not nearly so vital to life as electricity and running water. The United States remained at the vanguard of global productivity, leaving plenty of room for China and other developing countries to catch up. But rapid increases in productivity at the frontier are possible only if the right innovations occur. Transport and energy technologies had hardly changed in half a century. Lower taxes, the Republican Party's panacea, could not alter inertia. Some observers countered that Gordon erred in downplaying the contributions of the third revolution. For example, Diane Coyle (2012) asserted that IT improved productivity in many domains. "Cheap information processing on a massive scale underpins innovation in other sectors such as biotechnology and materials. These will prove as 'evolutionary' as some of the innovations of the 1870s or 1920s." Like rail transport and electricity in earlier times, she predicted, they will transform lives.

Some analysts said innovation depends on money. America's technological hegemony in the twentieth century resulted from heavy R&D investment by government and corporations. In the twenty-first century, however, U.S. spending on research and development declined as a share of GDP even as it rapidly increased in China. Chinese firms such as ZTE and Huawei filed more international patents than any U.S. company. To make matters worse, Chinese hackers were stealing U.S. industrial know-how and U.S. firms were conducting ever more of their R&D abroad, including major operations by Intel and Applied Materials in China (Fingleton 2013).

Niall Ferguson (2012) pointed to three factors likely to constrain the U.S. economy and three likely to boost it above and beyond others. America's lead in technological innovation was likely to diminish. Americans in 2008 had more patents in force than did applicants from elsewhere, but other nations were challenging the U.S. lead. Japanese filed more applications and received more patents than Americans. But Americans filed twice as many applications as South Koreans and three times more than did Germans or Chinese. American universities still dominated the top tiers of education but their preeminence could not continue unless U.S. primary and middle schools sharply improved. The unbridled rent-seeking of America's richest individuals and groups was eviscerating the entire society. The United States was coming to resemble China in the 1770s—described by Adam Smith as a "stationary" state in which growth was near zero and prosperity enjoyed mainly by a corrupt elite. The United States in 2013 was growing faster than Europe but plutocrats garnered the lion's share of the bounty.

Against these trends, demographics favored the United States. By 2020 only one-fifth of the population was likely to be older than sixty-four—a much smaller fraction than in Europe, Japan, or China. New finds in gas and oil were providing comparatively cheap energy that could fuel a renaissance in manufacturing. Like most countries, the United States was vulnerable to erratic climate change—but much less so than most of Asia.

These six factors did not exhaust the possibilities. The overriding question concerned China. Would the existing hegemon and rising challenger find a way to coordinate their complementary strengths for mutual gain or would they struggle in a new "cool" or even a hot war? Alarmed by China's rise, some believers in America's decline called for retrenchment to a Fortress

America in economics and world affairs. Instead of free trade, they urged a neo-mercantilist stance. Instead of leadership for peace and stability, they called for the United States to limit its military and political presence around the globe. Hawks went the other way. They demanded a military buildup to contain China.

Both declinists and hawks worried that if China's torrid economic growth continued, its GDP would exceed America's in several decades. Rising powers, they warned, clash with declining hegemons. They noted that Beijing brashly claimed most of the South China Sea; that China continued to advance in space and other technologies with military applications; and that its missiles menaced Taiwan, a friend of America for more than fifty years. However both declinists and hawks proceeded from a false assumption. Water shortages, pollution, and demographic problems were certain to slow if not derail China's rapid growth (Clemens 2012).

Taking into account the many factors that shape the global balance of power, Michael Beckley (2011, 43) concluded: "Over the last two decades, globalization and U.S. hegemonic burdens have expanded significantly, yet the United States has not declined; in fact it is now wealthier, more innovative, and more militarily powerful compared to China than it was in 1991." He noted, for example, that more than 90 percent of China's high tech exports were being produced by foreign firms. There was ever more foreign direct investment in China and fewer joint ventures in which technology is transferred.

The United States was not declining relative to China or any other power. But assertions to this effect are dangerous, because—if believed—they could push Washington or Beijing onto a collision course. The good news is that wars between upstarts and declining hegemons have been rare.[1] More "good" news: given the lethality of modern weapons, war is almost unthinkable between major powers. China's steady advances in military weaponry, beginning with a nuclear bomb in 1964, were impressive but not surprising for a country with millennia of technological innovation—and with long borders and vulnerable sea lanes to maintain.

Even better news: a combination of factors, both tangible and intangible, has reduced the frequency of big wars and the number of war deaths per capita. Images and news reports from Tibet, Syria, and elsewhere obscured the big picture, but the global trends are away from violence (Pinker 2011).

Under presidents George W. Bush and Obama, the large pot persisted in calling the kettle black. Washington alarums about Chinese military spending were risible given the Pentagon's well-funded programs to advance technology. As President Obama reminded the American people in 2011, planned reductions in U.S. defense spending would still give the Pentagon a budget larger than those of the next ten biggest military spenders combined. Leaving aside the outlays for Iraq and Afghanistan, U.S. defense outlays in 2011–12 were at least eight times those of China. Despite pressures to cut U.S. government expenditures, the U.S. Navy would not reduce its eleven aircraft carrier groups to ten. For its part, China floated just one refitted Ukrainian aircraft carrier that could move but not land even the vertical take-off planes for which it was designed.

For the foreseeable future, China would be far more vulnerable to exogenous events than the United States. China depended on imported commodities far more than the U.S.A. China had to increase its oil imports to cope with the demands of industry and a middle class yearning for private autos. The United States, by contrast, was producing more of its own gas and oil and had neighbors seeking to sell their carbon riches. Some analysts asked if the U.S. naval buildup aimed at a capacity to choke off China's imports of oil and other supplies. But this would be an act of war—a catastrophe for all parties.

Washington and Beijing possessed many assets, but showed limited "smart power" in dealing with each other. The words and deeds of each side risked becoming part of a self-fulfilling prophecy. Not even the United States would be safe if nuclear or cyber war shook the habitat and infrastructures on which life depends.

AGENTS AND STRUCTURES

Could American decline be explained by structures or individual agents? Many symptoms of decline emerged shortly after George W. Bush, along with Dick Cheney and other cronies, took executive power in 2001. Many analysts regarded the forty-third president as the worst in a century. Long the black sheep of his family and a recovering or recovered alcoholic, Bush had a history of wild bets and big losses in business, absorbed by rich benefactors. Many other members of Bush's cabinet and the Republican leadership in Congress conducted dubious financial arrangements that led to their resigning or being prosecuted for criminal actions (Morin and Clemens 2008).[2]

But this great (or bad) man argument ignores the role of structure. Nearly half the electorate voted for George W. not once but twice. Many voters continued to endorse Reagan and Bush policies in the Obama years. Some put "values" above their own material interests. Many did so because they got their "facts" and inspiration from right-wing talk shows and Fox News—virtual propaganda organs of certain moneyed interests. It was no accident that the most reactionary policies arose from the poorest and least educated states, also those with the highest rates of gun ownership and gun deaths.

The structure of public opinion, the power of Fox News, K Street lobbyists, and Republicans in Congress combined to block much of Obama's agenda. The president was a well-informed and energetic "agent," but was nearly paralyzed by other agents within the structures of American society. Even a Democratic majority in the Senate could do little to alter these dynamics. To secure cloture and have a chance at winning approval for any of his initiatives in the upper house, the president needed not a simple majority in the Senate but a supermajority. Sixty Senators had to agree before the upper house could even vote on a bill that some senators wanted to debate indefinitely. System failure and human failure combined to produce power outages in Washington and elsewhere.[3]

HUMAN CAPITAL AND SELF-ORGANIZATION

True fitness—wise use of hard and soft power to meet America's challenges— often seemed out of reach. Advances in science and technology could help address of the world's problems, but they are often Janus-faced, with a potential to destroy as well as construct. Globalization makes many challenges increasingly complex and resistant to facile remedies. American firms led the way in developing solar cells, but heavily subsidized Chinese firms then copied or adapted the technology to produce cells at cut-rate prices. Having blazed a trail only to lose market share, several U.S. firms collapsed in 2011. Hundreds of similar dilemmas dotted the horizon.

The United States survived and appeared to win the twentieth century's major hot wars and cold war. Whatever the country's mistakes, they were cushioned by a large margin for error. Yes, the United States might be able in the twenty-first century to fight anti-American forces in one or two small or medium-sized wars simultaneously. But what if it were challenged (as in World War II) by serious threats on many fronts? Yes, the country seemed to function better as it became more "wired," but what if hackers mangled the wiring or if a nuclear explosion over either coast or the Midwest knocked out electricity? Many vital industries resisted government pressures to raise their defenses against cyber and other attacks by state and nonstate actors.

To meet complex challenges requires deep and wide brain power. For the long term, it requires schools that generate world-class education—mastery of basic disciplines *and* a platform for unleashing great creativity. For the medium term, it means educating and reeducating an adult work force so that workers can learn, utilize, and improve on the latest technologies. For the near term, it demands leaders in politics, business, science, medicine, and other fields able and willing to make wise decisions and implement them.

Not only are useful solutions complex. They often involve great unknowns. Some observers placed great hope in technology, for example, classroom computers as a *deus ex machina* to save education. Ray Kurzweil (2005) expected the imminent unfolding of a great singularity as machines blended with bodies to produce improved and longer-lasting humans. However, the Pew Internet Project and Common Sense Media found in 2012 a widespread belief among teachers that pupils' constant use of digital technology was hampering their attention spans and ability to persevere in the face of challenging tasks. Some educators wanted to keep these tools from students until their late teens. If a few keystrokes did not produce an answer, some students gave up. They suffered also from a "Wikipedia problem"—an expectation that the Internet will quickly provide authoritative and adequate answers. Many teachers felt they had to be entertainers to hold students' dwindling attention (Richtel 2012).

There was also debate about careers. Not everyone will work in a laboratory or concert hall. How many young people should be trained to make the wheels spin on time? At what age should young people gear up for practical work? *Brave New World* projected a system that began in utero. Could a system be devised to meet public needs as well as individual aspirations and aptitudes?

Education is probably a necessary but insufficient condition for a healthy society. America's educational system, like most other social systems, had deep staying power but resisted fundamental change. Friedman and Mandelbaum (2011) surveyed the field and made a series of practical suggestions, for example, select, pay, train, and honor teachers as in Finland and some other countries. Identify and reward outstanding high school teachers, as Amherst College does each year, based on recommendations by its graduating seniors. But such changes would depend on altering an entire ethos and finding money when communities are loath to invest even in upkeep of bridges and roads. "Never mind teachers' salaries," some would say. "Let them be glad they still have jobs."

America's problems and difficulties are serious and generate many negative effects but need not be irreversible. They have not fundamentally affected the strength, competitive power, and development of the United States. Decline is not preordained but neither is an American renaissance. Many observers, both liberals and conservatives, home-grown and foreign, eschewed fatalism but questioned whether a dysfunctional political system and fraying culture could regain its fitness (Brzezinski 2012; D. Kagan 2012; Luce 2012b).

Howard Friedman worried that without major shifts in how Americans elect their officials, the United States "will increasingly move toward an aristocracy in which the majority of people have no say in their government's operations while the wealthy class purchases more and more . . . legislation" favorable to narrow privileged interests. To regain America's competitive edge, Friedman called for "competitive intelligence"—adapting best practices from world leaders. Putting this principle into practice, Friedman called for more progressive and less regressive taxation; raising the minimum wage; making corporate governance more transparent; raising teachers' salaries; and bolstering gender equality. Friedman recommended shifting the U.S. political system toward proportional representation to give women and minority interests more clout. To boost social equality, Friedman suggested birth grants or lump sum payments to every child at birth (Friedman, 2012, 219).

AN ACTION PROGRAM FROM THE HARVARD BUSINESS SCHOOL

Michael Porter and Jan Rivkin (2012) at the Harvard Business School proposed eight steps to improve the country's competitiveness: (1) Ease the immigration of highly skilled individuals so that the world 's best and brightest come and stay. (2) Simplify the corporate tax code to reduce rates but close loopholes. (3) Tax overseas profits only once—where they are earned—to encourage firms to bring their profits home. (4) Protect intellectual property and open access to foreign investment and services in China and other emerging markets. (5) Simplify and improve regulation of U.S. business—not to lower standards but to improve outcomes by cost-benefit analysis. (6) Enact a multiyear program with public-private partnerships to improve U.S. roads, ports, telecoms, and energy infrastructure. (7) Agree on a framework to develop new sources of gas and oil while protecting the environment. (8) Create a sustainable federal budget that includes revenue increases and spending reductions. Such measures could begin to transform the country in two or three years. Major reforms were also needed in education and health care, but would need more than three years to implement.

The Porter-Rivkin proposals appeared sound and could attract support from moderates among both Democrats and Republicans. But raising American fitness would require more than rewriting the tax laws. One reader observed that Porter and Rivkin failed to point out that "business leaders have responsibilities too which they have sorely neglected. The legal corruption and perversion of policy making and regulation that is fostered by lobbying financed and driven in large part . . . by businesses pursuing their own narrow interests is co-responsible for the dysfunctional state of U.S. politics, the flourishing of anti-competitive practices and the rejection of sensible regulations as well as the spreading disillusionment within our polity." Where are the business leaders of gigantic enterprises who could champion improved conditions for their employees, their employees' families, and their customers instead of focusing only on a narrow definition of shareholder value? "Compromise for the sake of the greatest good for the greatest number has become a dirty word in the world of business, like 'elite' in the language of talk radio." Business leaders too often blame their problems on others instead of striving to solve problems. "The disgraceful resistance to change of the titans in the financial sector is perhaps the most egregious and appalling example of private sector behavior and attitudes."

The proposals from the Harvard Business School amounted to tinkering with what Karl Marx termed the superstructure. Let us turn to Marx and two other voices from the mid-nineteenth century for broader perspectives.

THE *Communist Manifesto*

Karl Marx could say: I told you all this would happen. The plutocrats of the United States and other countries—Brazil, Russia, China, India, and much of

Europe—own a huge share of their countries' wealth. Naive idealists imagine that these riches were gained in a win-win effort that raised incomes for most people. But this was not the case in the late twentieth and early twenty-first centuries. Instead, huge fortunes were acquired at the expense of others—from the upper middle to the lowest income classes of their countries. The top 1 percent prospered because the remaining 99 percent did not.

Plutocracy means rule of the rich. The rich not only acquired material assets but used their wealth to perpetuate their dominant position by shaping politics, culture, religion, and even science. Plutocracy confirms the fundamentals of dialectical materialism. Economics is the base and everything else is superstructure—ideology, politics, law, and culture. The base consists of the means of production and production relations—who owns what and controls whom. In capitalist systems, private parties own the means of production. Striving for profit (surplus value), capitalists automate factories to reduce production costs, driving workers toward subsistence wages and, eventually, to revolution.

Why then, long after the *Communist Manifesto* and *Das Kapital,* is the capitalist world still capitalist and much of the former socialist world semi-capitalist? Marx would probably reply that capitalists found ways to delay revolution by paying their workers a living wage and providing a social welfare net. In part they paid for this by exploiting the resources and people of less developed countries. Still, the drive for surplus value does not relent. Factory owners in China as well as the United States export jobs to countries where labor costs are lower. They resist controls to curb environmental costs of their production. They employ lobbyists, lawyers, and accountants to minimize their tax burden. They pay the costs of elite education for their own children, helping to create dynastic plutocracies. They own or influence mass media to enforce a belief that the existing social order is just and the best of possible worlds. Even the Metropolitan Museum of Art honors a painter of tomato soup cans—implying that everyone in all classes enjoys this salty and low-cost commodity. Gone are the days when an artist such as George Bellows could reveal how drooling bourgeois brutes egged on proletarian boxers as they bloodied and maimed each other. American capitalists in the 1980s persuaded Congress to reduce regulation of the banking and other industries. Deregulation helped capitalists to act ever more like parasites—deriving more profits from financial activities than from manufacturing.

These trends cannot go on forever. Capitalists have perpetuated and broadened their realm in ways that I, back in 1848, could not imagine. Not only capitalists but ostensible communists have joined in this enterprise. They have enriched the few at the expense of the many by exploiting both human and material resources. The growing contradictions within the world system, however, will explode the system and produce a new and better way of life. Things will get worse before they get better.

A contemporary German analyst updated Marx. "Total capitalism," Jakob Augstein wrote (2012), "is America's true ruler, and it has the power to destroy the country." The functionaries of total capitalism "have no need of public hospitals or of a reliable power supply to private homes. The elite have their own infrastructure." But total capitalism "has left American society in ruins and crippled the government. America's fate is not just an accident produced by the system. It is a consequence of that system." The people and even the U.S. president are helpless in the face of power wielded by the military, the banks, and industry. "The checks and balances have failed. And a perverse mix of irresponsibility, greed and religious zealotry dominate public opinion." American citizens probably could not stop the country's decline "no matter how hard they tried. But they aren't even trying."

ISHMAEL ON COPING WITH COMPLEXITY

Dialectical materialism is deterministic. Most Americans prefer to believe in some version of individual free will. Who better to advise Americans on how to deal with complex challenges than Herman Melville's Ishmael? He was the sole survivor of a difficult quest across treacherous seas in quest of whales whose oil, like that now carried by tankers and pipelines, could light the homesteads and workplaces of Americans. The protagonist of *Moby Dick* ventured out on the *Pequod* more than 150 years ago. Melville tells us that Ishmael's voyage took place between what could be billed as "*Grand Contested Election for the Presidency of the United States*" and a "BLOODY BATTLE IN AFGHANISTAN." Here are six lessons Ishmael learned that may be useful to American and other denizens of the twenty-first century.

Lesson 1: Human Diversity and Merit

Ishmael learned to respect and appreciate human diversity—the very qualities that allow societies to explore and climb the highest peaks of complex and ever-changing fitness landscapes. With no room in the inn for sailors in New Bedford, Ishmael had to share a bed with another seaman. Learning that his prospective bedmate, Queequeg, had been a headhunter in the South Pacific, Ishmael fumed. He felt only disgust as the tattooed savage prayed before a wooden idol. Getting past surface differences, however, the two men quickly become fast friends. Ishmael discovered "how elastic our stiff prejudices grow when love once comes to bend them." At first he found Queequeg's pipe smoking in bed repugnant, but soon Ishmael liked nothing better than to have the savage smoking bedside him full of serene joy.

The "savage" proved a brave and generous soul. Twice he plunged into a stormy sea to save a shipmate—including one who had mocked him. Having rescued this bumpkin, Queequeg donned dry clothes, lighted his pipe-axe, and seemed to reflect: "It's a mutual, joint-stock world, in all meridians. We cannibals must help these Christians." For his part, Ishmael concluded: "We good Presbyterian Christians should be charitable . . . and not fancy ourselves so vastly superior to other mortals, pagans and what not, because of their half-crazy conceits. . . ."

When a ship owner demanded to know if Queequeg had converted, Ishmael asserted that that Queequeg was a "deacon of the First Congregational Church." Questioned on this matter, Ishmael explained that all humans belong to the "great and everlasting First Congregation of this whole worshipping world." Yes, some believers cherished "queer crotchets," but these did not touch "the grand belief; in that we all join hands." Persuaded, the otherwise dogmatic ship owner tightened the metaphor to all "*splice* hands."

Ishmael had assumed that Nantucketers were the best whale hunters in the world, but the *Pequod*'s owners selected its crew for their qualifications—not their origins or color. The three harpooners were all dark skinned: the cannibal Queequeg, a Gale Head Native American, and a six-foot five-inch black African, the tallest and one of the strongest men on board. Other crewmen came from Ireland, France, and India. The ship's elderly cook, a wise man with deep ironic humor, and child stowaway, Pip, were American-born blacks. Though Captain Ahab was a monomaniac, he virtually adopted Pip after the child twice fell overboard. Whatever their native ways and tongues, all the crew accepted the rigid discipline of ship life. All spoke to the captain and chief mates as "sir."

Lesson 2: How Sciences Can Jump Together

Ishmael shows us how to seek, unify, and utilize knowledge from every quarter. For Ishmael there was no rift between "two cultures," the literary and the scientific. Nor any gap between biology and art. He practiced what E. O. Wilson (1998) called "consilience"—letting every discipline "jump together" to fathom and make the most of our surroundings. Like many Americans, Ishmael interpreted many events through the lens of the Bible. But his insights gained from familiarity with the sacred texts and worldviews of other faiths. Steeped also in Greek and Roman mythology, Ishmael saw many parallels between travails on the *Pequod* and those of Odysseus and other ancient mariners.

By example, Ishmael advises us to read widely and deeply. To understand whales and whaling, he evaluates cetology reports in many languages. He compares species from Greenland to Japan. He studies artistic depictions of the whale from ancient Greece to the nineteenth century, but finds that most represent mere flights of fancy. Ishmael supplements and often challenges book learning by empirical testing. He dissects a whale and uses the tools of Euclid to analyze its anatomy. Even though Ishmael knows that whales suckle their young and are warm-blooded, however, he concludes that whales are "fish." Scientists in his time, as in ours, can err—especially when they become overconfident.

An evolutionist before Darwin's *Origin of the Species*, Ishmael studied whale fossils buried in layers of rock. From paleontology he inferred that whales had become larger and better adapted over time. He believed that God culled the "selectest champions" from the commons. An environmentalist before John Muir, Ishmael worried that that whale "fishers," like buffalo hunters on the great plains, were depleting their stock. Still, he noted that whales were congregating in larger groups for protection. So numerous and wily, he expected them to escape extinction. Like wishful thinkers today, Ishmael let hopes push aside reality.

Lesson 3: Fusing Theory and Practice

Literature and science, for Ishmael, should not be divorced from practical arts. He tells us how to splice a rope; forge a spear; boil blubber and store whale oil; fashion a wooden coffin; make and fit a prosthesis. Today he would review and test the "how-to" recommendations found in *Popular Mechanics*.

Lesson 4: Mysteries of the Heart

There are worlds within "objective" reality. Ishmael inquires into the human heart—why he and others risked their lives at sea. He saw the conflicts tearing the insides of first mate Starbuck and Captain Ahab—each having left a wife and children in Nantucket. Starbuck wished to end the mad chase for Moby Dick and return to the bosom of his family. He nearly persuaded Ahab to reverse course, but Ahab followed his own demons. Against his better judgment, Starbuck executed his captain's orders and helped bring on catastrophe.

Lesson 5: "Our Divine Equality"

Consilience includes ethics. Ishmael depicts not only the power and temper of the whale, but also its majesty and beauty. Unlike Ahab, Ishmael realizes that whale attacks on humans are usually a response to human aggression.

Ishmael observes how piety can cohabit with contradiction. One ship captain was a Quaker who would not bear arms against land invaders, but had himself "illimitably invaded the Atlantic and Pacific; and though a sworn foe to human bloodshed . . . spilled tuns upon tuns of leviathan gore." Another captain, also a pious Quaker, worried lest the pagan Queequeg lose his soul if he perished at sea. But this same captain had a "practical" bent and doled out "unmitigated hard work" so that, arriving home from a long voyage, most of his crew had to be carried to the hospital.

No matter the failings of individuals and misdeeds of corporations and nations, Ishmael believes that "man, in the ideal, is so noble and so sparkling" that all persons "should run to throw their costliest robes" over others' shortfalls—

just as God helped the convict John Bunyan, the paupered Cervantes, and the fallen Andrew Jackson. For each of us contains an "abounding dignity which has no robed investiture." It is a "democratic dignity which, on all hands, radiates without end from God; Himself! . . . The centre and circumference of all democracy! His omnipresence, our divine equality!"

Lesson 6: Empathy vs. Fanaticism

Ishmael talks to an America that perceives looming dangers on all fronts and yearns for radical remedies. Ishmael cautions all people to cultivate empathy and eschew black-and-white images. Like some Americans, Ahab ignores how he may have offended others and determines to take revenge on the monster that mutilated him. Single-minded, he abuses his own crew; disregards the economic stakes of the ship's owners; spurns intercourse with other ship captains except to learn if they have seen the white whale. Yes, he has a tender spot for little Pip and even for Starbuck, the only crewman who dares question his judgment. But Ahab is a fanatic. Ignoring every other consideration, Ahab seeks to destroy what he sees as Evil incarnate. In so doing he again wounds the great whale but destroys himself, his crew, and his ship. Only Ishmael survives, picked up by another whaling ship whose captain had asked Ahab for assistance after its own encounter with Moby Dick.

Who will save Americans—and humanity—if they go overboard?

AVOIDING THE LAST NEW MUMBO-JUMBO

Just as Henry David Thoreau was closing his experiment at Walden, Ralph Waldo Emerson in nearby Concord pondered the world. "Society," he wrote in 1847, "has at all times, the same want, namely, of one sane man with adequate powers of expression to hold up each object of monomania in its right relation." Writing as the United States seized northern Mexico, Emerson warned that "the ambitious and mercenary bring their last new mumbo-jumbo, whether tariff, Texas, railroad, Romanism, mesmerism, or California; and, by detaching the object from its relations, easily succeed in making it seen in a glare; and a multitude go mad about it." The opposite multitude, said Thoreau's mentor in Transcendentalism, are "are kept from this particular insanity by an equal frenzy on another crochet." Emerson hoped for one man with a "comprehensive eye" who could make illusions vanish and "return reason to the community."[4]

Emerson disdained the "practical" people who believe that "ideas are subversive of social order and comfort, and at last make a fool of the possessor." Like the grown-ups in Antoine de Saint-Exupéry's *The Little Prince* (1943), the practicals accept that "ordering a cargo of goods from New York to Smyrna; or, the running up and down to procure a company of subscribers to set a-going five or ten thousand spindles; or, the negotiations of a caucus, and the practising on the prejudices and facility of country-people, to secure their votes in November,—is practical and commendable."

Emerson believed that mankind had a deep stake in the illumination achieved by contemplative people. A life of action, he said, engenders costs. "Show me a man who has acted, and who has not been the victim and slave of his action. What they have done commits and enforces them to do the same again. The first act, which was to be an experiment, becomes a sacrament. The fiery reformer embodies his aspiration in some rite or covenant, and he and his friends cleave to the form and lose the aspiration." Actions of cunning, and stealing, efforts to ban reason and sentiment produce nothing but drawback and negation. "The measure of action is the sentiment from which it proceeds."

Quoting Talleyrand but again foreshadowing *The Little Prince,* Emerson advised that the way to judge a person is not to ask "Is he rich? Is he committed? Is he well-meaning? Has he this or that faculty? Is he of the movement? Is he of the establishment?" No, the question should be, "Is he anybody? Does he stand for something?" He must be "good of his kind"—real and admirable, not on the outside, but truly able.

What man can be honored "when he does not honor himself; when he loses himself in the crowd; when he is no longer the lawgiver, but the sycophant, ducking to the giddy opinion of a reckless public; when he must sustain with shameless advocacy some bad government, or must bark, all the year round, in opposition . . . ?"

Emerson saw the chaos of modern life: "There was never such a miscellany of facts. The world extends itself like American trade. We conceive Greek or Roman life,—life in the middle ages—to be a simple and comprehensive affair, but modern life to respect a multitude of things, which is distracting." We need people like Goethe, who saw how every fact and science weaves together.

Emerson worried too about self-righteous airs. He agreed with Goethe that "I have never heard of any crime which I might not have committed. "Conversing with Mephistopheles about Faust, Goethe's Lord is tolerant: "People will err," he says, "so long as they strive." The Lord ultimately forgave Faust his lapses because of his striving to build for humanity.

Emerson worried that many Americans show an unfounded respect for external shows of talent, "especially if it is exerted in support of any . . . interest or party." Instead, they should look to see "whether there be a man behind" what is said. Those who speak to the public are often the reflection of "some monied corporation, or some dangler, who hopes, in the mask and robes of his paragraph, to pass for somebody."

A truly worthy man exists—"not for what he can accomplish, but for what can be accomplished in him." His every word will be true and wake "nations to a new life." His every word will be carved "into the earth and sky; and the sun and stars were only letters of the same purport; and of no more necessity." He will "honor every truth by use."

Emerson would probably approve Google's informal slogan, "Don't be evil," but insist that the company and its leaders never compromise this standard.

Having endured a presidential election campaign in 2012 in which not only negative ads but outright lies, repeated over and over Goebbels-style, filled their TV screens and telephone receivers, many Americans hoped that their officials would do more to honor truth. The greatest asset for a country beset by many problems was that it continued to produce leaders whose personalities and accomplishments inspired the world—Rosalynn and Jimmy Carter, Melinda and Bill Gates, Michelle and Barack Obama, Hillary and Bill Clinton. Though the U.S. Congress had yet to respond, Al Gore and James Hansen sounded the alarm on climate change early and often Though racism continued to gnaw at America's innards, Martin Luther King Jr. and Lyndon Johnson had pushed public opinion to the point where members of minorities could become not only mayors and cabinet officers but even occupy the Oval Office. Ten of the world's great thinkers were based in Silicon Valley. Americans, some foreign-born, continued to win the lion's share of Nobel prizes. Daphne Koller, Andrew Ng, and Shai Reshef gave the world free access to world-class education; George Soros, a Hungarian-born, self-made billionaire and philanthropist, did more than any government to support movement toward a more open society in formerly communist countries. The United States did not spawn but it succored other champions of freedom and the rule of law such as Aung San Suu Kyi, Ai Weiwei, Chen Guangcheng, and Salman Rushdie.[5]

chapter nine

WHY IS SOUTH KOREA NOT NORTH KOREA?

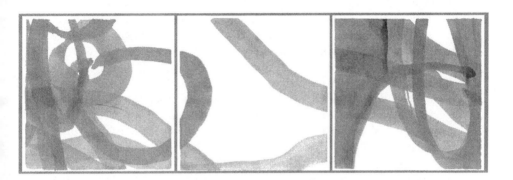

Until 1945, Koreans had long formed one of the most homogeneous societies on the planet. Partitioned at the thirty-eighth parallel in August 1945, the South and North became two different political systems and societies. In 1948, the South became a separate state, the Republic of Korea (ROK), as did the North, which called itself the Democratic People's Republic of Korea (DPRK). Following the Korean War (1950–53), the North industrialized much faster than the South. Starting in the 1970s, however, the ROK evolved into a near model of societal fitness while the DPRK remained a rogue state, dangerous to its own people and the world. While the *Gangnam Style* Psy led the world's popular hit parade and pranced for ROK voters in 2012, the North's soft power consisted in mass demonstrations to honor its dead demigods. Can complexity science shed light on this divergence?

CONTRASTS IN HUMAN DEVELOPMENT

By 2013, the Republic of Korea ranked twelfth of 186 countries on the UN Human Development Index (HDI) (up from twenty-sixth in 2007 and fifteenth in 2011). Norway was at the top in 2013, with the Democratic Republic of Congo and Niger at the bottom. The United States placed third; Japan, tenth; and Hong Kong, thirteenth. The ROK ranked well ahead of Singapore, eighteenth; Russia, fifty-fifth; China, 101st; and Mongolia, 108th. Given the lack of reliable data, the HDI did not rank North Korea. Its meager GDP and poor health would push the DPRK toward the bottom, though its extensive school enrollment would raise it somewhat. The UN Development Programme offered no data on the DPRK except to note that, in 2011, life expectancy at birth in the North was 68.8, much lower than 80.6 in the South.[1]

In 2013 South Korea's life expectancy at birth was 80.7; its mean years of schooling, 11.6, and expected years of schooling, 17.2; gross national income per capita, $28,231. If income were omitted (thus giving more weight to health and education), the country's HDI score increased from 0.909 to 0.949.

South Korea's rank on gender equality was twenty-seventh from the top (where The Netherlands was number one). Japan ranked higher (better) at twenty-first, while the United States ranked much lower—forty-second. The major difference was in maternal mortality: In the ROK there were sixteen deaths of mothers per one hundred thousand live births compared with twenty-one in the United States. On the other hand, income inequality in the ROK was greater even than in the United States. South Korea placed twenty-eighth from the best score on the inequality-adjusted HDI in 2011, while the United States placed twenty-third.

Human development numbers for South Korea rose rapidly in the late twentieth century. The absolute score for South Korea in 1980 was 0.634— far below the OECD average then of 0.749.[2] The ROK narrowed the gap with the OECD in 1990 and 2000 and went on to score higher than the OECD in 2005—0.866 versus 0.860. By 2011, the gap was still larger— ROK, 0.897, versus OECD, 0.873. Like other advanced industrial countries, the ROK advanced more slowly in the early twenty-first century. The UN Development Programme offered no data on the DPRK except to note that, in 2011, life expectancy at birth in the North was 68.8 years—much lower than the 80.6 in the South.[3]

The World Economic Forum ranked South Korea the nineteenth most competitive of 144 countries in 2012–13—behind Switzerland, ranked first; Singapore, second; the United States, seventh; Hong Kong, ninth; Japan, tenth; and Taiwan, thirteenth. On the other hand, the ROK ranked well ahead of three neighbors: China (twenty-ninth), Russia (sixty-seventh) and Mongolia (ninety-third). North Korea was not listed.[4]

The Bertelsmann Foundation Transformation Index gives a still broader set of measures. Political and economic developments (or lack thereof) put North Korea at 125th of 128 countries, with Somalia at the bottom. South Korea ranks eleventh on his list, behind the Czech Republic (first) and Taiwan (second), but ahead of Singapore (twenty-ninth), Russia (sixtieth), and China (eighty-fourth). The BTI gives South Korea a higher rank for economic development (seventh) than for political (twelfth). The measures employed are summed up in Figure 9.1.[5] As the graph makes clear, the web of fitness in the South reaches wide, while the North appears strong only in "stateness," but even this asset could prove shallow and feeble.

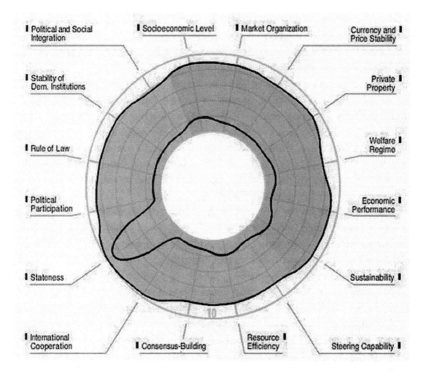

FIGURE 9.1. South Korea compared with North Korea, BTI 2012.

HOW TO ACHIEVE FITNESS: THE ROLE OF SELF-ORGANIZATION

As we saw in earlier chapters, complexity science notes three ways to promote and maintain fitness. First, natural *selection*. Small-scale genetic mutations and recombinations help some individuals and, in time, larger groupings to adapt, survive, and multiply in their ever-changing environment. Some players coalesce for shared purposes, for example, the tendency of states worried about the rise of China and North Korea's nuclear tests (the first in 2006) to gravitate toward Washington.

Second, *historical contingency*. The life cycle of political and other systems is often characterized by a long period of punctuated equilibrium terminated by a rapid decline or upsurge.

Third, *self-organization*—a capacity by members of a group to cooperate for shared goals without top-down commands. Self-organization can emerge without natural selection or climactic historical events.

Self-organization often gives rise to power laws in social systems, because of "preferential attachment"—the principle that in a network, a node with more connections is likely to attract more connections in the future. This explains why the rich get richer, and also how Psy's *Gangnam Style* music and dance could spread quickly from South Korea to diverse settings and applications across the globe in 2012–13.

Self-organization does not exist in a pure form anywhere in the world except perhaps among tribal groups in remote jungles or mountains. Still, some modern societies practice self-organization in many domains while others experience totalitarian dictatorship. Conforming to the expectations of complexity science, the DPRK is unfit because its top-down system stifles creativity, enterprise, cooperation, and even hard work. Freedom House ranks the DPRK as one of the least free societies in the world while the ROK places among the free (rated 1 for political rights and 2 for civil liberties).

Still, the high fitness achieved in the South appears at first glance to have arisen without much self-organization. The society's political and economic development took place under strong authoritarian rule from 1945 until the early 1980s. The South's GDP began its rapid advance under Park Chung Hee's dictatorship, which began with a military coup in 1961 and ended with his assassination in 1979 (Kim and Vogel 2011). Looking beneath the surface, however, we find that seeds of self-organization in South Korea began with land reforms launched by U.S. military authorities in 1948 and continued by President Syngman Rhee even during the Korean War. These reforms, like those in Japan and Taiwan, helped South Korea begin its transition from a limited access to an open access society in the political as well as the economic sphere. The reforms reduced disparities in wealth and generated private funds for educating a new generation of civil servants and entrepreneurs. They enabled a democratic student revolution in 1960 that demanded an end to corruption and to the Rhee presidency (You 2013).

Threats from the North and competition with the DPRK helped to limit extreme forms of rent seeking and corruption in the South. Land reform opened access to economic opportunities and facilitated a state monopoly of violence critical to later economic and political development. It also contributed to expanding education and establishing meritocratic and autonomous bureaucracy.[6]

In short, the "developmental state" of Park Chung Hee benefited from preexisting trends. Even under his dictatorship, self-organization emerged at a grassroots level. In the 1960s, the Planned Parenthood Federation of Korea began to organize "Mothers' Clubs" to promote family planning and community development. Following trends in civil society, the ROK government in the 1970s launched the New Village Movement to mobilize human and material resources. The relatively open access economy not only brought about rapid and sustained economic growth but also created increasing pressures for a more open politics that led, over time, to the democratic transition of 1987. Laws passed in the mid-1990s required that the government not lay the first brick on a new construction project without consulting everyone affected. Responding to popular protests in the 1990s, the Ministry of Construction and President Kim Young Sam cancelled a proposed dam at Youngwol. By the late 1990s and early twenty-first century, labor unions became more powerful and women's' rights achieved greater respect. (Clemens 2010b, 32–35, 224–25). The 1997 financial crisis was a critical point at which Korea could have reverted back to a limited access order. But the ROK weathered the 1997 storm and went on to become an open access society where democratic rule became the stable and accepted norm.

Still, family-owned business conglomerates—*chaebols* (a term that combines the words for "wealth" and for "clan") remained the key actors in South Korea's economic life, exerting great influence over politics. The Samsung Group in 2007 had revenues comparable to Malaysia's GDP; Hyundai, to New Zealand's. For South Korea, as for all the Asian "dragons" and "tigers," the term *self-organization* must be understood as the collaboration of private-sector elites with government officials and agencies to advance their own personal and institutional interests and those of the country. The model for such collaboration was set by the lower and middle ranking samurais who installed the Meiji emperor as the figurehead for Japanese unity in 1866. Theirs was more than a palace coup, for the agents of change in Japan pushed through educational reforms that quickly achieved universal literacy and military reforms that included universal conscription. A dynamic system of economic collaboration emerged, the *keiretsu,* a set of companies with interlocking business relationships and shareholdings. The member firms owned shares in each other's companies, centered on a core bank, thus insulating each entity from stock market fluctuations and takeover attempts, thereby enabling long-term planning in innovative projects. The U.S. occupation authorities decided in 1945–46 to abolish these networks but soon opted to revive them to make Japan a strong partner against communism. American-sponsored land reforms also helped integrate Japanese farmers in the body politic.

Arrangements similar to the *keiretsu* emerged in Singapore, Taiwan, South Korea, and—with deep differences, in Communist China after 1979. While South Korea's *chaebols* were modeled after Japanese groups, the Park Chung Hee regime gave the ROK's conglomerates more direct funding and controlled them more tightly than happened in Japan.[7] Conglomerates in Japan and South Korea evolved into publicly owned companies, but the founding families of Samsung and Hyundai probably exerted more control over these businesses in the early twenty-first century than did their Japanese counterparts. Although export-led industrialization helped to increase open access and competition in the ROK economy, collusion between government and the *chaebols* set limits to access and to competition.

Still, the differences between the ROK (and Japanese) systems and North Korean practice ran wide and deep. The DPRK system remained similar to that of the Stalinist USSR—all productive enterprises owned and controlled by the state and run by government employees. The government sometimes tolerated limited private trading and black market activities, but the political elite kept control of the overall economy and most other aspects of life.

Partnerships between economic and political elites generate risks as well as advantages. They can inhibit as well as stimulate innovation. And if one hand washes the other, one hand may also dirty the other. Some leaders of the largest South Korean *chaebol*, Hyundai, welcomed ROK president Kim Dae Jung's effort to meet DPRK leader Kim Jung Il in 2000. Pragmatic interests as well as ideals motivated Hyundai officials, for they hoped that better ties with Pyongyang might help Hyundai to employ North Korean workers at comparatively low wagers. Kim Dae Jung received the Nobel peace prize in 2000 for his "sunshine policy," but a major scandal soon erupted. Investigations revealed that the Hyundai Asan Corporation had given half a million dollars to the North just before the summit, an act that many South Koreans saw as a bribe. Responding to the scandal, the head of Hyundai Asan, the fifth son of Hyundai founder Chung Ju-yung, committed suicide in 2003. At the request of the ROK National Assembly, an independent counsel was established to investigate the alleged pay-off. Kim Dae-jung's chief of staff, Park Jie-won, who served as culture minister in 2000, was found to have taken 12.6 million dollars from Hyundai in April 2000. But after the first seventy-day stage of the investigation, ROK president Roh Moo-hyun rejected a request by the independent counsel to prolong the probe to uncover still other facts. In 2009, however, Roh Moo-hyun, by then retired, also committed suicide after he as well as his associates and family members were themselves accused of seeking and taking bribes.

While South Korea ranks very high on most measures of human development, its rating for honesty is low. The Corruption Perceptions Index of Transparency International in 2012 ranked South Korea as the forty-fifth least honest country in the world; To be sure, North Korea ranked much lower—near the bottom—at 174th. Japan placed seventeenth, the United States nineteenth, China eightieth, and Russia, 133rd. The ROK did better on some measures of transparency. On financial secrecy, for example, it ranked twenty-eighth, much higher than on corruption and bribery.[8]

More revelations of corruption appeared in 2012. The elder brother of sitting president Lee Myung-bak was arrested in July, accused of accepting more than a half-million dollars in bribes to help two banks avoid a government audit. Lee Sang-deuk had earlier served six terms as a parliamentarian and had been vice speaker of the National Assembly. He had enjoyed an unofficial role as "kingmaker" and "great problem solver." Prosecutors said the bankers had paid Mr. Lee to stop government regulators from shutting their savings banks down for lax oversight and capital shortages. The bankers themselves were charged with embezzlement and bribery, and their banks' operations suspended. Responding to the scandal, Kim Geo-sung, chairperson of Transparency International Korea, stated that "the country needs to develop more effective ethics and anti-corruption awareness education programs and build a culture in which citizens naturally feel a sense of social responsibility."

The revelations undercut any influence the sitting president might have had in nominating his successor. The woman whom Lee Myuyng-bak defeated when contending for the party's nomination in 2007, Park Geun-hye, won its backing in 2012 and went on to win the presidency in the December election. Her biggest problem, said a *Korea Times* commentator, did not arise from the economy or foreign affairs. Her worst enemy was widespread skepticism that she would serve the people—not the elites. Park's predecessor, Lee Myung-bak, achieved a great deal but he ignored advice from his own experts and scoffed at signs that his associates were corrupt. Before him, the late president Roh Moo-hyun called his administration a "participatory government" but failed to broaden a support base for his initiatives. The *Korea Times* commentator declared: "We don't need a leader we can call a father or mother. That time is gone. We need a peer as leader. We don't need our new president to be an updated version of Park Chung Hee, who had led our 'Miracle on the Han River.' "Instead, Koreans wanted a partnership with their president in which "we are equal stakeholders in national prosperity" (Oh 2013). Fair or not, such views showed that some thoughtful persons believed that "self-organization" was still weak in South Korea. Countering this trend, however, bombastic rhetoric and threats from the North in Spring 2013 pushed South Koreans to unite.

DO THE THEORIES OF PUNCTUATED EQUILIBRIUM AND CRITICALITY APPLY TO KOREA?

Both North and South were devastated by the war that raged in 1950–53. Starting slowly from a low base, the South's fitness began a rapid ascent in the 1970s and 1980s. This trend continued in the 1990s and early twenty-first century, though with some reversals and at a slower pace. Complexity science allows that the South's trajectory could persist for some time, but predicts that at some point it will either rise sharply or fall.

Complexity science cannot forecast when South Korea will reach the critical threshold that triggers a shift up or down. While mindful of many enabling factors ("adjacent possibles") that open avenues to further change, the science cannot predict whether human agency and *fortuna* will push fitness levels in any society into reverse or forward gear.

How does complexity science appraise North Korea's prospects? Clearing away the ruins caused by U.S. bombings, Kim Il Sung's regime in the mid-1950s found remnants of an industrial infrastructure established earlier by Japan in northern Korea, close to the country's mineral riches. Building on this base, comparatively weak in the South, the DPRK economy grew faster than the ROK in the late 1950s and 1960s. But then the North's development plateaued—stagnated—from the 1970s into the early twenty-first century. Despite the regime's devotion to *juche,* the North remained highly dependent on Russia and China for inputs of industrial know-how and machinery, oil, and food. Self-reliance in the North achieved little except where the regime prioritized its drives for nuclear weapon and missile development. Meanwhile, both Moscow and Beijing kept Pyongyang on a short leash. Limited fuel supplies meant that North Korean pilots could train very few hours—a mere twenty per year—in flight relative to those in neighboring countries.[9] Limited fuel supplies make it harder for a would-be defector to reach South Korea or Russia and more perilous, because ejection seats were disabled in peacetime. Still, the North appeared to maintain a fleet of Ukrainian-made "Colt" aircraft to ferry two regiments of sniper brigades to attack rear areas in the South. During Pyongyang's verbal fusillades in Spring 2013, one of its few shows of strength included the descent of five parachutists from an ancient Soviet helicopter onto DPRK turf close to the Yalu River.

Will the North's decade-long fitness plateau continue indefinitely? Complexity science says "no," but it cannot predict when a sharp change will occur or it what direction. The replacement of an ill, rather dour demigod by his much younger and more animated son in 2011–12 encouraged hopes that the new leader would give greater emphasis to raising living standards in the North and cultivate a more cheerful, if not more liberal, atmosphere. Whatever his stage appearances, however, the deeds of Kim Jong Un in 2012–13 pointed to a tightening of political controls at home and a ratcheting up of hostile rhetoric toward the ROK and the United States.

Kim Jong Un might manage to continue the fitness plateau realized under his father and grandfather, but his stand-pat policies did not promise an upward shift in DPRK fitness. At best they could help the regime hold onto power and compel its subjects to keep their shoulders to the wheel and avoid outward displays of discontent. In the second decade of the twenty-first century the North might well repeat portions of the Soviet experience in the 1970s and 1980s—growing military power accompanied by persistent economic and social stagnation, mere lip service to ideology, frequent reliance on food imports, and haphazard efforts to buy, copy, and steal foreign technology. A would-be savior of the Soviet system, Mikhail Gorbachev, appeared in 1985, but his reforms proved too little and too late. The Russian state remained in the 1990s, but the putative superpower had disappeared and lost more than half its former citizens and all its foreign subjects.

As in the former Soviet Union, any serious reforms in the DPRK must face the danger of rising expectations. This peril rises as information about the outside world penetrates Kim Jong Un's hermit kingdom. His regime sought to avoid a Ceaușescu or Gorbachev denouement, but it confronted a dilemma: Development requires being wired—not only at home but worldwide. Opening to the world, however, imperils regime and state security. Authorities try to tighten censorship but find it difficult to do so effectively. Tight controls can kill the golden goose of global networking while porous dikes let in waves of information that challenge the regime's raison d'être. Some DPRK reformers might argue that China's opening to the world did not dethrone the Communist Party. More cautious voices could reply, "Not yet, but just wait." The fact is that China's opening was gradual and closely monitored, but sooner or later could still jeopardize top-down rule. Having waited so long to liberalize, North Korea might find it hard to open up without destabilizing the regime.

FITNESS LANDSCAPES

Complexity theory accepts that societal fitness can be measured by absolute and relative standards. South Korea's fitness has increased for decades. The United Nations has few reliable statistics about human development in the DPRK, but we can be sure that the North's absolute scores have improved very little, if at all, and that its rank relative to South Korea, Japan, and China has declined. Its rank relative to Russia and Mongolia, however, may have experienced little change, for their HDI scores have plateaued or declined in recent years.

The fitness landscape of East Asia shows a series of peaks rising while that of the DPRK declines in absolute and relative terms. The North's leaders plod along in a sort of Death Valley. They would like to raise their peak but they value regime security over public weal. Their situation resembles that of East Germany as well as the USSR in the 1980s but with some important differences. The case of the German Democratic Republic is especially salient, because its lack of fitness contrasted sharply with the high fitness achieved by its West German neighbor, which was not only much larger but far more affluent and free. As North Koreans learn more about conditions in South Korea (as well as in China), pent-up pressures for change can only mount. Without a real parliament, elected by popular vote, however, the DPRK cannot readily implement the East German model, because the GDR parliament, chosen in a free election in 1990, voted to end the East German state and join a unified Germany (Clemens 2010b, 247, n. 15). From this perspective, a gradual change in North Korea and peaceful union with the South appear less likely than a convulsive end of the road for the system and its ruling dynasty. The critical grain of sand or "last straw" can come from many directions. Several may emerge at the same time—multiplying their corrosive effect.

INTERDEPENDENCE

Complexity science sees all living things as interdependent. The South accepts the reality of global interdependence and has managed to join—not stand apart from or castigate—global networks of trade, cooperation, and security. The export-led growth strategy exposed the South Korean firms to global competition, which limited the importance of collusive rent seeking and promoted learning and innovation. A South Korean diplomat, Ban Ki-moon, became UN secretary-general in 2007 and was elected for a second term in 2011. Fifty-three heads of state attended a nuclear summit conference held in Seoul in 2012.

The South benefits from global networks but also contributes to what amounts to a system of value creation for mutual gain. The North, in contrast to the South, has been a hermit kingdom. Often scorned and denigrated by its sometime patrons in Moscow and Beijing, Pyongyang has gone its own way, even developing nuclear weapons and long-range rockets. Making a virtue of necessity, it has developed these military technologies with little outside assistance, indeed, over the objections of Moscow and Beijing. A vicious cycle has formed as the DPRK tests weapons of mass destruction that elicit widespread condemnation, even by Beijing, and tighter sanctions, usually ignored by China. The more that the DPRK does its own thing, the greater its isolation. Unlike its erstwhile client, Myanmar, which decided that its growing isolation was a bad thing, Pyongyang has shown little sign that it wishes to join the family of nations. Even when its own harvests are poor and people are starving, Pyongyang has treated foreign food aid as an inconvenience and relief workers as scum. The strongest indication that the North valued some integration with the outside world came in the George W. Bush era when Pyongyang demanded the return of financial reserves frozen in a Macao bank as the price for proceeding with the arms accord agreed to on September 19, 2005.

POLICY IMPLICATIONS

HOW TO INCREASE FITNESS

The single best indicator of societal fitness is HDI rank. To improve human development, societies and governments must broaden and deepen education opportunities; bolster individual and public health; and raise incomes. The ROK has made significant progress on the first two goals but income inequality remains a major challenge—aggravated by worries that any redistribution of wealth will reduce economic dynamism. The DPRK provides many years of public education but vitiates its quality by extensive thought control and by permitting class origin to influence educational opportunities. Poor public health is tied to low incomes for most North Koreans. Only a sliver of DPRK society enjoys a comfortable standard of living and the health quality it affords.

There is no quick remedy for these problems. Radical if not revolutionary changes are needed.

As noted in previous chapters, most of the societies that rank in the top twenty places on the HDI share in three cultural revolutions that commenced in Central Europe five to six hundred years ago: demands for mass literacy, free thought, and respect for individual dignity. Western Christian influences did not impact Korea until the late nineteenth century, but some sixty or seventy years before Luther's challenge to Rome, the Chosun King Sejong the Great called on scholars to produce an alphabet that all Koreans could read. A decade before Gutenberg's press published its first Bible (not in the vernacular, but in Latin), Korean scholars in 1443–44 produced what became known as the *hangŭl* alphabet. Their project was described in a document entitled "The Proper Sounds for the Education of the People." Still, some scholars and some later kings preferred to keep the masses in the dark.[10] Thanks in part to pressures by Protestant missions, however, *hangŭl* became the standard script used in schools in the late nineteenth and early twentieth centuries. Church schools and other private schools for wealthy Koreans were established in the years just before the Japanese takeover.

Parts of the Bible were published in Korean in 1882; the New Testament in 1887; the entire Bible in 1911. Here are the first verses from the gospel according to St. John ("In the beginning was the Word . . ." as published by the Korean Bible Society in 1993:

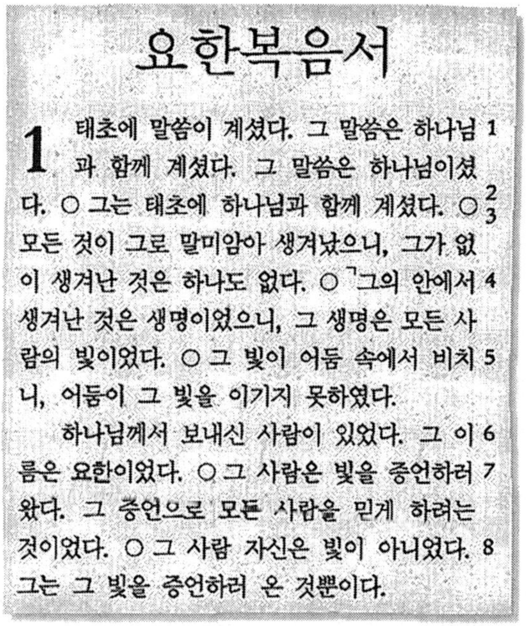

요한복음서

1 태초에 말씀이 계셨다. 그 말씀은 하나님 1 과 함께 계셨다. 그 말씀은 하나님이셨 다. ○ 그는 태초에 하나님과 함께 계셨다. ○ $^2_3$ 모든 것이 그로 말미암아 생겨났으니, 그가 없 이 생겨난 것은 하나도 없다. ○ 그의 안에서 4 생겨난 것은 생명이었으니, 그 생명은 모든 사 람의 빛이었다. ○ 그 빛이 어둠 속에서 비치 5 니, 어둠이 그 빛을 이기지 못하였다.

하나님께서 보내신 사람이 있었다. 그 이 6 름은 요한이었다. ○ 그 사람은 빛을 증언하러 7 왔다. 그 증언으로 모든 사람을 믿게 하려는 것이었다. ○ 그 사람 자신은 빛이 아니었다. 8 그는 그 빛을 증언하러 온 것뿐이다.

FIGURE 9.2. "In the beginning was the Word . . ."—in *Hangŭl*.

Somewhat later and more slowly than in Japan, literacy spread in Korea in the twentieth century. Free thought and free expression, however, were circumscribed by authorities. Japanese occupiers declared their language the official tongue and suppressed any signs of resistance. Anti-Japanese Koreans based outside the country could use Korean but they too had to observe the political correctness of their political faction. Opportunities for free thought and expression increased in the South after 1945, but U.S. and Korean authorities labored to curb political dissent. Confucian respect for seniority also played a role.[11] Not till the 1980s did free thought begin to flourish in South Korea. In the North, however, party-line orthodoxy ruled from 1945 into the twenty-first century. Yes, some innovations appeared under Kim Jong Un. The new leader seemed to approve of Mickey Mouse, but if his whims changed, even Mickey could be taboo. A domestic Intranet was accessible for some North Koreans, but the Internet was off limits except for a narrow elite.

Respect for individual dignity remained a challenge for South Korea in the twenty-first century. Even with a female president inaugurated in 2013, discrimination against women remained a fact of life. In the North, however, there was little if any respect for any form of human rights. The powerful did what they could and others what they must, with discipline and terror sustained by networks of informers and gulags. Corruption—much worse in the North than in the South—helped a few elites retain a comfortable life style while most people suffered and many hungered.

CAN OUTSIDERS HELP?

Assistance from outsiders can encourage positive behaviors but can also be abused. South Koreans made good use of U.S. assistance for many years after the Korean War. Outsiders cannot judge how effectively North Koreans utilized aid from Russia and China. More than sixty years after the 1953 Armistice, however, the DPRK still needed foreign assistance to meet its basic energy and food requirements. Mocking the principle of *juche,* Pyongyang relied on outside aid as a crutch, one that permitted the regime to plow precious resources into a large army and weapons development.

In the second decade of the second millennium, insecurities plagued Koreans on both sides of the DMZ. Many in the South felt anguish about economic security and worried about the North's tough talk and its tools of mass destruction. Leaders and publics in the North expressed (or feigned) anxiety about an attack by the United States and/or the ROK. They saw China as a rapacious or fair-weather friend. All the players in Northeast Asia shared a security dilemma: Fearing one another, they took ostensibly defensive steps that made each other feel less secure. The burden of defense was heavy but manageable for the United States and ROK; for the DPRK, however, it devoured resources desperately needed for the civilian economy, public health, and education. Beyond these burdens, the North's drive for a nuclear deterrent deepened its isolation.

Complexity science, like the worldviews of Buddhism and other philosophies, holds that all living things are mutually vulnerable and dependent. They are linked so closely that they can hurt—or help—one another. They can choose to go it alone, claiming and seizing whatever values they can. Or they can opt to create values for mutual gain. To be sure, no major actor has a clean record. North Korea has reason to distrust and dislike all its interlocutors in the erstwhile six-party talks. But the North failed to examine deeply the prospects for overcoming distrust. It rebuffed offers of a grand bargain by U.S. and South Korean authorities and scorned condemnations by the UN Security Council. Kim Jong Un in 2012–13 kept the North on a dead-end road to increased isolation. Refusing to talk, to explore possible compromises, and reneging on apparent accords, Pyongyang backed itself into a corner in which its tiny stock of advanced weapons offered a poor platform for meeting the challenges of twenty-first century complexity.

chapter ten

TOWARD A NEW PARADIGM FOR GLOBAL STUDIES

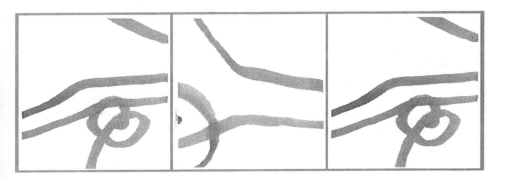

To avoid entrapment in the narrow choices posed by realist and idealist paradigms, analysts of international relations can fruitfully apply the basic concepts of complexity science to analyze the properties and patterns (if any) of global interdependence. To illustrate the value of these concepts to international studies, this chapter applies them to fourteen of the major challenges facing global political analysis, comparing their explanatory power with the insights generated by other approaches. The review suggests that, at a minimum, complexity science merits a place alongside the other paradigms used to study world affairs.

New scientific paradigms, once they have been widely accepted, do not necessarily weaken or disconfirm old scientific truths; but they often rearrange the configuration of truths in new and unanticipated ways. After Einstein and after quantum mechanics, we acknowledge the spheres where Isaac Newton's laws of mechanics obtain as well as the spheres where other laws take over" (Gardner 2011, 35). If complexity science becomes an accepted approach to world politics, there will still be a place for Hobbesian realism and Kantian-Wilsonian idealism. There will also be times and places where the insights of Karl Marx or J. Ann Tickner or Alexander Wendt provide the most useful path to understanding.

SALIENT PROBLEMS IN GLOBAL POLITICS:
INSIGHTS FROM COMPLEXITY SCIENCE

ISSUE I. FROM DESPOTISM TO CHAOS

The National Intelligence Council (2012) cautioned that at least fifteen countries were "at high risk of state failure" by 2030. Afghanistan and Pakistan were high on the list, with Burundi, Rwanda, Somalia, Uganda, and Yemen also in danger.

To adopt the language of complexity theory, all these countries lacked effective self-organization. Neither rigid hierarchy nor anarchy is conducive to fitness. Despotism often erupts into chaos while weak or no government elicits an iron fist. Without a strong political authority, Hobbes argued, there is war of all against all. Life is nasty, brutish, and short. To escape from this "state of nature," frightened but rational people submit to the authority of an all-powerful sovereign. Even then, however, Hobbes left the door open to anarchy, because no one could be expected to obey the sovereign if doing so endangered his or her own life. Whatever happened *within* the body politic, Hobbes posited that anarchy would remain *among* states, because no supranational Leviathan ruled over individual sovereigns.

Updating Hobbes, some realists have argued that less-developed societies need strong, authoritarian leadership to maintain stability. They have added that preaching democracy is futile where top-down rule accords with local values. Besides, despots may be useful to America if they sell oil at reasonable prices or permit U.S. forces on their soil.

The authoritarian prescription has proved shortsighted. Many of the despotic regimes long embraced by Washington have collapsed or are collapsing—generating enormous problems for their own peoples and for the United States. And when tyrants are overthrown, as in Somalia, the result is often a failed state—a danger to its own people and to outsiders. Decades of military dictatorship in Myanmar helped turn one of Asia's most bountiful countries into one of the poorest.

Unlike classical realists, structural realists do not concern themselves with top-down or bottom-up rule because domestic conditions are irrelevant to world politics, a sphere where, they believe, raw power settles everything. Structuralists ignore the roles of key individuals and the cultures that spawn and embrace them. Experience shows, however, that authoritarian dictators (for example, Hitler, Stalin, Pol Pot, Mao Zedong, Slobodan Milošević) and their regimes are lethal. Dictatorships started and lost most of the major wars of the twentieth century. Dictators killed more of their own people than perished in the century's major wars (Rummel 1996).

Many idealists do worry about despotisms and underdevelopment but often lack the means to achieve their ends. West European governments agonized about bloodletting in the former Yugoslavia but lacked the will and resources needed to stabilize the region. Only when the Clinton administration in 1995 decided to act—backing forceful diplomacy with military force—did the fighting halt (Holbrooke 1998). Later, in 2011, France and Great Britain deployed planes and other resources to help rebels overthrow Libya's dictator. Short on matériel and reconnaissance, however, they needed substantial American support.

Some forms of idealism such as Aryan supremacy and Islamic fundamentalism endorse top-down rule provided it conforms to their ideology.[1] Other idealisms such as environmentalism and feminism share no agreed framework for analyzing or coping with political malaise. Focusing on one issue, they often lack the broad programs and material resources needed to cope with complex challenges.

To overcome anarchy in world affairs, neo-Kantian liberals call for more democracy and a larger role for international law and organization. Many neoconservatives also espouse democracy but distrust or even disdain international law. Some idealists believe that outsiders need only replace dictatorships and impose the proper constitution and—eureka!—peace and progress will emerge. Some realists instead trust in the decisive use of hard power. The naïveté of both orientations was underscored by the difficulties experienced by the George W. Bush and Barack Obama administrations in their efforts at nation building in Iraq and in Afghanistan.

The origins of failed states and of terrorist movements are complex and poorly understood (Dorff 2005). But it seems clear that stability and fitness reinforce each other. Most of the countries ranked high on the HDI have also been among the most stable. Switzerland is the world's oldest democracy while the United States uses the world's oldest extant written constitution. Each country enjoys high living standards and boasts one of the world's most competitive economies. Still, democratic constitutions do not guarantee democracy or stability—witness the "crisis of classic modernity" that helped collapse the Weimar Republic (Peukert 1992).

Addressing what complexity science regards as fitness, Samuel P. Huntington in the 1960s argued that the crucial distinction between a politically developed society and an underdeveloped one is the number, size, and effectiveness of its organizations. If social change weakens the traditional bases of association, the achievement of a high level of political development depends on the capacity of the people to develop new forms of associations. Where civil society and organization are weak, politics is often confused and chaotic (Huntington 1968, 31). Thus, Egyptians came together in 2011 to overthrow a despot, but lacked broad institutions to provide for real self-organization. Only two powerful organizations remained—the military and its nemesis, the Muslim Brotherhood—banned for decades but possessing more organizational strength than any other civic group. Analogous problems challenge the entire Arab Spring.

Modernity often fosters stability over time, but the processes of modernization can generate instability. Social and economic change challenge the existing bases of community. So, as social forces multiply, political institutions must become more complex and variegated. Urbanization, literacy, education, and media exposure often enhance aspirations and expectations that, if unmet, galvanize individuals and groups to take political action. Without strong and adaptable political institutions, efforts to modernize a less-developed country can lead to violence and the destruction of the well-being sought by modernizers (Huntington 1968, 39–47).

ISSUE 2. HEGEMONIC WAR OR MUTUAL GAIN?

Focused on the structures of power, neorealists assume that the sole superpower will bully other actors—compelling them to bandwagon with or partner against it. Neorealists predict hegemonic war. Sooner or later, they expect, China and the United States will face off in a struggle for hegemony. This diagnosis fits some trends in the first years of the twenty-first century. In 2012, for example, the Obama administration opted to "pivot" from Iraq and Afghanistan to contain a rising China. But structural realism cannot explain why the same U.S. superpower, with even greater relative power in the 1990s, seldom acted unilaterally.[2] When the administrations of George H. W. Bush or Bill Clinton intervened on distant shores, they did so only after mobilizing large coalitions of UN or NATO members to follow America's lead. The son of George H. W. Bush, when he became the forty-third president, commanding the same relative power, leaned toward unilateral action. The contrasts in the policies pursued by the elder and younger Bush did not result from material factors but from intangibles, beginning with divergent belief systems and personalities.

For Waltz the structural realist, individuals and their domestic circumstances have little impact on world affairs. What counts is the distribution of material power. How illusory is the Waltz "theory of international politics" may be seen from a cursory look at the world scene in 2000, 2008, and 2012. By most material standards, the United States was the world's sole superpower at each juncture (see Tables 7.1 and 7.2 above). When the Clinton presidency ended, U.S. influence was very high. After eight years of George W. Bush, America's *material* power was still "hyper" but Washington's influence quite low. U.S. soft power recovered under President Obama but was much lower than in 2000.

Idealists disagree among themselves about war. Neo-Hegelians expected peace, because history has ended (Fukuyama 1992). "Endism" survived the Balkan wars of the early 1990s, because none of the protagonists fought for a transnational ideology. Soon, however, fundamentalist Muslims and Christians faced each other in global combat, making "endists" appear parochial as well as just plain wrong.

Hegemonic war is possible but avoidable. World history since 1945 falsifies assertions about the inevitability of hegemonic war. The largest empire ever, the British, devolved into a commonwealth. The French, Dutch, and Portuguese empires disintegrated after local wars but without hegemonic war. Starting in 1945, the two rival superpowers avoided hot war until the USSR imploded without a fight, whereupon the United States and its allies labored to *revive* Russia and other successor states. The United States need not fight a rising China. Both countries have deep incentives to cooperate on mutual interests such as renewable energy and security threats in Northeast Asia (Gross 2013; Gurtov 2013; Clemens 2012).

The future of world affairs is open-ended. Neither conflict nor harmony is assured between China and the United States. "There will not be any hegemonic power" in 2030, according to the National Intelligence Council (2012). Instead, "power will shift to networks and coalitions in a multipolar world." The best-case situation for global security, the report stated, would be a growing political partnership between the United States and China. But it could take a crisis to bring Washington and Beijing together—perhaps a nuclear standoff between India and Pakistan resolved only by bold cooperation between the United States and China. A worst-case situation could result from a stalling of economic globalization that blocked advancement of material well-being around the world. This scenario could arise from an outbreak of a global health pandemic leading to closed borders and economic isolationism.

Complexity science agrees with Hobbes about the perils of chaos but not with his proposed remedy of absolutist, top-down rule. Rather, complexity concurs with liberal peace theory: Republics rarely if ever fight one another and suffer less internal violence than authoritarian regimes. The originator of liberal peace theory, Immanuel Kant, counted on a system of self-organization similar to that practiced for centuries by the Hanseatic city-states.[3] Republics fought back when attacked in the twentieth century and won most of the century's major hot wars and the long cold war—in part because they were more fit than their adversaries.

Complexity science looks on the "balance of power"—whether seen as stable or fluid, equal or unequal—as an emergent structure, but one that depends on human decisions as well as the power alignment of its components. Neorealists expect that when a great power weakens, it will attack its rival in a desperate effort to retain its status or that the rising power will act to crush its weakening rival. This mechanical formula did not work as the Soviet empire eroded. Presidents Mikhail Gorbachev, George H. W. Bush, and Ronald Reagan finessed a peaceful evaporation of the erstwhile colossus.

Given that today's hegemon and all potential challengers are interdependent—above all, in security and economic terms—they can choose to cultivate their complementary assets for outcomes more useful to each side than conflict.

ISSUE 3. SECURITY DILEMMAS: CONFRONTATION OR NEGOTIATION?

Neither realists nor idealists provide satisfactory answers to the security dilemmas that confront political actors worldwide. Radical realists advise building up one's own power to stay ahead no matter the other side's response. Moderate realists advise a strategy of tit for tat, matching the other side's tough or conciliatory move in kind. But this approach can leave both sides on a treadmill of matching toughness with toughness.[4] Each will fear to take the first steps toward détente. Hopeful idealists will not win at this game either. Counting on win-win outcomes, their unconditional generosity can be abused by tough rivals.

How does complexity science deal with security dilemmas? It affirms that maximum creativity is often found at the edge of chaos. Security usually emerges from a dynamic interaction—not from some unchanging order. Further, complexity reminds us that even hostile rivals are interdependent—mutually vulnerable—and that their complex problems can benefit from mutual gain solutions. If either side feels itself disadvantaged, a deal will not be reached or will not endure. If one side plays the game as zero-sum, the other party will have to take protective measures. However, if an overt clash can be avoided and if habits of cooperation are cultivated, each side may gradually learn that "niceness" can pay (Goldstein and Freeman 1990).

Consider North Korea and the bomb. Realists tell us that each actor uses negotiation to pursue its own security objectives. North Korea explains that its nuclear weapons are meant to deter external threats. Paying scant attention to the four other participants in the six-party negotiations, North Korea focuses on the United States. The problems of Northeast Asia, however, are "too complex and the configurations of power too interlocking to permit overt hegemonic behavior" (Kerr 2005, 432).

Given the many complexities and asymmetries, negotiations with North Korea repeatedly hit dead ends. Some neorealists do not worry, however, because the proliferation of nuclear weaponry may buttress deterrence and stability. Indeed, the Bush administration may not have wanted an accord because a nuclear-armed North Korea offered the best rationale for building missile defenses in Alaska and California (Clemens 2005).

At the other pole, some idealists look for a win-win arrangement such as the 1994 Agreed Framework between Washington and Pyongyang that promised to meet each side's objectives but fell into desuetude. Some analysts explain that perceptions and misconceptions have blinded both sides to their true interests and kept them from a mutual-gain agreement. For more than five years, two ROK presidents offered unlimited "Sunshine" to Kim Jong Il despite his failure to reciprocate.

Complexity theorists would start by analyzing the extent of interdependence and what actions could enhance the fitness of each actor. They would analyze the military benefits and costs of nuclear weapons for North Korea and a putative missile defense for the United States. If Washington gave high priority to forestalling nuclear spread, it would offer a package of security as well as economic benefits meant to persuade Pyongyang to abjure weapons of mass destruction (Clemens 2010b and 2011). What looks like rational self-interest to a Westerner, however, might look like suicide to the regime in Pyongyang.

Would it be good for Iran too to get the bomb? Yes, said Kenneth N. Waltz (2012), because nuclear weapons would make Iran feel more secure. Once Israel and the United States accept the reality of a nuclear armed Iran, their incentives to attack or otherwise intervene in Iran will shrink. Since nuclear weapons provide deterrence, nuclear proliferation should improve global security. "More may be better."

The best argument against structuralist logic is human frailty. Granted that most politicians recognize the dangers of nuclear war, emotion-driven actions and mechanical accidents happen. The likelihood of a nuclear exchange increases with every actor with access to a nuclear trigger. Indeed, the first major book by Waltz outlined the case *against* the simplicities of structural realism. *Man, the State and War* (1959) argued that human nature and the state as well as the facts of international anarchy can generate war. As Waltz saw more than a half-century ago, individual humans and their enveloping political culture are the agents by which the structure of global power comes to life.

Individuals and political culture cannot be overlooked. Waltz expects every government to bow to what he sees as the logic of international power. He ignores Goethe's observation, cited in chapter 7, that "humans call it 'reason,' but use it only to be more brutish than any beast."

Laertes got it right: "Best safety lies in fear." Better to play it safe and distrust the simplistic nostrums of structural realism. Peace and security will not gain from wider access to weapons of mass destruction.

ISSUE 4. INITIATION AND SPREAD OF WAR

Realists and idealists disagree on the causes of war. Neither camp gives an adequate explanation. Some realists explain World War I by the challenge posed to Great Britain by the rise of German industrial and naval power. Lenin, also a materialist, argued that the capitalist drive for "surplus value" led imperialists to fight over overseas markets. Neither account explains why war began first between Austria-Hungary and Serbia and then spread to Germany, France, and Russia—with Great Britain entering only after Berlin violated Belgian neutrality. Idealists may talk about the absence of democratic restraints, but cannot explain why the war elicited strong public support across Europe— even by trade unionists who would soon be fighting their fellow workers.

Complexity scientists take account of individuals—their ideas, beliefs, and perceptions—but also of structures, such as Germany's ability to mobilize quickly and move its forces by rail. But complexity's greatest contribution is to see all of Europe as a network with important subsystems—alliances—that could be activated for war (Vasquez et al. 2011) A comparison of networks and ideas about structures helps explain why World War I began with a chain-gang effect, while World War II spread more slowly as each defender tried to pass the buck (Christensen and Snyder 1990). Analogous links pitted Hungarians against each other as well as against Turks in times past (Barabási 2010).

War as well as trade can lead to forms of cooperation. War requires in-group cooperation and often cross-border partnerships against external threats. Anthropological research shows that when population density increases within a region, conflict becomes a way for cooperators to acquire more resources and protect themselves against adversaries. Groups that successfully organize themselves to raid others acquire resources and a selective advantage against groups that are less well organized (Stanish and Levine 2011). Here we see the workings of coevolution and criticality. Inchoate political units may go to war several times. After several rounds, however, some units prevail over neighbors and establish organized states, whose leaders often feel they must continue to expand if only to protect their borders. Conflict may give way to a new equilibrium that lasts for some time until punctuated by a dramatic shift.

But cooperation without war can also enhance each actor's objectives. Despite news headlines, the historical record shows that violence within countries and across borders has decreased (Pinker 2011). Both moral repugnance and fear of modern weapons probably contributed to this decline, though similar sentiments did not throttle the guns of August 1914.

The NIC (2012) anticipated that in coming decades the risk of conflict *within* states, such as a civil war or an insurgency, would probably decline in Latin America. It would remain high, however, in sub-Saharan Africa, in parts of the Middle East and South Asia, and in some Asia-Pacific island hot spots. A more fragmented international system increases the risks of conflict between states. This danger will probably mount due to increased resource competition, the spread of lethal technologies, and spillover from regional conflicts. Future wars in Asia and the Middle East could include nuclear weapons. If any party used nuclear weapons, however, hopes that war could engender cooperation might well go up in smoke and clouds of radiation.

ISSUE 5. CLASHES OF CIVILIZATIONS

Samuel P. Huntington (1996) warned that clashes between civilizations were likely to replace the erstwhile struggles among fascism, communism, and Western democracy. Attributing such importance to the intangibles of culture made this thesis more idealist than realist. Still, Huntington applied a realpolitik viewpoint when he warned that the some Islamic countries and China, despite dissonance between their cultures, would team up against America.

Many realists complain that Huntington downgraded the role of national interest and turned the ideological superstructure into a foundation. But Huntington's thesis is congenial to hardliners in China and elsewhere who use it as a rationale to increase military spending. Also, some idealist theologians and theocrats cite it when arguing that their faith cannot coexist peacefully with infidel or apostate beliefs. But the thesis is anathema to the many idealists who believe that many (if not all) civilizations have their strong points and who call for mutual enrichment (Khatami 2001) or a higher synthesis (Toynbee 1979). Some Russian and Ukrainian scholars in the twenty-first century called for addressing shared economic and environmental concerns via a "partnership of civilizations" (Iakovets 2011).

The clash thesis prepares us for jihads and crusades, but the argument is too simplistic. The tension between the West and Islam includes a clash of cultures, but the deepest issues are mutual fear, strategic threats, real estate, oil, domestic politics, and the compulsions of individuals such as Osama bin Laden and George W. Bush. Furthermore, each "civilization" suffers from deep cleavages. Some Islamic elites (for example, in Qatar and Bahrain) cooperate with Washington while others seek to undermine U.S. influence. Paris and Berlin, although units in the same civilization as the United States, sought in the George W. Bush years to undercut U.S. policy and power. Leaders in each Western capital saw the threats and stakes differently—their disagreements amplified by personal animosities.

Complexity recognizes culture as a key variable shaping fitness within each society and across borders. Culture nurtures attitudes toward education, work and savings, and ethnic diversity (L. Harrison and Huntington 2000; L. Harrison 2006). It buttresses optimism against fatalism—confidence that life can become better versus acceptance of what is. But there is no inevitable clash. Many Americans and Chinese, for example, are quite comfortable with many features of each other's way of life.

The deepest impact of culture on IR is that countries in the tradition of West European Christianity are far more progressive (L. Harrison 2006) or fit (Clemens 2006) than most others. These differences in fitness, however, have encouraged both domineering behaviors and resentment.

Issue 6. The Rise and Fall of Empires

Why and how do empires rise and fall? Political realists point to the relationship between ends and means. Political actors expand their domain when they can but eventually suffer from overstretch. When ambition exceeds means, empires shrink or disappear (Kennedy 1987). A variation on this theme is that entire civilizations perish when they outstrip their material base by abusing their environment (Diamond 2005). Up-and-coming powers may attack a declining hegemon and try to administer a coup de grace (Gilpin 1988). But other analysts explain imperial dynamics by the energy and stagnation of ideas and ideals. Communist ideals helped to create and expand the Soviet empire. When they withered, the Kremlin's realm collapsed (Kotkin 2008).

The twists and turns of nations supply abundant grist both for realist and idealist theories, but most historical cases defy any monocausal accounting. Complexity science offers more nuanced and comprehensive explanations than any version of realism or idealism. As Ferguson (2010) put it, great powers and empires are "complex systems, made up of a very large number of interacting components that are asymmetrically organized." They may function quite stably for some time and appear to be in equilibrium. But a time may come when these complex systems "go critical." A small event—a kind of last straw—may set off a "phase transition" from a benign equilibrium to a crisis. The course of empire often coincides with the model of punctuated equilibrium. They may rise relatively quickly; plateau for decades or even centuries; and then collapse with near-blinding speed. What we know as Roman civilization collapsed within one generation. In China the transition from Confucian equipoise to anarchy took little more than a decade. The Romanov, Hapsburg, Hohenzollern, and Ottoman empires fell in less than a decade. The British, French, and Dutch empires disappeared quickly after World War II, the Soviet in the aftermath of the Afghan war. Defeats on the battlefield blended with severe economic problems to end systems that, a few years or decades earlier, had appeared strong if not invincible.

The fitness of any great power or empire depends on the interactions of many kinds of tangible and intangible factors as they coevolve and behave in nonlinear ways. The Kremlin's rocket and ground forces, for example, seemed to signify superpower, but this potential asset changed its sign from positive to negative: their very quantity and quality became a burden on the Soviet Union's overall fitness. Yes, the USSR gained influence from Angola to Grenada while America struggled with its Vietnam syndrome, but Soviet society paid a price: infant mortality mounted in the early 1970s. Several decades later, the United States veered along a similar track: U.S. military outlays in the early twenty-first century equaled those of most other countries combined, but America's ranking declined in overall competitiveness and in information technology (World Economic Forum 2011 and 2012). Infant mortality in the United States declined in the years 2005 to 2010 but remained nearly the highest for the thirty OECD member states. The number of overweight children declined a little after 2010, but one-third of Americans were obese—with grave implications for public health and productivity. Problems in these areas, of course, would echo in other domains. An entire way of life endangered itself. The United States risked fulfilling Arnold Toynbee's prediction for all civilizations: they rise in a creative response to challenges but eventually, wasted in war and other excesses, destroy themselves.

ISSUE 7. ETHNIC REPRESSION AND ETHNIC STRIFE

Ethnic conflict can arise from many sources but perceived injustice is the most common denominator; to deal with such perceptions and the underlying realities is extremely difficult. Power politicians such as Vladimir Putin say: "Crush the insurgency [as in Chechnya or from the "Pussy Riot"] at any cost." Idealists of different stripes offer a variety of opinions. Racial and cultural supremacists hold that their group should dominate others. Legalistic idealists and consociationalists urge rewriting the constitution to assure each group a share of political power and wealth.

Complexity helps us understand the relative successes and failures of various societies in coping with ethnic pressures. Only a society that is basically fit can meet the challenges of ethnic diversity. The United States, Switzerland, and Singapore have dealt with their particular problems in different ways, but with much greater success than their peers in the former USSR, the one-time Yugoslavia, or the still extant Sri Lanka (Clemens 2004, 288–302; Clemens 2010). Neither Switzerland nor Singapore faces such difficult ethnic challenges as the United States, but America has thrived on the edge of chaos. The affluence of Singapore, Switzerland, and the U.S.A. make it easier for them to deal with ethnic diversity, but they were not always rich. Today they are relatively fit *because* they have coped well with ethnic diversity. Their earlier fitness has nourished still greater fitness.

The diverse ethnic groups in the USSR, Yugoslavia, and Sri Lanka were also interdependent, with a capacity to help or harm each other, but they failed to collaborate for mutual gain. Their governments repressed ethnic problems until internal pressures pulled apart each system. Sri Lanka appeared to be one of the fittest developing countries in the 1960s, but the majority's intolerance and policies—reverse affirmative action—drove a minority into rebellion. Complexity science offers answers (sketched above in chapter 4) as to why much of the Balkans roiled in the 1990s while the Baltic republics experienced peace and made the most of new opportunities.

ISSUE 8. HAVES AND HAVE-NOTS

Disparities of wealth generate tensions within and across borders. Many realists are blasé. They say: "Inequality is natural. Live with it. Meanwhile, each government should do what it can to enhance its own power and wealth." Idealists disagree among themselves. Some opine that income disparities reflect God's will: "The poor you have always with you" (Matthew 26:11). Some take the opposite stance and demand that the rich share their wealth. Moderate voices in each camp call for all sides to "enlarge the pie."

The National Intelligence Council (2012) foresaw greater prosperity for many humans and immiserization for others. "The growth of the global middle class constitutes a tectonic shift," the study said. By 2030 billions of people will gain new individual power as they climb out of poverty. "For the first time, a majority of the world's population will not be impoverished, and the middle classes will be the most important social and economic sector in the vast majority of countries around the world." At the same time, however, half of the world's population will probably be living in areas that suffer from severe shortages of fresh water. The NIC opined that wise management of natural resources will be a crucial component of global national security efforts.

The NIC noted the problem of fresh water but failed to underscore its severity and the difficulties in coping with it. As noted above in chapter 7, more than 60 percent of the United States faced drought conditions in 2012. The challenges were many times more acute in China, where much water was unfit even for industrial use (Gall 2012).

Other important demographic trends will be aging populations in Europe, Japan, South Korea, and Taiwan, which could slow their economies further. The NIC report warned that Russia's economy would also suffer a relative decline, while the United States benefited from its domestic oil and natural gas supplies and new technologies to tap them. However, the NIC expected that "the health of the global economy increasingly will be linked to how well the developing world does—more so than the traditional West." If China or India stumbled and fell, however, this bet too would be off.

The intertwined concepts of interdependence, societal fitness, and coevolution point the way to a deeper understanding of inequality and what can be done about it. The basic reality is that interdependence links rich and poor on many levels. Suppliers and producers of goods and services, whether rich or poor, need providers and buyers. Rich and poor coevolve with the shared biosphere of planet Earth. High levels of fitness in some countries cannot be maintained without improving conditions in other, less fit countries. Chaos in Mexico or Haiti or Cuba adds to social problems in the United States. The affluent can buy protection from certain ills, but the rich as well as the poor are threatened by chaos—war, terror, epidemics, and climate change. Wealth offers no shield against nuclear fallout. Indeed, wealthy countries could well be the first targets for weapons of mass destruction.

Complexity implies that poverty cannot be ignored or remedied by simple redistribution, but can be ameliorated by improving each society's overall fitness. Human development is both the end *and* the means. Investment in human capital is key. It explains transitions from millennia of Malthusian near-stagnation to the Industrial Revolution to the emergence of modern human capital–based growth (Galor 2011). Foreign aid should therefore be directed to empower all those without resources to help themselves, for example, women without education or capital (Sachs 2005).

What is good for individual entrepreneurs may not benefit the commons. Requirements to use ethanol with gasoline helped boost profits for U.S. corn growers and gain votes for some politicians, but drove up the price of food worldwide—adding to other reasons for unrest (Lagi, Bar-Yam, and Bar-Yam 2012).

ISSUE 9. THE EMERGENCE OF CYBERPOWER

The rapid emergence of cyberpower is an important new factor in world affairs. Even as it bolstered an Information Age, the Internet also accelerated and deepened global interdependence. The growth of the World Wide Web made possible the nearly instantaneous and anonymous exchange of ideas and ideologies; the sharing and manipulation of previously protected and sophisticated technologies; vast and transparent social networking. These developments, in turn, tended to homogenize some cultures, castes, and classes. They also led to creation of complex virtual worlds and a wide dependence on the global grid from every sector of society. The low price of entry, anonymity, and asymmetries in vulnerability helped smaller actors to enjoy greater leverage in cyberspace than in many traditional arenas of world affairs. Thus, hackers in impoverished North Korea could wreak havoc in the computer networks of South Korea, one of the most wired countries in the world.

U.S. Secretary of Defense Leon B. Panetta in October 2012 spoke of the need to prepare for a possible "cyber–Pearl Harbor" attack on the United States. His concerns were shared by others who analyzed computer security. Richard A. Clarke, author of *Cyber War: The Next Threat to National Security and What to Do About It* (2010), complained that present efforts to make networks more secure were akin to putting a finger in a dike sure to leak elsewhere. The National Intelligence Council (2012) warned that terrorists in coming decades could mount a computer network attack in which the casualties would be measured not by the hundreds or thousands killed but by the millions severely affected by damaged infrastructure, such as electrical grids being taken down.

A pioneer in computer security, Peter G. Neumann explained that complex systems break in complex ways. He worried that flaws in contemporary hardware and software made it virtually impossible to identify the vulnerabilities in computer systems and ensure that they are secure and reliable. Borrowing from a common practice in biology, Neumann urged that we give computer systems multiple immune systems—a rows of sentinels (Markoff 2012).

The characteristics of cyberspace reduced some power differentials among actors and thus spurred the diffusion of power. The largest powers cannot dominate this domain so readily as at sea and in the air. Still, the diffusion of power via cyberspace in the early twenty-first century did not signify equality of power or the replacement of governments as the most powerful actors on the world stage (Nye 2010).

Mr. Y (2011) noted the minuses as well as the pluses: "The worldwide web has also facilitated the spread of hateful and manipulative propaganda and extremism; the theft of intellectual property and sensitive information; predatory behavior and the exploitation of innocence; and the dangerous and destructive prospect of cyber warfare waged from the shadows of non-attribution and deception. Whether this revolution in communication and access to information is viewed as the democratization of ideas, or as the technological catalyst of an apocalypse, nothing has so significantly impacted our lives in the last one hundred years."

Cyber warfare can not only threaten the other side's hard power (as when Chinese hackers roam Pentagon or Lockheed hard drives) but can also shape politics. Thus, *New York Times* reportage in October 2012 about the personal wealth of Chinese leaders (e.g., the $2 billion controlled by the family of the Prime Minister Win Jiabao) cast doubt on the regime's claims to executor of heaven's mandate. Chinese censors blocked the newspaper's English and Chinese Web sites but reports nonetheless pierced the Bamboo Curtain.

The United Sates has been a leader in IT but its computer-reliant infrastructure also make it exquisitely vulnerable to cyberattack. America's drones can track and kill opponents at a great distance, but these weapons also stir resentment in the minds and hearts of peoples that Washington would prefer to coopt.

Complexity science with its insights into networks and bursts of energy (Barabási 2003, 2010; Newman et al. 2006).will go further toward understanding these world shaping forces than exegesis of the Melian debate or the UN Charter.

ISSUE 10. TERRORISM

Each social malaise discussed here can encourage terrorist actions. Terrorists usually feel disenfranchised and think that violence against civilian and government targets is the best way to achieve their goals. Fundamentalist religion often plays a supporting role. It helps draw boundaries between "them and us." It rationalizes and sanctifies killing the innocent for a worthy cause. It blesses suicide as martyrdom. Mr. Y (2011) cautions that in "complex systems, adaptation and variation demonstrate that 'binning' is not only difficult, it often leads to unintended consequences." Labeling or binning Islamist radicals as "terrorists" leads to the erroneous perceptions that all Muslims are terrorists and that terrorists are faithful Muslims rather than apostates. Traditional realists pay little heed to the grievances that inspire terrorists. Instead, they urge tough policies to stamp them out. Some idealists, secular as well as religious, approve and justify terror as a weapon of the weak. Most liberal idealists abhor violence and call instead for dialogue and political-economic reform.

Complexity endorses force as needed to defend society and maintain order, but seeks to understand and ameliorate the social conditions that give rise to terrorist movements. Today's "Islamic" terrorists come mainly from societies where ruling elites hoard education, wealth, and power (Anonymous 2004). Most terrorists do not seek to "destroy freedom" but rather to oust an alien military presence (Pape 2005).

Complexity's emphasis on self-organization helps to explain the resilience of terrorist networks. Al-Qaeda ("the base" in Arabic) gains strength from decentralization. It exploits modern technologies to share information, coordinate action, and shape public opinion. Yes, the "base" could atrophy or implode if its top leaders were gone (Cronin 2006, 2009), but al-Qaeda had a hydra-headed quality. Osama Bin Laden's death did not shut down the movement. Hard-pressed in Afghanistan, al-Qaeda became more active elsewhere, including Yemen and Mali. Still, terrorist movements do not endure forever. Like imperial and other political systems, terrorist organizations (such as tsarist Russia's *Narodnaya Volya*) can plateau for long periods and then collapse.

Like terrorist networks, fundamentalist movements should be seen as emergent systems. Charismatic leaders also play an essential role in fundamentalist religions. But their prospects, like those of al-Qaeda, are uncertain. Religious worldviews are self-limiting—absolutist and ascetic in a multicultural and materialistic world. Some fundamentalists want to rule the world but many are parochial or particularistic. If they take part in normal political life, the pressures to compromise can dilute their zeal (Almond, Appleby, Sivan 2003). In 2011–12, Hamas in Gaza agreed to cooperate with the Palestinian Authority on the West Bank.

Complexity sheds light on the strengths of decentralized networks, but it also reminds us of the dense and complex strengths of modern states. A terrorist attack with a nuclear or other weapon of mass destruction, of course, would raise the pressures on these states to new levels.

Complexity theorists advise matching the solution to the problem. "In a complex war, the organization of forces is as important as the size of the forces." A huge army with tanks and guided missiles was appropriate to expel Saddam Hussein from Kuwait. A far more fine-tuned operation—"a distributed decision process, involving many networked people with different sources and types of information"—may be needed to subdue terrorists (Bar-Yam 2004, 110).

ISSUE 11. CRIME ACROSS BORDERS

Transnational crime cannot be well understood or controlled by state-centric realisms or utopian idealisms. Just as complexity helps explain the resiliency of al-Qaeda, it also contributes to our understanding of "how smugglers, traffickers, and copycats are hijacking the global economy" (Naím 2005). As Mr. Y (2011) puts it: "Criminal networks prey upon and contribute to the disenfranchisement of a sizeable portion of the population in many underdeveloped nations." Many of these activities profit from the self-organized fitness of their networks.

Banks in many Western as well as developing countries facilitate tax fraud and money laundering. Police networks such as Interpol try to break up international crime, but self-organization of the police is weak relative to that of criminal gangs. Most police are still nationalist while their opponents are cosmopolitan. The tools for fighting international crime need updating for a globe on which illicit activities cross borders with lightning speed.

Sanctions on the banking systems of North Korea and Iran probably constrained their abilities to transfer funds to and from foreign clients as well their delivery of hard cash to ruling elites in Pyongyang and Tehran.

ISSUE 12. HUMANS AND THE BIOSPHERE: RAPE OR POSITIVE SYMBIOSIS?

The biosphere shapes and is shaped by everything that happens on the world stage. These interactions shape the dynamics of climate change, resource scarcity, protracted social conflicts, socioeconomic transitions, stock market fluctuations, and the rhythms of environmental negotiations.

Globalization, the borderless nature of the Internet, and the proliferation of nonstate actors and ideologies underscore the "interconnectivity of today's strategic ecosystem" (Mr. Y 2011). Disease and starvation have often taken a greater toll than combat in wartime. Less than optimal living standards produced more early deaths than all the wars of the twentieth century (Morrison and Tsipis 1998, 26).

Many realists regard "nature" as just one more resource to be exploited in the quest for power. They ignore the interdependence of humans with their biosphere. Raping nature can boomerang. Entire civilizations have collapsed because they abused their habitats and failed to adapt to environmental change (Diamond 2005).

Ignoring the biosphere concept spelled out by a leading Soviet scientist in 1924, the Soviet regime pursued hard power as if the biosphere would tolerate any human behavior and continue to sustain a would-be superpower.[5] Post-Soviet Russia continues the onslaught. Dirty economic activity results in 300,000 to 350,000 deaths per year. Whereas many Americans think it patriotic to seek preservation of the county's environment, many Russians have regarded such attitudes as treasonous (Yablokov 2005). Of course Russia as well as the United States, China, Japan, and other countries are pockmarked with environmental hot spots.

International law has helped conserve some domains of the environment, for example, Antarctica. But idealistic calls to act and think "Green" have achieved only modest success. They run a losing race against greed, comfort, and convenience. To aggravate matters, some "children of Abraham" cite Genesis to prove that God meant man to dominate all creation.

Rooted in evolutionary biology as well as human history, complexity science reminds us that the fitness of each society depends on its coevolution with other actors and with their shared environment. Indeed, complexity encourages us to examine the fitness not just of individual societies but also that of the entire global system. The entire system can and should be studied for its ability to sustain human and other life forms, now and in the future. Biological diversity is not only an aesthetic and sentimental value but also a vital ingredient in human survival (Wilson 1993). How ecology and international studies could learn from one another is explored in Clemens (1972–73).

While realists and idealists leaned toward single-factor diagnoses and prescriptions, geographers and environmentalists addressed twenty-six different levels of the environmental and economic problems besetting the grand rivers and catchment areas in five different countries affecting and affected by pollution in the Baltic region (Furberg 2006). Assuming that science knew the answers, political and economic actors at each level would have to make the necessary decisions and take the appropriate actions to ameliorate the accumulating bundles of problems. UNESCO encouraged the Estonian Ministry of the Environment and the RF Ministry of Natural Resources to design and carry out a plan to cope with the economic and environmental challenges in the Narva–Lake Peipsi basin by 2007. Years later, however, as a Krylov fable has it, "the load was still there"—unmoved.[6]

ISSUE 13. CROWD-SOURCING REFORM AND WISDOM

Peoples across the world want political reform. Neither "might makes right" nor anarchy offers much promise. Making use of the new technologies of social networking, Democrats helped to elect a black American president in 2008 and 2012. Tea Party activists and other Republicans began tapping similar techniques to oppose him in 2010 and 2012.

Looking around the globe, we see that variants of self-organization brought profound change to Iran (1979), Poland and Czechoslovakia (1980s), the Baltic countries (1987–1991), Slovenia, Croatia, and Bosnia (mid-1990s), Serbia (2000), Georgia (2003), Kyrgyzstan (2005), and Ukraine (2004–05). Ukraine's Orange Revolution won at the polls in 2004–05 but aborted when members of the old elite regained control and neutered self-organization.

Texting helped Filipinos in 2000 to topple President Joseph Estrada; Spanish supporters of José Luis Rodríguez Zapatero to coordinate the 2004 ouster of the People's Party in four days; anticommunist Moldovans in 2009 to turn out twenty thousand protesters in just thirty-six hours; Tunisians, Egyptians, and Libyans to topple authoritarian regimes in 2011; Syrian dissidents to expose the brutality of government forces in 2012.

Starting in 2011, there were open struggles across the Arab world between self-organizers and despots. Both sides made use of the new social media, though some governments also deployed police clubs and army tanks. Graphs assembled by data scientist Kovas Boguta revealed a sharp increase in tweets concerning events in Egypt from January 24 to 27, 2011—just before the Hosni Mubarak regime took major Internet service providers off-line. Tweets from Egypt nearly disappeared for the next five days, but tweets from users outside Egypt sharply increased. Service within Egypt resumed on February 2, after which messages from within and from outside Egypt increased, becoming much more frequent than before the shutdown on January 28.[7] When Egypt's new government failed to act in 2012–13, however, self-help collectives (many led by members of the Muslim Brotherhood) formed in Cairo to rebuild a decrepit infrastructure and carry out some basic services.

Table 10.1 shows how Internet usage can correlate with political stability or with rebellion. Wide access to the Internet could reflect a syndrome of openness and self-organization, as in Iceland. Indeed, three of the most stable Islamic countries—Qatar, Kuwait, and the United Arabic Republics—also had the highest percentages of their population using the Internet. The UAR and Qatar (along with Brunei) also ranked among the top forty countries on the HDI. On the other hand, access to the Internet helped fuel rebellion where Internet usage was more limited, as in Tunisia and Egypt. Bahrain, the second-highest Islamic country in Internet usage and fourth-highest Islamic country on the HDI, experienced massive unrest put down only by massive force. Other Islamic countries facing large-scale unrest included Libya, Pakistan, Nigeria, and Iran. Each had many Internet users but were not included in the broadband survey summarized in Table 10.1. Defying any simple correlation, Turkey—a NATO ally and perennial candidate for EU membership—ranked low on Internet usage and in HDI placement. Bottom line: Even limited numbers of persons with access to the Internet can act as a critical mass.[8]

Authoritarians in oil-rich Saudi Arabia tried to buy off discontent among Shiia citizens and guest workers. Other Arab regimes also sought to purchase stability with money. "Some had enough cash for new subsidies and direct handouts, as well as to pay their military and security forces more and reinforce their tools and methods of crowd control" (Bremmer 2011). Bahrain, the world's only Shiia-majority country still governed by a Sunni monarch, remained on edge in 2011–13. It counted on deep-pocketed friends in Saudi Arabia—determined to prevent Bahrain's unrest from spilling over into their oil-rich Eastern Province, where most Saudi Shiia lived. Some Shiia in Bahrain hoped to gain more rights and political representation, as well as cash payments and jobs, even as King Hamad bin isa Al Kalhifa retained his throne.

The winds from Tunisia blew eastward toward Syria, Jordan, and even to Sudan, but not south toward sub-Saharan Africa, where levels of education and access to the Internet were much lower. Most important, civil society was weak. Regime change took place relatively often in sub-Saharan Africa, but usually by military coup (as in Mali in 2012), not by the liberating energies of self-organization. There were few organizations with the power

TABLE 10.1. Percentage of Individuals in Islamic Heritage Countries Using the Internet in 2011 (global sample n = 92)

World Rank	Country	%	HDI Rank
1 (tops)	Iceland	95.0	14
8	Qatar	86.2	37
23 (for comparison)	United States	77.9	4
24	Bahrain	77.0	42
29	Kuwait	74.2	63
35	UAR	70.1	30
36 (for comparison)	Israel	70.1	17
38	Oman	68.0	89
43	Malaysia	61.0	61
44	Bosnia	60.0	74
49	Brunei	56.0	33
54	Lebanon	52.0	71
57	Morocco	51.0	130
59	Azerbaijan	50.0	76
62	Albania	49.0	70
64	Saudi Arabia	47.5	56
65	Kazakhstan	45.0	68
73	Turkey	42.1	92
79	Tunisia	39.1	94
85	Egypt	35.6	113
89	Jordan	34.9	95
90	Maldives	34.0	109

Source: http://www.broadbandcommission.org/Documents/bb-annualreport2012.pdf (accessed 10/30/2012)

to challenge the authority of rulers, to organize dissenters, and to articulate alternative ideas of government that ordinary people would be willing to give their lives for. "Civil society organizations are often weak because they are divided along ethnic lines, and many nongovernmental organizations are simply revenue-generating activities, so they are not very helpful in building the values of a deep civil society."[9]

Conditions were ripe in each country. The *ancien régime* was rigid, corrupt, insensitive, and incompetent. Each revolution took advantage of recent advances in communication technology—tape recordings, television, and, in recent years, social networking via the Internet—that permitted people to self-organize and evade centralized dictation. High levels of education and rising gender equality helped mobilize large segments of the population. However where civil society was weak, as in Egypt, it was hard to cultivate self-organized governance after the dictators were gone.

Crowd-sourcing became a major source of news when the rulers of Iran and other repressive regimes banned professional journalists from covering antiregime demonstrations. The competitive landscape changed when the Internet allowed insurgents to play by different rules from incumbents. Access to the Internet helped Iranian Greens in 2009 to mobilize for democracy but met stiff government repression.[10] Digital networks acted as a "massive positive supply shock to the cost and spread of information, to the ease and range of public speech by citizens, and scale of group coordination" (Shirky, in Gladwell and Shirky 2011). Like David against Goliath, social media allowed committed individuals and groups to play by new rules.

Of course, technology can liberate or repress. It can foster creativity and public spirit (Shirky 2010) or stifle free thought. Chinese authorities tried in 2011 to shield its citizens from news about people power in Egypt. Beijing limited coverage of the Egyptian protest movement to its external news services and warned that Chinese web sites that did not censor comments about Egypt would be "shut down by force." In 2011–12 Chinese dissidents used the instant messaging service QQ to protest corruption. But in 2012 Chinese authorities shut down dozens of web sites accused of spreading "rumors" about infighting between top leaders and passing "slurs" about the riches accumulated by Chinese elites.

While Chinese authorities could still limit access to information in the early twenty-first century, the long-term costs to the regime and the country could be high. Blocking open discussion of hard choices, authorities risked more blunders such as building the Three Gorges Dam.

More than two decades after the demise of the USSR, most of the formerly communist-controlled regimes in Eastern Europe maintained high levels of political and economic freedom. In oil-rich Russia, Azerbaijan, and Kazakhstan, however, authorities promised bread more than freedom, and throttled serious challenges to authoritarian rule.

But the Putin regime failed to silence Russians demanding free and fair elections in 2011–12. The ever-widening swath of Russians with access to the Internet (more than 40% of the population in 2012) implied that efforts at mind control would encounter mounting difficulties.

Besides repressing information about elections, the Kremlin sought to control news about Chechnya and other trouble spots in the Caucasus. The reign of silence was abetted by U.S. reluctance to offend a regime that facilitated America's "war on terror." Starting in 2001, however, the on-line service *Caucasian Knot* [*Kavkazkii uzel'*] utilized a virtual office and, by 2012, some fifty correspondents to provide objective reporting from twenty locations in the North Caucasus and beyond.[11] Nearly two million readers tapped into this service each month (vanden Heuvel 2012)—including Russian officials who tolerated its existence because they wanted unvarnished information, often withheld by their viceroys in places such as Kabardino-Balkaria where, the

Caucasian Knot reported, some 173 persons died in armed conflict in 2011.[12]

Dissidents in many countries—from Soviet-era Lithuania to the Serbia of Slobodan Milošević to Burma under military dictatorship—adopted and adapted the nonviolent strategy and tactics formulated in Boston by Gene Sharp (2005 and earlier). But some protestors used violence to pursue their goals. In Kyrgyzstan, for example, young people learned in 2010 that mobs wielding sticks and iron rods could oust corrupt leaders and convince other politicians to behave in certain ways.[13] To persuade people to unlearn and disavow street violence would be a long-term challenge for Kyrgyz authorities (McGlinchey 2011, 93). At the other extreme, neither peaceful nor forceful protests appeared to be feasible in North Korea where citizens found it dangerous to show "voice" by arranging a secretive exit or even by engaging in market activities. Yes, authorities in Pyongyang showed visitors students at an elite institution busy at computers but with no access to the World Wide Web.

ISSUE 14. AGENTS AND STRUCTURE, FREE WILL AND FORCES

Neither realism nor idealism can satisfactorily explain the relative impacts of agents and structures. Neorealists contend that structures of power explain who does what and why on the world stage, but fail to explain the often decisive roles played by key individuals and soft variables such as culture. Exponents of voluntarism and Zeitgeist, on the other side, allow too little room for structures of hard power. Complexity science is alert to all levels of action—from individuals to the biosphere. It integrates all forms of power and thought into analysis of relative fitness and fitness landscapes. It recognizes the role played by contingency and looks for Black Swans at the tail of normal distributions.

Structures condition but seldom determine human behavior. Most important, they can permit actors to choose and follow certain courses of action. Cooperation needs to grow as societies become more complex. Instead of viewing humans as passive agents responding to larger factors, analysts should see people as individuals engaged in strategic and adaptive decision making—seeking not only to survive but to thrive in their physical and social environment. In short, these processes result from the amalgamated behaviors of multiple agents.

Complexity science sees that changes in the natural and cultural landscape present both challenges and opportunities for strategic decision making by individuals and by groups of individual agents. This perspective emphasizes factors that are culturally created and controllable. It views exogenous factors less as stresses that dictate new and costly reorganizations and more as circumstances that permit the creation of cooperative organizations not feasible in previous environmental and cultural contexts (Stanish and Levine 2011).

Structures, if kneaded in constructive ways, may help to harvest wisdom on complex and difficult choices. Putting individuals into groups where their combined expertise may shed light on difficult issues such as climate change can reduce the supposed distinction between agent and structure (Klein 2011; Keller 2011; Holman 2011; Hernandez 2011a and 2011b). This is the goal of the MIT Deliberatorium, discussed later in the next chapter.

chapter eleven

CHALLENGES TO COMPLEXITY SCIENCE

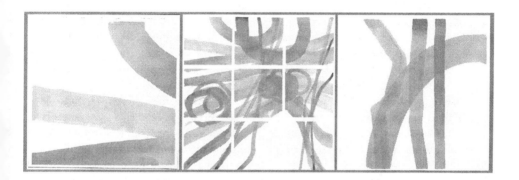

Complexity science hearkens to Albert Einstein's advice: "Everything should be made as simple as possible, but no simpler." In 1952, while still in college studying applied mathematics, Peter G. Neumann talked with Einstein for two hours over breakfast—a meeting that filliped a lifelong romance with both the beauty and perils of complexity. "What do you think of Johannes Brahms?" Neumann asked. "I have never understood Brahms," Einstein replied. "I believe Brahms was burning the midnight oil trying to be complicated." A computer scientist with a guiding concern for security, Neumann in the twenty-first century called for redesigning systems starting from a "clean slate" (Markoff 2012)—in effect, a paradigm shift.

BEYOND DESCRIPTION

Can students of world affairs find a useful "clean slate"? Having looked at perennial and contemporary issues, this book argues that a paradigm based on interdependence and complexity offers a broad and insightful framework for analyzing the past and present of global politics.

To what extent do any of the existing approaches to international studies help us anticipate alternative futures or prescribe policy?

From Machiavelli to Hans J. Morgenthau and John J. Mearsheimer, realists posited that global actors will continue, as in the past, to struggle for power. Led by Kenneth W. Waltz, neorealists add that—responding to the shifts in the structure of power—weaker states will balance against or align with stronger ones.

Idealists in the tradition of Kant and Woodrow Wilson predict that democracy will conduce to peace. If democracy is imperfect, however, all bets are off—due to "poor implementation" or "path-dependency" (Mansfield and Snyder 2005). Another set of idealists, Iran's theocrats, blame their country's woes not on themselves but on the Great Satan (Bellaigue 2005).

Our knowledge of world affairs will not be advanced by dogmatic assumptions about the inexorable quest for power or the need to establish democracy or some other ideal. Forecasts based on such assumptions sometimes seem to explain important phenomena, at least in some respects, but sometimes not. Most such forecasts are hard to confirm or falsify. If they prove wrong just once, followers of Karl Popper will say that they have been falsified.

Nothing is predetermined. Sound analysis must take account of trends while trying to think of all the contingencies that can stop, reroute, or supersede them. The *Global Trends 2030* analysis by the National Intelligence Council (2012) is a model of such analysis. The study stresses that the future "is malleable" and lists important "game changers" that will most influence the global scene through 2030. The list includes a crisis-prone world economy, shortcomings in governance, conflicts within states and between them, the impact of new technologies, and whether the United States can "work with new partners to reinvent the international system." Failing to flesh out some of the darkest and most preferable scenarios possible, however, the analysis is somewhat abstract and may not spur policymakers to take and implement unpalatable but needed decisions. The NIC conceded that its earlier reports sometimes underestimated the speed at which changes arrive on the global scene.

Mindful of complexity and contingency, complexity science offers no flat-out predictions. Still, the hypothesis advanced in chapter 2 is supported by experience. *Complexity science contends that top-down rule is inimical to human development and that self-organization is the key to societal fitness. High levels of fitness and human development are most likely to be found in communities that practice self-organization while avoiding the polar opposites of anarchy and despotism. As outlined in Table 2.1, this diagnosis describes and explains the main obstacles to development and to world peace.*

Still, an understanding of each actor's fitness and the global fitness landscape permits some "if, then" exploration of alternative futures. If a political-social-economic system loses fitness, it will wither unless negative trends are reversed. Thus, the growing shortfalls in Soviet fitness were evident in the upturn in the country's infant mortality in the early 1970s (Davis and Feshbach 1980), because infant mortality reflects many dimensions of fitness. Despite deepening public health and environmental challenges, the Kremlin continued to direct massive resources to its military. Priority to military developments also retarded the system's ability to stay abreast of what Zbigniew Brzezinski (1970) termed the technetronic revolution.

For decades before the Soviet collapse, however, realists looked at the Kremlin's hard power—its armed forces and natural resource endowment—and expected the Soviet empire to endure.[1] Taking note of Soviet expansion from Angola to Grenada, some forecast a steadily growing Soviet empire. Fixed on geopolitical continuity and system inertia, realists were not prepared for the system's implosion. Meanwhile, idealists of various stripes regarded the Soviet system as inhuman, but that opinion did not help them predict its demise. Inhuman systems can exist for long periods.

As the social fabric of the USSR weakened, however, the empire wilted from within. Each time Soviet dominion was challenged by its putative al-lies—by East Germans in 1953, by Hungarians in 1956, by Czechs and Slovaks 1968—Moscow delayed action ever longer and killed fewer rebels. When Poland's Solidarność movement in the 1970s began organizing anticommunist activities in neighboring countries, the Kremlin opted not to use Soviet forces but instead let its clients in Warsaw impose martial law. By the late 1980s the three Baltic countries were proclaiming the priority of their laws over those framed in Moscow (Clemens 1988, 1991). Facing strong independence movements, Soviet troops killed fewer than forty persons in Latvia and Lithu-anian and none in Estonia. A military goliath was disarmed by a radical soft power—a singing revolution (Šmidchens 2013; Clemens 2009).

The low fitness of post-communist Russia was again evident in public health statistics in the 1990s.[2] Thanks in part to government largesse permitted by higher oil and gas prices on the world market, life expectancy in Russia improved in the early twenty-first century. For men it climbed from 57.6 in the Yeltsin era to 60.1 in 2011, while for women it reached 73.2. Still, in 2012 some 2,500 *more* people died than were born in the RF, and infant mortality *rose* to 8.7 deaths per thousand births, up from 7.1 in 2011 after a dozen years of decline. New forms of network power took shape in the Putin era—computerization with guns plus updated forms of bribes and personal connections, long known as *blat* (Kononenko and Mosches 2011). Complexity science would warn, however, that top-down manipulation and rent-seeking will never optimize fitness or competitive ability. As Anders Åslund (2013) noted, there were many reasons why Putin's regime could prove unstable:

- All power was centered in one person.

- Russia's economy depended on high oil prices, which might again fall.

- Regimes with high-level corruption are unstable, but campaigns against corruption can trigger high-level resistance.

- The regime's practice of meeting nearly every protest with repression could generate still more opposition.

- The Kremlin's anti-American campaigns undermined prospects of cooperation with the only superpower.

- Putin's bullying worsened Russia's relations with its post-Soviet neighbors. Not mentioned by Äslund, Putin's abusive treatment of the RF's non-Russian republics such as Tatarstan threatened the federation's unity and provoked calls in Kazan for "confederation like the EU."

The imminent collapse of the Yugoslav Federation could also be discerned from its declining fitness. The Federation's gross domestic product shrank for most of the 1980s—the worst performance in all of Eastern Europe. The two fittest republics, Slovenia and Croatia, were first to split from Belgrade's domination.

Attuned to complexity, analysts of world affairs will anticipate what Machiavelli termed *fortuna*—all the chance factors that open or close the door to change. Virtually unpredictable coincidences and events may accelerate or thwart the apparent dynamics of history and the efforts of governments and other actors to shape them. Thus, in 1981 an individual gunman (backed perhaps by some communist authorities) tried to assassinate Pope John Paul II. The structure and the voluntarist act were there but the bullet missed. It wounded but did not kill the pope, whose personal presence and whose policies continued to undermine the communist realm. Would the Soviet empire have expired when it did if the Polish-born Pope John Paul II had been killed instead of wounded by an assassin's bullet?

A perfect storm may arise from many sources. Chance events include mood changes, near misses and lucky hits, riots, last-minute decisions, voter turnouts, sharper than usual fluctuations in weather (an early or weak monsoon), economic dislocations (George Soros versus the Bank of England), swings in voter moods (a French *non* in 2005 to the proposed European Union constitution as a protest against President Jacques Chirac). Wise planners, of course, will try to erect defenses against tsunamis and other changes of fortune. As Machiavelli noted in *The Prince,* XXV, the very best leaders will not stick to old routines but expect the unexpected and adapt as new conditions emerge.

Given a political condition of anarchy, or top-down rule, or self-organization, complexity science is probably correct to forecast the kinds of outcomes outlined above in Table 2.1. This diagnosis also generates a foundation for assessing alternative futures and for suggesting wise policy recommendations.

POLICY GUIDANCE

Is global politics and economics winner-take-all or win-win or something more open-ended? What are the policy implications of the various paradigms? Realists call for more power while idealists seek realization of their ideals. Policymakers often emphasize one approach to the neglect of the other.

Ultrarealists say that world politics is a zero-sum struggle. Some idealists contend that IR is or should be a win-win, positive-sum collaboration. Other analysts expect a negative-sum future as humans destroy themselves and their environment. These diverse expectations have practical consequences: ultrarealists pursue hard-line policies of conquest and deception that often backfire; ultraliberals count on win-win outcomes that risk abuse by hardliners.

Cynical realism can exert a heavy toll. Soviets, even when they talked "peaceful coexistence," seldom escaped the "*kto kovo* [who will destroy whom]" mentality bequeathed them by Lenin and Stalin. The resultant policies cut them off from mutual gain endeavors such as the Marshall Plan.

U.S. policy during and after the cold war was heavily influenced by the "lessons of Munich." George F. Kennan ("Mr. X" in 1947) called for containing the USSR but also for cultivating the fundamental values and well-being of the United States—close to what complexity scientists would term America's "fitness." For decades Washington heeded the first part of Kennan's advice while assigning a subordinate role to the second part. In Washington, no less than in Tehran, fanaticism sometimes crowded out sober thinking. The zero-sum unilateralism of the George W. Bush administration alienated America's friends and inspired its enemies. Washington's expanding dedication to military assets and operations shortchanged other ingredients of fitness—even science. Candidate Mitt Romney in 2012 called for spending 4 percent of GDP on defense regardless of specific threats to U.S. security. A deep concern for mutual vulnerability—system-wide as well as domestic—would provide a sounder premise for policy.

Complexity science acknowledges that politics is often played as a zero-sum game but contends that most cross-border interactions are variable-sum: one side only may win; or both; or neither. Losses and gains can be absolute or relative. As Mr.Y (2011) puts it, the uncertainty and change produced by today's complex, open system affords both "opportunity and hope. . . . Competitors are not necessarily adversaries." To be a "*winner* does not demand a *loser.*"

Neither cynical nor naive, complexity science perceives world affairs in all their variable-sum conditionality. Accordingly, it recommends that actors seek mutual gain by strategies of contingent cooperation—what Mr. Y calls the leveraging of "converging interests and interdependencies."[3]

Complexity science cautions us not to expect "security" from a rigid hierarchy of power. Challenging dogmatic Marxists and other critics, Mikhail Gorbachev in the late 1980s averred that policy must no longer be guided by class or national interests but by "all-human" interests (Clemens 1990). Using nearly the same language as Gorbachev, Mr. Y asserted that "in our complex, interdependent, and constantly changing global environment security is not achievable for one nation or by one people alone; rather it must be recognized as a common interest among all peoples. Otherwise, security is not sustainable, and without it there can be no peace of mind."

Humans cannot arrange nature or world affairs to go on as a static idyll. Healthy systems operate close to the edge of chaos where they can be maximally creative. Skillful players accept that everything is dynamic and that nature itself evolves through strategies of risk taking (Marshall and Zohar 1997, 134–35). Mindful of interdependence, complexity warns us to plan for the system effects of tsunamis, violence, epidemics, and waves of displaced persons. Mr. Y urges us to think in terms of "strategic ecology."

Complexity science suggests that human development programs as well as preventive diplomacy limit state failure and related violence. The notion of "global governance" by governments, NGOs, the UN, corporations—by all stakeholders who can play a useful role—amounts to an application of complexity science to world affairs Nonstate actors as well as some governments and international organizations have taken some steps to reverse environmental degradation, for example, by curbing products that deplete the ozone layer. They have also cultivated a foundation for future action by building a scientific consensus on threats such as climate change.

A world affairs perspective informed by complexity science would focus on the long-term fitness of each society, beginning with one's own, and that of the entire planet. If policymakers shared this perspective, it would fundamentally alter the framework by which they debate whether to conduct more nuclear tests, curb global warming, and permit sales of patented drugs in developing countries. Alert to the likelihood of unforeseen side effects, a complexity perspective would restrain grandiose schemes to alter the flow of rivers, replace traditional grains with newly engineered varieties, or insert exotic fishes into established water systems (such as Lake Victoria). It would discourage the logic of collective action that says, "What we do for our private gain won't affect the big picture."

The MIT Deliberatorium aims to help large numbers of people, distributed in space and time, combine their insights to find well-founded solutions for complex multistakeholder, multidiscplinary problems such as sustainability, climate change policy, and complex product design. It uses "argument mapping" to identify an issue (like the trunk of a tree) about which there are ideas (like branches), some pro and some con (like leaves on the branches). From knowledge sharing the deliberative process seeks synergetic problem-solving The open-source movement and Wikipedia encouraged Deliberatorium's founder Mark Klein to infer that many people are not selfish utility-maximizers but individuals who want to make the world a better place (Duval 2010,

160–70). The present book, too, proposes that deeper understanding of our interdependent complexity will help people cope with challenges to their own and the planet's well-being.[4]

ICARUS OR THE WRIGHT BROTHERS?

A brutal test of any paradigm is: What does it add to untutored common sense? The basic concepts of realism and idealism (old and new varieties) come readily to any thoughtful person, especially one who reads a major newspaper or interacts with persons from different cultures. These concepts include visions of power/influence, offense/defense, expansion/contraction, beliefs/sentiments, and perception/misperception. But these concepts do little to sharpen our ability to understand world affairs. (Wilson 1988, 183–84). This is not the case with concepts such as societal fitness, punctuated equilibrium, and self-organized criticality. Having borrowed many of these concepts from biology and other disciplines and applied them to global interactions, complexity can truly deepen our understanding of international and other social systems.

Using these concepts, a complexity paradigm can contribute fundamental insights helpful to grand as well as to micro and partial theories in social sciences. Seeking to explain the fitness of all life forms, complexity science provides a broader lens for analyzing the power and influence of nonstate actors as well as states. Emphasizing the coevolution of each actor with its rivals and partners, and with their shared habitat, complexity can help global studies make stronger connections with kindred disciplines such as political economy and ecology. For the same reason, complexity science helps analysis of IR to connect with historical studies of the rise and fall of states and entire civilizations. All these linkages tap and boost the consilience of social and natural sciences, ethics and religion, and aesthetics (Wilson 1998).

Some critics contend that, at best, the premises of complexity science do no more than confirm intuitive assumptions and thus serve no function except as metaphors. Defenders reply that reframing of basic visions is valuable in itself. Metaphors can change how we perceive and act (Hendrick 2010, 388).

One of the most penetrating critiques of complexity science in political science is that of Earnest and Rosenau (2006). They contend that human societies and their authority structures cannot be explained by analogies to beehives, anthills or bird swarms and cannot be reproduced or predicted by computer simulations. Politics—especially international politics—cannot be understood as biology writ large. According to Earnest and Rosenau, efforts to mimic human society by computer simulations of artificial society ignore the unique place of political authority among humans. Agent-based modeling is unsuited to a field where political authority simplifies the inherent complexity of social life.

Defenders of complexity science reply that there is no reason why an agent-based approach must exclude the human agents who shape the system. A broad understanding of complexity will assess not only structures and processes but also human choice. While structure limits options, it also confronts individuals with choice. They may pursue one course or another. Outcomes depend heavily on how well actors interpret the structure and chart their course.

The stiff standards articulated by Earnest and Rosenau also challenge existing paradigms of realism and idealism. The demand that a valid theory of international relations take full account of "who the actors are" undercuts neorealist theory and some idealisms no less than it does complex systems theories. The grander the theory to which international relations scholarship aspires, the more difficult it will be to find an approach that meets the standards of physical sciences. Humans are far more complex than quarks—or jaguars. Neither politics nor biology is conducive to deductive, "nomothetic" models. Classical Newtonian models are too mechanical, too deterministic, and too experimental. In the study of complex systems, they give way to probabilism, synergism, emergence, and the methods of observation and comparison. This transformation has affected relativity and quantum physics and may well be the appropriate approach to employ in social sciences (Almond et al. 2003, 116–17).

Realism and idealism no less than complexity approaches confront the V–N dilemma. The more *variables* we attempt to weigh, the more difficult it becomes to study a large *number* of cases from which to generalize. Complexity science proffers no easy solutions to this dilemma, but its framework is more suited to wrestle this challenge than any monocausal approach.

Complexity science is very far from producing a comprehensive theory. Its supporters do not agree on which puzzles need to be or can be tackled. They disagree on which methods are best or even feasible. Still, the basic concepts of complexity science offer the basis for a paradigm shift in comparative politics and international studies—a framework that could open the door to significant theoretical and practical advances. To eschew the pitfalls of a false paradigm is no small thing. Astronomers could never understand their subject so long as they assumed that the sun circles the earth. Similarly, investigators of world affairs will never draw a true picture of their field so long as they posit that raw material power or the ascendancy of certain ideas is the prime mover in world affairs.

Walt Whitman summed up how a complexity perspective could alter world affairs in his *Salut au Monde*. Having hailed the rivers, mountains, deserts, nations, and religions of the world—its vast material and spiritual beauty, Whitman concluded:

> My spirit has pass'd in compassion and determination around the
>   whole earth
> I have look'd for equals and lovers and found them ready for me
>   in all lands,
> I think some divine rapport has equalized me with them.

Complexity science, we conclude, will not melt like the wings of Icarus. Like the Wright Brothers in 1903, it is ready to fly—primitive but with an expansive future.

afterword

SCIENCE AND ART IN THIS BOOK: EXPLORING THE GENOME TOGETHER

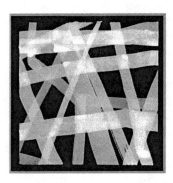

Too often, science and art are spoken through their antagonisms—science is seen as dealing with truth, whereas artists deal with ego and expression. But for myself and many other artists, our pursuit is not one of personal expression, but of interrogation. Interacting with life scientists, I see with increasing clarity that both science and art are about knowledge. Collaboration between them can deepen our understanding of this beautiful and complex world.

The illustrations in this book derive from a "Data Set" of watercolors, born out of my conversations with scientists at the Broad Institute of M.I.T. and Harvard University. These watercolors are painted on 3-by-3 grids of 8-inch square sheets of paper, which I then scanned into my computer. Not only did the work allow me to explore what I was learning about science, but also, by serendipity, helped me to develop a "high-throughput" drawing process, which formed a kind of experimental data. The process yielded a data base of serial images that could be shifted, sorted, analyzed, and reworked in a variety of ways. When reorganized, the images produced patterns like those seen in some pages of this book.

From the data we can discern patterns. From the patterns we can extract new meaning. In the same way that experimental results can raise more questions than they answer and lead to new hypotheses to be tested, an image in my database could be removed from its original series and serve as the seed for a new grid. Within the digital environment, I can remove a mark from a painting and begin a new one around that single element. The database has thus become a way for me to use image-making to process the science that I've learned and to develop a multi-dimensional tool to create new images, some of which appear in this book.

Western science tends to isolate the system it is studying from its environment. Until now this has been one of its strengths. Scientists can talk about the "organs" of a cell without mentioning the cell itself. In the realm of genetics, DNA is almost always isolated from the genome's epigenetic features. The context is assumed. We often see the genome depicted as a one-dimensional string of A's, T's, G's, and C's. In "reality," however, it is a three-dimensional chemical structure with shape and action and a place in the cell. To work around this we played with different ways of contextualizing this process, finally settling on the idea of sizing the elements—DNA, histone proteins, cells—so that each element is mapped within the next. The resulting image illustrates epigenetics in a new, contextual way.

This experience underscored the rising importance of dimensionality to contemporary science. This is a dual problem, involving both understanding and communication. How do you conceptualize and manipulate a space in many dimensions? How do you collapse that space into the two or three dimensions that we have evolved to navigate intuitively? And how do you represent it in such a way that it is understandable to others?

Exploring this dynamic view brought me to wonder about time-based networks. A typical view of networked elements, such as genes, will show all measured relationships between the elements. In a complex process, such as stem cell differentiation, this leads to what is expressively called a "hairball," where there are so many connections that the parts are no longer visible. By giving time properties to the edges in such a network, one could begin to see operative connections for a given time point or cell state. These actual links may be more informative in this context than the full set of all possible connections. In this case, of course, less is more.

From my own experiences moving around the globe and adopting new cultures, I know how long it takes to learn the shape of a new space and transform it into something significant. Clearly this is only the first stage of my own investigation, which I call my *défrichage*—French for the clearing that happens before wild, forested land can be planted. I know that the images I have created so far are only superficially connected to the science, but they are also a necessary point of departure. My ultimate interest is in finding visual analogs for complex ideas in the genomic sciences, and through them to discover emergent features of a larger worldview in today's culture. In this way my own objectives converge with those of this book.

DANIEL KOHN

NOTES

CHAPTER ONE. WHY A SCIENCE OF COMPLEXITY?

1. Unlike the administrators of *The Hunger Games,* who sponsored assassination and civil war to allocate scarce resources among their subjects, Roth and Shapley developed algorithms showing how best to bring contending parties together for mutual benefit. They pointed the way to stable outcomes—allocation of benefits in cases when there are many possible options but the parties perceive no gain from seeking a different match.

2. Healthy heartbeats display a complex set of multifractal properties while heartbeats of people with congestive heart problems are generally monofractal (McNeil 1999; also Goldberger 1996; more references at www.physionet.org).

3. Cohen and Stewart (1994, 3) contrasted "simplicity" with "complicity." The first refers to "the tendency of simple rules to emerge from underlying disorder . . . in systems whose large-scale structure is independent of the fine details of their substructure." By contrast, "complicity is the tendency of interacting systems to coevolve in a manner that changes both, leading to a growth of complexity from simple beginnings—complexity that is unpredictable in detail, but whose general course is comprehensible and foreseeable." The authors maintain that simplicities of form, function, or behavior emerge from complexities on lower levels because of external restraints. Simple rules emerge from underlying disorder and complexity in systems whose large-scale structure is independent of the details of their substructure. See also Casti 1994 and Buchanan 2000.

4. Goethe, according to Emerson, regarded a leaf, or the eye of a leaf, as a key unit of botany, and saw that every part of the plant was only a transformed leaf to meet a new condition; and, by varying the conditions, a leaf may be converted into any other organ, and any other organ into a leaf." In like manner, in osteology, Goethe assumed that one vertebra of the spine might be considered the unit of the skeleton; the head was only the uppermost vertebra transformed. "The plant goes from knot to knot, closing, at last, with the flower and the seed. So the tape-worm, the caterpillar, goes from knot to knot, and closes with the head. Men and the higher animals are built up through the vertebrae, the powers being concentrated in the

head." In every field Goethe went to the core. In optics "he rejected the artificial theory of seven colors, and considered that every color was the mixture of light and darkness in new proportions."

5. For complexity science at the Santa Fe Institute, see http://www.santafe. edu/; at the New England Complex Systems Institute, http://necsi.org/necsi/; at the Northeastern University Center for Interdisciplinary Research on Complex Systems, http://www.circs.neu.edu/; at the Northeastern University Center for Complex Network Research, http://www.barabasilab.com/; at the George Masson University Center for Social Complexity, http://socialcomplexity.gmu.edu/; at the European Union's Complex Systems Network of Excellence (EXYSTENCE), www.complexityscience. org; at the Department of Biology, Calgary University, http://www.bio.ucalgary.ca/; at the Center for Complex Systems Research, University of Warsaw, http://www.iss. uw.edu.pl/osrodki/obuz/OBUZNEW_ENG/obuz.htm. In Paris, Edgar Morin (2008) was a virtual center.

6. Quantum physics once seemed like the last nail in the coffin of pure reason. According to George Musser (2012), however, it provides a model for human behavior in which irrationality makes total sense.

7. Longo, Maël, and Kauffman (2012) argue that there is no place in biological evolution for the physics worldview of law-entailed dynamics. They point to the variability of the very contexts of life—interactions among organisms, biological niches, and ecosystems. These contexts are ever-changing, intrinsically indeterminate, and unprestatable. No one can know ahead of time the niches that constitute the boundary conditions for selection. Looked at broadly, the space of possibilities cannot be prestated mathematically. No laws of motion can be formulated for evolution. Life goes on in a web of enablement and radical emergence. Still, mutations and other causal differences put nonconservation principles at the core of evolution, unlike physical dynamics, based largely on conservation principles. A conceptual frame of "extended criticality" (discussed below in chapter 2) can benefit the study of life processes.

8. Later on, as weaponry became less dependent on physical strength, women too could pull triggers and push buttons to kill. In the twenty-first century, American and some other women could not only vote and occupy high offices but even fight on the front lines.

9. In this vein, Darwin noted that if two tribes fight, the tribe with "a great number of courageous, sympathetic and faithful members, who were always ready to warn each other of danger, to aid and defend each other" is more likely to prevail.

10. Mephistopheles heaped scorn on jurisprudence as well as on philosophy and theology. "The sense of what is right and wrong, born within us, is not discussed by this profession" (*Faust* I, 1970–79).

11. For these and other uses of the word, see "complex" in the *Oxford English Dictionary*.

12. IR scholars who have drawn on studies of evolution and/or complexity include Axelrod 1984, 1997a., 1997b, 2006; Modelski 1996; Jervis 1997; Axelrod and Cohen 1999; Clemens 2001, 2002, 2010; Hoffmann, M. 2005; the editor and other contributors to N. Harrison 2006; Axelrod 2006; Kavalski 2008; Albert, Cederman, and Wendt 2010. All these authors provide extensive bibliographies to relevant social science and other scientific literature.

13. James (2002) suggests revisions to structural realism that, he argues, make it the most reliable approach to the study of international relations.

14. For an effort to document these four dimensions in the 1960s, see Clemens 1965.

15. For a unified growth theory, however, see Galor 2011.

16. For expert introductions to complexity, see Morin 2008; Mitchell 2008; and Page 2011.

17. For life sciences, "evolution by natural selection . . . has taken on the solidity of a mathematical theorem." Darwin's *On the Origin of Species* (1859) is arguably "history's most influential book" (Wilson 2006, 13).

18. See, however, Somit and Peterson 1992 and 2008. On the first political-military rivalries, see Cioffi-Revilla 1998.

19. Given this state of affairs, the tem complexity *science* should be used instead of *theory* in Clemens 2001, 2002, and 2010.

20. The two viewpoints are implicit in the Melian debate recounted in Thucydides, *Peloponnesian War*, Book V:84–116.

21. Neoconservatives among Washington's power elite seem to be close to wealth and power but claim to be devoted to democratic ideals. Many observers—conservatives as well as liberals—believe that the George W. Bush administration dissipated American power by throwing U.S. forces—very many but still too few—into Iraq (for example, Haass 2005 and Walt 2005).

22. For a dialogue between realists (including Morgenthau) and utopians, see *Salzburger Humanismusgespräch* 1970.

23. The temperament of a human infant, for example, will be conditioned not only by the parents' genes, emotions, and overall health but also by the time of year in which it is conceived and, of course, by the culture into which it is born (Kagan 2011).

24. Analysis of and citations to leading works may be found in C. Weber 2005. Her chapters deal with realism, idealism, constructivism, gender, globalization, clash of civilizations, and empire. Examples of many theories applied to a single case may be found in Sterling-Folker 2006.

25. Exceptions include Corning 2000; Smith and Stevens 1997; Somit and Peterson 1997.

26. Savagery, for Hobbes, was exemplified in the New World (Muloney 2011).

27. See the debate on rational choice and security studies in Brown 2000.

28. *Hamlet*, Act 2, Scene 2: 239–51; italics added.

CHAPTER TWO. BASIC CONCEPTS OF COMPLEXITY SCIENCE

1. The modernist city planning of Jean-Baptiste Colbert and Le Corbusier aimed to maximize access for authorities and central control. The chaos of city slums cannot be good for human development but neither are the orderly spaces of a planned city such as Brasilia. Compare the images of public areas in older towns such as São Salvador and São Paulo with the access-only-by-autos residential areas of Brasilia (Scott 1998, 122–24). Similarly, the straight-line layout of many colleges is probably less conducive to creative exchanges than the crisscrossing paths of other institutions, for example, within the Harvard Yard. Given the layout of their buildings, it is amazing that so many MIT people escape from linear thinking.

2. Two useful tools for resilience building in social-ecological systems are structured scenarios and active adaptive management, according to Folke et al. (2002). These tools require and facilitate a social context with flexible and open institutions

and multilevel governance systems that allow for learning and increase adaptive capacity without foreclosing future development options.

3. The UNDP produced its first HDI in 1990 and progressively refined its methodology and data-gathering and analytical techniques. Reliable data is difficult to obtain from many countries—especially when trying to reconstruct the facts to analyze trends extending back into the 1970s and 1980s. North Korea's reported life expectancy, for example, is probably quite inflated.

4. See reports by Freedom House (2010) and Transparency International, (2009). There is less overlap with the Index of Economic Freedom produced by the Heritage Foundation (2011).

5. The World Economic Forum in 2010 ranked Singapore number one in competitiveness and the United States as number four. Singaporeans, however, created very little even though the city-state's pupils scored high on standardized tests. Some Americans, in contrast, continued to innovate despite deepening shortfalls in education. In 2012 the forum ranked Switzerland number one; Singapore, number two; and the USA number seven.

6. Some 52 percent of Turkmens reported themselves as "thriving" in 2010 while only one percent admitted to suffering. More Belarusians and Kosovars claimed to be thriving (29%) than did Poles or Slovenes—even as the political and economic systems of Belarus and Kosovo were among the most repressive and backward in Europe. Cheerful Latin Americans reported high levels of satisfaction. Some 58 percent of Brazilians reported themselves as thriving compared to 57 percent of U.S. respondents; Costa Ricans reported higher satisfaction than Canadians (Gallup 2010).

7. The *Global Peace Index* produced by the World Peace Forum (2010) is singularly blind to these nuances.

8. If two countries existed isolated from each other, such as the Aztec and Chinese empires in 1500 CE, and if we could agree what value to measure, we could plot the rise and fall of their individual peaks. If the value measured were health, we might find that one of these polities had a higher life expectancy. The relative height of each peak would reflect not only each polity's policies but also the challenges and opportunities presented by its physical environment and by third parties. Since the Conquistadors virtually wiped out the Aztec way of life, we could say that the Aztec peak fell while China's remained upright despite pressures from ascendant Western powers and Japan's Rising Sun.

9. Each dimension summarizes many related variables. "Brain power," for example, seeks to summarize education at all levels *and* the dynamism of each country's scientific and research institutions. Time horizons are also imbedded in these estimates. China's "economic power" here is discounted mindful of resource challenges likely to become more severe.

10. Kant posited the synergy of representative government, a spirit of trade, hospitality to foreigners, plus a growing body of law and organization to govern transactions across borders. Kant's vision reflected the system developed by the Hanseatic merchants in city-states such as Königsberg, where Kant lived. Their way of life offered a model of self-organization, domestically and across borders—a system quite different from the extremes of hierarchy and anarchy prevalent in the Holy Roman Empire. For nearly four centuries the Hansas enjoyed long periods of peace and prosperity, until absorbed by larger "nation" states and empires—less than a century before Kant's birth (Clemens 2001, 26–30).

11. For a primer, see Payne and Nassar 2003.

12. See United Nations Development Programme 2010a and Transparency International 2010.

13. Some East Asian countries climbed higher on both indexes in later years. In 2011–12, for example, three Asian countries with mixed cultural backgrounds ranked in the top twenty for honesty: Singapore placed sixth, Hong Kong twelfth, and Japan fourteenth.

CHAPTER THREE. A CRUCIAL TEST CASE:
WHY THE BALTIC IS NOT THE BALKANS

1. For a very different slant, consider *War Again* and *Bulgarian Chicks* by Balkan Beat Box, a U.S.-Israeli group that recorded albums in many places including Belgrade with Serbian musicians. Lyrics and images on YouTube (accessed Oct. 25, 2012).

2. Non-Slovenes who left in the 1990s, when they returned, did not easily obtain citizenship or recognition as national minorities. Discrimination against Roma was manifest in Doleniska/Posavie. Efforts to build a mosque in Ljubljana met considerable resistance. Slovenes, a visiting U.S. scholar concluded, were "xenophobic" (Pozun December 2004).

3. Riots in Albania in 1997 arose from the collapse of pyramid investment schemes.

4. Roughly 20 percent of Estonia's residents in 2003 were not citizens. They could not vote in national elections or in the referendum on EU accession, but they were allowed to vote in local elections. Russian remained the language of instruction in localities where most children spoke Russian at home (*Nations in Transit 2004*). By 2011, more Russian speakers had become citizens and could speak Estonian.

5. Only one-third of Russian speakers in Latvia thought the 2002 parliamentary elections were free.

6. http://www.freedomhouse.org/sites/default/files/Graphs%202012.pdf (accessed 10/22/12).

7. For an explanation, see Adam 2009.

8. Frol Kozlov and Jerry Hough agreed on this proposition, challenged by Clemens 2000.

9. In 1990, thousands of Russian workers mingled with Soviet officers in a Tallinn square under a banner proclaiming "The People and the [Soviet] Army Are One." Author's observation and photos.

10. In the 1980s, most economies in Eastern Europe were floundering, but Yugoslavia's performed the worst—losing 1 percent annually in the 1980s except in 1986, when it grew by 3.5 percent. According to official statistics (possibly inflated) Bulgarian and Romanian economies also did well in 1986, growing by 5.5 and 7.3 percent respectively (Hafner and Lajh 2003, 34–35).

11. Estonia derived some energy from oil shale. Until the early twenty-first century, Lithuania had nuclear power, while Russia relied heavily on Baltic refineries and ports to process and deliver its oil to Western markets.

12. While poverty may have driven some African insurgencies, a study by the World Bank (Collier 2003) probably erred in minimizing political and other motives for civil war (Klem 2004; Kahl 2004). The World Bank analysis left out how some politicians instigate violence to protect or expand their own power.

13. On migrations in Croatia, for example, see Crkven 1997.

14. A broad survey found that, after controlling for per capita income, more ethnically or religiously diverse countries were no more likely to experience significant civil violence in the years after the collapse of communism The factors likely to trigger civil war were not ethnic or religious but underlying conditions such as poverty and political instability (Fearon and Laitin 2003). Large-N surveys, of course, do not capture the features of specific cases. Kosovars were relatively poor while most Estonians and Slovenians were relatively well off. Poverty in Narva aggravated political discontent, but few Russian speakers there wished to rejoin Russia.

15. A Californian transplanted to Ljubljana in the 1990s found that Slovenes and some "southerners" displayed "a certain wry wisdom, a cockeyed sense of humor, a melancholy knowledge of the reality of human nature all of which seems to be absent from the American sensibility." Slovenes were quick to distinguish between "ours [*naša*]" and "southerners [*južnjaki*]" (other South Slavs) and "Albanians [*Čefuri*]." An American with her blue U.S. passport was marked "*tujka* [foreigner]," but got quicker and perhaps better treatment in medical clinics and from government bureaucrats than did refugees from the other ex-Yugoslav republics with their red passports. The native Californian observed, however, that the erstwhile Yugoslavs exhibited "an odd combination of openly-expressed prejudice accompanied by a weary and heart-rending tolerance" that was probably "a truer reflection of the human condition than America's openly-expressed tolerance accompanied by the weary prejudices . . . hidden behind the . . . the bullying tendency to eradicate every difference with a shallow phrase" (Debeljak 2004, 105).

16. Believing he had collaborated with the Soviet KGB, many Estonians took umbrage when the head of the Orthodox faith in Estonia was brought to Moscow as Patriarch Aleksei.

17. After 1991 Estonians were inclined to transfer control of Orthodox churches to Orthodox authorities in Istanbul rather than in Moscow. This orientation did not oppose Orthodoxy but sought only to curtail Russian influence. Within a few years, all parties worked out a compromise solution.

18. The Chechen separatist leader Dzhokhar Dudaev (1944–1996) was a hero in Estonia because, as commander of the Soviet base near Tartu, he had refused to use force to crush the Estonian independence movement.

CHAPTER FOUR. CULTURE AND THE
CAPACITY TO COPE WITH COMPLEXITY

1. *Pretty Village, Pretty Flame* (*Lepa sela lepo gore*)—a 1996 Serbian film based on an incident in 1992.

2. The folktale *Miorita* is shared by Romanian speakers in Moldova as well as in Wallachia (Babuts 2000). For people in Bucharest, *Miorita* probably symbolizes the unity of Romania's three major provinces. In Chișinău, however, the poem could recall that Moldova had a separate and unique past and underscore the willingness of powerful elites in Wallachia and Transylvania to kill Moldovans for reasons of envy and greed. Early in the twenty-first century Moldovans had incomes much lower than Romanians but most seemed to cherish their independence despite the many problems it occasioned.

3. When I visited Zagreb in March 1953, Young Communists showed me photos of Stepinac consorting with German and Ustaša officials. By that time Stepinac

had been transferred from prison to house arrest in his home village Krašić, some fifty kilometers from Belgrade. Arriving in Krašić, then several hours by bus from Zagreb, I asked Stepinac about this wartime behavior. He replied that his conscience was clean—"*Mein Gewissen ist rein.*"

4. Stepinac did not publicly condemn Catholic clergy and laypersons who helped draw up racist laws that led to massacres of Roma, Orthodox Serbs, and antifascist Croats Had he spoken publicly, a Croatian colleague writes, "it would have meant Jasenovac death camp for him. . . . People easily forget how Ustašes killed or sent to Jasenovac not only Serbs and Communists but also prominent members of HSS [Stjepan Radić's peasant party]. In Banja Luka, for example, the Ustašes killed every prominent member of HSS, none was spared."

5. The sheer chaos of Romanian life after Ceauşescu made it more likely that even constructive legislation such as Iliescu's language reforms would spark conflict.

6. Opponents said Iliescu had been too close to Ceauşescu, was Gorbachev's puppet, had fostered corruption, and even that he was guilty of "crimes against humanity."

7. Rolandas Paskas, however, was ousted from the Lithuanian presidency for alleged ties with a Russian businessman.

8. Landsbergis had long held a distorted view of Martin Luther King Jr., he told me in 1996, because Soviet media had cast King as a sort of Uncle Tom for capitalist imperialism.

9. Dates for hundreds of languages are at www.worldscriptures.org. The site oversimplifies in some cases but it includes not just the dates for Bible publication in southern Estonian (no longer spoken) and Tallinn Estonian but also for Eastern and Western Livonian, each spoken now by only a hundred or so persons.

10. For the larger pattern, see Hroch 1985.

11. About 80 percent of Estonians could read in 1881—a higher percentage even than in Finland, Sweden, Scotland, or Germany (Hasselblatt 1996, 51–61). According to Imperial Russian census of 1897 census, 96.1 percent of the Estonian population ten years and older in the Baltic Provinces could read, with male and female literacy levels virtually the same (Raun 2003, 136). Literacy in most of Central Asia, however, was only one-third of Russian in 1900.

12. In 2002 the editor of *Journal of Baltic Studies* in a book review derided complexity science for giving no practical advice except to cooperate.

13. Valkov (2009) challenged the hypothesis that there is a cohabitation of civic engagement with democratic institutions and practices.

14. The New Testament was published in Bulgarian in 1840, the entire Bible in 1864. Of Orthodox countries, Romania was the first to publish the Bible in the vernacular. Part of the Bible was published in 1553, the entire New Testament in 1648, the complete Bible in 1688—probably in a very limited edition. Parts of the Bible were translated and published for speakers of Romanian Macedonian in 1889 and for Romani Vlach in 1980.

15. Questioning the role played by tradition, one Serbian educator argued that paternalism and personal rule derived from the ruling elite's need to strengthen state power (Rosandić 2000, 14).

16. The Polish-Lithuanian Commonwealth was a model of cosmopolitan live-and-let-live in many respects. When Ukrainian nobles did not get the same rights as others, however, their allegiance switched from the Commonwealth to Russia.

CHAPTER FIVE. COMPLEXITY SCIENCE AS A
TOOL TO UNDERSTAND THE NEW EURASIA

1. The Bertelsmann Foundation criteria for economic transformation are broader and more solicitous of social welfare than the laissez-faire standards of the Heritage Foundation Index of Economic Freedom, cited below in Table 5.4. Regardless of a country's democracy score, Heritage might approve its economic freedom, e.g., Singapore's.

2. Ownership of the mine was divided between the Mongolian government (34%) and Canadian-listed Turquoise Hill (66%), which was controlled by Rio Tinto (headquartered in London but managed from Melbourne).

3. Besides these clashes, Azerbaijan fought Armenia, Russia fought Chechens and Dagestanis, Tajiks fought Tajiks. Given their other characteristics, these players are listed in zones D and E.

4. For background and recent developments in the Caucasus, see De Waal 2010.

5. On the reversal of ethnic cleansing in Bosnia, however, see Toal and Dahlman 2011.

6. Of eighty regions in the Russian Federation, Tatarstan ranked 4th—just below St. Petersburg—on the Human Development Index; Chechnya, 71st; and Tuva 80th. See hdr.undp.org/en/reports/europethecis/Russia/Russia_NHDR_2010_EN.pdf (accessed 07/29/11).

7. Not only was the Soviet system faulty but it elicited bad leaders. Recalling her encounters with the Soviet leaders in the 1950s and 1960s, Galina Vishnevskaya (the leading soprano at the Bolshoi Theater in those years) found them to be "men of crude manners, sparse education, a worm's eye view of the larger world and unspeakable conceit. They were the tip of the Mafia and they didn't make much attempt to conceal it. The number of times I had to sing to the chomping jaws of our drunken leaders is too many to remember" (Clark 2012). Gorbachev, the last Soviet president, was of much higher caliber than most of his predecessors. By his time, the system was collapsing.

8. Buddhist and Confucian traditions did not prevent Mongolia, Japan, South Korea, and other Asian countries from becoming politically free.

9. The "demolition of democracy" was feared by some opposition parties in Hungary, according to *The New York Times,* December 22, 2011.

10. The BTI included two sets of rankings: one for the present "status"—each country's rank for what has been achieved, and one for "management," a capacity for transformation, with allowance for the difficulties. This chapter uses only the status rankings.

11. The value-laden term *transitional* was not altogether appropriate. First, "highly advanced" countries such as the Czech Republic were certainly not "developing" in the sense, say, of India. Nor were they transitional. For many years the Czech Republic had already become a functioning democracy with a market economy. Second, "transitional" and other categories such as "advanced" and "blocked" implied a deterministic trajectory. As a comparison of the rankings across the years demonstrates, states could "advance" or fall back. Third, many governments may not want their countries to "develop" as the Bertelsmann Foundation would like. Turkmenistan's leaders, for example, may not have wanted a market economy or democracy under law.

12. United Nations Development Programme 2010a; Bertelsmann Foundation 2011; Transparency International 2010.

13. Regardless the "objective" trends, each individual feels his or her milieu individually. In October 2012 I met a well-dressed, healthy-looking Georgi, packing groceries in Boston. He had departed Bulgaria a few months before. He had a decent job as a photographer in Sofia, but could not abide the pervasive corruption. He knew four languages but little English. Still, at age fifty-three, he left everything for a new life. "How about Bulgaria and the European Union?" I asked in Russian. His reply: "EU good, Bulgaria bad."

14. Citing a range of sources, the BBC reported on October 24, 2012, that Estonia's GDP fell 14.3 percent in 2009 but then grew at 2.3 and 7.6 percent in 2010 and 2011. Slovenia's fell by 8 percent in 2009; rose by 1.4 percent in 2010 and then shrank again in 2011 by 0.2 percent. Slovakia's GDP fell by 4.9 percent in 2009 but then grew at better than 3 percent in 2010–11.

15. For a complex system analysis, see Lagi and Bar-Yam 2012.

16. World Health Organization, 2011, Suicide rates per one hundred thousand by country, at http://www.who.int/mental_health/prevention/suicide_rates/en/ (accessed 11/14/12).

17. Fourth place was occupied by Sri Lanka (31 per 100,000), but its data dated from the 1990s, and probably reflected the chaos of the country's long civil war.

18. World Health Organization, 2012, at http://www.who.int/mental_health/prevention/suicide/suicideprevent/en/. (accessed 11/12/2012).

19. The statistics had to be treated with caution. Few attempts at suicide "succeed"—perhaps only one in twenty. Families and authorities in many countries underreport suicide as a cause of death. Data from less-developed countries are often missing or incomplete. The erstwhile model developing country Sri Lanka reported very high levels of suicide, but its health services and government statistics were much stronger than in most of Southeast Asia or Africa.

20. To track teenage suicides, the WHO surveyed sixty-three countries in 1995 and ninety countries in 2004. Seven of the top ten in 1995 were post-communist: Russia, Lithuania, Kazakhstan, Latvia, Estonia, Belarus, and Kyrgyzstan. Five of these countries ranked in the top ten again in 2009, while Latvia and Kyrgyzstan fell into the second tier (11 to 20), their places taken by Turkmenistan and Ukraine. The rates for some countries increased—Russia, Kazakhstan, Estonia, and Ukraine; Belarus remained the same; rates in Latvia and Kyrgyzstan dropped (Wasserman et al. 2008; Efimova et al. 2011).

21. Around the world, an average of seven out of every one hundred thousand teenagers commited suicide each year in the late 2000s. In Russia, that number was twenty-two per hundred thousand, and in two regions, Tuva and Chukotka, more than one hundred per hundred thousand. Yearly, more than 1,700 Russians between fifteen and nineteen took their lives (Efimova 2011) but more than six thousand did so if the cohort includes all those from fifteen to twenty-four (WHO 2012a).

22. Impressions from many visits to Yugoslavia and the Soviet and post-Soviet realm, starting in 1953, including a year at Moscow State University, 1958–59. See also Appelbaum 2012.

23. Albanian dissident Lirak Bejko, aged forty-seven, burned himself in October 2012 to protest delays in government-promised compensation for communist-era political prisoners.

24. Men serving in the military provided a special case: Suicides in the U.S. armed forces exceeded battle deaths during Obama's first term.

CHAPTER SEVEN. HYPERPOWER CHALLENGED: PROSPECTS FOR AMERICANS

1. How these assets shifted over time is analyzed in Clemens 2000 and 2004. Hard, soft, and smart power are analyzed in Nye 2010.

2. Speaking of Faust, the Lord said, *"Es irrt der Mensch, so lang er strebt."*

3. The Afghan and Iraq campaigns launched after 9/11/2001 appeared a decade later as even more momentous failures.

4. The U.S. score on the HDI rose from 0.810 in 1980 to 0.857 in 1990. By 2000 it was 0.893; by 2010, 0.902 The average HDI scores for advanced industrial countries in the OECD also leveled off in the early twenty-first century, but the OECD average climbed from 0.723 in 1980 to 0.853 in 2010. China's ascent was much steeper. Its HDI score rose from 0.368 in 1980 to 0.663 in 2010. The world average, including, of course, the poorest countries, rose from 0.455 in 1980 to 0.624 in 2010—a bit lower than China's score.

5. http://www.brookings.edu/papers/2011/1113_recovery_renewal.aspx#story (accessed 11/14/11).

6. For systematic updates on these and other issues, see the Renewing America blog, scorecards, and reports at Council on Foreign Relations 2012.

7. *The Economist*, October 22–28, 2011, 118; also "Debts and Deficits Compared," *The New York Times*, September 30, 2011, A9.

8. *The Economist* October 22–28, 2011, 17.

9. BBC at http://www.bbc.co.uk/news/business-15748696 (accessed 11/18/11).

10. Each source of market income before taxes was less evenly distributed in 2007 than in 1979. Business income and capital gains grew faster than labor income. Government transfers and federal taxes helped even out income distribution by some 20 percent in 2007, but this equalizing effect had been much larger in 1979. The equalizing effect declined because the share of transfer payments to the lowest-income households declined while the overall average federal tax rate fell (Congressional Budget Office 2011).

11. *Citizens United v. Federal Election Commission*, 558 U.S. 08-205 (2010).

12. Human rights groups in Switzerland and Canada urged the arrest of the forty-third president and his vice president for violating international conventions.

13. http://www.theworld.org/2011/11/makana-sings-occupy-protest-song-to-apec-leaders/ (accessed 11/16/11).

14. In a future North America, rulers maintain control through an annual televised survival competition pitting young people selected by lottery from each of twelve districts against one another. Sixteen-year-old Katniss takes her younger sister's place and, with her bow and arrows, "wins."

15. A CBS poll published after the 2008 elections found that most Americans rejected the theory of evolution. Instead, 51 percent of Americans reported that God created humans in their present form. Three in ten conceded that humans had evolved but that God had guided the process. Another 15 percent stated that humans evolved and that God was not involved. The results dovetailed with those of a CBS survey after the 2004 elections.

16. Analysis of the one hundred-plus freshman class of legislators elected in 2010 showed that half denied the existence of man-made climate change and that 86 percent opposed any climate change legislation that increased government revenue. See http://thinkprogress.org/politics/2010/11/03/128002/gop-frosh-class/?mobile=nc (accessed 4/12/12).

17. The District of Columbia led with 45.7 percent followed by Massachusetts with 36.7 percent—more than twice the 15.3 percent of graduates in West Virginia. The D.C. also led the country in shootings, while Hawaii and Massachusetts had the fewest. See www.statemaster.com for many other rankings.

18. U.S. Bureau of Justice Statistics (2011–12), Total Correctional Population, at http://bjs.ojp.usdoj.gov/index.cfm?ty=tp&tid=11 (accessed 04/13/12).

19. Black males, with an incarceration rate of 4,749 inmates per 100,000 U.S. residents, were incarcerated at a rate more than six times higher than white males and 2.6 times higher than Hispanic males. Black females, with an incarceration rate of 333 per 100,000, were more than two times as likely as Hispanic females and over 3.6 times more likely than white females to have been in prison or jail. U.S. Bureau of Justice Statistics (June 23, 2010) at http://bjs.ojp.usdoj.gov/content/pub/press/pim09stpy09acpr.cfm, (accessed 10/28/11).

20. Kentucky: A Data-Driven Effort to Protect Public Safety and Control Corrections Spending at http://www.pewcenteronthestates.org/report_detail.aspx?id=61357 (accessed 10/27/11).

21. Data for 2009: gun deaths, 31,347—10.2 per 100,000; suicides by guns, 18,735—6.1; motor vehicles deaths, 34,485—11.2. FastStates at http://www.cdc.gov/nchs/fastats/suicide.htm (accessed 12/15/12).

22. Excerpts in the *Congressional Record*, July 21, 2003, at http://www.fas.org/irp/congress/2003_cr/h072103.html (accessed 2/15/04).

CHAPTER EIGHT. WHAT FUTURE FOR THE AMERICAN DREAM?

1. Yes, Imperial Germany challenged Great Britain before 1914, but World War I erupted for other reasons. The relatively peaceful implosion of the USSR in 1991 showed that war between weakening great powers and their rivals is not inevitable Indeed, the weakening Soviet regime in the 1980s concluded many arms control and other cooperative arrangements with the West. But the system was sick and the Soviet empire disappeared without a whimper.

2. Before becoming vice president, Dick Cheney as Halliburton CEO had sited company offices beyond reach of U.S. tax collectors and used a subsidiary to do business with Iran, in violation of U.S. law. During the Bush-Cheney reign Halliburton won many noncompetitive contracts from the government even after inspectors found the company often overcharged for goods and services. Mitt Romney and his Bain Capital Company exploited U.S. tax loopholes by extensive use of offshore tax havens.

3. Both system and human factors helped bring on the power outage that swept across a large swathe of the American southwest on September 8, 2011 —the region's worst cascading blackout in fifteen years. It started at a substation near Yuma, Arizona, where a utility employee "was doing some work" on faulty equipment. Something happened to cause the substation to shut down, disconnecting a 500kV transmission line and disrupting the electricity supply to Yuma's ninety thousand residents. The

immediate power shortage at Yuma caused the current suddenly to reverse its direction. This produced a violent fluctuation in line voltage that fed back through the grid to trip switches at substations throughout the San Diego area. Many power stations shut down automatically to protect themselves from voltage swings.

With a major plant disconnected and the umbilical cord from Arizona effectively severed, the delicately balanced grid serving San Diego quickly became unstable. Such problems would normally be resolved by ratcheting up the output of surrounding power stations. But with little base-load capacity in the area, standby plants for meeting peak demand could not be spun up fast enough to stabilize the voltage. The overloaded grid promptly crashed, causing prolonged blackouts across the region.

4. Quotes are from "The Writer" (1847), published in Emerson 1927.

5. For background, see *Foreign Policy* 2012.

CHAPTER NINE. WHY IS SOUTH KOREA NOT NORTH KOREA?

1. http://hdrstats.undp.org/en/countries/profiles/KOR.html and http://hdr. undp.org/en/statistics/ (both accessed 2/27/2013).

2. OECD = Organization for Economic Cooperation and Development—an international economic organization founded in 1961 with thirty-four member countries in 2013, each of them with a high score for human development and democracy.

3. http://hdrstats.undp.org/en/countries/profiles/KOR.html; and http://hdr. undp.org/en/statistics/ (both accessed 2/27/2013).

4. http://www3.weforum.org/docs/CSI/2012-13/GCR_Rankings_2012-13. pdf (accessed 2/27/2013).

5. The graphs and facts underlying each measure are given at http://www. bti-project.org/country-reports/aso/ (accessed 2/27/2013).

6. You (2013) showed that comparison of the Korean experience with those of Taiwan and the Philippines reveals the critical importance of land reform. In Taiwan, the success of land reform also helped to remove the privileged landed class and to develop the economy without excessive distributive struggle, which eased the democratic transition and consolidation processes. In the Philippines, however, the initial failure of land reform in the absence of an external threat (as in South Korea and Taiwan) led to continuous distributive struggles, which made democratic consolidation difficult and helped the insurgencies to continue.

7. E-mail communication by Ezra F. Vogel, 2/28/2013.

8. http://cpi.transparency.org/cpi2012/ (accessed 2/27/2013).

9. Hours of in-flight training per year for military pilots in Japan were 148; in China, from 80 to 130; in Russia, from 25 to 80; in the United States, from 189 to 365 (International Institute for Strategic Studies 2008). No data were given for South Korea.

10. Until the early twentieth century, *hangŭl* was denigrated as vulgar by many of the literate elite who preferred the traditional *hanja* writing system. They gave it such names as *Achimgeul*: "writing you can learn within a morning"; *Eonmun*: "vernacular script"; and *Amgeul*: "women's script."

11. When I lectured in Seoul and in Taipei in 1970, only senior professors and white-haired journalists commented or raised questions, while younger professionals and students kept their views to themselves. Their deference recalled the old Korean

saying: "One should not step even on the shadow of one's teacher." Two and three decades later, younger intellectuals not only spoke up but openly challenged their elders.

CHAPTER TEN. TOWARD A NEW PARADIGM FOR GLOBAL STUDIES

1. Most faiths, including Islam, can pick and choose from an abundance of instructions in their sacred texts and interpretations. Praxis, in any case, may not square with theory. For many examples, see Sajoo 2010.

2. See the review of Mearsheimer 2001 by Rosecrance 2002: 153–55.

3. For details, see above, page 216, note 10.

4. Mutual defection can be avoided if the first player to move takes a conciliatory step. and the other side reciprocates (Axelrod 1984). In real life, however, there is no discrete first step, because interactions usually go back for decades if not centuries.

5. The geochemist Vladimir I. Vernadskii (1989) adapted the idea of the biosphere from Theilhard de Chardin and went on to develop the concept of noosphere—the realm of human thought and action. For literary depictions of the environmental destruction brought on by Soviet rule, see Rasputin 1989 and 2004.

6. http://www.unesco.org/water/wwap/case_studies/peipsi_lake/peipsi_lake. pdf (accessed 05/11/11).

7. Boguta's sample consisted of Mideast Twitter users who included the keywords ("hashtags") #Jan25 and #Tahrir in messages (Bartholet 2011, 106).

8. Many Turks experienced a nationalist thrill in 2012 when they saw a film celebrating the conquest of Constantinople in 1453. Still others rallied round the regime when shots were exchanged with Syria.

9. Achille Mbembe, an historian at Witwatersrand University in Johannesburg, quoted in. Baldauf 2011.

10. However, many Iranians stayed up in the early hours in February 2012 to access coverage of the Oscars where *The Separation* won best foreign language film award—a film produced but not distributed in Iran. Still, some authorities in Tehran expressed pleasure that the Iranian film prevailed over an Israeli competitor.

11. A conventional office would invite a violent intervention.

12. http://kabardino-balkaria.kavkaz-uzel.ru/ (accessed 4/12/12).

13. Some of their peers, flush and buoyant from summer jobs in the United States, could be seen using computers in a Cape Cod public library to keep up on events back home.

CHAPTER ELEVEN. CHALLENGES TO COMPLEXITY SCIENCE

1. Convergence or parallel evolution? Two experts predicted the latter (Brzezinski and Huntington 1963). For the denouement, see Kotkin 2008.

2. For males, from 65.0 in 1987 to 57.6 in 1994; for females, from 74.6 in 1987 to 71.2 in 1994, after which averages improved.

3. For many case studies suggesting the utility of contingent cooperation, see Clemens 2004a.

4. On linking the science of opinion polling to the ideals of democracy, see Fishkin 2009.

REFERENCES

Acemoglu, D., and J. A. Robinson. 2012. *Why nations fail: The origins of power, prosperity, and poverty*. New York: Crown, Random House.

Adam, F., P. Kristan, and M. Tomšič. 2009. Varieties of capitalism in Eastern Europe with special emphasis on Estonia and Slovenia. *t-Communist Studies* 42, no. 1 (March): 65–81.

Ahrens, G-H. 2007. *Diplomacy on the edge: Containment of Ethnic Conflict and the Minorities Working Group of the Conferences on Yugoslavia*. Baltimore: The Johns Hopkins University Press.

Albert, M., L-E. Cederman, and A. Wendt, 2010. Eds. *New systems of world politic*. New York: Palgrave Macmillan.

Alker, H. R., and S. Fraser. 1996. On historical complexity: "Naturalistic" modeling approaches from the Santa Fe Institute, American Political Science Association Annual Meeting, San Francisco.

Allison, G. T. 1971. *The essence of decision: Explaining the Cuban missile crisis*. Boston: Little, Brown.

———, and P. Zelikow. 1999. *The essence of decision: Explaining the Cuban missile crisis*. 2nd ed. New York: Longman.

Almond, G., A. R. Appleby, and E. Sivan. 2003. *Strong religion: The rise of fundamentalisms around the world*. Chicago: University of Chicago Press.

Anonymous (M. Scheuer). 2004. *Imperial hubris: Why the West is losing the War on Terror*. Washington, DC: Brassey's.

Appatova, S. 2008. *Negotiating strategies in contemporary politics: The cases of Hungary and Romania during EU accession negotiations*. Boston University Political Science Department, unpublished Directed Study.

Appelbaum, A. 2012. *Iron curtain: The crushing of Eastern Europe, 1944–56*. New York: Penguin.

Aslund, A. 2013. Nine reasons why stability in Russia may be illusive. *Moscow Times*, Jan. 22.

Augstein, J. 2012, Destroyed by total capitalism. *Spiegel Online International*, November 5.

Axelrod, R. M. 1984 and 2006. *The evolution of cooperation*. Revised ed. New York: Basic Books.

———. 1997a. *The complexity of cooperation: Agent-based models of competition and cooperation*. Princeton: Princeton University Press.

———. 1997b. The dissemination of culture: A model with local convergence and global polarization. *Journal of Conflict Resolution* 41: 203–26.

———, and M. D. Cohen. 1999. *Harnessing complexity: Organizational implications of a scientific frontier*. New York: The Free Press.

Babuts, N. 2000. "Morita": A Romanian ballad in Homeric perspective. *Symposium* 54, no. 1.

Baldauf, S. 2011. Why Tunisia's winds of change aren't blowing south to sub-Saharan Africa, *Christian Science Monitor*, Feb. 1.

Barabási, A-L. 2003. *Linked: How everything is linked together and what it means*. New York: Plume.

———. 2010. *Bursts: The hidden patterns behind everything we do*. New York: Dutton, 2010.

Bartholet, J. 2011. Young, angry, and wired. *National Geographic* 220, no. 1 (July): 102–107.

Bar-Yam, Y. 2004. *Making things work: Solving complex problems in a complex world*. Cambridge, MA: NECSI Knowledge Press.

Beckley, M. 2011. China's century? Why America's edge will endure, *International Security* 36, no. 3 (Winter 2011/12): 41–78.

Bellaigue, C. de. 2005. *In the rose garden of the martyrs: A memoir of Iran*. New York: HarperCollins.

Berčič, B., ed. 1968. *Abhandlungen über die slowenische Reformation*. Munich: Rudolf Trofnik.

Bertelsmann Foundation. 2011. At http://www.bertelsmann-transformation-index.de/en/ (accessed 07/21/11).

Binnendijk, H., and R. L. Kugler. 2006. *Seeing the elephant: The U.S. role in global security*. Washington, DC: National Defense University Press and Potomac Press.

Bloom, P. 2012. The original colonists, *The New York Times*, May 11.

Bremmer, I. 2011. Is the Arab spring losing its spring? At http://english.aljazeera.net/indepth/opinion/2011/04/2011479616652196.html# (accessed 04/12/11).

Brookings Institution. 2011. http://www.brookings.edu/papers/2011/1113_recovery_renewal.aspx#story (accessed 11/14/11).

Brown, M. E., ed. 1996. *Debating the democratic peace: An* International Security *reader*. Cambridge: MIT Press.

———, et al. 2001. The causes of internal conflict: An overview. In *Nationalism and ethnic conflict,* rev. ed., 3–25. Cambridge: MIT Press.

Brown, M. E., O. R. Cote Jr., S. M. Lynn-Jones, and S. E. Miller, eds. 2000. *Rational choice and security studies: Stephen Walt and his critics*. Cambridge: MIT Press.

Broz, S. 2001. Good people in times of evil. *Agni,* Boston University 54: 46–78.

Brzezinski, Z. 1970. *Between two ages: America's role in the technetronic era*. New York: Viking.

———. 2011. How to stay friends with China. *The New York Times*, Jan. 2.

———. 2012. *Strategic vision: America and the crisis of global power*. New York: Basic Books.

————, and S. P. Huntington. 1963. *Political power: USA/USSR.* New York: Viking.

Buchanan, M. 2000. *Ubiquity: The science of history, or why the world is simpler than we think.* London: Widenfeld and Nicolson.

Bucharest Summit Declaration. 2008. http://www.nato.int/docu/pr/2008/p08-049e. html (accessed 4/24/10).

Burg, S. L., and P. S. Shoup. 1999. *The war in Bosnia Herzegovina: Ethnic conflict and international intervention.* Armonk, NY: M. E. Sharpe.

Carr, E. H. 1940. *The twenty years' crisis: An introduction to the study of international relations.* London: Macmillan.

Casti, J. L. 1994. *Complexification: Explaining a paradoxical world through the science of surprise.* New York: HarperCollins.

Cederman, L-E. 1997. *Emergent actors in world politics: How states and nations develop and dissolve.* Princeton: Princeton University Press.

Chapais, B. 2008. *Primeval kinship: How pair-bonding gave birth to human society.* Cambridge: Harvard University Press.

Christensen, T. J. 2006. Fostering stability or creating a monster? The rise of China and U.S. policy toward East Asia. *International Security* 31, no. 1 (Summer): 81–126.

————, and J. Snyder. 1990. Chain gangs and passed bucks: Predicting alliance patterns in multipolarity. *International Organization* 44: 137–68.

Cioffi-Revilla, C. 1998. *The first rivalries: Comparative international relations and the origins of world politics.* Boulder: LORANOW Project, Department of Political Science, University of Colorado.

Clark, A. 2012. Diva who shed hardship to dazzle Rostropovich and the West. *Financial Times,* Dec. 15/16.

Clarke, R. A., and R. Knake. 2012. *Cyber war: The next threat to national security and what to do about it.* New York: HarperCollins.

Clemens, W. C. Jr., ed. 1965. *World perspectives on international politics.* Boston: Little, Brown.

————. 1972–73. Ecology and international relations, *International Journal* 28:1–27.

————. 1973. Review of *Foreign Policy. Foreign Policy* 10: 182–85.

————, 1978. *The U.S.S.R. and Global Interdependence: Alternative Futures.* Washington, D.C.: American Enterprise Institute.

————. 1981. Will the Soviet empire survive 1984? *Christian Science Monitor,* July 10.

————. 1988. Estonia, A place to watch. *The National Interest* 13: 85–92.

————. 1990 and 2011. *Can Russia change? The USSR confronts global interdependence.* Boston: Unwin Hyman; London: Routledge.

————. 1991. *Baltic independence and Russian empire.* New York: St. Martin's.

————. 2000a. *America and the world, 1898–2025: Achievements, failures, alternative futures.* New York: St. Martin's.

————. 2000b. Could more force have saved the Soviet system? *Journal of Cold War Studies* 21: 116–23.

————. 2001. *The Baltic transformed: Complexity theory and European security.* Lanham, MD: Rowman and Littlefield.

————. 2002. Complexity theory as a tool for understanding and coping with ethnic conflict and development issues in post-communist Eurasia. *International Journal of Peace Studies* 7, no. 2: 1–15.

———. 2004a. *Dynamics of international relations: Conflict and mutual gain in an era of global interdependence.* 2nd ed. Lanham, MD: Rowman and Littlefield.

———. 2005. Negotiating to control weapons of mass destruction in North Korea, *International Negotiation: A Journal of Theory and Practice* 10: 453–86.

———. 2006. Understanding and coping with ethnic conflict and development issues in post-Soviet Eurasia. *Complexity in world politics: Concepts and methods of a new paradigm,* ed. N. Harrison, 73–93. Albany: State University of New York Press.

———. 2009. Culture and symbols as tools of resistance. *Journal of Baltic Studies* 40, no. 2 (June): 169–77.

———. 2010a. Ethnic peace, ethnic conflict: Complexity theory on why the Baltic is not the Balkans. *Communist and Post-Communist Studies* 43: 245–61.

———. 2010b. *Getting to yes in Korea.* Boulder: Paradigm.

———. 2011. Time for a grand bargain in Northeast Asia. *Bulletin of the Atomic Scientists,* October 24. At http://thebulletin.org/web-edition/op-eds/time-grand-bargain-northeast-asia.

———. 2012. Why pick a fight with China? *Global Asia* 7, no. 1 (Spring): 116–19.

———, with Jim Morin. 2004b. *Bushed! What passionate conservatives have done to America and the world.* Skaneateles, NY: Outland Books.

Clover, C. 2012. Russian "civilization" concept stirs resentment. *Financial Times,* Dec. 12, 4.

Cohen, J., and I. Stewart. 1994. *The collapse of chaos: Discovering simplicity in a complex world.* New York: Penguin.

Collier, P., et al. 2003. *Breaking the conflict trap: Civil war and development policy.* New York: Oxford University Press.

Collins, S. 2008. *The hunger games,.* New York: Scholastic Press.

Congressional Budget Office. 2011. *Trends in the distribution of household income between 1979 and 2007* (October). At http://cbo.gov/sites/default/files/cbofiles/attachments/10-25-HouseholdIncome.pdf (accessed 4/12/12).

Cooper, J. 2011. Fixing Congress (speech at the Harvard Law School). At http://cooper.house.gov/images/stories/here.pdf (accessed 4/12/12).

Council on Foreign Relations. 2012. Renewing America. At http://www.cfr.org/projects/world/renewing-america/pr1527 (accessed 12/15/12).

Coyle, D. 2012. Letter, *Financial Times,* October 8.

Crkven, I. 1997. *Croatian ethnic territory and the multiethnic composition of Croatia as a result of population migrations.* Zagreb: Pregledni rad.

Cronin, A. K. 2006. How al-Qaida ends: The decline and demise of terrorist groups. *International Security* 31 (Summer): 7–48.

———. 2009. *How terrorism ends: Understanding the decline and demise of terrorist organizations.* Princeton: Princeton University Press.

Čuješ, R. P. 1985. *Slovenia: A land of cooperators.* Willowdale, Ontario: Slovenian Research Centre.

D'Anieri, P. J. 1999. *Economic interdependence in Ukrainian-Russian relations.* Albany: State University of New York Press.

Davis, C., and M. Feshbach. 1980. *Rising infant mortality in the U.S.S.R. in the 1970s.* Washington, DC: U.S. Department of Commerce, Bureau of the Census.

Davis, E. 1917. When peace without victory was a failure. *The New York Times Magazine,* Nov. 11, 69.

Dawkins, R. 1996. *The blind watchmaker: Why the evidence of evolution reveals a universe without design.* New York: W. W. Norton.

Debeljak, E. J. 2004. Five Little Negroes and other songs: A lesson in political correctness from the former Yugoslavia. *Common Knowledge* 10, no. 1: 105–18.

Denby, D. 2012. Kids at risk: "The Hunger Games" and "Bully," *The New Yorker,* April 2: 68–70.

De Waal, T. 2010. *The Caucasus: An introduction.* New York: Oxford University Press.

Diamond, J. M. 1997. *Guns, germs, and steel: The fates of human societies.* New York: W. W. Norton. 2005.

———. 2005. *Collapse: How societies choose to fail or succeed.* New York: Viking.

Dorff, R. H. 2005. Failed states after 9/11: What did we know and what have we learned? *International Studies Perspectives* 6: 20–34.

Doyle, M. W. 1977. *Ways of war and peace: Realism, liberalism, and socialism.* New York: W. W. Norton.

———. 1997. *Ways of war and peace: Realism, liberalism, and socialism.* New York; W. W. Norton.

Durham, W. H. 1991. *Coevolution: Genes, culture, and human diversity,* Stanford: Stanford University Press.

Duval, J. 2010. *Next generation democracy: What the open-source revolution means for power politics.* New York: Bloomsbury USA.

Earnest, D. C., and J. N. Rosenau. 2006. Signifying nothing? What complex systems theory can and cannot tell us about global politics. In *Complexity in World Politics,* ed. N. Harrison, 143–63. Albany: State University of New York Press.

Efimova, A. I. et al. 2011. *Smertnost' rossiiskikh podrostov ot samoubiistv.* Moscow: RF Ministry of Health and Social Development and UNICEF (1,000 copies printed).

Elman, M. F., ed. 1997. *Paths to peace: Is democracy the answer?* Cambridge: MIT Press.

Emerson, R. W. 1850. *Representative men and other essays.* Boston: D. C. Heath, 1927 (reprint).

Epstein, J. M., and R. Axtell. 1996. *Growing artificial societies: Social science from the bottom up.* Washington, DC: Brookings Institution.

EU Commission. 2011. Mechanism for cooperation and verification for Bulgaria and Romania. Feb. 18, 2011. At http://ec.europa.eu/dgs/secretariat_general/cvm/progress_reports_en.htm (accessed 5/10/11).

Falk, R. A. 2008. *The costs of war: International law, the UN, and world order after Iraq.* New York: Routledge.

Fearon, J. D., and D. Laitin. 2003. Ethnicity, insurgency, and civil war. *American Political Science Review* 97, no. 1: 75–90.

Feldstein, M. S. 2010, U. S. growth in the decade ahead. NBER Working Paper No 15685, January.

Ferguson, N. 2003. Why America outpaces Europe clue: The God factor, *The New York Times* June 8.

———. 2010. Complexity and collapse, *Foreign Affairs* 89, no. 2 (March/April): 18–32.

———. 2011. *Civilization: The West and the rest.* New York: Penguin.

Fingleton, E. 2013. America the innovative? *New York Times,* March 31.

Fishkin, J. S. 2009. *When the people speak: Deliberative democracy and public consultation.* New York: Oxford University Press.

Flannery, T. 2011. *Here on Earth: A natural history of the planet,* Toronto: HarperCollins.

Flögel, M., and G. Lauc. n.d. *War stress—Effects of the war in the area of the former Yugoslavia.* Faculty of Pharmacy and Biochemistry, University of Zagreb.

Folke, C., S. Carpenter, T. Elmqvist, L. Gunderson, C. S. Holling, and B. Walker. 2002. Resilience and sustainable development: Building adaptive capacity in a world of transformations. *Ambio: A Journal of the Human Environment* 31, no. 5: 437–40.

Foreign Affairs. 2011. Is America over? 90, no. 6 (Nov.-Dec.).

Foreign Policy. 2012. 100 top global thinkers 2012. Annual Special Issue (Dec.).

Freedom House. 2001. Country Ratings. At http://www.freedomhouse.org/ratings/index.htm (accessed 04/06/02).

———. 2004. *Nations in transit 2004.* Lanham, MD: Rowman and Littlefield.

———. 2006. *Nations in transit 2006.* Lanham, MD: Rowman and Littlefield.

———. 2007. *Nations in transit 2007.* Lanham, MD: Rowman and Littlefield.

———. 2009. *Nations in transit 2009.* At http://www.freedomhouse.org/uploads/nit/2009/Tables-WEB.pdf (accessed 04/19/10).

———. 2010. *Freedom in the world 2010: The annual survey of political rights and civil liberties.* Lanham, MD: Rowman and Littlefield.

Freeland, C. 2012. *Plutocrats: The rise of the new global super-rich and the fall of everyone else.* New York: Penguin.

Friedman, H. 2012. *The measure of a nation: How to regain America's competitive edge and boost our global standing.* Amherst, NY: Prometheus.

Friedman, T. L. 2007. *The world is flat: A brief history of the twenty-first century.* New York: Picador/Farrar, Straus and Giroux.

———. 2012. Elephants down under. *The New York Times,* March 28, A25.

Friedman, T. L., and M. Mandelbaum. 2011. *That used to be us: How America fell behind in the world it invented and how we can come back.* New York: Farrar, Straus and Giroux.

Fukuyama, F. 1992. *The end of history and the last man.* New York: Avon.

Furberg, D. 2006. Preparation of a pilot multi-thematic GIS database in the framework of the DatabasiN Project, UNDP/GRID-Arendal. At http://enrin.grida.no/databasin/pilotdb/Pilot%20Database%20Report.pdf (accessed 5/11/11).

Gabora, L. 1997. The origin and evolution of culture and creativity, *Journal of Memetics—Evolutionary Models of Information Transmission* 1. At http://cfpm.org/jom-emit/1997/vol1/gabora (accessed 4/05/12).

Gall, N. 2012. Water in China. *Braudel Papers* (São Paolo) 46: 1–8.

Gallup. 2010. Global wellbeing surveys find nations worlds apart. At http://www.gallup.com/poll/126977/global-wellbeing-surveys-find-nations-worlds-apart.aspx (accessed 4/9/12).

Galor, O. 2011. *Unified growth theory.* Princeton: Princeton University Press.

Galtung, J. 1996. *Peace by peaceful means: Peace and conflict, development and civilization.* Thousand Oaks, CA: Sage.

Gardner, H. 2011. *Truth, beauty, and goodness reframed: Educating for the virtues in the twenty-first century.* New York: Basic Books.

Gell-Mann, M. 1994. *The quark and the jaguar: Adventures in the simple and the complex.* New York: W. H. Freeman.

Gertner, J. 2012. *The idea factory: Bell Labs and the great age of American innovation.* New York: Penguin.

Gilpin, R. 1988. The theory of hegemonic war. *Journal of Interdisciplinary History* 18, no. 4 (Spring): 591–613.

Girusov, E. 2004. The noospheric imperative for *paideia* in the twenty-first century. In *Educating for democracy: Paideia in an age of uncertainty,* ed. A. M. Olson, D. M. Steiner, and I. S. Tuuli, 43–49. Lanham, MD: Rowman and Littlefield.

Gladwell, M., and C. Shirkey. 2011. From innovation to revolution. *Foreign Affairs* 90, no. 2 (March-April): 153–54.

Goldberger, A. L. 1996. Non-linear dynamics for clinicians: Chaos theory, fractals, and complexity at the bedside. *Lancet* 347: 1312–14.

Goldin, C. D., and L. F. Katz. 2008. *The race between education and technology.* Cambridge: Harvard University Press.

Goldstein, J. S., and J. R. Freeman. 1990. *Three-way street: Strategic reciprocity in world politics.* Chicago: University of Chicago Press.

Gordon, R. J. 2012. Is U.S. economic growth over? Faltering innovation confronts the six headwinds. NBZER Working Paper No. 18315, Aug.

Gould, S. J. 1989. *Wonderful life: The Burgess Shale and the nature of history.* New York: W. W. Norton.

———. 2002. *The structure of evolutionary theory.* Cambridge: Harvard University Press.

Greenblatt, S. 2011, *The swerve: How the world became modern.* New York: W. W. Norton.

Greenwald, G. 2011. *With liberty and justice for some: How the law is used to destroy equality and protect the powerful.* New York: Metropolitan Books.

Grodona, M. 1996. *El mundo en clave.* Buenos Aires: Planeta.

Gross, D. 2013. *The China fallacy: How the U.S. can benefit from China's rise and avoid another cold war.* New York: Bloomsbury.

Gurtov, M. 2013. *Will this be China's century? A skeptic's view.* Boulder: Lynne Rienner.

Haass, R. N. 2005. *The opportunity: America's moment to alter history's course.* New York: Public Affairs.

Hafner, D. F., and D. Lajh, 2003. *Managing Europe from home: The Europeanisation of the Slovenian core executive.* Ljubljana: FDV.

Harris, S. K. 2011. *God's arbiters: Americans and the Philippines, 1898–1902.* New York: Oxford University Press.

Harrison, L. E. 2006. *The central liberal truth: How politics can change culture and save it from itself.* New York: Oxford University Press.

———, and S. P. Huntington, eds. 2000. *Culture matters: How values shape human progress.* New York: Basic Books.

Harrison, N. E., ed. 2006. *Complexity in world politics: Concepts and methods of a new paradigm.* Albany: State University of New York Press.

Hasselblatt, C. 1996. Die Bedeutung des Nationalepos Kalevipoeg für das nationale Erwachen der Esten. *Finnisch-Ugriche Mitteilungen,* Band 20: 51–61.

Hastings, A. 1997. *The construction of nationhood: Ethnicity, religion, and nationalism.* New York: Cambridge University Press.

Hatemi, P. K., and R. McDermott. 2011. The normative implications of biological research. *PS. Political Science & Politics* 44, no. 2 (April): 325–29.

Hausmann, R., C. A. Hidalgo et al. 2011. *The atlas of economic complexity: Mapping paths to prosperity.* At http://www.cid.harvard.edu/documents/complexityatlas.pdf (accessed 11/17/11).

Hawking, S. W. 2003. *The theory of everything: The origin and fate of the universe.* Beverly Hills: New Millennium.

Hendrick, D. 2010. Complexity theory and conflict transformation. In *Oxford international encyclopedia of peace,* ed. N. J. Young, 4 vols., 1: 386–89. New York: Oxford University Press.

Heritage Foundation. 2002. *The 2002 index of economic freedom.* At http://cf.heritage.org/index/indexoffreedom.cfm (accessed 5/2/03).

———. 2011. *Index of economic freedom.* At http://www.heritage.org/index/ (accessed 10/5/11).

Hernandez, R. 2011a. Digital + diversity: What does your newsroom reflect? *OJR: The OnLine Journalism Review* Jan. 4. At http://www.ojr.org/ojr/people/webjournalist/201101/1926/ (accessed 9/22/11).

———. 2011b. What if we are part of the voiceless community? *OJR: The OnLine Journalism Review* June 27. At http://www.ojr.org/ojr/people/webjournalist/201106/1987/ (accessed 9/22/11).

Hoffmann, M. J. 2005. *Ozone depletion and climate change: Constructing a global response.* Albany: State University of New York Press.

Hoffmann, S. H., ed. 1960. *Contemporary theory in international relations.* Englewood Cliffs, NJ: Prentice-Hall.

Holbrooke, R. C. 1998. *To end a war.* New York: Random House.

Holland, J. H. 1998. *Emergence from chaos to order.* Reading, MA: Addison-Wesley.

Holman, P. 2011. *Engaging emergence: Turning upheaval into opportunity.* San Francisco: Berrett-Koehler.

Horgan, J. 1996. *The end of science: Facing the limits of knowledge in the twilight of the scientific age.* Reading, MA: Addison-Wesley.

Hroch, M. 1985. *Social preconditions of national revival in Europe: A comparative analysis of the social composition of patriotic groups among the smaller European nations.* Cambridge: Cambridge University Press.

Huntington, S. P. 1996. *The clash of civilizations and the remaking of world order.* New York: Simon and Schuster.

———. 1968/2006. *Political order in changing societies.* New Haven: Yale University Press.

Iakovets, Iu. V. 2011. *Dolgostrochnaia strategiia energoekoligicheskogo partnerstva tsivilizatsii.* Moscow: MICK.

Interethnic riot in March 1990. *Divers [sic] Bulletin* 11 (139), March 28, 2005. At http://cm.greekhelsinki.gr/index.php?cid=431&sec=192 (accessed 09/12/07).

International Institute for Strategic Studies. Annual. *The Military Balance.*

International Studies Quarterly. 1996. Special Issue: Evolutionary paradigms in the social sciences 40, no. 3 (September).

Jackson, P. T. 2011. *The conduct of inquiry in international relations: Philosophy of science and its implications for the study of world politics.* London and New York: Routledge.

Jacquin-Berdal, D. et al., eds. 1998. *Culture in world politics.* New York: St. Martin's.

James, P. 2002. *International relations and scientific progress: Structural realism reconsidered.* Columbus: Ohio University Press.

———. 2011. Symposium on interdisciplinary approaches to international studies: History, psychology, technology studies, and neuroeconomics. *International Studies Perspectives* 12, no. 2 (May 2011): 89–93.

Jervis, R. 1997. *System effects: Complexity in political and social life.* Princeton: Princeton University Press.

Johnson, C. 2008. Partitioning to peace: Sovereignty, demography, and ethnic civil wars. *International Security* 324: 140–70.

Judah, T. 2000. *The Serbs: History, myth, and the destruction of Yugoslavia*, 2d ed. New Haven: Yale University Press.

Kagan, J. 2011. The tapestry of variation in human traits, International conference on complex systems. Boston (June 30).

Kagan, R. 2012. *The world America made*. New York: A. A. Knopf.

Kahl, C. H. 2004. Review of Collier et al. 2003. At http://www.wilsoncenter.org/index.cfm?topic_id=1413&fuseaction=topics.item&news_id=56795 (accessed 04/22/10).

Kant, I. 1795. *Zum ewigen Frieden* (1983. *Perpetual peace and other essays*). Indianapolis: Hackett), 107–43.

Kaplan, M. A. 1957. *System and process in international politics*. New York: Wiley.

Karatnycky, A., A. Motyl, and A. Piano, eds., 2001. *Nations in transit, 1999–2000: Civil society, democracy, and markets in East Central Europe and the newly independent states*. New York: Freedom House.

Kates G. 2012, A spate of teenage suicides alarms Russians. *The New York Times*, April 20, A4.

Kauffman, S. A. 1993. *The origins of order: Self-organization and selection in evolution*. New York: Oxford University Press.

———. 1995. *At home in the universe: The search for the laws of self-organization and complexity*. New York: Oxford University Press.

———. 2000. *Investigations*. New York: Oxford University Press.

———. 2008. *Reinventing the sacred: A new view of science, reason, and religion*. New York: Basic Books.

———. 2011. What price value? At http://www.npr.org/blogs/13.7/2011/08/01/138866819/what-price-value#more (accessed 08/08/11).

Kavalski, E. 2008. The complexity of global security governance: An analytical overview. *Global Society: Journal of Interdisciplinary International Relations* 22, no. 4: 423–43.

Kavčič, V. 1969. *The golden bird: Folk tales from Slovenia*. Cleveland: World.

Keller, M. 2011. Crowdsourced knowledge: Peril and promise for conceptual structures research. In *Conceptual structures for discovering knowledge*. Lecture notes in artificial intelligence (Springer, LNAI). Volume 6828, ed. S. Andrews, S. Polovina, R. Hill, and B. Akhgar.

Kennedy, P. 1987. *The rise and fall of the great powers: Economic change and military conflict, from 1500 to 2000*. New York: Random House.

Keohane, R. O., and J. S. Nye Jr. 2011. *Power and independence*. 4th ed. Boston: Longman.

Kerr, D. 2005. The Sino-Russian partnership and U.S. policy toward North Korea: From hegemony to concert in Northeast Asia. *International Studies Quarterly* 49: 411–37.

Khatami, M. 2001. *Dialogue among nations*. Paris: UNESCO.

Kim, Byung-Kook, and E. Vogel, eds. 2011. *The Park Chung Hee era: The transformation of South Korea*. Cambridge: Harvard University Press.

Klein, M. 2011. How to harvest collective wisdom on complex issues: The MIT deliberatorium. Cambridge: MIT Center for Collective Intelligence.

Klem, B. 2004. A commentary on the World Bank report "Breaking the conflict trap." Netherlands Institute of International Relations "Clingendael." At www.nbiz.nl/publications/2004/20040100_cru_working_paper_25.pdf (accessed 04/22/10).

Klemenčič, M., and Z. Mitja. 2004. *The former Yugoslavia's diverse peoples: A reference sourcebook*. Santa Barbara: ABC-CLIO.

Kolsto, P., ed. 2002. *National integration and violent conflict in post-Soviet societies: The cases of Estonia and Moldova*. Lanham, MD: Rowman and Littlefield.

Kononenko, V., and A. Moshes, eds. 2011. *Russia as a network state: What works in Russia when state institutions do not?* New York: Palgrave Macmillan.

Kostecki, W. 2002. Prevention of ethnic conflict: Lessons from Romania, Berlin. *Berghof Occasional Papers* 19.

Kotkin, S. 2008. *Armageddon averted: The Soviet collapse, 1970–2000*. New York: Oxford University Press.

Krasner, S., ed. 1990. *The ubiquity of chaos*. Washington, DC: American Association for the Advancement of Science.

Kropotkin, P. [1902]. *Mutual aid: A factor of evolution*. Boston: Extending Horizons.

Krugman, P. 2012. Defining success down in the Baltics, Conscience of a liberal blog, July 1 (accessed 07/07/12).

Kuhn, T. S. 1970. *The structure of scientific revolutions*. Rev. ed. Chicago: University of Chicago Press.

Kurzweil, R. 2005. *The singularity is near: When humans transcend biology*. New York: Viking.

Laar, M. 1992. *War in the woods: Estonia's struggle for survival, 1944–1956*. Washington, DC: The Compass Press.

Lagi, M., Yavni Bar-Yam, Yaneer Bar-Yam. 2012. The food crises: The US drought. *New England Complex Systems Institute Report,* July 23.

Lagi, M., and Y. Bar-Yam. 2012, The European debt crisis: Defaults and market equilibrium. *New England Complex Systems Institute Report*, Sept. 27.

Laitin, D. 1998. *Identity in formation: The Russian-speaking populations in the near abroad*. Ithaca: Cornell University Press.

———. 2003. Three models of integration and the Estonian/Russian reality. *Journal of Baltic Studies* 34, no. 2: 197–223.

Larrabee, F. S. 1977. Balkan security. *Adelphi Papers* 135. London: International Institute for Strategic Studies.

La Vecchia, C., F. Lucchini, and F. Levi. 1994. Worldwide trends in suicide mortality, 1955–1989. *Acta Psychiatrica Scandinavica* 90, no. 1 (July): 53–64.

Lepore, J. 2002. *A is for American: Letters and other characters in the newly United States*. New York: A. A. Knopf.

Leustean, L. N. 2008. Orthodoxy and political myths in Balkan national identities. *National Identities* 10, no. 4: 421–32.

Levin, S. A. 1999. *Fragile dominion: Complexity and the commons*. Reading, MA: Perseus.

Lewin, R. 1992. *Complexity: Life at the edge of chaos*. New York: Macmillan.

———, and B. Regine. 2000. *The soul at work: Listen, respond, let go: Embracing complexity science for business success*. New York: Simon and Schuster.

Lieven, A. 1993. *The Baltic revolution: Estonia, Latvia, Lithuania and the path to independence*. New Haven: Yale University Press.

Lincoln, D. 2012. The universe is a complex and intricate place. *Scientific American* 307, no. 5 (Nov.): 38–43.

Lind, M. 2012. *Land of promise: An economic history of the United States*. New York: HarperCollins.

Longo, G., M. Montévil, and S. Kauffman. 2012. No entailing laws, but enablement in the evolution of the biosphere. *Physics Arx,* Jan. 11. At http://arxiv.org/abs/1201.2069 (accessed 12/23/12).

Luce, E. 2012a. America's dream unravels. *Financial Times,* March 31/April 1.

———. 2012b. *Time to start thinking: America in the age of descent.* New York: Atlantic Monthly Press.

Lük, A. N. et al. 2000. *Managing the mix thereafter: Comparative research into mixed communities in three independent successor states.* Ljubljana: Inštitut za narodnostna vprašanja.

Lumsden, C. J., and E. O. Wilson. 1981. *Genes, mind, and culture: The coevolutionary process.* Cambridge: Harvard University Press.

MacDorman, M. F., and T. J. Mathews. 2008. Recent trends in infant mortality in the United States. Washington, DC: National Center for Health Statistics. NCHS Data Brief No. 9 (October).

Magocsi, P. R. 2002. *Historical atlas of Central Europe.* 2nd ed. Seattle: University of Washington Press.

Mann, T. E., and N. Ornstein. 2012. *It's even worse than it looks: How the American constitutional system collided with the new politics of extremism.* New York: Basic Books.

Mansfield, E. D. and J. L. Snyder. 2005. *Electing to fight: Why emerging democracies go to war.* Cambridge: MIT Press.

Markoff, J. 2012. Killing the computer to save it. *The New York Times,* October 30, D1, 4.

Marshall, I., and D. Zohar. 1997. *Who's afraid of Schrödinger's cat: All the new science ideas you need to keep up with the new thinking.* New York: William Morrow.

Maruca, R. F. 2000. Competitive fitness. *Harvard Business Review* 78 (July-Aug.).

May, R. 2012. In finance, too, complex ecosystems can be vulnerable. *Financial Times,* Oct. 20.

McGlinchey, E. 2011. Exploring regime instability and ethnic violence in Kyrgyzstan. *Asian Policy* 12 (July): 79–98.

McKibben, B. 2010. *Earth: Making a life on a tough new planet.* New York. Times Books.

McNeil, T. 1999. Explorations. *Bostonia* (Summer): 30–31.

Mearsheimer, J. J. 2001. *The tragedy of great power politics in war and peace.* New York: W. W. Norton.

Minelli, A., and G. Fusco, eds. 2008. *Evolving pathways: Key themes in evolutionary developmental biology.* Cambridge: Cambridge University Press.

MISK (Mezhdunarodnyi institute P. Sorokina-N. Kondrat'eva). At http://www.library.newparadigm.ru/ (accessed 7/21/11).

Mitchell, M. 2008. *Complexity: The guided tour.* New York: Oxford University Press.

Modelski, G. 1996. Evolutionary paradigm for global politics. In Special issue: Evolutionary paradigms in the social sciences. *International Studies Quarterly* 40: 321–42.

Monten, J. 2006. Thucydides and modern realism. *International Studies Quarterly* 50: 3–25.

Morgenthau, H. J. 1978. *Politics among nations: The struggle for power and peace.* 5th ed. New York: A. A. Knopf.

Morin, E. 2008. *On complexity: Advances in systems theory, complexity, and the human sciences.* Cresskill, NJ: Hampton Press.

Morin, J., and W. C. Clemens Jr. 2008. *Ambushed: A cartoon history of the George W. Bush administration*. Boulder: Paradigm.

Morrison, P., and K. Tsipis. 1998. *Reason enough to hope: America and the world in the twenty-first century*. Cambridge: MIT Press.

Mr. Y [W. Porter and M. P. Mykleby]. 2011. A national strategic narrative. Washington, DC: Woodrow Wilson Center. At http://www.wilsoncenter.org/events/docs/A%20National%20Strategic%20Narrative.pdf (accessed 07/08/11).

Mrak, M., et al., eds. 2004. *Slovenia: From Yugoslavia to the European Union*. Washington, DC: World Bank.

Mulloney, P. 2011. Hobbes, savagery, and international anarchy. *American Political Science Review* 105, no. 1 (Spring 2011): 189–204.

Murray, C. 2012. *Coming apart: The state of white America, 1960–2010*. New York: Crown Forum.

Musser, G. 2012. A new Enlightenment. *Scientific American* 307, no. 5 (November): 77–81.

Naím, M. 2005. *Illicit: How smugglers, traffickers, and copycats are hijacking the global economy*. New York: Doubleday.

Naselenie SSSR 1988: Statisticheskii ezhegodnik, 1989. Moscow: Finansy i statistika.

National Intelligence Council (NIC). 2012. *Global trends 2030: Alternative worlds.* At http://www.dni.gov/index.php/about/organization/national-intelligence-council-global-trends (accessed 12/12/12).

Neumann, I. B. 2008. Russia as a great power, 1815–2007. *Journal of International Relations and Development* 11, no. 2 (June): 128–51.

Newman, M., A-L. Barabási, D. J. Watts, eds. 2006. *The structure and dynamics of networks*. Princeton: Princeton University Press, 2006.

Noah, T. 2012. *The great divergence: America's growing economic inequality crisis and what we can do about it*. New York: Bloomsbury.

Nocera, J. 2011. The last moderate. *The New York Times,* September 6.

Norkus, Z. 2007. Why did Estonia perform best? The north-south gap in the post-socialist economic transition of the Baltic states. *Journal of Baltic Studies* 38, no. 1: 21–42.

Norloff, C. 2010. *America's global advantage: US hegemony and international cooperation*. Cambridge: Cambridge University Press.

Nye, J. S., Jr. 1990. *Bound to lead: The changing nature of American power*. New York: Basic Books.

———. 2004. *Soft power: The means to success in world politics*. New York: Public Affairs.

———. 2010. *Cyberpower*. Cambridge: Harvard University Belfer Center for Science and International Affairs. At http://belfercenter.ksg.harvard.edu/files/cyber-power.pdf (accessed 04/12/11).

———. 2011. *The future of power*. New York: Public Affairs.

Oh, Young-jin, 2013. Park's worst enemy. *Korea Times,* Feb. 25.

Olson, A. M., D. M. Steiner, and I. S. Tuuli, eds. 2004. *Educating for democracy: Paideia in an age of uncertainty*. Lanham, MD: Rowman and Littlefield.

Packer, G. 2011. The broken contract, *Foreign Affairs* 90, no. 6 (Nov.-Dec.): 20–31.

Page, S. E. 2011. *Diversity and complexity:* Princeton: Princeton University Press.

Pape, R. A. 2005. *Dying to win: The strategic logic of suicide terrorism*. New York: Random House.

Parent, J. M., and P. K. MacDonald. 2011. The wisdom of retrenchment. *Foreign Affairs* 90, no. 6 (Nov.–Dec.): 32–47.

Payne, R. J., and J. R. Nassar. 2003. *Politics and culture in the developing world.* New York: Longman.

Pei, M. 2012. China's troubled Bourbons, Project Syndicate, Nov. 3. At http://www.project-syndicate.org/commentary/rising-political-uncertainty-in-china-by-minxin-pei.

Pentland, A. ("Sandy"). 2011, How networks shape human behavior. Cambridge, MA: New England Complex Systems Institute, Lecture on March 4.

———. 2008. *Honest signals: How they shape our world.* Cambridge: MIT Press.

Perc, M. 2012. Evolution of the most common English words and phrases over the centuries. *Journal of the Royal Society Interface* 9 (July): 3323–28.

Pérez-Peña, R. 2012. Studies find more students cheating, with high achievers no exception, *The New York Times,* Sept. 7.

Perica, V. 2002. *Balkan idols: Religion and nationalism in Yugoslav states.* New York: Oxford University Press.

Peukert, D. J. K. 1992. *The Weimar Republic: The crisis of classical modernity.* New York: Hill and Wang.

Pickering, P. M., and M. Baskin. 2008. What is to be done? Succession from the League of Communists in Croatia. *Communist and Post-Communist Studies* 41, no. 4 (Dec.): 521–40.

Pinker, S. 2011. *The better angels of our nature: Why violence has declined.* New York: Viking.

Pontin, J. 2012, Why we can't solve big problems. *MIT Technology Review* (Nov.–Dec.).

Porter, M., and J. Rivkin. 2012. What Washington must do now, The world in 2013. *The Economist,* Nov. 21: 50, and http://www.economist.com/news/21566902-eight-point-plan-restore-american-competitiveness-what-washington-must-do-now/comments#comments (accessed 12/6/12).

Posen, B. R. 1993. The security dilemma and ethnic conflict. *Survival* 3, no. 51: 27–47.

Pozun, B. 2004. E-mail from Ljubljana (Dec. 30).

Putnam, R. D. 1993. *Making democracy work: Civic traditions in modern Italy.* Princeton: Princeton University Press.

———. 2000. *Bowling alone: The collapse and revival of American community.* New York: Simon and Schuster.

Rasputin, V. G. 1989. *Siberia on fire: Stories and essays.* De Kalb, IL: Northern Illinois University Press.

———. 2004. *Na rodine: rasskazy i ocherki.* Moscow: Algoritm.

Raun, T. 2003. Nineteenth- and early twentieth-century Estonian nationalism revisited. *Nations and Nationalism* 91: 129–47.

Reeves, J. 2012. For Mongolia, two symbolic steps in the wrong direction. *PacNet* 82 (Honolulu) (Dec. 6).

Regine, B. 2010. *Iron butterflies: Women transforming themselves and the world.* Amherst, NY: Prometheus.

Richards, D., ed. 2000. *Political complexity: Nonlinear models of politics.* Ann Arbor: University of Michigan Press.

Richardson, M. B. 2003. The metamorphosis of the Lithuanian wayside shrine, 1850–1990. Unpublished PhD dissertation, Boston University.

Richtel, M. 2012. For better and for worse, technology use alters learning styles, teachers say. *The New York Times*, Nov. 1: A20.

Ridley, M. 2002. The evolution revolution. *The New York Times Book Review*, March 17, 11.

Rockefeller Foundation. 2012. http://www.rockefellerfoundation.org/bellagio-center/residency-program/bellagio-poptech-fellows (accessed 10/27/12).

Roe, P. 2002. Misperception and ethnic conflict: Transylvania's societal security dilemma. *Review of International Studies* 28: 57–74.

Rosandić, R. 2000. Grappling with peace education in Serbia. *Peaceworks* 33. Washington, DC: United States Institute of Peace.

Rosecrance, R. N. 2002. War and peace. *World Politics* 55: 137–66.

Rosenau, J. N. 1990. *Turbulence in world politics: A new theory of change and continuity.* Princeton: Princeton University Press.

———. 2003. *Distant proximities: Dynamics beyond globalization.* Princeton: Princeton University Press.

———. 2005. Declaration of interdependence. *International Studies Perspectives* 6, no. 1: Back cover.

Rothstein, E. 2005. Saul Bellow, Saul Bellow, let down your hair. *The New York Times*, May 9, A17, 23.

Roubini, N. 2011. China's bad growth bet, April 14, 2011. At http://www.project-syndicate.org/commentary/roubini37/English (accessed 04/21/11).

Rummel, R. J. 1996. *Death by government.* Brunswick, NJ: Transaction.

Sachs, J. D. 2005. *The end of poverty: Economic possibilities for our time.* New York: Penguin.

Sajoo, A. B., ed. 2010. *A companion to Muslim ethics.* London: L. B. Tauris.

Salzburger Humanismusgespräch. 1970. *Der Friede im nucklearen Zeitalter: Eine Kontroverse zwischen Realisten u. Utopisten.* Munich: Oskar Schatz.

Scott, J. C. 1998. *Seeing like a state: How certain schemes to improve the human condition have failed.* New Haven: Yale University Press.

Serres, M. 2011. Eduquer au XXIe siècle. *Le Monde. Dossiers & Documents* 410 (July–Aug.): 18.

———. 2008. *Here comes everybody: The power of organizing without organizations.* New York: Penguin.

Sharp, G. 2005. *Waging nonviolent struggle: 20th century practice and 21st century potential.* Boston: Extending Horizons.

Shirky, C. 2010. *Cognitive surplus: Creativity and generosity in a connected age.* New York: Penguin.

Siegel, A., and I. Etzkorn. 2013. *Simple: Conquering the crisis of complexity.* New York: Twelve.

Singer, J. D. 1970. Escalation and control in international conflict: A simple feedback model. *General Systems* 15: 163–73; and 1971 *Bulletin of Peace Proposals* 24: 334–38.

———. 1999. Prediction, explanation, and the Soviet exit from the cold war. *International Journal of Peace Studies* 4, no. 2: 47–59.

Singh, G. K., and S. M. Yu. 1995. Infant mortality in the United States: Trends, differentials, and projections, 1950 through 2010. *American Journal of Public Health* 85, no. 7 (July): 957–64.

Šmidchens, G. 2007. National heroic narratives in the Baltics as a source for nonviolent political action. *Slavic Review* 66, no. 3: 484–508.

────. 2013. *The power of song: Nonviolent national culture in the Baltic Singing Revolution*. Seattle: University of Washington Press.

Snyder, J. 2000. *From voting to violence: Democratization and nationalist conflict*. New York: W. W. Norton.

Snyder, T. 2003. *The reconstruction of nations: Poland, Ukraine, Lithuania, Belarus, 1569–1999*. New Haven: Yale University Press.

────. 2010. *Bloodlands: Europe between Hitler and Stalin*. New York: Basic Books.

Somit, A., and S. A. Peterson, eds. 1992. *The dynamics of evolution: The punctuated equilibrium debate in the natural and social sciences*. Ithaca: Cornell University Press.

────. 2008. *The failure of democratic nation-building: Ideology meets evolution*. New York: Palgrave Macmillan.

Spruyt, H. 1994. *The sovereign state and its competitors: An analysis of systems change*. Princeton: Princeton University Press.

Stephan, A., and J. J. Linz. 2011. Comparative perspectives on inequality and the quality of democracy in the United States. *Perspectives on Politics* 9, no. 4 (Dec.): 841–56.

Sterling-Folker, J., ed. 2006. *Making sense of international relations theory*. Boulder: Lynne Rienner.

Stiglitz, J. E. 2012. *The price of inequality*. New York: W. W. Norton.

────, and L. Bilmes. 2008. *The three trillion dollar war: The true cost of the Iraq conflict*. New York: W. W. Norton.

────, A. Sen, and J-P. Fitoussi. 2010. *Mismeasuring our lives: Why GDP doesn't add up*. New York: Perseus.

Sunstein, C. 2013. *Simpler: The future of government*. New York: Simon and Schuster.

Swartz, M. 2002. Translations of *The Qu'ran*. Unpublished research, Boston University.

Talbeb, N. N. 2007. *The black swan: The impact of the highly improbable*. New York: Random House.

────. 2011. A map and simple heuristic to detect fragility, antifragility, and model error. International Conference on Complex Systems, Boston, July 1.

────. 2012. *Antifragile: Things that gain from disorder*. New York: Random House.

Tanner, M. 1997. *Croatia: A nation forged in war*. New Haven: Yale University Press.

Tismaneanu, V. 1998. *Fantasies of salvation: Democracy, nationalism and myth in post-communist Europe*. Princeton: Princeton University Press.

Toal, G., and C. T. Dahlman. 2011. *Bosnia remade: Ethnic cleansing and its reversal*. New York: Oxford University Press.

Tolstoy, L. N. 1852. *Detstvo, otrochestvo, iunost'*. Moscow: Detgiz, 1960.

Tomasello, M. 2009, *Why we cooperate*. Cambridge: MIT Press.

Tough, P. 2012. *How children succeed: Grit, curiosity, and the hidden power of character*. New York: Houghton Mifflin Harcourt.

Toynbee, A. J. 1979. *An historian's approach to religion*. New York: Oxford University Press.

Transparency International. 2002. Corruption perceptions index 2002. At http://www.transparency. org/cpi/2002/cpi2002.en.html (accessed 1/6/03).

────. 2009. Global corruption report 2009. At http://www.transparency.org/publications/gcr (accessed 11/5/09).

────. 2010. Corruption perceptions index 2010. At http://.transparency.org/publications/gcr (accessed 4/20/11).

────. 2011. Corruption perceptions index 2011. At http://cpi.transparency.org/cpi2011/ (accessed 4/13/12).

United Bible Societies. 2012. World scriptures. At http://www.worldscriptures.org/index2.html. (accessed 4/12/12).

United Nations Development Programme. 2003. *Human Development Report 2003*. New York: Oxford University Press.

———. 2006. *Human Development Report 2006*. New York: Oxford University Press.

———. 2007. *Human Development Report 2007–2008*. New York: Palgrave Macmillan.

———. 2009. *Human Development Report 2009*. New York: Palgrave.

———. 2010a. *Human Development Report 2010* at http://hdr.undp.org/en/reports/global/hdr2010/chapters/ (accessed 9/1/10).

———. 2010b. http://hdr.undp.org/en/statistics.hdi (accessed 10/2/11).

———. 2011. *Human Development Report 2011*. New York: Palgrave Macmillan.

———. 2013. *U.S. health in international perspective: Shorter lives, poorer health.* Washington, DC: National Academies Press.

Valkov, N. 2009. Membership in voluntary organizations and democratic performance: European post-communist countries in comparative perspective. *Communist and Post-Communist Studies* 42, no. 1 (March): 1–21.

vanden Heuvel, K. 2012. A brave and independent Russian editor. *The Nation* (April 9).

Van Evera, S. 1994. Hypotheses on nationalism and war,. *International Security* 18, no. 4: 5–39.

Vasquez, J. A. 1997. The realist paradigm and degenerative versus progressive research programs: An appraisal of neotraditional research on Waltz's balancing proposition. *American Political Science Review* 91: 899–912.

———, P. F. Diehl, C. Flint, and J. Scheffran. 2011. Forum on the spread of war, 1914–1917: A dialogue between political scientists and historians. *Foreign Policy Analysis* 7, no. 2 (April): 139 ff.

Vernadskii, V. I. 1989. *Biosfera i noosfera*. Moscow: Nauka.

Wade, N. 2006. *Before the dawn: Recovering the lost history of our ancestors.* New York: Penguin.

Walt, S. M. 2005. *Taming American power: The global response to U.S. primacy.* New York: W. W. Norton.

Waltz, K. N. 1959. *Man, the state, and war: A theoretical analysis.* New York: Columbia University Press.

———. 1979. *A theory of international politics.* New York: McGraw-Hill.

———. 1986. Reflections on *Theory of International Politics*: Response to my critics. In *Neorealism and its critics,* ed. Robert O. Keohane. New York: Columbia University Press.

———. 2000. Structural realism after the cold war. *International Security* 25, no. 1: 5–41.

———. 2012. Why Iran should get the bomb: Nuclear balancing would mean stability. *Foreign Affairs* (July/Aug.).

Wasserman, D., Q. Cheng, and G-X. Jiang. 2008. Global suicide rates among young people aged 15–19. *World Psychiatry* 4, no. 2: 114–20.

Weber, C. 2005. *International relations theory: A critical introduction.* New York: Routledge.

Wendt, A. 1999. *Social theory of international relations.* Cambridge: Cambridge University Press.

West, J. 2011. The complexity, simplicity, and unity of living systems from cells to cities: Toward a quantifying, unifying framework of biological and social structure, organization, and dynamics. International Conference on Complex Systems. Boston (July 1).

White, J. 2012. Long on rabbits, short on foxes. *Financial Times*, Oct. 26.

Wilson, E. O. 1975. *Sociobiology: The new synthesis.* Cambridge: Harvard University Press.

———. 1993. *Diversity of life.* New York: W. W. Norton.

———. 1998. *Consilience: The unity of knowledge.* New York: A. A. Knopf.

———. 2012. *The social conquest of Earth.* New York: W. W. Norton.

———, ed. 2006. *From so simple a beginning: The four great books of Charles Darwin.* New York: W. W. Norton.

World Bank. Annual. *World Development Report.*

World Bible Society. 2011. www.worldscriptures.org (accessed 07/20/11).

World Economic Forum. 2011. http://www.weforum.org/issues/global-competitiveness (accessed 4/15/11).

———. 2011. http://www.weforum.org/reports/global-information-technology-report-2010-2011-0 (accessed 4/15/11).

———. 2012. Global competitiveness index 2012–2013 rankings. At www.weforum.org/gcr (accessed 10/14/12).

World Health Organization. 2011. Suicide rates per 100,000 by country, year, and sex (Table). At http://www.who.int/mental_health/prevention/suicide_rates/en/ (accessed 11/12/12).

———. 2012a. Suicide prevention (SUPRE). At http://www.who.int/mental_health/prevention/suicide/suicideprevent/en/index.htm (accessed 11/12/12).

———. 2012b. Country reports and charts. At http://www.who.int/mental_health/prevention/suicide/country_reports/en/ (accessed 11/12/2).

World Peace Forum. 2010. *World Peace Index 2010.* Seoul: World Peace ports/en/ Forum.

Wright, Q. 1955. *The study of international relations.* New York: Appleton-Century-Crofts.

Yablokov, A. 2005. Economic growth and environmental security in Russia. *Meeting Report* 22. Washington, DC: Kennan Institute.

You, Jong-sung, 2013. Transition from a limited access order to an open access order: The case of South Korea. In *The shadow of violence: Politics, economics, and the problem of development,* ed. D. North, J. Wallis, S. Webb, and B. Weingast. Cambridge: Cambridge University Press.

Young, N. J., ed. 2010. *Oxford international encyclopedia of peace.* 4 vols. New York: Oxford University Press.

Zewail, A. 2012. Will America kill the curiosity that sent the rover to Mars? *Christian Science Monitor,* Aug. 20.

Zimmer, C. 2011. From single cells, a vast kingdom arose. *The New York Times,* March 15, D3–6.

Zimmerman, W. 1999. *Origins of a catastrophe: Yugoslavia and its destroyers.* New York: Times Books (first published 1996).

INDEX

Abkhazia, 76, 77, 107
accidents and coincidence, 6–9, 204
Acquis Communautaire, 45
Adamkus, Valdas, 62, 85
Adams, Ansel, 126
Adams, John, 127
adaptability:
  Baltic mythology, 57
  "competitive intelligence," 155
  complex systems, 14
  environmental change, 194
  human evolution, 6–11
  institutional strength and moderniza-
    tion, 182
  internal and external fitness, 28
  natural selection, 23–24
  resilience building in social and
    ecological systems, 215–16n. 2
  ROK and DPRK, 167
  self-organization structures, 24
  The Prince (Machiavelli), 204
"affluenza," 99
Afghanistan:
  state failure, 180–81
  U.S. intervention and nation-building,
    29, 70, 119, 138, 144–45, 152, 158,
    181–82, 193
  U.S. withdrawal (2014), 145
agent-based systems:
  explanation and modeling, 30, 111–
    12

modeling challenges, 207–08
  United States, 127
Ai Weiwei, 163
Akayev, Askar, 68
alcohol consumption, 102
al Qaeda, 21, 25, 145, 193
Albania
  cultural heritage and key indicators,
    89–94
  designation by Slovenians, 218
  EU accession, 46
  Internet usage, 115, 197
  Lirak Bejko, self-immolation, 222
  post-communist transition, 40, 41
  riots (1997), 217
  semi-consolidated democracy, 43–44,
    84–86
  transparency, 96
  Zone B societies, 75–77
Albright, Madeline, 21
Aleksei (Orthodox Patriarch), 218
Alexander I, Tsar, 64
Alexander the Great, 23
alternative scenarios, 34
altruism, 9–10
anarchy:
  exploitation and fitness, 4
  fluctuation in Russia and Ukraine,
    68–69
  Hobbesian conception, 3
  neorealism, 21, 185

anarchy *(continued)*
  order-chaos spectrum, 23, 114,
    180–81, 202
  self-organization, 32–35, 125–26
  Zone E societies, 80
Anna Karenina, 98
Appeasement, 28–29
Aristotle, 33
"Arkan" (Serbian underworld figure), 60
Armenia:
  conflict with Azerbaijan, 76–77,
    107–08, 220n3
  cultural heritage and key indicators,
    89–94
  dependence on Azeri energy, 110
  downward trajectory of democracy, 91
  human development, 76–77
  Nagorno-Karabakh, 76
  Russian support, 52
  semi-consolidated authoritarianism, 84
  Zone C societies, 76, 86
Armstrong, Lance, 137
Articles of Confederation, 25
Ashton, Catherine, 79
Asian Financial Crisis (1997), 169
Atlantic Community, 25
Atlantic Grupa, 79
Aung San Suu Kyi, 163
austerity:
  Estonia and Latvia, 96, 97
  Hungary, 111
  Romania, 85
  Slovenia, 74
Austrian Empire, 65
Axis, 29
Azerbaijan
  Armenia, 76–77, 107–08, 220n3
  civil society trends, 87
  consolidated authoritarian regime, 84
  cultural heritage and key indicators,
    89–94
  "curse of oil," 81
  democracy trajectory, 91
  energy, 53, 81, 107–08, 110
  human development, 79–80
  Internet usage, 114, 197
  Nagorno-Karabakh, 76

regression of judicial independence,
    85
rent-seeking, 114
top-down control, 114, 198
Zone D societies, 79–80

Bahrain:
  cultural heritage and key indicators, 94
  elite cooperation with U.S., 187
  Internet usage, 197
  revolts (2011), 53, 196
Balkan Beat Box, 217n1.
Balkan region:
  alternative futures, 69–70
  casualties from post-communist
    transition, 40–41
  comparisons with Baltics, xviii, 36–70,
    189
  democracy scores, 43
  downward democratic trajectory, 44
  "Endism," 182
  ethnic conflict, 51–52
  HDI scores, 43
  independent media scores, 43
  individual leaders, 58–63
  myths and mythmaking, 55–58
  Ottoman rule, 53
  political, economic and human
    development, 42–44
  self-organization, 63–67
  top-down rule, 65–69
  Zone C societies, 76
Baltic region
  alternative futures, 69–70
  casualties from post-communist
    transition, 40
  comparisons with Balkans, xviii,
    36–70, 189
  energy, 112, 217n11
  ethnic balance), 41, 42, 43
  German and Soviet interference, 65
  independence (1920), 65
  individual leaders, 61–62
  intermarriage, 41
  links to Western institutions, 44–46
  literacy, 64, 219n11
  myths and mythmaking, 55–58

nonviolent challenges to Soviet
	power, 48–53, 203
political, economic and human
	development, 42–44
pollution, 195
Popular Fronts, 65
Russian population, 41–42
self-organization, 63–67
self-organized criticality, 112
Slavic minorities and secession, 50
Swedish rule (promotion of literacy
	and education), 63
transfer to Russian control, 63
Zone A societies
Ban Ki-moon, 56, 174
Bearslayer, The, 57–58, 64
Bejko, Lirak, 222
Belarus:
	co-evolution, 110
	consolidated authoritarianism, 43, 84
	cultural heritage and key indicators,
		88–96
	energy, 87, 112
	ethnic balance, 109
	federation attempt with Lithuanians,
		Poles, 65
	fitness, 69, 82, 113
	Internet usage, 115
	National Endowment for Democracy
		(U.S.), 68
	suicide, 85, 98–99, 101, 103, 106, 221n20
	"thriving" disparities, 216n6
	top-down rule, 80
	Zone D societies, 79, 86

Belgium, 99
Bell Labs, 139
Bertelsmann Foundation Transformation
	Index (BTI), xv, xvii, xxii, 26, 88,
	90–93, 117, 166–67, 220–21n10, 11
Bible:
	distribution in Sweden, 116
	publication dates, 117, 219n9
	publication in Bulgarian, 219n14
	publication in Croatian, 66
	publication in East and West Livonian,
		219n9

publication in Estonian, 63–64
publication in French, 116
publication in Italian, 116
publication in Korean, 175
publication in Latvian, 63–64
publication in Lithuanian, 63–64
publication in Romani Vlach, 219n14
publication in Romania, 219n14
publication in Romanian
	Macedonian, 219n14
publication in Serbian, 67
publication in Slovene, 66
publication in Southern and Tallinn
	Estonian, 219n9
vernacular publication (across post-
	communist world), 116–17
bipolarity, 13
Bismarck, Otto von, 19
Black Swans, xiii, 9, 22, 199
blat, 102, 203
Borisov, Boyko, 75
Bosnia and Herzegovina, 42
	census (2013), 46
	cultural heritage and key indicators,
		89–94
	Dayton Peace Accords (1995), 40,
		46
	downward democratic trajectory, 44
	economic and political development
		(compared with Estonia), 48
	elections (and ethnocentrism), 69–70
	ethnic cleansing (reversal), 220n5
	EU accession, 46
	income, 68
	Internet usage, 115, 197
	Izetbegović, Alija, 60
	literacy, 68, 118
	lycée, 67
	political, economic, and human
		development, 42–44
	separation from Yugoslavia, 49
	Srebrenica Massacre (1995), 56
	suicide, 98
	top-down rule, 66
	transitional regime, 84
	U.S./NATO intervention, 53
	Zone C societies, 76–78, 86

Boston Marathon bombings (2013), 113
brain mapping, 2
Brave New World, 137, 155
Brazauskas, Algirdas, 61
Brezhnev era stagnation, 72
Bucharest Summit Declaration (2008),
    44, 45
Bulgaria
    Acquis Communitaire, 45–46
    Borisov, Boyko, 75
    consolidated democracy, 44
    corruption, 86, 91
    cultural heritage and key indicators,
        89–94, 97
    decline of media independence, 44
    "Georgi" (interview subject), 221n13
    independent media scores, 43
    Internet usage, 115
    Macedonia (conflict with Serbia), 66
    matica, 7
    regression of judicial independence,
        85
    religious tension, 52, 53
    Roma, 86
    semi-consolidated democracy, 43, 84
    upward democratic trajectory, 91
    Whose Song Is This?, 69
    Zone B societies, 77
Bush, George H.W., 11, 49, 134,
    182–83
Bush, George W.:
    2000 election, 135
    veterans services, 138
    decline of American fitness, 129, 141,
        149, 153, 182
    Haliburton contracts, 223
    military expenditures, 29, 138, 152
    nation-building, 181
    neoconservativism, 215n21
    No Child Left Behind, 141
    North Korea, 174, 184
    political cohesion, 134–35
    public opinion, 28, 144, 153
    tax policies, 133, 138
    unilateralism, 144, 182, 205
Butkevikius, Algirdas, 83, 85

Carson, Rachel, 128
Carter, Jimmy, 11, 19, 128, 134, 163
Carter, Rosalynn, 163
casinos, 136
Catherine the Great, 21
Ceauşescu, Nicolae, 61, 173, 219n6
Center for Nonviolent Resistance, 68
chaebols, 169–70
Chancery Slavic, 64
chaos theory, 4, 5
Chechnya, 28, 53, 80, 108, 189, 198,
    220n3, 4, 6
Chen Guangcheng, 102, 163
Cheney, Dick, 153, 223n2
Chetniks (Yugoslavia), 59
Chile, 36–37, 88
China (PRC):
    16th CCP Conference (2012), 88
    anarchy, 188
    Ai Weiwei, 163
    Chen Guangcheng, 102, 163
    comparative assets 28, 31–32
    competitiveness, 166, 216
    control of ethnic minorities, 109
    corruption, 170
    cultural heritage and key indicators,
        36–37, 90, 95–96, 222n4
    Cultural Revolution, 72
    defense expenditures, 27, 152–53
    Deng Xiaoping, 72, 104
    downward democratic trajectory, 91
    female infanticide, 109
    historic resilience, 216
    historical power assets, 122–23
    intellectual property, 156
    interdependence with U.S., 4, 13,
        125–26, 183
    Internet usage, 115
    leadership transition (2012), 88
    Leninist capitalism, 72
    Mao Zedong, 72, 180
    military pilot training, 224n9
    North Korea, 83, 172–74, 176
    pollution, 190
    rising influence, 24, 129–32, 142,
        150–52, 167, 182, 187

Shanghai Cooperation Organization, 110
suicide, 98, 101, 103–104
tensions with Mongolia, 76, 87
Zone F societies, 82–83, 87–88
Chirac, Jacques, 204
Chu, Steven, 139, 140
Chung Ju-yung, 170
civil society:
 Azerbaijan, 87
 Balkans, 57
 Baltics, 65
 Bulgaria, 86
 Egypt, 197
 fitness and associations, 181
 importance, 115
 New Village Movement, 168
 Popular Fronts, 65
 Romania, 85
 South Korea 168
 Sub-Saharan Africa, 196–97
 Ukraine, 87
clash(es) of civilizations, 51–53, 186–87
class struggle, 3
climate change, 27, 125, 140–41, 151, 163, 190, 194, 200, 206, 223n16
Clinton, Bill, 21, 28, 134, 135, 163, 181–82
Clinton, Hillary, 21, 163
coevolution:
 applications, 207
 criticality and the spread of war, 186
 definition, 29
 emergence, 29–30
 genes and behavior, 10
 importance to fitness, 194–95
 inequality, 190
 post-Soviet Eurasia, 110–13
 United States, 127
"commodity curse," 81
Commonwealth of Unrecognized States, 77
Community for Democracy and Rights of Nations, 77

Comparative Democracy, Independent Media, and Human Development (2009), 43
comparative historical sociology, 15
competitiveness (measurement of), 26, 27
"complect," 14
complex adaptive system (CAS):
 concept definition, 14
 coral reef example, 24
 threats to system viability, 149
complexity science:
 agents and structure, 199–200
 alternative scenarios for fitness and regime type, 34

 clashes of civilization, 186–87
 communities, 8
 "crisis of," 12
 crowdsourcing, 195–99
 cyberpower, 191–92
 definition, xvii, xviii
 despotism vs. chaos, 180–82
 ethnic conflict, 189
 hegemony vs. cooperation, 182–83
 inequality, 189–91
 rise and fall of empires, 187–89
 security dilemmas, 184–85
 spread of war, 185–86
 terrorism, 192–93
 the environment, 194–95
 transnational crime, 193–94
 utility, xix
Congress Party (India), 33
conscience, 11
consciousness, 11
conserving innovations, 10
consilience, xv, xix, 159–60, 207
consolidated democracies:
 definition and examples, 42–44, 74
 liberal peace theory, 108
 Zone A societies, 83–84
constructivism, xii, xviii, 18, 22, 46, 215n24
Copernicus, 17
Corruption Perception Index (CPI), 35–37, 91–92, 95–96, 117

corruption:
Albania, 44, 91, 96
Belarus, 79
Bulgaria, 45, 86, 91, 221n13
China, 198
Czech Republic, 91
Denmark, 91
fitness landscapes, 113
Georgia, 119
Hungary, 85
Iceland, 91
Lithuania, 85
Mongolia, 91
Norway, 91
place in complexity science, 27
Romania, 45, 85, 91, 219n6
Russia, 204
Slovakia, 91
South Korea, 168, 170–71
Sweden, 91
U.S., 156
Zone A societies, 74
Zone B societies, 75–76
Ćosić, Dorica, 56
Counter-Reformation, 65, 66
creativity, 4, 6, 26–27, 34, 63, 102, 108, 125, 154, 168, 184
Croatia:
armed conflict with Serbia, 60
Bible publication, 66
Croatian Democratic Union (HDZ), 60
Croatian Diet, 66
cultural heritage and key indicators, 89–94
Dayton Peace Accords (1995), 40, 46
education, 66–67
EU accession, 46, 60, 78–79
Gotovina, Ante, 78
income, 68
internal migrations, 217n13
Josipović, Ivo, 78
Krajina, 50
Krajina, 50, 78
literacy, 66–67
Markač, Mladen, 78
Marković, Ante, 60

Pavlović, Ante, 59
political, economic, and human development, 42–44
Radić, Stjepan, 219n4
recent tensions with Serbia, 78
Reformation, 66
semi-consolidated democracy, 42, 43, 84
separation from Yugoslavia, 49, 66, 204
Serbian populations, 50
Social Democratic Party, 60
stagnant trajectory of democracy, 91
Stepinac, Alojzije, 59, 219n3 and 4
suicide, 98
Tuđman Franjo, 60
Ustaša, 59
war crimes acquittals, 78
World War II, 59
Zone C societies, 76–77
Cuba:
corruption, 96
cultural heritage and key indicators, 89–94
freedom rankings, 87–88
health and education systems, 26, 80, 132
Missile Crisis, 13, 15, 125
persistence of communism, 71
suicide, 98–100, 104
Zone D societies, 79–80
Cultural Revolution (China), 72
culture:
autocatalytic nature, 11
clashes of civilization, 186–87
conservation innovations, 10
consilience, 159
cultural zones, 88–91
cyberpower, 191
evolution, 2
fitness, xv, xvii, 35–40, 71–72, 116–18
kto kovo, 61
Marxist assumptions, 21
myths and mythmaking, 55–57
nationalism and xenophobia, 69
rational choice theory, 22
Reformation in Lithuania, 64

self-organization (Balkans vs. Baltic), 66–68
structural realism, 180, 185, 199
suicide, 98
Turkey and EU accession, 46
U.S., 127–28, 137, 141, 148, 155
Czech Republic, 26
Acquis Communitautaire, 45
Bible in vernacular, 117
Challenges to USSR (1968), 203
consolidated democracy, 42
corruption, 91
cultural heritage and key indicators, 89–94
democracy ratings, 84
EU accession, 44, 45
Havel, Vaclav, 102
income, 96
Internet usage, 115
NATO accession, 44
partnership with Western institutions, 44
post-Communist transition, 40
purchasing power, 97
self-organization, 63, 195
Slovaks, relations with, 46
"transitional" terminology, 220n11
Zone A societies, 74

Dačić, Ivica, 78, 79
Dagestan, 80, 81, 220
Dayton Peace Accords (1995), 40, 46
de Chardin, Theilhard, 225n5
democracy:
Baltics vs. Balkans, 39
Czech Republic, 220n11
democracy scores, 42–44, 83–94, 117
democratic peace theory (see "liberal peace theory)
democratization (risks of partial processes), 107–08
dictatorship of the majority, 63, 116
egalitarianism, 33, 160–61
energy exporters, 81
ethnic conflict, 108
fitness, 4, 71
futility of preaching democracy in top-down cultures, 180

Green Movement (Iran), 198
Hungary, 220
liberal peace theory, 107, 202
neo-Kantian liberalism, 181
OECD, 27–28, 166, 188, 222n4, 224n2
opinion polling, 226n4
participation (U.S.), 148
self-organization, 33–34, 63
state stability, 181
Turkmenistan, 221n20
Zone A societies, 72–75
Zone B societies, 75–76
Zone C societies, 76–79
Zone D societies, 79–80
Zone E societies, 80–82
Democratic Republic of Congo (DRC), 26, 165
Democratic Study Group, 134
Deng Xiaoping, 72, 104
Department of Homeland Security, U.S., 138
diamat, 101
diplomatic constellations, 15
Director of National Intelligence, U.S., 138
Đilas, Milovan, 59
DPRK (see "North Korea")
Drnovšek, Janez, 60
Dudaev, Dzhokhar, 218n18
Dust Bowl, 127–28

economic determinism, 50–51, 156–58
economic freedom:
Azerbaijan, 198
Baltic states, 39–40
Belarus, 79
BTI, 88, 220
Cuba, 91
cultural heritage, 93–95
Eastern Europe, 198
Heritage Foundation Index of Economic Freedom, 74, 88, 216, 220n1
Kazakhstan, 198
Russia, 198
Ukraine, 87

ecosystems, 12–13, 111, 214n7
Eduard Shevardnadze, 68, 118
education:
  Baltic Russians, 41
  brain power formulation, 216n9
  communism, 82, 101
  Croatian Serbs, 50
  Cuba, 25–26, 80
  culture, 187
  Finland 104–05
  foreign aid, 190
  HDI, xvii, 25
  IHDI (gender), 26
  innovation, 216
  Korea (historic), 175
  measurement, 26–28
  modernization, 182
  Mongolia, 75
  North Korea (DPRK), 174–75
  Russia, 81
  Saudi Arabia, 25
  self-organization, 197
  Serbs, 52, 67, 69
  Singapore, 216
  South America, 216n5
  South Korea (ROK), 168–69, 171
  Sub-Saharan Africa, 196
  Sweden and its Baltic provinces, 64
  terrorism, 192–93
  United States, 25, 124–25, 128, 132–
    36, 140–41, 148, 150–51, 154–57,
    216n5
  USSR, 220n7
  war-induced values, 69
  World Economic Forum, 216
egalitarianism, 33, 160–61
Egypt, 53, 68, 181, 195–98
Einstein, Albert, 16, 179, 201
Eisenhower, Dwight D., 105, 128
elemental interaction, 14
emergence:
  definition, 29, 30
  evolution, 214n7
  global governance, 35
  post-communist fitness, 110–11
  United States, 127

emergent structures:
  definition, 30
  Baltic states, 65
Emerson, Ralph Waldo, xv, 1, 5, 23, 25,
    161–63, 213, 224n4
emissions, 12
empathy, 10
English language, 10, 24
environmental change 8
Estonia:
  Aleksei (Orthodox Patriarch), 218
  consolidated democracy, 43, 84
  cultural heritage and key indicators,
    89–93
  Dudaev, Dzhokhar, 218n18
  economic and social development 48
  Hanseatic League, 63
  historic literacy rates, 219
  income and purchasing power, 96–97
  Independence (1920), 65
  Internet usage, 115
  Kelam, Mari-Ann, xxii
  Kelam, Tunne, 61
  Laar, Mart, 61
  literacy, 63–64
  Meri, Lennart, 61
  non-citizen residents, 217n4
  Red Army Memorial incident, 41
  Russian population, 41
  Rüütel, Arnold, 61
  self-organization, 64–65
  Son of Kalev, The, 57–58, 64
  suicide, 98, 101, 103, 106
  Swedish rule, 64
  Taagepera, Rein, 62
  Vīķe-Freiberga, Vaira, 62
  Zone A societies, 74–75
Ethiopia, 36
ethnic conflict:
  Albania, 75
  elite factors, 58, 59
  ethnic cleansing, 41, 51, 52, 53, 54
  ethnocentrism, 66
  explanations, 46, 47, 48
  Kyrgyzstan, 80
  minorities, 108, 109

predictions, 114–16
Romania, 85
European Bank for Reconstruction and
  Development, 79
European Central Bank (ECB), 111
European Coal and Steel Community,
  13
European Convention on Human
  Rights, 85
European Court of Human Rights, 85
European integration, 13
European Network of Transmission
  System Operations, 112
European Recovery Program, 124
European Union:
  Acquis Communautaire, 45
  Albania, 46, 86
  Bosnia census (2013), 46
  Bulgaria, 45, 75, 86, 221n13
  Croatia, 46, 60, 76, 78
  Cyprus, 46
  Czech Republic, 45
  Estonia, 45, 217n4
  European Central Bank (ECB), 111
  European Coal and Steel Community,
    13
  European Convention on Human
    Rights, 85
  European Court of Human Rights,
    85
  Eurozone crisis, 74, 96–97, 112–13
  expansion (2004–13), 445–46, 75
  EXYSTENCE, 214n5
  French anti-Constitution vote (2005),
    204
  Greece, 97, 112
  Hungary, 45, 85, 111
  Iceland, 46
  importance as Western institution, 25,
    44, 70, 110–11
  income and purchasing power, 96–97,
    111, 112
  Ingalina nuclear power plant, 112
  Latvia, 45
  Lithuania, 45, 112
  Macedonia, 46

Montenegro, 46
Poland, 45
purchasing power of member and
  candidate states, 97
Romania, 45, 61, 75, 86
sanction threats, 45
Serbia-Kosovo mediation, 46
Serbia, 46, 78
Slovakia, 45
Slovenia, 45, 74
Turkey, 46, 196
evolution, 2, 214n7 and n9, 222n15
exogamy, 8
exotic species, 12
exploitation (linkages with mutual gain,
  fitness), 4
external fitness, 27–28, 31
extractive institutions, 33
eyes, 8

failed states, 35, 180–81, 206
famine (North Korea), 83
Faust, 14, 19, 144–45, 162, 214n10,
  222n2
federation attempt (Poles, Lithuanians,
  and Belarusians), 65
Ferghana Valley, 80
fields of diplomatic constellations, 15
fields of historical sociology, 15
Finland, 64, 98–101, 104–05, 112, 148,
  155, 219n11
First Party (Latvia), 42
fitness:
  acquisition, 116–18
  China, 150–53
  differences between ROK and
    DPRK, 173
  diversity, multiculturalism, 62, 63
  domestic, 27, 28
  (as) explanatory variable, 71, 72
  fitness landscapes, 31, 113
  fitness matrix, 36
  how to achieve, 23
  linkages with exploitation, mutual
    gain, 4
  measurement, xvii

fitness *(continued)*
  relative fitness, 31
  societal, xvii
  United States, 147–55
  virtuous circle, 62
Ford, Gerald, 124, 134, 136
Ford, Henry, 126
Fox News, 153
fracking, 139
fractal properties, 5
France, 99, 116, 159, 181, 185
free riders, 10
Freedom House Index of Political and
    Civil Liberties, xvii, 26
Fukushima nuclear power plant, 112
Fukuyama, Francis, 20, 182

G.I. Bill, 124
Gaddafi, Muammar al-el, 53
Gagauz, 77
Galileo, 17
Gates, Bill, 163
Gates, Melinda, 163
Gedankenfabrik, 14
Genes, 10
Geni coefficient, 26
Georgia:
  Abkhazia, 76–77, 107
  challenge to Soviet power (1989), 48
  Internet usage, 115
  Ivanishvili, Bidzina, 119
  Kmara, 68
  reliance on Azeri energy, 110
  Rose Revolution, 68
  Saakashvili, Mikheil, 118–19
  Shevardnadze, Eduard, 118
  South Ossetia, 76
  transitional-hybrid regimes, 84
  war with Russia (2008), 76
  Zone C societies, 76–77
German empire, 65
Gingrich, Newt, 134–36
global governance, 35
Global Trends 2030, 202
Goethe, 5, 14, 19, 23, 25, 162, 185,
    213n4
Gorbachev, Mikhail S., 48–49, 51, 103,
    172–73, 183, 205–06, 219–20

Gore, Al, 135, 140, 163
Gotovina, Ante, 78
Grand Duchy of Lithuania, 64
Great Britain, 21, 122, 148, 181, 185,
    223n1
Great Depression, 124
Greece, 3, 13, 36–37, 40, 44, 93, 97,
    111–12, 132, 159
Greenpeace, 21
Gross domestic product (GDP), 25
"group-think," 30
Guatemala (U.S. intervention), 125
Guildenstern (in *Hamlet*), 22
Gulf War, 13
gun violence (United States), 142–44

Habsburg rule (Croatia, Slovenia), 66
Hamlet 22, 100
hangŭl, 175
Hanseatic League, 35, 63–64, 183, 216,
    225n3
happiness, 26–27, 92
Haradinaj, Ramush, 78
hard power:
  comparative resources, 32
  cyberpower, 192
  Realism, 181, 199
  United States, 124
  USSR, 49, 194, 203

Harmony Center (Latvia), 42
Harvard Business School Action Plan,
    156
Harvard Coop, 126
Harvard-MIT Index of Economic
    Complexity (IEC), xvii, 26, 113
Havel, Vaclav, 102
HDI (adjusted for inequality), 26
HDI scores, 37, 43, 73, 92, 93, 117, 130
HDI trends, 43, 73, 93, 130
heartbeats (multifractal vs. monofractal),
    213n2
Hegel, 19, 182
Heritage Foundation Index of
    Economic Freedom, 74, 88, 91,
    216, 220n1
historical contingency, 24
Hitler, 15, 28–29, 59, 65, 180

Hobbes, Thomas, 3, 20–21, 35, 179–80, 183, 215n26
Honesty scores (*see* Corruption Perceptions Index)
Hong Kong, 26, 95–96, 100, 148, 165–66, 217n13
HSS party (Yugoslavia), 219n4
human capital (and Malthusian stagnation), 68–69
Hungary (debt crisis), 111–12
Hungary:
  consolidated democracy, 84
  democracy (erosion), 91, 220n9
  democracy ratings, 84–85
  income and purchasing power, 96–97
  Internet usage, 115
  political, economc, and human development, 40, 42, 44–45, 74
  Romania, 61, 111
  self-organization, 63
  suicide, 98, 100
  Targu Mures, 41
Hunger Games, The, 137, 213n1, 222n14
Hus, Jan, 116
Hussein, Saddam, 60, 193

IBM, 21
idealism, xviii, 18–22, 179, 181, 188, 193, 199, 207–08, 215n22, 24
Iliescu, Ion, 61, 219n5, 6
incarceration policies (U.S.)142
income:
  fitness (ROK), 174
  fitness measurement, 6, 25–26, 34
  health disparities (U.S.), 147–48
  human capital (Slovenia), 68
  income inequality (ROK), 166
  income inequality, 82, 189
  purchasing power, 96–97
  recent trends and austerity, 95–97
  wealth inequality (U.S.), 124, 132–34, 157, 222n10
Index of Economic Complexity (IEC), xvii, 26, 133
India, 33, 36–37, 124, 131, 183, 190, 220–21n11
individual dignity, 11, 63, 65, 71–72, 116, 161, 175–76

Indochina (U.S. intervention), 105, 123–25, 135, 188
Industrial Revolution (first), 149
Inequality-adjusted HDI (IHDI), 26
infant temperament, 215n2223
Ingalina nuclear power plant, 112
Inner Mongolia, 75–76
innovation vs. competitiveness, 216n5
intellectual production, 3
Intergovernmental Panel on Climate Change (IPCC), 140
International Monetary Fund (IMF), 28
Internet, 114–15, 154–55, 176, 191, 196–98
"invisible hand," 3
Iran, 11, 125, 144, 184, 194–96, 198, 202, 223n10, 225n10
Iraq, 13, 29, 60, 70, 138, 144, 152, 181–82, 215n21
irredentism, 56, 60, 66, 76, 82
Ishmael (lessons on complexity), 158–61
Islamic fundamentalism, 60, 79–80, 181
Israel, 21, 36–37, 125, 144, 185, 197, 217n1
Ivanishvili, Bidzina, 119
Izetbegović, Alija, 60

Jagiello dynasty (Lithuania), 61
Japan:
  competitiveness, 148–51
  democracy, 220
  demographics, 190
  Fukushima nuclear power plant, 112
  historical power assets, 122–25, 131
  keiretsu, 169
  manufacturing, 132
  Meiji Restoration, 33, 169
  military pilot training, 224n9
  occupation of Korea, 176
  shogunate, 33
  stagnation, 28
  suicide, 99, 105
Jeremić, Vuk, 56
jihadists, 13, 125, 187
John Paul II (Pope), 59
John, Wycliffe, 116
Josipović, Ivo, 78

K Street lobbying, 153
Kalevipoeg (see "*Son of Kalev, The*")
Kant, Immanuel, 19, 35, 63, 179, 18,
    202, 216n10
Karađorđević dynasty (Serbia), 59
Kazakhstan
    challenge to Soviet power (1986), 48
    coevolution, 110
    consolidated authoritarianism, 84–85
    cultural heritage and key indicators,
        89–94
    energy, 81, 108–09
    Internet usage, 115
    revolt against Soviets (1986), 48
    suicide, 98–101, 103, 106, 221n16–21
    Zone D societies, 79–80
keiretsu, 169
Kelam, Mari-Ann, xxii
Kelam, Tunne, 61
KelKel (Kyrgyzstan), 68
Kennan, George F., 205
Kennedy, John F., 15, 125, 128
Kennedy, Robert F., 15
Kepler, 17
Khlomov, Kiril, 99
Khrushchev, Nikita S., 15, 82, 125
Kim Dae Jung, 170
Kim Geo-sung, 171
Kim Il Sung, 171
Kim Jong Il, 170, 184
Kim Jong Un, 172, 176–77
Kim Young Sam, 169
kin group, 8–10
King Mindaugas, 57
King, Martin Luther, Jr., 219n8
Kingdom of Serbs, Croats, and Slovenes,
    59
Kissinger, Henry, 19, 126
Klein, Mark, 206
Kmara, 68
Knežević, Aleksandar, 60
Koller, Dapphne, 163
Korea, Republic of (*see* "South Korea")
Korea, Democratic People's Republic of
    (*see* "North Korea")
Korean alphabet, 175
Korean War, 165

Kosovo:
    conflict and separation from Serbia,
        44, 49, 78–79
    elections and ethnocentrism, 69–70
    EU accession, 46
    Haradinaj, Ramush, 78
    human capital (vs. Slovenia), 68
    Kosovo Pole, 57
    semi-consolidated authoritarianism,
        43, 84, 86
    Thaçi, Hashim, 79
    U.S./NATO intervention, 46, 53
    war crime allegations, 78–79
Koštunica, Vojislav, 67
Krajina (Croatia), 50, 78
Kropotkin, Petr (Prince), 126
kto kovo culture, 61, 205
Kučan, Milan, 60
Kuwait, 13, 53, 193, 196–97
Kuznetsov, Eduard, 102
Kyrgyzstan:
    Akayev, Askar, 68
    Ferghana Valley, 80
    KelKel (Kyrgyzstan), 68

Laar, Mart, 61
Labor Party (Lithuania), 83
Lāčplēsis (see "*Bearslayer, The*")
land reform (Korean, Taiwan,
    Philippines), 224n6
Landsbergis, Vytautas, 61–61, 85, 102,
    219n8
Laos, 71, 83, 87, 90–91, 95
Latvia:
    austerity, 97
    Bearslayer, The, 57
    challenges to USSR, 51, 203
    consolidated democracy, 43, 89
    cultural heritage and key indicators,
        89–93
    ethnic balance, 41–43, 48–49, 109,
        217n9
    EU, 111
    First Party, 42
    Hanseatic League, 63
    Harmony Center, 42
    income and purchasing power, 96–97

Independence (1920), 65
Internet usage, 115
literacy, 63–64
Occupation Museum, 57
People's Party, 42
Popular Fronts, 50
self-organization, 64–65
Škele, Andris, 62
suicide, 98, 101, 103, 105–06, 221n20
support for self-determination of
    SSRs, 53
survival of Christianity, 53
Swedish rule, 64
Zone A societies, 74–75
League of Nations, 21, 126
League to Enforce the Peace, 126
Lee Myuyng-bak, 171
Lee Sang-deuk, 170
levels of analysis, 15
levels of complexity, 21
liberal institutionalism, 20
liberal peace theory, 35, 63, 107–08, 183
Libya, 21, 44, 53, 181, 195–96
life expectancy, xvii, 9, 25, 27, 31, 75, 81,
    99, 104–05, 147, 150, 166, 203, 216n3
literacy:
    Baltic, 64, 65, 219n11
    communist systems, 118
    fitness, 11, 71–72, 116, 175
    Islamic world, 118
    Japan and Korea, 175–76
    Russia and Central Asia, 219n11
    Serbia, 67
    Yugoslav republics, 68
Lithuania
    2008 Law on Citizenship, 42
    austerity, 97
    Brazauskas, Algirdas, 61
    Butkevikius, Algirdas, 83–85
    cultural heritage and key indicators,
        89–93
    discrimination (Jews, Roma), 42
    domestic political intrigues, 83–85
    great power history, 64
    HDI, 74, 117
    income and purchasing power, 96–97
    Independence (1920), 65

Ingalina nuclear power plant, 112
Internet usage, 115
King Mindaugas, 57
Labor Party (Lithuania), 83
Landsbergis, Vytautas, 61–61, 85, 102,
    219n8
literacy, 63–64
Migration Department, 42
Paksas, Rolandas, 83–85
Polish, Russian populations, 42
Reformation, 64
self-organization, 64–65
Social Democrats (Lithuania), 83
Solidarność, 62
suicide, 85, 98–106
Vil'no University, 64
Vilnius (Polish population, street
    names), 42
Visaginas nuclear plant referendum,
    112
Volga Federal District, 81
Zone A societies, 74–75
Little Prince, The, 161
livestock, 11
Ljubuški, 60
Lončar, Budimir, 61
Lotka-Voltera model, 29
Luce, Henry, 121
Lukashenko, Aleksandr, 86–87
Luther, Martin, 11, 64, 116
lycée, 67

Macedonia:
    Bible publication, 219n14
    cultural heritage and key indicators,
        89–94
    elections and ethnocentrism, 69, 70
    EU accession, 46
    literacy, 68
    nationalism, 52
    purchasing power, 97
    semi-consolidated democracy, 42, 43,
        44, 84
    separation from Yugoslavia, 52
    Serbian-Bulgarian conflict, 66
    U.S./NATO intervention, 53
    Zone C societies, 76

Machiavelli, Niccoló, 3, 10, 19, 202, 204
Makana, 137
Mao Zedong, 72, 180
March on the Drina, 56
Markač, Mladen, 78
Marković, Ante, 60
Marseillaise, 57
Marx, Karl, 2–3, 18–19, 29, 50, 134, 136, 156–57, 179
material production, 3
materialist dialectic, 3
materialistic realism, xviii
maticas, 67
matrix of fitness, 36
May-Widmer stability theorem, 12
Mbembe, Achille, 225n9
McNamara, Robert S., 15
Medvedev, Dmitri A., 99
Meir, Golda, 21
Melville, Herman, 126, 158
Mephistopheles, 14, 124, 144, 162, 214n10
Meri, Lennart, 61
Mihailović, Dragoljub-Draža, 59
Milanović, Dafina, 60
military flight training, 224n9
millet system (Ottoman), 66
Milošević, Slobodan, 49–50, 52, 59–63, 67–68, 78, 180, 199
Miorita, 218n2
MIT Deliberatorium, 206
MIT/Club of Rome, 128
Mladić, Ratko, 59–60
Moby Dick, 158
modernization, 66, 182
Moldova:
    crowd-sourcing (2009 protests), 195
    cultural heritage and key indicators, 89–93
    cultural heritage and key indicators, 89–94
    ethnic balance, 77, 109
    Gagauz, 77
    Internet usage, 115
    Miorita, 218n2
    Romanian state visit, 61
    Russian and Ukrainian minorities, 77

transitional-hybrid regime, 84
Transnistria, 77
    Zone C societies, 76–77, 86
Mongolia, 75–76, 82, 87, 90–91, 95, 109, 165–66, 220n2
monogamy, 9
Montenegro:
    cultural heritage and key indicators, 89–93
    EU accession, 46
    Internet usage, 115
    literacy, 68
    semi-consolidated democracy, 42–44, 84
    separation from Yugoslavia, 52
    Zone C societies, 76–77, 86
moral code, 11
Mostar, 60
Mothers Clubs (ROK), 168
Moynihan, Daniel P., 55
Mubarak, Hosni, 68, 196
Muir, John, 126
multipolarity, 13
mutation, 23–24
mutual gain
    linkages with exploitation, fitness, 4
    mutual vulnerability, 3
    zero-sum competition, 213
mythmaking, 55, 56, 57. 58

Nagorno-Karabakh, 76–77, 113
NASA, 140
National Defense University (U.S.), 20
National Endowment for Democracy, 68
National Institutes of Health, 140
National Intelligence Council, 183, 190, 191, 202
National Rifle Association (NRA), 144
National Science Foundation (NSF), 140
National Skills Coalition, 31
nationalism, 46–48, 56, 59–61, 66, 69, 81–82
Nations in Transit (democracy ratings), 43, 83–84, 217n6
NATO, 25, 28, 44, 46, 49–50, 61, 75, 86, 110–11, 119, 144, 154, 182, 196

natural selection, xiv, 5, 18, 23–25, 167, 217214n7, 9
neo-Darwinians, 18
neorealism, 14–15, 18, 21, 35, 46, 48–49, 52, 182–84, 199, 202, 208
Neumann, Peter G., 191, 201
New Deal, 124
New Village Movement (ROK), 168
Newsroom, The, 147
Ng, Andrew, 163
Nigeria, 36, 37, 196
Nikolić, Tomislav, 78
1984, 137
No Child Left Behind, 141
Nobel Prize, xiii, 1, 3, 16, 27–28, 124, 126, 133, 139–40, 144, 163, 170
non-state actors, 25
noosphere, 225n5
North Korea (DPRK), 26
    comparison with South Korea, 165–77
    comparisons with East Germany (GDR), 173
    cybercrime, 191
    dependence on USSR, PRC, 172, 176
    famine, 83
    fitness landscape, 173
    Kim Il Sung, 171
    Kim Jong Il, 170, 184
    Kim Jong Un, 172, 176–77
    Mickey Mouse (appearance with Kim Jong Un), 176
    nuclear program, 174, 184–85
    ongoing isolation, 174
    prospects of improving fitness, 174–77
    punctuated equilibrium, 171–73
    sanctions, 194
    statistical abnormalities, 216
    Sunshine Policy, 170
Norway:
    cultural heritage and key indicators, 91–93
    external fitness, 113
    fitness parameters, 26–28
    income and purchasing power, 96–97
    suicide, 105

surplus, 132
Utøya Island massacre (2011), 113

nuclear war, 9, 185

Obama, Barack, 12, 21, 28–29, 105, 129, 131, 135–38, 140–41, 144–45, 149, 152–53, 163, 181–82, 222n24
Obama, Michelle, 163
Obrenović dynasty (Serbia), 59
Occam's Razor, 14–15
Occupation Museum (Latvia), 57
Occupy Wall Street movement, 129
OECD, 28
Office of Information and Regulatory Affairs, 12
OneGoal, 141
Orange Revolution (Ukraine), 68, 80, 87, 195
Origin of the Species, 159, 215n17
Otpor!, 67–68
Ottomans:
    historical power assets, 122
    millet system, 66
    path dependency of Christian churches, 53
    rule over Serbia, 59, 66, 108
overstretch, 138
Oyu Tolgoi mine, 76

pair-bonding, 8
Paksas, Rolandas, 83–85
Pakistan, 144–45, 180, 183, 186
paradigm shift, 17
paradigms, 16–19, chps 10 and 11
parameters of power, 122, 131
Park Chung Hee, 168
Partisans (Yugoslavia), 59
Pavlović, Ante, 59
Pax Americana, 13
Pax Romana, 13
Peace Corps, 124
Peasants' Revolt (1524–25), 116
People's Party (Latvia), 42
People's Republic of China (PRC (*see* China)
Perry, James "Rick," 141

Petraeus, David, 145
Piłsudski, Jósef, 65
Plato, 19, 33
pluralism, 33, 60
Poland:
 "Christ of nations," 56
 Acquis Communitautaire, 45
 consolidated democracy, 42
 cultural heritage and key indicators,
  89–94
 EU accession, 44, 45
 Eurozone, 112
 income and purchasing power, 96–97
 Internet usage, 115
 NATO accession, 44
 partnership with Western institutions,
  44
 Piłsudski, Jósef, 65
 Polish-Lithuanian Commonwealth,
  57–58, 220n16
 post-communist transition, 40
 self-organization, 63–64, 195
 Solidarność [Solidarity], 203
 Walesa, Lech, 102
 Zone A societies, 74

Political and Economic Transformation
 (BTI ratings trends across Eurasia),
 88–91
Politics, The (Aristotle) 33
polygamy, 9
Popper, Karl, 202
Popular Fronts (Baltic States), 65
Pora, 68
Power, Samantha, 21
practical falsifiability, 19
Pretty Village, Pretty Flame, 56, 218
Pridnestrovian Moldavian Republic
 (PMR), 77
printing press, 11
"Proper Sounds for the Education of
 the People," 175
Protestantism, 64–67, 116, 175
punctuated equilibrium, xix, 24, 113,
 128–29, 149–53, 167, 171–73, 188,
 207
purchasing power, 96–97

Putin, Vladimir, 31, 80–81, 87, 110,
 118–19, 189, 198, 203–04

Qu'ran, 118
quantum mechanics/physics, 5, 16, 117,
 208, 214n6.

"Race to the Top," 141
Radić, Stjepan, 219n4
Rand, Ayn, xviii
rational choice, xii, xviii, 22, 46, 215n27
Reagan, Ronald, 29, 124, 128, 134, 136,
 138–39, 153, 183
Realism (political), xviii, 19–21, 30, 35,
 46–47, 114, 126, 129, 171, 180–81,
 184–95, 199, 202–08, 214n13,
 215n22 and 24
reciprocity, 10
reductionism, 5
Reformation, 11, 64–67
Renaissance, 11
Republic, The (Plato) 33
Republican Guard (Albania), 75
Reshef, Shai, 163
resilience:
 definition, 23
 influence in world affairs, 28
 self-organization and terrorism, 193
 self-regulation among American
  students, 141
 structured scenarios and active
  adaptive management, 215n2
 technological effects, 14
resource base, 11
Rice, Susan, 21
Roh Moo-hyun, 170
Romania
 Bible publication, 116, 219
 Ceauşescu, Nicolae, 61, 173, 219n5, 6
 economic growth (1980s), 217n10
 EU accession, 45–46, 111
 Iliescu, Ion, 61, 219n5 and 6
 Internet usage, 115
 language reforms, 50, 219n5
 Miorita, 218n2
 NATO, 44–45, 111
 post-communist transition, 40–42

purchasing power, 97
semi-consolidated democracy, 43–44, 84
state church sponsorship, 53
Transylvania (and Hungarian minority), 50, 52, 56, 61
Zone B societies, 75, 85
Rome, 24
Roosevelt, Eleanor, 126, 134
Roosevelt, Franklin D., 126
Roosevelt, Theodore, 126
Rose Revolution (Georgia), 68
Rossiskaia, 81
Rousseau's "general will," 66
Rushdie, Salman, 163
Russia/Russian Federation:
acquisition of Baltics, 64
alcohol, impact of, 102
Alexander I, Tsar, 64
blat, 102, 203
Brezhnev era stagnation, 72
Catherine the Great, 21
Chechnya, 28, 53, 80, 108, 189, 198, 220n3, 4
Chechnya, 28, 53, 80, 108, 189, 198, 220n3, 4, 6
consolidated authoritarianism, 43–44
Dagestan, 80, 81, 220
disengagement from Balkans, 49
economic and social development 48
energy leverage, 112–13
energy, 81
fitness, 28, 31–32, 34, 190, 203–04
Geni coefficient, 82
Georgia, 76
Gorbachev, Mikhail S., 48–49, 51, 103, 172–73, 183, 205–06, 219–20
IHDI, 26, 81, 82
Medvedev, Dmitri, 99
Narodnaya Volya, 193
National Endowment for Democracy, 68
post-communist transition, 40
Putin, Vladimir, 31, 80–81, 87, 110, 118–19, 189, 198, 203–04
religious revival, 53
rossiskaia, 81

Russian Empire, 65
Sakharov, Andrei D., 102
self-organization, 109–10
serfdom, 64
Sevastopol naval base, 82
Soviet collapse, 202–04
Sputnik, 128
suicide, 86, 99, 101, 102
top-down government, 68–69
Transnistrian Republic, 77
Yeltsin, Boris, 31
Zone F societies, 80–81
Rüütel, Arnold, 61

Saakashvili, Mikheil, 118–19
Sakharov, Andrei D., 102
Salut au Monde, 209
Salzburger Humanismusgespräch, 215n22
Sanford, Mark, 145
"sapiens paradox," 11
Saudi Arabia, 25–26, 132, 196–97
Schumpeter, Joseph, 17
Second Industrial Revolution, 149
Sejong the Great, 175
self-interest, 10
self-organization:
Balkans, 66–68
Balts, 63–65
definition, 4, 24, 30
differences between ROK and DPRK, 167–71
Russia, 109, 110
Slovenia, 66
self-organized criticality, 112–13
Separation, A, 225
September 11 attacks, 29
Serbia
"Arkan" (Serbian underworld figure), 60
"Greater Serbia," 49
attempts to maintain Yugoslav federation, 49
cultural heritage and key indicators, 89–94
Dačić, Ivica, 78, 79
Dayton Peace Accords (1995), 40, 46
education, 52, 67, 69

Serbia *(continued)*
  historic regional tensions, 52
  independence from Ottomans, 67
  invasion of Croatia, 60
  Jeremić, Vuk, 56
  Karađorđević dynasty, 59
  Knežević, Aleksandar, 60
  Kosovo, 44, 52
  Koštunica, Vojislav, 67
  Krajina, 50
  March on the Drina, 56
  Milanović, Dafina, 60
  Miloševic, Slobodan, 49–50, 52,
    59–63, 67–68, 78, 180, 199
  Ministry of Education, 52
  Mladić, Ratko, 59–60
  Montenegro, 52
  national elections, 2000, 67
  Nikolić, Tomislav, 78
  Obrenović dynasty, 59
  Otpor!, 67–68
  Ottoman rule, 59
  Pretty Village, Pretty Flame, 56
  relations with Croatia, 59–61, 78
  self-organization, 67, 68
  semi-consolidated democracy, 42, 43,
    84
serfdom, 64
Sevastopol naval base, 82
Sharp, Gene, 68
Short Catechism, 116
simplicity vs. complicity, 213n3
"Singing Revolution," 58
Široki Brijeg, 60
Škele, Andris, 62
Slovakia, 40
Slovenia, 26
  Bible publication, 66
  consolidated democracy, 84
  construction bubble, recession and
    austerity, 74
  cultural heritage and key indicators,
    89–94
  Drnovšek, Janez, 60
  elections (2011, 2012 elections), 74
  ethnic minorities, 41
  EU accession, 45–46
  fitness, 26

  folk tales, 65
  income, 68
  Kučan, Milan, 60
  literacy, 69
  political, economic, and human
    development, 42–44
  Reformation, 66
  self-organization, 63–65
  Stanovnik, Janez, 60
  sub-regional identity, 218n15
  suicide, 98, 101, 104, 106
  Zone A societies, 72–75
Social Darwinism, xviii, 3
Social Democratic Party (Croatia), 60
Social Democrats (Lithuania), 83
social development (Estonia vs. Bosnia),
  48
societal security dilemma, 47–50
soft power, 11, 32
Solidarność, 62
Somalia, 26, 32–35, 166, 180
Son of Kalev, The, 57–58, 64
Soros, George, 204
South Korea (ROK):
  Ban Ki-moon, 56, 174
  Bible publication, 176
  Buddhist-Confucian traditions and
    democracy, 220n8
  chaebol
  Chung Ju-yun, 170g
  comparison with North Korea,
    165–77
  corruption, 170
  cultural heritage and key indicators,
    89–94
  "developmental state," 168
  fitness landscape, 173
  hangŭl 175
  Hyundai, 170
  interdependence and global networks,
    174
  Kim Dae Jung, 170
  Kim Geo-sung, 171
  Kim Young Sam, 169
  land reform, 168
  Lee Myuyng-bak, 171
  Lee Sang-deuk, 170
  literacy, 175–76

Mothers Clubs (ROK), 168
New Village Movement (ROK), 168
Park Chung Hee, 168
Park Geun-hye, 171
Park Jie-won, 170
"Proper Sounds for the Education of
    the People," 175
Roh Moo-hyun, 170
Sejong the Great, 175
self-organization, 168
Sunshine Policy, 170
Syngman Rhee, 168
South Ossetia, 76
South Serbs, 59
Southwestern U.S. Blackout (2011), 223,
    224n3
Soviet collapse, 202–04
Sputnik, 128
Srebrenica Massacre (1995), 56
Sri Lanka (civil war), 221
stability (May-Widmer theorem), 12
Stalin, 15, 29, 65, 180, 205
Stanovnik, Janez, 60
Star Spangled Banner, 57
Stepinac, Alojzije, 59, 219n4
structural realism (see "neorealism")
structured scenarios and active adaptive
    management, 215–16n3
suicide:
    Belarus, 103
    challenges to fitness paradigms,
        98–105
    China, 104
    Cuba, 104
    Finland, 104, 105
    Kazakhstan, 103
    Latvia and Estonia, 103
    Lithuania, 102
    rates, 85
    Russian Federation, 102
    Slovenia, 104
    United States, 105
Sunshine Policy, 170
superspreaders, 12
supranational authority, 35
sustainability, 27
Sweden, 53, 64, 91, 99, 105, 112, 116,
    148, 219n11

Switzerland, 99, 132, 142, 148, 166, 181,
    189, 216n5
syllogism, 14
synergistic relationships, 9
Syngman Rhee, 168
Syria, 53, 152, 195–96, 225n8
system effects, 14, 206

Taagepera, Rein, 62
Targu Mures (Hungary), 41
tax cuts (United States), 132–34
teaching, 10
terrorism, 29
Thaçi, Hashim, 79
Thatcher, Margaret, 21
Thiel, Peter, 139
Third Industrial Revolution, 150
Thoreau, Henry David, 126, 161
"thriving" disparities, 216n6
Thucydides, 3, 20, 149, 215n20
Tickner, J. Ann, 179
Tito, Josef Broz, 52
Tokyo, 11
Tolstoy, Lev, 98, 99
top-down rule, 35, 65–69
transnational actors, 25
"transitional" terminology, 220–21n11
transparency (ratings trends across
    Eurasia), 91–95
Transparency International Corruption
    Perceptions Index (2012), 85
Transparency International, xvii
transparency, 27
Transylvania, 41, 50
Tuđman Franjo, 60
Tunisia, 53, 195–97
Turkey, 40, 44, 46, 75, 88, 132, 196–97
    Ottomans:
        historical power assets, 122
        millet system, 66
        path dependency of Christian
            churches, 53
        rule over Serbia, 59, 66, 108
Tygart, Travis, 137
Tymoshenko, Yulia, 87

Ukraine:
    agriculture, 109

Ukraine *(continued)*
cultural heritage and key indicators, 89–94
hybrid-transitional democracy, 43–44, 84, 87
income, 96
nationalism, 56
Orange Revolution, 68, 80, 87, 195
oscillation between anarchy and chaos, 68–69
Pora, 68
self organization, 195
suicide, 88, 221
Sevastopol naval base, 82
Tatars (return to Crimea, voting rights in Ukraine), 82
Tatarstan, 80
Tymoshenko, Yulia, 87
Zone E societies, 80–82
UN Gender-rrelated Development Index (GDI), 74
Undeutsche (Hanseatic city-states), 63
unified growth theory, 215n15
unilateralism, 144
unipolar moment, 129
unipolar system, 13
unipolarity, 13
United Arab Emirates, 36
"united Europe," 13
United Kingdom (*see* "Great Britain")
United Nations, 25–26, 56, 126
United States:
9/11 attacks (*see* "September 11 attacks")
agent-based systems, 127
Armstrong, Lance, 137
Articles of Confederation, 25
basic resources, 129–31
Bell Labs, 139
Boston Marathon bombings (2013), 113
brain power, 138–42
Bush, George H.W., 11, 49, 134, 182–83
Bush, George W.:
2000 election, 135
veterans services, 138

decline of American fitness, 129, 141, 149, 153, 182
Haliburton contracts, 223
military expenditures, 29, 138, 152
nation-building, 181
neoconservativism, 215n21
"No Child Left Behind," 141
North Korea, 174, 184
political cohesion, 134–35
public opinion, 28, 144, 153
tax policies, 133, 138
unilateralism, 144, 182, 205
Carter, Jimmy, 11, 19, 128, 134, 163
Carter, Rosalynn, 163
casinos, 136
Cheney, Dick, 153, 223n2
Chu, Steven, 139, 140
Clinton, Bill, 21, 28, 134, 135, 163, 181–82
Clinton, Hillary, 21, 163
coevolution, 127
complexity, 125–29
congruity with international institutions, 142–44
culture, 128
debt ceiling crisis, 135
Department of Homeland Security, 138
Director of National Intelligence, U.S., 138
economic power and well-being, 132–38
Eisenhower, Dwight D., 105, 128
emergence, 127
fitness landscapes, 128
Ford, Gerald, 124, 134, 136
Ford, Henry, 126
Fox News, 153
fracking, 139
Gingrich, Newt, 134–36
Gore, Al, 135, 140, 163
guns
Indochina (U.S. intervention), 105, 123–25, 135, 188
interdependence, 126
K Street lobbying, 153
Kennedy, John F., 15, 125, 128

Kennedy, Robert F., 15
Khrushchev, Nikita S., 15, 82, 125
Koller, Daphne, 163
McNamara, Robert S., 15
military might, 138
National Defense University (U.S.), 20
National Endowment for Democracy, 68
National Institutes of Health, 140
National Intelligence Council, 183, 190, 191, 202
National Rifle Association (NRA), 144
National Science Foundation (NSF), 140
National Skills Coalition, 31
New Deal, 124
Ng, Andrew, 163
"No Child Left Behind," 141
Obama, Barack, 12, 21, 28–29, 105, 129, 131, 135–38, 140–41, 144–45, 149, 152–53, 163, 181–82, 222n24
Obama, Michelle, 163
Occupy Wall Street movement, 129
Office of Information and Regulatory Affairs, 12
Perry, James "Rick", 141
Petraeus, David, 145
political cohesion and justice, 134–38
power and hegemony, 121–25
Power, Samantha, 21
public safety, 142–44
punctuated equilibrium, 128, 129
Reagan, Ronald, 29, 124, 128, 134, 136, 138–39, 153, 183
Reshef, Shai, 163
Roosevelt, Eleanor, 126, 134
Roosevelt, Franklin D., 126
Roosevelt, Theodore, 126
Sanford, Mark, 145
self-organization, 125–28
Southwestern U.S. blackout (2011), 223n3
Star Spangled Banner, 57
tax cuts, 132–34
Tygart, Travis, 137
Wilson, Woodrow, 19

University of Belgrade protests (1998), 67
urban planning and Le Corbusier, 215n1
USSR (see "Russia")
Ustaša (Croatia), 59
Utøya Island massacre (2011), 113

vernacular catechism (Estonia, Latvia), 63
Vernadskii, Vladimir I., 225
Vīķe-Freiberga, Vaira, 62
Vil'no University, 64
Vilnius (Polish population, street names), 42
Visaginas nuclear plant referendum, 112
Volga Federal District, 81
Vukovar, 78

Wagner, Richard, 1
Walesa, Lech, 102
war and peace (Lithuania and Croatia), 47
war crimes (2012 Yugoslav tribunal and acquittals), 78
"war on terror" (U.S.), 119
Warsaw Pact, 25
wealth extraction, 136
weapons, 8
Wendt, Alexander, 179
"wet robots," 2
Whitman, Walt, 126
Whose Song Is This?, 69
Wilson, E.O., xix
Wilson, Woodrow, 19
World Bank, 28
World Trade Center attacks (see "September 11 attacks")
World Wide Web (growth, structure), 24

xenophobia (Slovenia), 217n2

Yeltsin, Boris, 31
Yugoslavia:
    breakup, 60–61
    casualties from post-communist transition, 40–41
    Chetniks, 59
    Ćosić, Dorica, 56

Yugoslavia *(continued)*
Dayton Peace Accords (1995), 40, 46
Djilas, Milovan, 59
ethnic tension and conflict, 51–53
HSS party, 219n4
Kingdom of Serbs, Croats, and
Slovenes, 59
Mihailović, Dragoljub-Draža, 59
Ministry of Education (1993 language
laws), 52
Tito, Josef Broz, 52

Zimmerman, Warren, 59

Zone A: Peace, Progress, and
Democracy, 72–75
Zone B: Flawed Freedom, 75
Zone C: Turmoil and Slow
Development, 76–79
Zone D: Statism and Stagnation, 79,
80
Zone E: Between an Iron Fist and
Anarchy, 80–82
Zone F: Economic Advance Without
Political Freedom, 83
zones of development (trends across
post-communist Eurasia), 72–83